Where Matters

Imagine a hospital where equipment never goes missing, patients never wait unnecessarily, and staff focus on care instead of logistics. In *Where Matters: Healthcare's Playbook for Location-Based Services 2.0 and AI*, this vision becomes reality through care traffic control (CTC), a revolutionary framework that brings the precision and reliability of aviation traffic control to healthcare operations.

Drawing from decades of experience in both aviation and healthcare, the authors reveal how location-based services and digital twin technologies can transform healthcare operations from reactive to predictive, from fragmented to orchestrated, from inefficient to optimized. This isn't just another technology book – it's a blueprint for operational revolution.

Through the compelling journey of Edenvale General Hospital, readers witness the dramatic transformation that occurs when real-time location intelligence meets operational excellence. From reduced costs and improved patient satisfaction to enhanced staff productivity and safety, the results are nothing short of extraordinary.

Learn how to:

- Create a hospital command center that rivals the sophistication of air traffic control
- Deploy automation that enhances rather than replaces human capabilities
- Transform chaotic workflows into synchronized symphonies of efficiency
- Build a digital twin that makes the invisible visible and the impossible achievable
- Generate immediate returns while building toward long-term transformation

Whether you're a healthcare executive seeking operational excellence, a technology leader navigating digital transformation, or an improvement professional driving change, *Where Matters: Healthcare's Playbook for Location-Based Services 2.0 and AI* provides the roadmap, tools, and insights you need. Each chapter includes specific guidance for improvers, leaders, and vendors, ensuring practical application across all stakeholder groups.

This isn't just about tracking assets or monitoring workflows – it's about fundamentally reimagining how healthcare operations can work. Through real-world examples, practical frameworks, and proven methodologies, *Where Matters: Healthcare's Playbook for Location-Based Services 2.0 and AI* shows you how to turn this vision into reality. Join the operational revolution that's transforming healthcare – because in the future of healthcare operations, where matters.

Where Matters
Healthcare's Playbook for Location-Based Services 2.0 and AI

Ali Youssef
Paul E. Zieske

Foreword by John D. Halamka, MD, MS

CRC Press
Taylor & Francis Group
Boca Raton London New York

CRC Press is an imprint of the
Taylor & Francis Group, an **informa** business

Designed cover image: Shutterstock Image ID 451890163

First edition published 2026
by CRC Press
2385 NW Executive Center Drive, Suite 320, Boca Raton FL 33431

and by CRC Press
4 Park Square, Milton Park, Abingdon, Oxon, OX14 4RN

CRC Press is an imprint of Taylor & Francis Group, LLC

ISBN: 978-1-041-03808-5 (hbk)
ISBN: 978-1-041-03812-2 (pbk)
ISBN: 978-1-003-62548-3 (ebk)

DOI: 10.1201/9781003625483

Typeset in Sabon
by SPi Technologies India Pvt Ltd (Straive)

Contents

Foreword

By John D. Halamka, M.D., M.S.

For the past 40 years, I have worked at the intersection of healthcare delivery, information technology, and public policy. I have seen the rapid evolution of electronic health records, the translation of machine learning from bench to bedside, and the rise/fall of many innovations.

When I speak with healthcare leaders around the world, none of them want technology for technology's sake. They want to solve specific business problems. These typically include revenue challenges, hiring/retaining clinicians, and mitigating the burnout that some many caregivers are feeling.

At the same time we are trying to address issues of productivity, efficiency, and quality in healthcare, the world is experiencing demographic shifts. Every industrialized country (except Israel) has a birth rate less than replacement. The result is fewer trainees in medicine. Lifespans are increasing which require more services to more people. The impending supply/demand mismatch of the next decade is already being felt in many areas with long appointment waiting times and challenges finding appropriate caregivers.

Technology is not only an enabler to help us with these challenges, it is our best answer to ensure a bright future of wellness, prevention, and early diagnosis. At the 2025 World Economic Forum in Davos, digital health transformation was a key topic across government, academia, and industry stakeholders.

One such technology is location services which helps us understand many aspects of a patient care journey. What is a patient's level of activity in the home (we can measure their daily routines and even identify falls). As patients transition from their daily lives to a caregiving location (which still could be their home), where are the services, supplies and equipment they need during the care process? Where are their blood samples and medications? Where are the devices that support them (glucometers, EKG machines, defibrillators).

Adding "Where" to our process optimization activities gives us an entirely new range of opportunities to optimize the care experience. Fifteen years ago I coined the term "Care Traffic Control" to describe a more proactive approach to ambulatory and inpatient operations. This has led to the idea of control towers in many hospitals internationally.

In this book, Paul Zieske gives us a glimpse of the future of healthcare that is proactive, easy to navigate, and optimizes the shortest path from sickness to wellness. With a new set of technology tools we can ensure the right patient receives the right care in the right setting at the right time by the right person. The concept of digital twins will enable us to test many care paths and select the right one based on precision medicine and personalization.

COVID taught us how to embrace new care models. We embraced remote patient monitoring, telehealth, and new classes of caregivers (community paramedics assisting with care in the home). Regulatory changes enabled different workflows and reimbursement possibilities.

There is no better time to introduce a new class of automation into our healthsystem design. We have the technologies, policies, and cultural change needed to add "where" to our existing "what" and "who".

John D. Halamka MD, MS

Authors

Ali Youssef My fascination with wireless technology has been the driving force of my 25-year career in healthcare technology. As Director of Medical Device and Emerging Technology Security at Henry Ford Health, I've transformed my passion for wireless innovation into practical solutions that enhance patient care and operational efficiency.

My journey with wireless technology began with early Wi-Fi implementations in healthcare, where I discovered the transformative potential of indoor positioning and Internet of Things (IoT) connectivity. This revelation led me to explore location-based services (LBS) in healthcare operations, becoming an advocate for their adoption across the industry.

I've shared my expertise through co-authoring *Wi-Fi Enabled Healthcare* (2014) and contributing a chapter on medical device security in *The Rise of the Intelligent Health System* (2024). My work emphasizes practical applications of wireless technology while maintaining robust security measures.

As a HIMSS Fellow and Wireless Chair for the Intelligent Hospital Association since 2015, I continue to advocate for innovative uses of wireless technology in healthcare settings. My certifications (CISSP, CCSP, HCISPP, CISM, CPHIMS, and CWNE) reflect my commitment to mastering both technical and healthcare-specific challenges.

Through my role on the AAMI Healthcare Technology Leadership Committee and Editorial Board, I help shape the future of healthcare technology, particularly in IoT and LBS. I remain passionate about bridging the gap between emerging wireless technologies and their practical application in healthcare, always seeking new ways to improve patient care through technological innovation.

Paul E. Zieske With 34 years in designing and building complex systems, I have used emerging technologies in every phase of their maturity. I have worked at large organizations, like the FAA (Federal Aviation Administration) and Westinghouse, down to my own startup. I have worked in industries like aviation, automotive, banking, retail, and healthcare. I have been in engineering, product management, project management, consulting, and leadership. I have enjoyed the many experiences that helped me hone my skills and find where my passions lie. My journey has brought me to a place where I want to share what I have learned along the way.

My career journey started at Westinghouse in their Air Traffic Control radar division where I eventually left to join the FAA. In the FAA, I moved from radar to creating a distributed system of weather cams that were viewable on the Internet in 1998 (https://weathercams.faa.gov). That project revealed some of the potential for using the Internet as more than a marketing channel so I left the FAA to join an Internet consultancy. MarchFIRST was introducing some of the biggest brands on the Internet for the first time. It was an exciting time that was called the Internet boom.

Like all booms, they are temporary, and I found in healthcare an opportunity to help an industry that was in great need. While working at Henry Ford in Detroit, I saw location services technologies that were maturing and worked with the Henry Ford Innovation Institute to create a new product. This product was designed to address the delays that were a source of constant frustration in hospitals. NavvTrack was tapping into my experience from Air Traffic Control and the new technologies that would enable an indoor traffic control system.

It was clear that the success of this type of product would be based on the success of the concept that provided the vision for it and that was care traffic control. At the same time, it was clear that the concept would only take hold if people were aware of it. Why Where Matters (https://whywherematters.com) was created to be a source of information and education on the concept of care traffic control. This book provides a foundation for the subject matter that Why Where Matters provides.

In my personal life, I am a multisport athlete and have completed seven Ironmans, five Boston Marathons, and many other endurance events. I love the challenge of preparing and completing events that test you in so many ways. My wife and I have grown children, and we have three Great Danes that we love and spend our time with.

Introduction

It is unnecessary to detail the reasons why healthcare needs to improve. Every healthcare improvement book has plenty of data to support the troubled times that healthcare is going through. This book is not about the "why." This book is about the "how." This book performs the highwire act of being both visionary yet feasible, inspiring yet practical and valuable yet frugal. It is a textbook, a manual, and a story.

The unending drive for efficiency in healthcare operations is fraught with complexity. It has fueled the use of concepts from quality science like total quality management (TQM), lean, and Six Sigma by performance improvement teams and healthcare consultants. There are examples of high reliability from industries like aviation that are offered as aspirational models for healthcare. You will hear words like systemization and the comparisons with manufacturing that uses lots of automation. There are many research papers and even some proof points like Virginia Mason and Mayo who have made meaningful progress. With so much useful information available, there has been little progress toward the kind of improvement initiatives that have revolutionized other industries.

In *Where Matters*, we are tapping into other industries, the digital transformation and even looking at Industry 4.0 and its drive toward using technology to finish what the quality revolution started. Emerging technologies like the digital twin, Internet of Things (IoT), artificial intelligence (AI), and cloud computing are part of the ecosystem. Aviation and air traffic control is an industry that provides an example to draw parallels and best practices.

CARE TRAFFIC CONTROL AND LOCATION-BASED SERVICES

The book intends to describe a framework and a process to realize the potential of these technologies. By looking at aviation and air traffic control, we can find features that have led to the reputation of reliability found there. We are calling the framework "Care Traffic Control."

The common thread that runs through the fabric of waste in healthcare is "motion." Lean is so bold as to say all motion is waste. Wasted motion equates to wasted time and wasted time equates to wasted money. It is not just time and money; there are safety and quality issues that are attributed to these location and motion problems. Location and motion are spatial problems, and location-based services are the technologies that are designed and built to solve spatial problems. Motion has spatial and temporal components, so designing systems is as much about when as it is about where.

AI AND ITS ROLE IN SYSTEMS ARCHITECTURE

The thread that we will be pulling slowly at first, but aggressively toward the end, is AI. We are not going to get into the specific types of AI or what algorithm might be best suited for a specific problem. Our intention is to create a place in the architecture where AI can thrive. This will make it much easier to address those details when the time comes.

AI is the study of rational agents, and of course, humans are the best rational agents in our known world. The dramatic emergence of AI offers us a new way to look at improvement. When we break down the dynamics of an organization along the lines of rational agency, we can model the outcomes in ways we never could before. This makes the application of AI something we can do strategically because we already know how the organization looks, as a hierarchical agent architecture. We will get utility from this exercise in the beginning of our AI journey, when there might be no AI agents, and we will gain an extreme advantage from having a model to plot the rest of the journey. We can take this as far as our imaginations and the limitations in the state of the art for sensors and AI will let us. The technology will advance, but the agent architecture will remain intact.

WHERE MATTERS IS MORE THAN LOCATION-BASED SERVICES

Location-based services are very complex, and because it is an emerging area of technology, it is being left to the vendors and integrators to dictate the direction these products take. This is creating a gap between the improvers and users who are embedded in the healthcare system and the technologists that are trying to deliver solutions. For legacy location services, you see a core set of use cases that are employing location technologies that persist in creating many point solutions that don't work together, even as the underlying tech improves. As the number of point solutions increases, it calls into question the return on investment (ROI) that comes from this technology.

Location offers powerful context, and we are going to look at how location and other contextual information can be used to make systems aware and more intelligent. The intention is to steer the market toward a platform-oriented architecture that can provide valuable contextual information to any system that needs it.

INTRODUCING EDENVALE GENERAL HOSPITAL

To illustrate what the care traffic control journey might look like, we include examples from a fictional hospital called Edenvale General Hospital (EGH). Because many of these are new concepts, describing what they might look like in the real world will be helpful. The concepts leave room for many ideas not captured in the Edenvale examples, so we encourage readers to imagine their own innovations. The Epilogue includes a wrap up of what a mature version of the concept looks like at EGH.

WHERE MATTERS AS A PLAYBOOK

This book offers a crawl-walk-run approach to help flatten the maturity curve. We offer descriptions of existing technologies and enumerate the critical capabilities that are necessary for success. The goal is to remain somewhat vendor neutral and offer an evidence-based approach to architecting enterprise solutions. As we develop the vision for this, we will describe what Location-based Services 2.0 might look like. Some of these solutions are not yet available in the market but that makes it even more important to offer this framework for inspiring the market to action.

We call this a playbook because we are offering ways to get started, but we also want to help more progressive healthcare systems to push forward with the more visionary aspects. This is a bit of a dilemma because the playbook cannot be a one-size-fits-all. Hopefully, the Edenvale journey and maturity model at the end of the book will outline what progress might look like. At the end of each chapter, you will find the "Playbook" section. It has three audiences in mind.

The first audience is the "Improver." The improvers are healthcare systems employees, consultants, and anyone assigned the role of executing an improvement in a healthcare system. These are people who are actively engaged in change.

The second is the leader. These are people who sponsor, champion, and evangelize these initiatives. This is all the way at the top of the organization down to the supervisor who is responsible for changing specific workflows.

Last are creators. The creators are the vendors, inventors, and researchers who create ecosystems of technologies that are required for this to all work. This is all the way to big-tech like Microsoft who has amazing cloud features that are trending toward this already. It is also down to the gritty startups that have the speed and agility to create proof points that are necessary to gain traction.

Healthcare systems need to understand the terminology and the complexity of these systems. The closer you get to a point solution, the simpler the solution is, but when you want to create an enterprise architecture for real-time healthcare, it is like 3D chess. That is the education in this book is such an important step. The background chapters in the beginning will help technical leaders and operations executives with terms and concepts. In later chapters, they will become familiar with what is possible so that they can influence vendors to keep pushing forward with both capabilities and interoperability.

HOW THE BOOK IS ORGANIZED

The book is divided into three sections to provide better indexing for the subject matter. Although it is sequenced and designed to build on previous topics, it is also modular so that individual chapters can offer insights without the complete background. That is why some repetition is necessary, so please bear this in mind when you see things you might have seen before.

Section 1 is called background, and here is where we look at the history of location services and take a broad look at the technologies that make up this space. We will also look at what the next evolution of the location services might look like. We will touch on some emerging technologies that are showing promise here as well. Some of these technologies will not be used in later sections of the book, but we feel they are important to understand.

In this section, we establish some background knowledge for how the field of AI is influencing systems architecture. We will introduce the concept of agents and how they can be used in systems architecture. By starting with an architectural foundation, we can build a system that can use minimal automation or become fully automated when the elemental components are ready for adoption.

Section 2 is called care traffic control. Here, we dig deeper into the concept of care traffic control and how it can revolutionize healthcare operations. In this section, we only touch on the process changes and go deeper into the tech and the care traffic control ecosystem.

This is where we show how to build an architecture using the concepts coming from robotics and automation that were described in the previous section. This "agent architecture" is an architecture that applies specifically to CTC and its use of location-based services and sensors.

Section 3 offers a methodology that can be used to implement care traffic control and its automation. Because performance improvement is a driving factor in CTC, the section starts by establishing some techniques from improvement science. In this section, we look at a key component of digital transformation and real-time healthcare and that is simulations. We also lay out the steps that can be used to get a feedback system in place to create changes that can be sustained. At the end of the section, we offer a maturity curve to measure progress toward a fully mature and optimizing system.

Section I

Background

Section 1 establishes the foundational knowledge necessary to understand the evolution and implementation of location-based services in healthcare environments. This section explores both historical context and cutting-edge technologies, providing essential background for the care traffic control concept that will be developed in later sections. By examining established concepts from computer science and improvement science, we build a framework for understanding how location-based services can revolutionize healthcare operations.

Chapter 1 – History of Location Services traces the fascinating evolution of location tracking technology from its origins in World War II radar systems to modern healthcare applications. This chapter explores how early military innovations in friend-or-foe identification evolved into RFID and eventually gave rise to the sophisticated real-time location systems used in healthcare today.

Chapter 2 – Location Services Technologies provides a comprehensive overview of current location tracking technologies, including RFID (Radio Frequency Identification), BLE (Bluetooth Low Energy), UWB (Ultra Wideband), Wi-Fi, and other solutions. This chapter examines the capabilities, limitations, and optimal use cases for each technology, helping readers understand how to select the right solutions for their specific needs.

Chapter 3 – Location-Based Services 1.0 examines the first generation of location-based services in healthcare, analyzing both their transformative potential and implementation challenges. This chapter explores why despite promising benefits, many early adoption efforts struggled to deliver expected returns.

Chapter 4 – Location-Based Services 2.0 introduces the next evolution of location-based services, showcasing how rethinking system architecture with an enterprise approach can maximize value across an organization. This chapter outlines key characteristics that differentiate LBS 2.0 from earlier approaches.

Chapter 5 – Maps and Geospatial Science delves into geographic information systems (GIS) and their expanding role in indoor environments. This

DOI: 10.1201/9781003625483-1

chapter demonstrates how decades of GIS advancement can be leveraged for indoor location services.

Chapter 6 – Pervasive and Mobile Computing explores the concept of ubiquitous computing and its implications for location-based services. This chapter examines how computing technology embedded throughout the environment enables new capabilities.

Chapter 7 – Artificial Intelligence and Rational Agents provides essential background on AI concepts and rational agents, preparing readers for their specific applications in later sections. This chapter establishes key principles that will inform the design of location-aware systems.

Chapter 8 – Digital Twin introduces the broad concept of digital twins while focusing on aspects relevant to care traffic control. This chapter lays the groundwork for understanding how digital twins can transform healthcare operations.

Chapter 1

History of location services

Ali Youssef

The evolution of location services represents one of healthcare's most transformative technological developments, though its origins lie far from hospital walls. This technology, which today helps hospitals track everything from vital medical equipment to vulnerable patients, began its journey in the urgent necessities of World War II. The progression from military radar systems to modern healthcare applications illustrates how technological innovations can transcend their original purposes to solve complex challenges in entirely different domains.

Location services has evolved from simple tracking systems to sophisticated platforms that provide real-time intelligence about the movement of people and assets throughout healthcare facilities. This evolution reflects a broader transformation in healthcare operations – from reactive management to proactive, data-driven decision-making. Today's healthcare providers leverage location services to enhance patient safety, optimize workflow efficiency, and improve resource utilization in ways that would have been impossible just decades ago.

This chapter traces the fascinating journey of location services technology, from its wartime origins through its commercial development and ultimately to its crucial role in modern healthcare. We will explore how early radar and identification systems laid the groundwork for radio frequency identification (RFID) technology, and how subsequent innovations led to the development of real-time location services (RTLS) and other advanced tracking solutions. Understanding this history provides valuable context for healthcare leaders and technologists working to implement these systems today.

By examining the key developments, challenges, and breakthroughs in location services technology, we can better appreciate both its current capabilities and its future potential in healthcare settings. This historical perspective also offers insights into how healthcare organizations can effectively adopt and adapt these technologies to meet their specific needs.

DOI: 10.1201/9781003625483-2

MILITARY ORIGINS

RFID technology has a fascinating history. Sir Robert Alexander Watson-Watt, a Scottish physicist and engineer, is credited with the discovery and development of radar technology. In the 1930s, Watson-Watt, along with his team, conducted extensive research and experiments that led to the realization of radar's potential for detecting and tracking objects using radio waves. In 1935, Watson-Watt presented a groundbreaking report to the British Air Ministry, highlighting the feasibility of using radio waves to detect aircraft. This report laid the foundation for the development of the chain home (CH) radar system, a vital defense mechanism during World War II. Like many other groundbreaking inventions, RFID evolved out of necessity during a time of war.

During the war, radar technology could detect approaching airplanes, but there was no way to distinguish between friendly and enemy aircraft. German engineers, however, discovered that the radar signal reflected off an airplane changed when the plane performed a rolling maneuver. They cleverly used this technique to differentiate between German and non-German warplanes, marking the inception of the first passive RFID system.

As the war progressed, the British, being in close proximity to Germany, realized the need for proactive detection of enemy bombers. They installed towers across the country and developed the CH radar system, which successfully detected approaching aircraft. However, they soon recognized the necessity for a more advanced system to differentiate between friendly and unfriendly planes. This led to the development of the identify friend and foe (IFF) system, one of the earliest forms of active RFID. It involved transponders, receivers, and messages containing data like aircraft ID, speed, altitude, and other useful metrics. By the 1940s, the British had installed transponders and receivers on their own aircraft, enabling them to identify and engage enemy planes while in the air (Figure 1.1).

For his groundbreaking achievements, Sir Robert Alexander Watson-Watt was knighted in 1942 and is widely recognized as the "father of radar." His pioneering research and inventions laid the groundwork for the modern radar systems that we rely on today in various applications, including aviation, meteorology, and navigation (Figure 1.2).

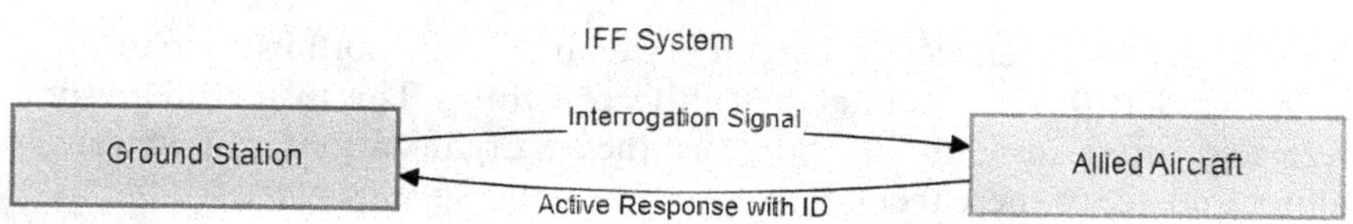

Figure 1.1 Identify friend and foe (IFF) system diagram.

Figure 1.2 British bombers WW2.

EARLY RFID DEVELOPMENT

The foundational elements of radar technology, such as signal transmitters and receivers, gradually evolved into what we now know as passive and active RFID. The official credit for the invention of RFID goes to Harry Stockman, who published a research paper titled "Communications by Means of Reflected Power" in October 1948. Stockman conducted experiments with radio, light, and sound wave transmissions, focusing on the theory of reflected power. He even envisioned potential civilian applications for this technology.

After the war ended and Stockman's research became widely known, excitement surrounding RFID technology continued to grow, especially in the 1950s. Research and development efforts intensified, exploring the use of RFID in high-risk industries such as coal mining, oil exploration, and nuclear installations. Advancements were also made in aircraft radar systems and anti-theft system development.

The 1970s witnessed significant advancements in RFID technology. In 1983, the first US-based patent using the term "RFID" was granted to American inventor Charles Walton. The US government began experimenting with using RFID to track nuclear materials. Scientists at the Los Alamos National Laboratories, who developed the technology, went on to create automated toll payment systems. These early experiments paved the way for companies developing systems using low radio frequencies. Many of these systems are still in use today, tracking everything from cows to validating car keys for specific vehicles.

COMMERCIAL EVOLUTION

Over time, engineers started exploring ultra high frequency (UHF) RFID systems, which offered increased range and faster, more robust data transmission. Although the discovery was made by IBM engineers, Intermec purchased the patent and played a significant role in making the technology more mainstream. In 1999, the Auto-ID Center at MIT played a crucial role in networking RFID tags and linking them to Internet-accessible databases. The center also helped establish standards for the RFID industry, which were soon followed by ISO standards. This revolutionized the supply chain industry, enabling vendors to provide real-time notifications to consumers about shipped products. Two MIT professors, David Brick and Sanjay Sarma, contributed to the maturation of RFID research, but it was the adoption of RFID by the Department of Defense that truly helped commercialize the technology.

In 2003, RFID gained significant traction in the retail sector when Walmart mandated that its top 100 suppliers use RFID tags on pallets delivered to their stores. By 2006, retailers recognized the value of automating merchandise tracking within their stores. Coupled with the decreasing cost of technology, this development served as a catalyst for RFID adoption.

RFID found extensive use in manufacturing, retail, and logistics, effectively automating these sectors. It proved its value in various applications, including inventory management, par level management, and asset tracking from manufacturing facilities to point-of-sale locations. This provided valuable insights into timing, efficiency, and demand.

As RFID continued to gain traction, it expanded into new domains. It began being used to track people at entry points to trade centers, conferences, and amusement parks. Institutions started relying on RFID as an added security measure for access control and tracking purposes, whether it was tracking books in libraries or opening hotel room doors. In 2007, RFID integration into US passports served as a fraud deterrent.

HEALTHCARE ADOPTION

As RFID technology progressed and RTLS emerged, the number of use cases multiplied. In 2005, RFID started making inroads into the healthcare sector. The healthcare industry recognized the potential for reducing labor costs, improving processes, and establishing stronger partnerships with suppliers. Initially, RFID deployments in healthcare were at the departmental level and driven by early adopters. Literature reviews began to emerge, highlighting

RFID's benefits in patient tracking and inventory management. By 2006, the healthcare RFID market had reached $90 million. Hospitals primarily aimed to enhance patient care, achieve efficiency wherever possible, and generate cost savings. Drug manufacturers also relied on RFID to combat the issue of counterfeit drugs, estimated to be around 7% of all drugs in circulation. The U.S. Food and Drug Administration (FDA) released guidance on using barcodes for hospital-administered drugs, further fueling the market's growth to $2.1 billion by 2016 as healthcare organizations turned to RFID for compliance monitoring and reporting.

While passive RFID was ideal for retail applications, healthcare use cases often required active RFID or RTLS. Active RFID tags, powered by batteries, enabled real-time location tracking and provided continuous location data. Healthcare institutions were particularly interested in using the technology for asset management and ensuring proper par levels. They focused on guaranteeing that assets were in the right location at the right time and received appropriate cleaning and maintenance. RFID became the go-to technology for tracking small, inexpensive assets, while RTLS became the preferred choice for larger, costlier assets. By tracking assets within healthcare facilities, organizations could analyze workflows, optimize asset utilization, and ensure medical devices received proper servicing and cleaning. Additionally, RFID technology assisted in theft prevention.

The successful tracking of assets led to further exploration of tracking staff to optimize clinical workflows. With real-time visibility of staff locations, schedules could be adjusted, and patient timing expectations could be communicated proactively. Digital whiteboards integrated the capability to highlight provider details when they entered patient rooms. Tracking staff members also contributed to improving safety and reducing liability, particularly in cases of duress alerting. Behavioral health institutions benefited from the ability to locate employees instantly, offering them a sense of security. Tracking staff also facilitated nurse call automation, accurately detecting when a nurse entered a room. Real-time, actionable data from these applications opened new avenues for improvement and optimization (Figure 1.3).

RFID technology proved invaluable in addressing critical healthcare challenges such as infant protection and patient elopement. It enabled the detection of infant movement and alerts if they were taken outside designated areas. RFID bands ensured that each infant was correctly assigned to their mother, minimizing confusion and reducing the risk of infant abductions within hospitals. Moreover, RFID played a prominent role in hand hygiene compliance, a crucial aspect of preventing hospital-acquired infections. Automated reminders prompted staff to sanitize and wash their hands before engaging with patients, while adherence to hand hygiene protocols could be tracked and monitored. In case of disease outbreaks, RFID technology facilitated contact tracing and provided visibility into infection control.

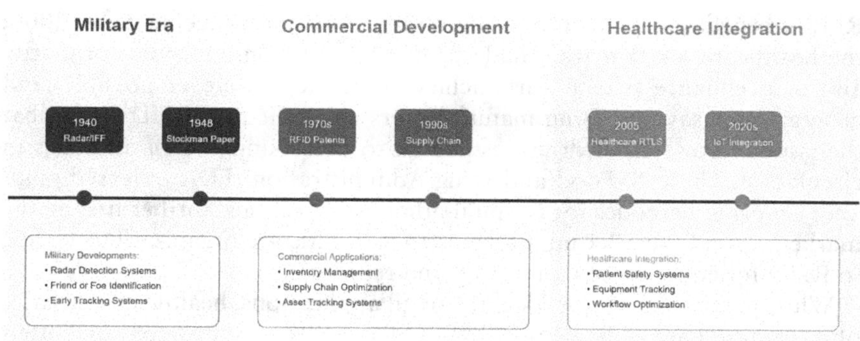

Figure 1.3 Location-based services timeline. WW2 to healthcare present day.

The emergence of Wi-Fi and Bluetooth technologies expanded the possibilities for leveraging RFID and RTLS. The proliferation of Wi-Fi-enabled devices allowed for location tracking without dedicated tags. Wi-Fi radios in devices could function like tags, utilizing triangulation techniques to determine approximate asset locations and analyze people density in specific areas. Bluetooth further extended the capabilities by enabling more advanced functionality using energy-efficient built-in bluetooth low energy (BLE) radios in devices.

With the growing focus on Wi-Fi and BLE, RFID adoption expanded into areas such as wayfinding and patient engagement. Hospitals began exploring indoor GPS-like functionality, catering to individual preferences based on a phone's location within the facility. Proximity detection enabled personalized experiences and services. The synergistic use of RFID, RTLS, Wi-Fi, and bluetooth technologies facilitated more advanced use cases and delivered increased value. From its origins as a tool for warfare, RFID had found its way into healthcare, significantly contributing to improving patient care and saving lives.

Location services have undergone a remarkable evolution in the healthcare industry, revolutionizing the way hospitals operate and enhancing patient care. From the early adoption of RFID technology for asset tracking and patient safety to the integration of RTLS, hospitals have harnessed the power of location-based data to optimize workflows, improve efficiency, and deliver better outcomes.

The implementation of location services in healthcare was initially driven by the need for asset management and optimization. Hospitals struggled to keep track of vital equipment and supplies, leading to inefficiencies and unnecessary costs. As RFID technology advanced and RTLS emerged, healthcare institutions saw an opportunity to address these challenges and unlock new possibilities for operational excellence.

One of the primary applications of location services in hospitals is asset tracking. By attaching RFID tags or utilizing RTLS-enabled devices, healthcare organizations can monitor the location and movement of critical assets such as medical equipment, wheelchairs, infusion pumps, and more. This real-time visibility enables staff to quickly locate and retrieve necessary equipment, eliminating time wasted searching for items or ordering replacements. As a result, staff productivity increases, patient care is expedited, and the overall efficiency of the hospital improves.

Location services in healthcare have come a long way, and boy, have they revolutionized the industry! It's like having a personal GPS system for every aspect of hospital operations. From keeping track of medical equipment to optimizing workflows and ensuring patient safety, location services have become the go-to solution for healthcare institutions.

CURRENT TECHNOLOGIES

Now, let's talk about some of the advanced technologies that have taken location services to the next level. One of the most exciting additions is ultra-wideband (UWB) technology. UWB uses short-range radio waves to provide highly precise location data that can pinpoint the exact location of people and objects within a few centimeters.

With UWB, hospitals can achieve unparalleled accuracy in tracking assets and personnel. Imagine being able to locate a specific medical device within seconds, even in a large facility. That means less time wasted searching for equipment and more time spent on patient care. It's a game-changer for improving efficiency and reducing costs.

But UWB is not the only technology making waves in the world of location services. We also have BLE- and Wi-Fi-based solutions that offer their own set of advantages. BLE, for instance, is energy-efficient and perfect for tracking smaller assets or even patients. Hospitals can attach BLE-enabled tags to items like medication carts or attach them to patients' wristbands for accurate and real-time tracking.

On the contrary, Wi-Fi-based solutions leverage existing Wi-Fi infrastructure to provide location data. It's like turning the hospital's Wi-Fi system into a giant tracking system. By analyzing Wi-Fi signals and using triangulation techniques, hospitals can determine the approximate location of assets and staff members. It's a cost-effective solution that doesn't require additional infrastructure, making it a popular choice for many healthcare facilities.

These advanced location services technologies have opened up a world of possibilities for hospitals. Apart from asset tracking and workflow optimization, they have paved the way for innovative use cases. For example, hospitals can now implement wayfinding systems to guide patients and visitors through complex facilities. Imagine arriving at a hospital and immediately receiving turn-by-turn directions to your destination.

Moreover, patient engagement has reached new heights with the integration of location services. Hospitals can create personalized experiences based on a patient's proximity to different areas within the facility. Imagine receiving notifications on your smartphone about nearby amenities, appointment reminders, or even educational content tailored to your specific needs. It's all about enhancing the patient experience and making them feel cared for at every step of their healthcare journey.

But location services don't stop at asset tracking and patient engagement. They also play a crucial role in ensuring patient safety and security. Infant protection systems, powered by location services, provide an extra layer of security to prevent infant abductions. By monitoring the movement of infants and alerting staff if they are taken outside designated areas, hospitals can quickly respond and ensure the safety of these vulnerable patients.

Additionally, location services contribute to infection control efforts. Hand hygiene compliance is a top priority in healthcare, and location-based systems can help hospitals monitor staff interactions and remind them to sanitize their hands before and after each patient encounter. By promoting proper hand hygiene, hospitals can significantly reduce the risk of hospital-acquired infections and enhance patient safety.

The future of location services in healthcare is brimming with potential. As technology continues to advance, we can expect even more precise and efficient solutions. Imagine a world where hospitals can predict patient flow, optimize resource allocation, and prevent bottlenecks before they even occur. With the integration of artificial intelligence (AI) and predictive analytics, location services will become invaluable tools for healthcare administrators, allowing them to make data-driven decisions and improve patient outcomes.

REAL-WORLD APPLICATION: LOCATION SERVICES IN ACTION

Emergency response scenario

In a busy 2-million-square-foot hospital, a critical situation unfolded that would demonstrate the vital importance of modern location services. David, a post-stroke patient, became disoriented and wandered from his room on the neurology floor. Within minutes of his departure, his absence triggered a series of automated responses that would have been impossible in the pre-location services era.

System response

The hospital's location services system activated through a sophisticated network of integrated technologies. David's RFID-enabled wristband continuously transmitted his location data, while building access points tracked his movement patterns throughout the facility. Security cameras enhanced with AI integration provided visual confirmation of his path, while mobile staff devices received instant alerts with his current location information. This multi-layered approach ensured continuous tracking and monitoring.

Coordinated response

The system's effectiveness was particularly evident in how it enabled a coordinated response across multiple departments. As soon as David's unauthorized departure was detected, the system generated immediate notifications to nursing staff and the security team. Unlike traditional search protocols that might involve time-consuming manual searches of multiple floors, the location services system provided continuous, real-time updates of David's position within the facility.

The strategic deployment of response teams showcased the system's sophisticated coordination capabilities. Security personnel received constant location updates, while the system identified and alerted the nearest available staff members. The system calculated and distributed the most efficient intercept routes, allowing response teams to approach from multiple directions while avoiding redundant coverage of the same areas.

Outcome and impact

Through this coordinated effort, staff located David within minutes, finding him in a non-clinical area of the hospital. The quick response prevented potential complications and demonstrated the transformative impact of modern location services. What might have previously required hours of searching was resolved in minutes, with minimal disruption to hospital operations.

The response time reduction proved crucial for patient safety, while the precise deployment of resources demonstrated remarkable operational efficiency. Throughout the incident, team members maintained seamless coordination through the integrated communication system. The entire event was automatically documented, providing valuable data for future analysis and protocol refinement.

Lessons learned

This incident highlighted the importance of system integration in modern healthcare facilities. The seamless interaction between multiple technologies – from RFID tracking to security systems – created a comprehensive safety net that proved highly effective in an emergency situation. The successful resolution demonstrated how well-integrated location services can transform routine protocols into sophisticated response mechanisms.

Staff readiness played a crucial role in the system's effectiveness. The team's ability to respond to automated alerts and coordinate their efforts through the system showed how technology can enhance rather than replace human judgment and action. Clear protocols and trained staff turned the system's capabilities into effective action.

Broader implications

David's case illustrates the evolution of location services from simple tracking systems to comprehensive safety and security solutions. The technology now serves as an integral component of modern healthcare operations, supporting both routine activities and emergency responses. The integration of real-time location data with automated alerts and coordinated response protocols has created new possibilities for patient care and safety.

This real-world application demonstrates how far location services have come from their military origins. The technology now serves as an essential component of healthcare safety and efficiency, while pointing toward future possibilities as these systems continue to evolve and integrate with other healthcare technologies. The successful resolution of David's case suggests that future developments in location services will continue to enhance healthcare providers' ability to ensure patient safety while optimizing operational efficiency.

Chapter 2

Location services technologies

Ali Youssef

In today's fast-paced healthcare environment, the demand for efficiency and accuracy has never been higher. Location-based services (LBS) has emerged as a transformative solution, offering enterprise applications designed to track and locate assets, devices, and personnel within the complex healthcare ecosystem. From sprawling hospitals to neighborhood clinics and home care settings, LBS technology continues to demonstrate its remarkable utility through widespread adoption across the healthcare industry.

Consider the daily challenges faced by clinical staff, particularly nurses who stand at the forefront of patient care. Their responsibilities span carrying out physician orders, monitoring vital signs, administering medications, serving as a bridge between doctors and patient families, and overseeing the use of essential medical equipment. A properly configured LBS system can eliminate the often-frustrating process of locating necessary medical equipment. In hospitals, a phenomenon known as "device hoarding" occurs when staff hide devices for personal use due to difficulties in finding them when urgently needed. This practice creates particular challenges for biomedical professionals responsible for maintaining and upgrading these devices. LBS offers a solution that not only pinpoints equipment location but also provides real-time status updates, indicating whether a machine is ready for use or requires maintenance.

This chapter focuses exclusively on LBS as a local positioning system within hospital facilities. At its core, this technology involves attaching a transmitter, commonly referred to as an LBS tag, to the desired asset. The Radio Frequency (RF) receiver then communicates the tag's information to software that presents a graphical interface for real-time monitoring of its status and location. Various LBS technologies utilize different wireless mediums for communication. Some systems directly interface with the hospital's Wi-Fi network, while others employ alternative wireless technologies. We will explore several different mediums that facilitate LBS, and many of these technologies can be integrated with Wi-Fi to enhance location accuracy.

DOI: 10.1201/9781003625483-3

Our exploration of these technologies will provide a comprehensive understanding of:

1. The fundamental principles behind each location tracking method
2. The strengths and limitations of various technologies
3. Implementation considerations for healthcare environments
4. Integration capabilities with existing systems
5. Future trends and emerging technologies

Whether you are an engineer tasked with implementing LBS or an executive seeking to understand the myriad use cases that can drive operational efficiencies, this chapter aims to provide the essential knowledge needed to make informed decisions about LBS in healthcare.

CORE TECHNOLOGIES

The foundation of modern healthcare location services relies on several key technologies, each offering unique advantages and specific use cases. Understanding these core technologies is essential for implementing effective location-based solutions in healthcare environments. Let us examine each technology, starting with the most established and moving toward emerging solutions.

Zigbee technology

Zigbee represents a fundamental technology in indoor positioning and asset tracking, offering capabilities particularly suited to healthcare LBS. Operating on global license-free bands (2.4 GHz, 900 MHz, 868 MHz), Zigbee employs mesh networking that allows data to "hop" between nodes, creating a robust and flexible network architecture.

In healthcare applications, Zigbee's meshing capabilities prove particularly valuable. Nodes can function as transmitters, receivers, or both, creating a self-healing network that maintains functionality even if individual nodes fail. With typical data rates of 20-250 kbps and indoor ranges of 10-100 meters, Zigbee provides reliable coverage for most healthcare facilities.

For asset tracking applications, Zigbee achieves impressive battery life through sophisticated sleep/wake duty cycling. Tags wake periodically to transmit location data, then return to sleep mode, conserving power. Location accuracy typically ranges from 1 to 3 meters, depending on the density of receivers deployed throughout the facility. This accuracy level suits most healthcare asset tracking needs while maintaining cost-effectiveness.

Wi-Fi-based solutions

Wi-Fi-based location services offer a compelling advantage: they leverage existing network infrastructure. Two primary approaches exist for implementing Wi-Fi location services:

The first approach utilizes a sensory network overlay, deploying separate receivers to detect LBS tags. This method functions similarly to a wireless intrusion prevention system (WIPS) overlay, allowing continued client service during LBS operation. However, it requires additional hardware investment.

Alternatively, the Wireless Access Point (WAP)-based approach uses existing access points as receivers for tags. While eliminating the need for extra hardware, this method requires careful consideration of AP resources, as LBS processing competes with client service demands.

Both approaches rely on several key location determination methods:

- Received signal strength indication (RSSI) for distance estimation
- Time of flight (ToF) calculations for precise positioning
- Time difference of arrival (TDoA) for multilateration

Success with Wi-Fi LBS typically requires careful attention to AP density, with an ideal spacing of 15-30 feet for room-level accuracy. Many hospitals require additional APs due to signal-blocking building materials. Combining Wi-Fi with supplemental technologies like infrared (IR), Bluetooth low energy (BLE), or ultra-wideband (UWB) can enhance precision significantly.

Infrared systems

Infrared (IR) technology enables precise indoor positioning through ToF measurements. IR emitters flood areas with invisible light pulses, while sensors on tags detect these pulses when in range. This system offers several distinct advantages:

- Accuracy within one meter due to narrow beam characteristics
- High resolution for exact positioning
- Minimal interference with other wireless signals
- Cost-effective emitter and sensor components
- Simple installation with standard power requirements

However, IR systems face certain limitations. Opaque objects block IR signals, restricting range and requiring clear line-of-sight. Signal accuracy degrades with wider beam dispersion, and tags must maintain direct line-of-sight to emitters for reliable operation.

Modern IR systems often incorporate exciters that activate tags when entering a zone, enabling:

- Location reporting only when necessary
- Extended battery life through low-power listening modes
- Enhanced accuracy through precise timing of exciter signals

Ultrasound systems

Ultrasound location tracking relies on high-frequency sound waves for precise positioning. Operating at frequencies from 20 kHz up to 10 MHz, these systems use wavelengths ranging from 6 mm to 0.06 mm. The technology employs a network of emitters that broadcast encoded ultrasound pulses, while sensors pick up and decode these signals for location determination.

Ultrasound offers distinct advantages in healthcare settings:

- Achieves precise room or zone-level accuracy (within inches)
- Signals remain confined within room boundaries
- Experiences minimal interference with other wireless systems
- Requires relatively inexpensive infrastructure

However, certain considerations effect implementation. Ultrasound waves can be absorbed and distorted by air, limiting effective range. Accuracy depends heavily on sensor density, and while line-of-sight isn't strictly required, it improves performance significantly. Digital signal processing extracts location data from ultrasound signals, while directional sensors enhance position calculation through angle of arrival measurements.

Ultra-wideband (UWB) technology

UWB represents the cutting edge of indoor positioning accuracy. UWB systems operate across a wide spectrum of radio frequencies (3.1 GHz to 10.6 GHz), transmitting low-power signals over short durations. Unlike conventional narrowband technologies, UWB eliminates the need for carrier waves and leverages precise time measurements for positioning.

Key advantages of UWB include:

- Centimeter-level accuracy for precise positioning
- Superior performance in environments with signal interference
- Effective operation in non-line-of-sight conditions
- Seamless coexistence with other wireless technologies
- Enhanced location security through signal properties

Implementation considerations include higher infrastructure costs compared to narrowband solutions, requirements for careful calibration and positioning, and potential integration challenges with legacy Wi-Fi systems. However, UWB's unmatched accuracy makes it invaluable for applications requiring precise location data, such as surgical asset tracking or sensitive equipment monitoring.

Bluetooth low energy (BLE)

BLE technology offers an ideal balance of power efficiency, cost-effectiveness, and accuracy for healthcare indoor positioning. Operating in the 2.4 GHz industrial, scientific, and medical (ISM) band with adaptive frequency hopping, BLE provides typical data rates of 1 Mbps and approximately 30-meter indoor range under optimal conditions.

BLE systems offer several compelling advantages:

- Ultra-low power consumption enabling long battery life
- Small, lightweight beacons that install easily
- Mesh networking capabilities for redundant coverage
- Native integration with mobile devices
- Reasonable accuracy using trilateration algorithms
- Built-in encryption and privacy protocols

However, implementers should consider certain limitations:

- Lower precision compared to some alternative technologies
- Signal absorption by human bodies affecting performance
- Frequency hopping can limit data rates
- Potential interference in high-density deployments

The combination of low cost, low power requirements, and scalable architecture makes BLE an optimal choice for many healthcare LBS applications, particularly when exact room-level accuracy isn't critical. Technology Selection and Integration.

When implementing location services in healthcare environments, organizations often find that no single technology provides a complete solution. The key lies in selecting complementary technologies based on specific use cases and requirements. Consider these factors when choosing technologies:

- Accuracy requirements
- Asset type and tracking needs
- Clinical vs. non-clinical applications
- Safety-critical vs. convenience tracking
- Infrastructure considerations
- Existing wireless networks
- Building construction materials
- Power availability

- Network capacity
- Cost factors
- Initial hardware investment
- Installation requirements
- Ongoing maintenance
- System scalability
- Integration requirements
- Existing clinical systems
- Security protocols
- Regulatory compliance
- Future expansion needs

Organizations increasingly adopt hybrid approaches, combining multiple technologies to achieve optimal coverage and accuracy while managing costs effectively. For example, using BLE for general asset tracking while employing UWB in areas requiring precise positioning creates a cost-effective, comprehensive solution (Figure 2.1).

HOW LBS WORKS

To comprehensively understand the functioning of LBS, it is imperative to delve into the technical underpinnings of location determination methods. LBS relies on a combination of techniques, including received signal strength (RSS), time of arrival (ToA), TDoA, and angle of arrival (AoA), to accurately calculate the position of assets or individuals within a given environment. The following section will provide a technical exploration of these fundamental concepts.

Received signal strength (RSS) analysis

RSS is a fundamental technique employed in LBS for estimating the distance between a transmitter and a receiver based on the strength of the received signal. It involves the measurement of the power level of the signal received from the transmitter. By analyzing these RSS data from multiple receivers, the system can estimate the distance between the transmitter and each receiver.

However, it is important to note that RSS-based calculations can be susceptible to several factors that affect signal propagation. Obstructions like walls or materials with high attenuation properties, such as lead lining, can distort the RSS readings. This distortion results in non-uniform range measurements, leading to variations in the estimated location. To address these challenges, RF engineers often employ propagation models like the inverse square law to calculate distances between transmitters and receivers.

Technology	Accuracy	Range	Power Needs	Cost	Best Use Cases
UWB	10-30cm	Up to 50m	Medium	High	Surgical Asset Tracking High-Value Equipment
BLE	2-5m	Up to 30m	Low	Low	General Asset Tracking Staff/Patient Location
WiFi	5-15m	Up to 100m	Medium	Medium	Zone-Level Tracking Mobile Device Location
IR	Room-level	Line of Sight	Low	Low	Room Presence Detection Staff Workflow Analysis
Ultrasound	Centimeter	Room-based	Medium	Medium	Precise Indoor Positioning Critical Asset Location

Figure 2.1 Table of locator technologies.

The inverse square law describes how the intensity of the RSS is inversely proportional to the square of the distance from the transmitter. While this law provides a predictable means of calculating distance when the device is near the receiver, its accuracy diminishes as the device moves farther away. Additionally, for locations with obstacles and complex environments, RF fingerprinting is used. RF fingerprinting involves creating a map of consistent RSS measurements across the facility to establish x/y coordinates on each floor. Changes in the environment necessitate re-measuring these fingerprint data, which can be resource intensive.

Time of arrival (ToA) technique

ToA is another critical method employed in LBS, focusing on measuring the time taken for a signal to travel from a transmitter to a receiver. This is often referred to as ToF. To accurately locate an asset or individual, at least three sensors are required. When the distances from these three different sensors to the transmitter are known, the location can be determined by finding the intersection point of the three circles with their radii representing the calculated distances.

However, achieving precise ToA measurements necessitates the synchronization of all nodes within the network. Ensuring this synchronization can be a complex task, particularly when dealing with a network comprising numerous devices.

Time difference of arrival (TDoA) approach

TDoA leverages the principles of multilateration or hyperbolic positioning to determine the location of the asset or individual being tracked. Much like ToA, TDoA relies on the measurement of the difference in travel times from each sensor to calculate the distances between each sensor and the transmitter. This calculation results in multiple hyperbolas, and the point of intersection of these hyperbolas provides the location of the transmitter.

Angle of arrival (AoA) method

AoA focuses on measuring the angle between the direction of an incident wave and a reference direction, often referred to as orientation. In the context of LBS, AoA requires an antenna array for each node to accurately determine the direction of incoming signals. By measuring the angles of arrival from multiple antennas, the system can triangulate the location of the transmitter.

One challenge associated with AoA is its susceptibility to multipath interference, which can impact the accuracy of angle measurements, particularly in environments with reflective surfaces.

In summary, today's real-time location services offer outstanding technologies like UWB, BLE, and Wi-Fi to enable healthcare facilities to track assets and people with accuracy, efficiency, and privacy. By assessing use cases, accuracy needs, and infrastructure, healthcare IT leaders can determine the right technology or combination to optimize workflows and patient outcomes. A tailored LBS approach can transform hospital operations.

CORE GEOSPATIAL CONCEPTS

Position

Position is a fundamental concept in geospatial technology, referring to the precise location of an object or entity described by coordinates. These coordinates typically include latitude and longitude but can also incorporate altitude for three-dimensional positioning. There are various types of coordinate systems used in geospatial applications, including geographic coordinate systems (GCS) that use latitude and longitude on a spherical model of the Earth, projected coordinate systems that transform the spherical Earth onto a flat plane for mapping purposes, and local coordinate systems used for smaller areas or specific projects.

Global positioning system (GPS) data is a prime example of time-delimited position data. GPS satellites transmit signals that receivers use to calculate their position on Earth. The data typically includes latitude, longitude, altitude (if available), and a timestamp. GPS accuracy can vary depending on factors such as the number of visible satellites, atmospheric conditions, obstructions like buildings or mountains, and the quality of the receiver. Advanced positioning techniques like differential GPS (DGPS) and real-time kinematic (RTK) GPS can provide even higher accuracy, down to centimeter-level precision in some cases.

Presence

Presence refers to the existence of an object or entity within a designated space. This concept is crucial for many LBS, as it allows for context-aware applications and services. When an object's presence in a specific space is known, various attributes of that space can be associated with the object. This contextual information can include environmental data such as temperature, humidity, or air quality, demographic information, points of interest, and regulatory zones like speed limits or restricted areas.

There are several methods for determining presence, including geofencing, which creates virtual boundaries around real-world areas, indoor positioning systems that use Wi-Fi, Bluetooth beacons, or other technologies to determine presence within buildings, and short-range technologies like radio frequency identification (RFID) and Near Field Communication (NFC) for detecting presence in specific locations.

The applications of presence data are diverse and impactful. In retail analytics, it can be used to understand customer behavior in stores. Smart home automation systems can adjust settings based on occupancy. Security systems can detect unauthorized presence in restricted areas. Location-based mobile marketing can deliver targeted content to users in specific locations. These applications demonstrate the power of presence data in creating more responsive and context-aware environments.

Proximity

Proximity describes the spatial relationship between two or more objects, typically in terms of distance or relative position. This concept is crucial for many LBS and applications. Proximity can be categorized in various ways, such as distance-based (measured in units of length like meters or miles), time-based (estimated travel time between objects), or relative (describing position using terms like "near," "far," or "between").

Calculating proximity can be done using different methods depending on the application. Euclidean distance measures the straight-line distance between two points, while Manhattan distance is used to determine distance in a grid-like path. Network distance measures the distance along a network of roads or paths, which is particularly useful for navigation and routing applications.

The applications of proximity data are numerous and varied. Friend finder apps can alert users when contacts are nearby, enhancing social connections. Location-based reminders can trigger notifications based on proximity to a place, improving personal productivity. In fleet management, proximity data can be used to optimize routes and dispatch the nearest vehicles, increasing operational efficiency. Augmented reality applications can use proximity data to display information about nearby points of interest, creating immersive and informative experiences.

Data fusion and sensor integration

The combination of different types of geospatial data and sensor inputs can significantly enhance the utility and accuracy of LBS. This process, often referred to as "data fusion" or "sensor fusion," allows for more robust and context-aware applications. The benefits of data fusion are numerous. It can improve accuracy by combining multiple data sources to reduce errors and uncertainties. It enhances context awareness by integrating complementary information about the environment from different sensors. Data fusion can also overcome individual sensor limitations, compensating for weaknesses in single sensor systems. Additionally, it provides continuity of service, allowing other data sources to maintain functionality when one fails.

In mobile devices, sensor fusion is widely used to enhance LBS. For example, combining GPS data with accelerometer readings can improve positioning accuracy when GPS signals are weak and enable dead reckoning for brief periods without GPS. The fusion of compass and accelerometer data provides more accurate orientation and heading information, compensating for magnetic interference. Integrating GPS with Wi-Fi and cellular data enables faster position acquisition (A-GPS) and improves indoor positioning where GPS signals are weak. The combination of barometer and GPS data can enhance altitude measurements, improving vertical positioning in multistory buildings.

Advanced fusion techniques are continuously being developed to further improve the accuracy and reliability of location data. Kalman filtering is a mathematical method for optimally combining data from multiple sources, widely used in navigation and tracking applications. Particle filters are useful for non-linear systems and complex environments, providing robust positioning in challenging scenarios. Machine learning approaches are increasingly being applied to identify patterns and relationships in multisensor data, enabling more intelligent and adaptive location services.

Location fidelity

Location fidelity refers to the confidence level associated with location information. It is a crucial concept for understanding the reliability and usefulness of location data in various applications. Location fidelity is described by the percentage confidence that an object is located within a specific space. It comprises three main components: the size of the area (the physical dimensions of the space in question), the composition (the nature and characteristics of the space), and the level of confidence (the probability that the object is actually within the defined area).

There are several levels of location fidelity, each suited to different applications and use cases. Venue fidelity refers to a high confidence that an object is somewhere within a building or large facility, typically covering areas of 10,000 to 1,000,000 square feet. This level of fidelity is useful for retail analytics, large event management, and coarse-grained presence detection. Zone fidelity narrows down the location to a specific area within a venue, covering areas of 1,000 to 10,000 square feet. This is applicable in scenarios like department-level retail analytics, airport security zones, and hospital ward management.

Room fidelity provides high confidence that an object is within a specific room or small area, typically 100 to 1,000 square feet. This level of precision is valuable for smart home automation, office space utilization analysis, and museum exhibit interactions. Precise location fidelity offers high confidence in the exact coordinates of an object, usually within 1–10 feet. This level of accuracy enables applications like indoor navigation, asset tracking in warehouses, and augmented reality experiences.

Route fidelity is a unique category that focuses on the path an object has taken or is taking, combining multiple location points over time. This is particularly useful for navigation systems, fleet tracking, and geofence-based services.

Several factors affect location fidelity, including sensor accuracy, environmental factors like signal interference and physical obstructions, temporal aspects (how recently the location was determined), movement (whether the object is stationary or in motion), and system calibration. Improving location fidelity often involves techniques such as sensor fusion, machine learning to improve predictions based on historical data, crowdsourcing to refine location information, and regular system calibration to ensure optimal performance.

The location engine

The location engine is a crucial component in LBS, responsible for processing raw location data and providing meaningful, actionable information to applications and users. It's a software system that ingests data from various location-aware sensors and other sources, processes this data, and outputs refined location information. The primary functions of a location engine include data collection and normalization, position calculation and refinement, context enrichment, location prediction and tracking, and geofencing and proximity alerts. It is often the goal with these types of engines to promote a single pane of glass view for all location events.

A typical location engine consists of several key components. The data input module collects raw data from various sources such as GPS receivers, Wi-Fi access points, cellular network information, Bluetooth beacons, IR, and other types of sensors. It then normalizes this data into a standard format for processing. The position calculation module applies algorithms to determine position based on the available data, using techniques like trilateration and fingerprinting.

The context enrichment module adds additional information to raw position data, potentially including reverse geocoding to convert coordinates to addresses, point of interest association, and semantic labeling (e.g., identifying locations as "home," "work," or "commuting"). The prediction and tracking module estimates future positions based on historical data and current trajectory, applies smoothing algorithms to reduce jitter in location data, and handles transitions between indoor and outdoor environments.

The geofencing and proximity module manages virtual perimeters, triggers alerts when objects enter or exit defined areas, and calculates proximity between objects or points of interest. Finally, the Application Programming Interface (API) and integration layer provides interfaces for applications to request and receive location data, manages privacy settings and data access controls, and supports various output formats and protocols.

Modern location engines often incorporate advanced features to enhance their capabilities. Machine learning integration can improve location accuracy over time by learning from historical data, adapting to individual user patterns and behaviors, and enhancing prediction capabilities for future locations. Privacy-preserving techniques are increasingly important, implementing data anonymization and encryption, supporting differential privacy for aggregate location data, and providing user controls for data sharing and retention.

Energy optimization is another crucial aspect, with intelligent management of sensor usage to minimize battery drain, adaptive sampling rates based on activity and environment, and leveraging of low-power positioning technologies when appropriate. Many location engines now employ a cloud-edge hybrid processing model, distributing computation between mobile devices and cloud infrastructure to enable real-time processing for latency-sensitive applications and support offline functionality when network connectivity is limited.

The design and implementation of location engines face several challenges and considerations. Balancing accuracy with battery life is an ongoing challenge, requiring adaptive algorithms that adjust based on required accuracy and available power. Indoor positioning remains a significant challenge, necessitating the integration of alternative technologies like Wi-Fi RTT, UWB, and BLE beacons to overcome the limitations of GPS in indoor environments.

Privacy and security are paramount concerns, requiring robust measures to protect user location data from unauthorized access and ensure compliance with regulations like General Data Protection Regulation (GDPR) and California Consumer Privacy Act (CCPA). Scalability is another critical factor, as location engines must handle large volumes of location data in real time and support millions of concurrent users and devices. Cross-platform compatibility and the ability to adapt to various environmental factors also pose ongoing challenges in the development of effective location engines.

Chapter 3

Location-based services 1.0

Ali Youssef

The experience of location-based services has a history of promise and peril for healthcare organizations. The ability to find people and things in a complex environment like healthcare opens an array of opportunities for improvement. No one debates this but location services can be like playing 3D chess with the infrastructure, use cases, and software solutions that are out there.

In the early 2000s, healthcare organizations began exploring innovative ways to manage their complex environments more efficiently. This exploration led to the emergence of Location Services 1.0, a first-generation suite of comprehensive, technology-driven solutions designed to track and manage people, equipment, and resources within healthcare facilities. These systems, primarily based on real-time location system (RTLS) technology, held the promise of revolutionizing healthcare operations and patient care.

The core of Location Services 1.0 was built upon RTLS technology, comprising several key components. Small tags, attached to people or assets, emitted signals for location tracking. These signals were detected by sensors installed throughout the facility. A dedicated wireless network, either Wi-Fi or a dedicated frequency, transmitted the location data to a software platform, where it was processed, visualized, and integrated with other hospital systems. The most common technologies employed in these systems were radio frequency identification (RFID), which used radio waves for short-range tracking; infrared (IR), utilizing infrared light for line-of-sight tracking; and ultrasound, employing high-frequency sound waves for precise indoor positioning. Each of these technologies had its own strengths and limitations, often leading to the development of hybrid systems that combined multiple approaches for more comprehensive coverage.

Location Services 1.0 was designed to address a wide range of healthcare challenges, with several key use cases driving its adoption. Asset management and par-level management were primary applications, allowing hospitals to track medical equipment to reduce loss and rental costs, and improve utilization. Patient tracking capabilities offer the potential to optimize patient flow and reduce wait times. Staff tracking aimed to improve workflow efficiency and response times. Other important use cases included

DOI: 10.1201/9781003625483-4

infection control, environmental monitoring for temperature-sensitive assets like pharmaceuticals, infant protection in maternity wards, and safeguarding patients with cognitive impairments who might be prone to wandering. In addition, the icing on the cake was use cases like hand hygiene tracking.

These various applications formed what was often described as a "hub and spoke" model, with the RTLS technology at the center and the different use cases radiating outward like spokes on a wheel. This model was both appealing and challenging for healthcare organizations. While it offered the potential for a comprehensive solution to multiple healthcare management issues, it also presented significant implementation and integration hurdles.

Despite the promising potential of Location Services 1.0, the infrastructure requirements were often extensive, necessitating the installation of numerous sensors throughout the facility, the deployment of a dedicated wireless network, integration with existing IT systems, and sometimes even physical modifications to buildings for sensor placement. These requirements led to high initial costs and potential disruptions to hospital operations during installation. The costs were so astronomical at times that hospital administrators questioned the value of these types of platforms.

The use of active RFID tags introduced ongoing maintenance challenges. These tags typically required battery replacements every one to two years, a significant task in a large hospital tracking thousands of assets. Healthcare organizations needed to develop processes for managing tag inventory, as well as for attaching and removing tags from assets and people as needed.

COMMON LOCATION SERVICES USE CASES

The following use cases represent the most widely adopted applications of location-based services in healthcare environments. While these use cases have demonstrated value individually, their implementation as point solutions often leads to the challenges discussed earlier in this chapter.

Asset tracking and management

Asset tracking represents one of the most financially compelling use cases for location services in healthcare. By attaching RTLS tags to mobile medical equipment, hospitals can monitor the real-time location, status, and utilization of critical assets. The solution typically requires comprehensive coverage throughout the facility, with receivers or exciters installed in corridors, patient rooms, and storage areas. Beyond simple location tracking, advanced implementations include maintenance status monitoring, par-level management, and utilization analytics. The technology dependencies include reliable tag-to-receiver communication, accurate zone-level positioning, and integration with computerized maintenance management systems (CMMS) and inventory management platforms.

Healthcare organizations implementing asset tracking often see immediate returns through reduced equipment loss, improved utilization rates, and decreased rental costs. However, the infrastructure requirements can be substantial, necessitating careful planning of receiver placement and network design to ensure adequate coverage while managing installation costs.

Staff duress

Staff duress systems, also referred to as staff safety, panic buttons, or code white in some hospitals, provide healthcare workers with wearable panic buttons that can summon immediate assistance in threatening situations. These systems require precise and persistent location accuracy to direct response teams to the exact location of an incident. The infrastructure typically includes personal alarm devices (often integrated into ID badges), strategically placed receivers throughout the facility, and integration with security systems and communication platforms. Critical areas like emergency departments and behavioral health units often require enhanced coverage density to ensure reliable operation.

The effectiveness of staff duress systems depends heavily on rapid response capabilities and accurate location determination. Implementation requires careful consideration of alarm routing, response protocols, and coverage verification, particularly in areas with complex architectural features or potential RF interference. Integration with existing security systems and communication platforms is essential for a coordinated response.

Patient tracking

Patient tracking solutions help healthcare facilities monitor patient movement throughout their care journey, from admission through discharge. These systems typically utilize wristbands with embedded RTLS tags and require coverage in all patient care areas, waiting rooms, and transition zones. The infrastructure must support accurate zone-level positioning and integrate with admission-discharge-transfer (ADT) systems, electronic health records (EHRs), and patient flow management platforms.

Successful implementation requires careful attention to privacy considerations and integration with clinical workflows. The technology must be robust enough to maintain consistent tracking while being unobtrusive to patient care activities. Integration with other hospital systems enables automated updates to patient status and location information, improving overall operational efficiency.

Infant protection

Infant protection systems represent a specialized application of location services focused on preventing infant abduction and ensuring proper mother–baby matching. These systems require exceptionally reliable coverage in maternity units, including patient rooms, nurseries, and exit points. The infrastructure typically includes tamper-resistant tags, door-locking mechanisms, and specialized monitoring equipment. Integration with access control systems and nurse call platforms is essential for comprehensive security.

The critical nature of infant protection demands redundant systems and fail-safe mechanisms. Implementation requires careful consideration of tag attachment methods, door control integration, and alarm response protocols. Regular testing and maintenance procedures are essential to ensure system reliability.

Hand hygiene compliance

Hand hygiene monitoring systems use location technology to track healthcare worker compliance with hand-washing protocols. These systems require specialized sensors near hand-washing stations and sanitizer dispensers, combined with personnel tracking capabilities. The infrastructure must support the detection of staff presence near hygiene stations and the accurate measurement of washing duration and frequency. Integration with infection control systems and compliance reporting platforms enables comprehensive monitoring and intervention programs.

Implementation success depends on accurate detection of hygiene events and reliable staff identification. The system must balance the need for detailed compliance monitoring with practical workflow considerations and privacy concerns. Regular calibration and maintenance of dispensing sensors are essential for accurate data collection.

Elopement/wandering prevention

Elopement monitoring systems protect at-risk patients, particularly those with cognitive impairments or dementia, from leaving designated safe areas unattended. These systems require comprehensive coverage at all potential exit points and throughout patient care areas, utilizing a combination of wearable tags and strategically placed sensors. The infrastructure must support immediate detection of unauthorized movement patterns and integrate with door-locking systems, nurse call platforms, and security systems. Critical areas such as memory care units and behavioral health departments often require enhanced coverage density to ensure reliable perimeter control.

Implementation requires careful consideration of patient dignity while maintaining safety, including discreet tag designs and thoughtful integration with normal care workflows. The system must balance security requirements with the practical needs of patient care, incorporating flexible zone definitions for different times of day or patient risk levels. Successful deployment depends on reliable door control integration, clear staff notification protocols, and regular testing of response procedures. Integration with other clinical systems helps ensure that patient risk levels and monitoring requirements are consistently updated as conditions change.

Wayfinding

Wayfinding solutions help patients, visitors, and staff in navigating complex healthcare facilities efficiently. These systems require comprehensive indoor positioning infrastructure, including beacons, Wi-Fi access points, and other location technologies throughout the facility. The implementation must support accurate position determination and provide intuitive user interfaces through mobile applications or kiosk systems. Integration with appointment scheduling systems and facility management platforms can enable personalized navigation experiences.

Effective wayfinding implementation requires careful attention to user experience design and consideration of various user groups' needs. The system must maintain accuracy across different device types and platforms while providing clear, contextual guidance. Regular updates to routing information and point-of-interest data are essential for maintaining system utility.

The complexity and friction of Location Services 1.0 systems often exceeded the technical capabilities of many healthcare IT departments. Specialized knowledge was required for system maintenance, and organizations frequently struggled with troubleshooting and optimizing performance. Scaling the system as needs evolve has proven to be challenging for many institutions.

Integration with existing hospital systems was another significant hurdle. Healthcare organizations often encounter compatibility issues with legacy software, data standardization problems, and complexity in achieving real-time data synchronization. These integration challenges could limit the effectiveness of the location services and reduce the potential benefits (Figure 3.1). What use is a staff duress platform with lag?

User adoption presented yet another challenge. Many healthcare organizations faced resistance from staff members concerned about privacy implications, particularly in relation to personnel tracking. There was often a significant learning curve associated with the new technologies, and inconsistent use could lead to incomplete data, reducing the system's overall effectiveness.

The high costs associated with Location Services 1.0 necessitated careful cost-benefit and return on investment (ROI) analysis. Healthcare organizations had to consider not only the initial hardware and software purchases but also the expenses related to installation, infrastructure modifications, ongoing maintenance and support, and staff training and change management. Against these costs, they weighed potential benefits such as improved asset utilization, enhanced patient safety and satisfaction, increased operational efficiency, better infection control, and reduced equipment loss and theft.

However, many healthcare organizations found that realizing these benefits required implementation across multiple use cases. This led to what became known as the "hub and spoke" dilemma, where partial implementation often failed to justify the high costs of the system. Organizations

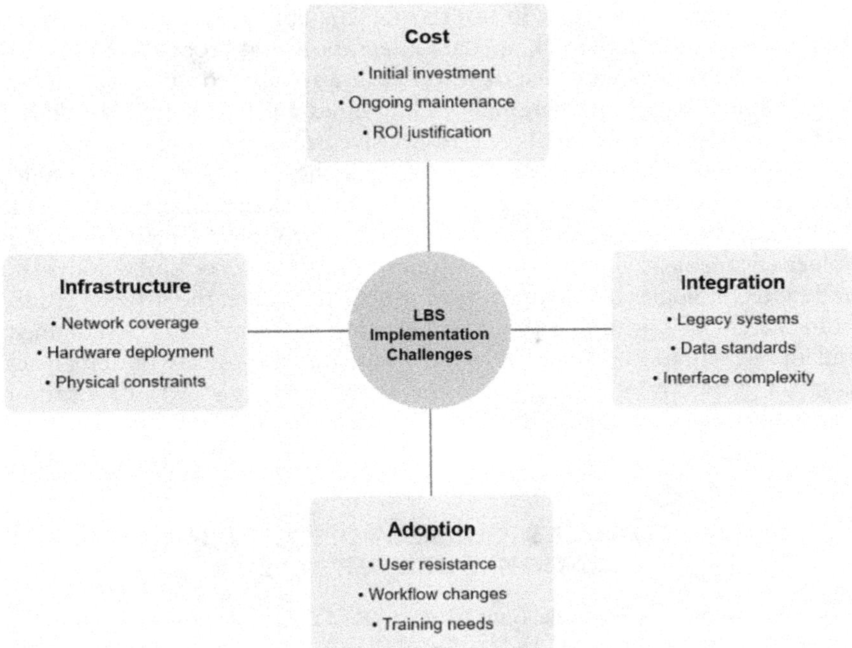

Figure 3.1 LBS implementation challenges diagram.

frequently found themselves caught between the high costs of full implementation and the limited benefits of partial deployment.

As healthcare organizations grappled with the challenges of Location Services 1.0, technology began to evolve. There was a shift toward more cost-effective technologies like Bluetooth low energy (BLE), which promised easier implementation and lower ongoing maintenance costs. The integration of location data with advanced analytics opened up possibilities for predictive insights, potentially increasing the value proposition of these systems. There was also a movement toward more flexible, scalable architecture, addressing some of the limitations of the first-generation systems.

These developments set the stage for what would become known as Location Services 2.0, which would address many of the limitations of the first-generation systems while building on their foundational principles. The evolution of these technologies reflected a growing understanding of the unique needs and challenges of healthcare environments, as well as advancements in the underlying technological capabilities.

It should not be understated that Location Services 1.0 represented a significant step forward in healthcare technology, offering the promise of improved efficiency, safety, and patient care. While implementation challenges and high costs limited widespread adoption, the lessons learned from these early systems paved the way for more advanced and accessible location-based technologies in healthcare. The core principles of Location Services 1.0 – real-time tracking, data integration, and process optimization – remain relevant as we move forward. Future systems continue to build on these foundations, leveraging new technologies and approaches to deliver on the promise of truly intelligent, responsive healthcare environments.

The journey of Location Services 1.0 in healthcare illustrates the complex interplay between technological innovation and practical implementation in healthcare settings. It underscores the importance of careful planning, stakeholder engagement, and ongoing optimization in the successful deployment of new technologies. As healthcare continues to evolve, the insights gained from the era of Location Services 1.0 continue to inform the development and implementation of new solutions aimed at improving the efficiency, safety, and quality of patient care. This is fueling a new wave of location-based services 2.0 adoption.

EDENVALE'S JOURNEY – DISCOVERING LOCATION-BASED SERVICES 1.0

When Sarah Chen, Edenvale General Hospital's ED Director, first brought up the idea of RTLS in the capital budget meeting, she came prepared. "We're wasting an average of 45 minutes per shift searching for equipment," she explained, spreading photos across the conference table showing IV pumps hidden in utility closets and portable monitors stashed behind curtains. "Our nurses are hoarding equipment because they can't find what they need when they need it."

The initial ED implementation seemed like a clear success. Within three months, equipment search times dropped dramatically, and staff reported higher satisfaction. The system paid for itself just by reducing rental costs for specialty beds and pumps that were previously "lost" in the department.

This success quickly caught the attention of other department leaders. Dr. James Martinez from Labor & Delivery advocated for an infant protection system after a near-miss event, emphasizing the need for real-time monitoring of every infant in their unit to meet Joint Commission requirements. Security Director Mark Thompson pushed for staff duress capabilities following several incidents in the ED and Behavioral Health units, stressing that every second counts when situations escalate. Meanwhile, the Clinical Engineering department head, Tom Wilson, wanted hospital-wide equipment tracking to address missed preventive maintenance deadlines and reduce replacement costs for misplaced equipment.

However, each implementation brought its own set of challenges. The infrastructure demands were substantial: the ED system required dedicated Wi-Fi access points, the infant protection system needed proprietary sensors, the staff duress system required its own receivers, and Clinical Engineering's solution demanded different hardware. Each system also required its own network configuration.

The software complexity became overwhelming for CIO Johnathon Bennett's IT team. They found themselves maintaining five different software platforms, multiple unintegrated databases, separate login credentials, different mobile apps, and incompatible data formats between systems. The financial impact also raised concerns, with CFO Robert Chen noting that annual maintenance contract costs were exceeding initial capital investments for some systems, while vendors continued raising their subscription fees for proprietary hardware.

User adoption varied significantly across departments. While ED nurses embraced their equipment tracking system and L&D staff consistently used the infant protection system, other units showed only sporadic usage. Many staff members complained about juggling multiple apps and interfaces, and the training requirements became increasingly burdensome.

The IT team made several attempts at integration, exploring options from creating a "single pane of glass" view to investigating middleware solutions and application programming interface (API) options. Each attempt, however, only revealed new technical challenges. The situation reached a critical point during a Joint Commission survey when a simple question about maintenance history and current location of critical care equipment couldn't be answered comprehensively, despite having multiple tracking systems in place.

This experience taught Edenvale several crucial lessons about technology selection, operational impact, strategic planning, and vendor management. They learned that point solutions created long-term integration challenges, while proprietary systems limited future flexibility. Infrastructure and maintenance costs often exceeded initial projections, and user adoption suffered from system complexity. The lack of an enterprise-wide strategy limited benefits and created departmental silos, making ROI difficult to measure across fragmented systems.

Vendor management became increasingly complex as multiple relationships required careful handling. Contract negotiations grew more challenging, support quality varied significantly between vendors, and upgrade cycles weren't synchronized, creating additional operational challenges.

Even with the bad experiences with RTLS, RFID, and, frankly, location-based services in general, Edenvale saw the amazing potential of the technology. Many of the systems worked adequately, but fragmentation of the disparate infrastructures and software was killing the ROI. They had many point solutions, and some were spread around IT so that no one IT department owned these systems. Each of them was supported by some outside integrator and there was little internal talent that knew Internet of Things (IoT) or the architecture overall. The hospital was under tremendous financial pressure, and Johnathon was charged with getting the IT spend down. During their most recent IT financial assessment, these systems seemed to be breaching the spend threshold they had set for flagging total cost of ownership (TCO). Location-based services was on the hot seat.

The applications portfolio VP was Suresh Mehta, and he asked to talk to the departments that were using these systems to see where they were at with them. If they were not happy, perhaps some of them should be wound down. None of the departments wanted to part with the systems, even though they had complaints about them. He asked them about how they measured the return they got from the system, and none of the departments had anything measurable to work with. ROI wasn't their problem. Johnathon was in a dilemma. He decided to create a steering committee to find ways to get these systems.

The steering committee was led by Suresh, and he invited the infrastructure directors and the operational department leaders to be part of the steering committee. The operational departments that were requested to join were the departments that were using location-based systems.

In the first meeting, the first thing he noticed was that there was a commitment to people using the systems, but having the technical discussions and the business discussions in the same meeting was fruitless. Now, two committees were needed: an LBS Steering Committee and an LBS Technical Steering Committee. This was becoming a lot of work.

In his one-on-one with Johnathon, Suresh was honest about the load that the location-based services steering was putting on him. They decided it was time to get a program manager to take over the program. Imani Jefferson was a participant in the Request For Pricing (RFP) for the new RTLS, and she had pointed out to Suresh the state of the overall program. Because there wasn't really any LBS program, it was noted but tabled until now. Imani was excited but also realistic about the challenge.

Imani was introduced at the monthly LBS Steering Committee meeting and spent the meeting listening and getting a sense of where the users were with the systems. At the end of the meeting, she asked if she could talk to users from the systems in each of the departments. The department directors said, "sure."

The technical steering committee hadn't had its first meeting yet, so Imani organized it and kicked it off. She started the meeting by showing everyone the inventory she prepared for each application and each infrastructure. This was what she got from Suresh. In the meeting, she found out there were systems that neither of them even knew about. There were applications that used different infrastructures in different parts of the building, and there were different versions of the applications in different departments. Ouch!!

Last, she met with the vendors that were supporting some of the systems like the Nurse Call system and new RTLS that was going to support the new

CMMS. The topics were going to be ROI and support Service Level Agreements (SLAs). The discussion about supporting SLAs was short. They were vague and hard to measure, but there were some SLAs. When she talked to the RTLS vendor about ROI, he said that ROI was going to be a challenge without expanding the system first. That was not good news. This was going to be a classic chicken-egg situation, and the climate for new investment in location-based services was not there.

The technical steering committee was in agreement on several fronts. The way toward ROI was through consolidating infrastructure and applications wherever possible. The other point of agreement was that they needed a location-based services architect. This ROI challenge was going in the wrong direction. When Imani met with Suresh and told him they needed an LBS architect, he said, "you're hired." She laughed, but he didn't laugh. She asked if he was serious, and he said, "first, they don't exist and second you are more than qualified. You know more about this stuff than anybody in the organization." Now she had two important roles and a big challenge in front of her.

Imani got access to every system she could and started learning how they worked. Consolidation would be hard, but there was hope. The CMMS was modular enough that you could present a group of users with the location of equipment without giving them access to the entire CMMS. Maybe that would allow the deprecation of one of their applications. It would require convincing surgery to switch applications. Next was the infrastructure. The new RTLS was able to integrate with the nurse call system, so they could deprecate some of the old infrastructure there. When they looked at the numbers, that still was not going to get them the savings they needed. They went back to the RTLS integrator, and he said they would need to expand the system and add valuable use cases.

Imani knew that Edenvale had a performance improvement team and that they had some ongoing projects that might benefit from LBS. When she met with the director of PI, she learned they had a project to do Periodic Automatic Replenishment (PAR) stocking of IV pumps. She was shocked when she found out it had been tabled and asked why. Apparently, the stakeholders couldn't agree on the process. She asked what technology they were planning to use, and the director said none. It was going to be all process changes with the Central Sterile processing team and the patient care units. She showed the director what they could do with the technology, and the PI director had no idea this was possible. This might solve their problems. If they had the feedback from LBS, it would be able to calm the concerns that were being aired.

Edenvale was getting ready to upgrade their IV pumps, and the timing was good because they knew they had a flow issue with them and there was a lot of hoarding going on. They didn't now want to move forward the old broken process with their new fleet of pumps. Imani was excited to talk to Suresh about it. Suresh said let's take it to the steering committee and asked for a proposal. When they got the price tag from the RTLS vendor for the project, it was more than they expected. They thought they were back to square one.

Imani had heard about care traffic control and knew it was a promising approach to location-based services. She found a consultant who was recommended by the integrator, and his name was Derek Frazer. She met with Derek and explained what they were going through, and he offered to help them with a strategy to get LBS on track to ROI. Imani went to Suresh, and he had that look that means, when are we going to save money instead of spending more. Suresh knew the feeling that Imani had of being overwhelmed and needing help, and he agreed to the engagement.

Derek said that before we even talk about care traffic control, we need to get your LBS 1.0 issues fixed. We are going to measure the LBS 1.0 ROI and use it to get you to LBS 2.0. Imani asked, "What is LBS 2.0? Derek said let's get this strategy done, and we can talk about LBS 2.0 and start looking at care traffic control. Imani agreed.

Derek said, "We are going to operate with some themes. They are:"

1. Earn the right to do the next project
2. ROI is more than dollars, but that's where you start
3. Everything starts with the maps
4. Mobile apps for mobile work
5. Workflows are king, so measure them precisely
6. Use what you already have
7. Minimal new infrastructure

Derek said, "you will get to know these themes as we move forward."

Table 3.1

Problem	*Impact*	*Initial solution*
Fragmented Systems	High TCO	System Inventory
No Central Ownership	Support Issues	Steering Committee
Limited IoT Expertise	Maintenance Challenge	Program Manager
Unknown Systems	Cost Control Issues	Technical Assessment

Chapter 4

Location-based services 2.0

Paul E. Zieske

LOCATION-BASED SERVICES 2.0

This chapter is a visionary look at the location-based services that fit the concept of care traffic control. Even though some of this has yet to be seen in the market, it is important to plant a flag where the industry should go and set a course to get there. There is a starting point and many steps we can take as the market takes shape, so there is no point in waiting for it.

The next evolution of location-based services will see the creation of a digital twin for the enterprise workplace. This will allow process improvements and automation to be modeled before it is implemented. Even though this sounds aspirational, the components of this digital twin are available now. It is much more a matter of architecture than raw materials. To illustrate this, we have included a maturity curve section in Chapter 20.

A point of contrast between LBS1.0 and Location-based Services 2.0 (LBS2.0) is where it sits in the organization's technology stack. Where LBS1.0 is a list of separate point solutions, LBS2.0 involves a platform that services an entire enterprise. That platform has connectors that provide location data to other core systems, and it serves the unique needs of individual departments. It pulls in location data from sensors that cover wide areas of geography and processes the data to get it where it needs to go.

In LBS2.0, there is an emphasis on geospatial processing, geographic information systems (GIS), and mobile devices. Maps in LBS2.0 are a critical part of the digital twin as they are the digital representation of the geography, the buildings, and spaces in the building. This, combined with sensors, allows for higher levels of automation than ever before. Geospatial processing is necessary for the expanding use of sensors and new features. This version of a digital twin includes IPS to track mobile workflows. The digital twin will expand the use of mobile devices like iPhones and Android, and these will become a vital part of mobile workflows. Workflow automation is enabled by combining mobile devices with this new emphasis on GIS and the sensors that are a part of the digital twin. LBS2.0 expands situational

DOI: 10.1201/9781003625483-5

awareness and automation to a new level and drives changes in the way work is managed and services are delivered.

We promised the use of slogans and alliteration so we will offer a slogan here. LBS2.0 is "Mobile first and workflows last and last." Mobile first was famously coined by Facebook because Mark Zuckerberg recognized that people were more engaged with their mobile devices and by focusing on that user experience, they would be more engaged. When we think of location-based services, they are, by definition, mobile. By making the mobile device location aware, indoors and out, the possibilities are endless. Saying "work-flows last," means a system that is built into the workflows is not easily abandoned. We also mean that anything we do in care traffic control can be packaged into a mobile workflow.

Instead of an Real-Time Locator System (RTLS) that is the center of a suite of applications that are using it, the RTLS is just a sensor that contributes real-time data to the digital twin. This allows the application of the location sensors to be tuned to the workflow, and it ensures that the performance of the system meets the expectations of the users.

When there is a platform for location, there will also be the ability to integrate with more systems. A care traffic control system will make many other systems location aware, and that will spawn a new era of automation for the systems that drive the expansion of location-based services and change the way we think about enterprise operations.

CHARACTERISTICS OF LOCATION-BASED SERVICES 2.0

Ubiquity

The most recognizable feature of the next evolution of location services will be their eventual geographic expansion throughout the entire enterprise. Location-based services are following the same arc as other technology domains that have enabled amazing user experiences and growth in productivity. If we remember how enterprise Wireless Fidelity (WIFI) advanced, it was established in isolated areas until the value of expanding it throughout the building had become obvious. Additionally, the ecosystem of endpoint devices, like smartphones and tablets, needed to be ready for that expansion. WIFI enabled mobility, but the devices that were connecting to the WIFI needed to generate the demand before the expansion could occur.

Location services are different from WIFI because the ubiquity for location services does not have to come from a single system, as there are strengths and weaknesses in technologies that need to be considered. The locating and tracking of objects and mobile devices have value everywhere, and this type of foundational ubiquity will become the norm with LBS2.0, just like it has for WIFI.

Automation

Another characteristic of LBS2.0 will be the trend toward automation. Currently, most location-based services are used for observation. That observation is usually used to create situational awareness with limited or no automation. The observation can help determine where things are to make it easier for people to do their jobs. For example, if a patient has an RTLS-enabled wristband, and the last known location of the patient is an east exit, this can be observed on a map. This observation contributes to situational awareness and will determine if the patient has possibly eloped.

Location fidelity is advancing as is the geographic ubiquity which creates the ability to do more advanced automation. This automation will enable control mechanisms that can remove some of the human effort from processes and workflows. In our previous example, sensing the patient's location at the exit can trigger notifications to security automatically. In the case of infant security, the unauthorized exit of an infant from the nursery can automatically lock the doors in the L&D department. Both use cases come from the more abstracted use case of loss prevention automation.

Workflows

Even though automation can be used effectively for use cases, solutions that are built around workflows will have the most benefit to the user. When location-aware workflow automation is a part of the work that is being done, the users will adopt it. Use cases are sometimes seen as adding to the workload. Using an RTLS to find equipment requires bringing up the system, locating what you want, and orienting yourself to find it. If finding equipment is built into the workflow, then the system is already aware of what you want and why you want it.

The need for locating mobile devices, like Android and iOS devices, will be just as important as the need to locate objects like equipment and supplies. Indoor positioning (indoor GPS), dependent and independent surveillance for tracking objects, and an enterprise location engine to process all the location inputs into useful information. Geospatial information should be based on standards and should cover whole buildings. This is where geographic information systems (GIS) become a critical part of the foundation of an enterprise approach to location services. In Chapter 1, section "Current technologies", we will talk about an indoor mapping standard that has been adopted by the GIS community. When someone is doing work that requires them to go somewhere or find something, the user experience will be on a mobile device. Additionally, for LBS2.0, the mobile device will be a part of a distributed context aware system, where the mobile device is doing some of the work of the system it supports.

The line between the tracking work and the equipment and supplies that are part of the work will disappear. From the perspective of functionality, workflow automation is the centerpiece of LBS2.0. With workflows front and center, finding the things that are necessary to do the work is built into the workflow automation. With the ability to track the work, the concept of "closing the loop" will be a critical part of workflow automation. Mobile workflows have a goal, and there is a repeatable cycle involved in them. Closing the loop means the mobile part of the workflow will be tracked from beginning to end so that the outcome can be measured, and the completion can be fully represented. This is vital to situational awareness and where automation makes inroads toward significant productivity gains.

Enterprise location engine

The operational digital twin is used to automate workflows, but it also supplies location information to other core systems. It is helpful to understand the relationship the digital twin has to the existing healthcare information systems. There are two types of systems that use location services. The first are systems that are *enhanced* by adding the context that comes from location but are not dependent on location to provide their value. The second system is a location-*dependent system* because to provide the service it is designed for requires location. LBS1.0 is mostly based on those location-dependent systems. The wheel of use cases described in Chapter 1, section "Commercial evolution" is all location-dependent. The digital twin services the needs of the entire enterprise and enhances the core systems that the enterprise depends on. These location-aware core systems will benefit the organization even more than the location-dependent systems. The core systems are where the enterprise's most important data lies, and adding location as context to that data is immensely valuable. The need to supply all these systems with location data will create the need for a platform that is a part of the digital twin that we will call the enterprise location engine.

Dependent	*Location enhanced*
• Employee Duress	• EHR – patient location, caregiver location, equipment location
• Patient Elopement	• ERP – location of amount-based supplies, procedural supplies
• Rounding	• CMMS – equipment location
• Hand Hygiene	• ITSM – location of worker responding to work orders
• Infant Protection	• LIM – lab sample location
• Loss Prevention	• Access Management – identity and physical access
• Wayfinding	• Security – location of officers and security personnel
• Nurse Call Cancel	• Pharmacy – medication deliveries

The enterprise location engine is where the location data is ingested from the sensors, processed, and matched with the identity for what is being located. For instance, the RTLS will locate the tag that is attached to the medical device, but the identity of the medical device should be sourced from the computerized maintenance management system (CMMS). Throughout the book, we apply the use of alliteration to define terms that we will use to develop concepts. Starting with identity, which takes the form of people and property, and the location data, which takes the form of position, proximity, presence, and possession. Location is sourced from mobile devices, independent surveillance, dependent surveillance, and crowdsensing.

The location engine, as described in Chapter 1, section "Early RFID development", is designed to provide location information only from the infrastructure it supports. An RTLS has a location engine that tracks the location of the tags that are a part of that system and can offer no additional location information. That first level of location information is important, but to take full advantage of indoor positioning, crowdsensing, or cameras, an overarching layer is needed. This layer of processing can combine multiple location inputs and use statistical processing to improve the certainty of the location information.

All the location inputs have areas of geographic coverage and different levels of certainty that contribute to the location fidelity of the digital twin. To get the highest location fidelity, we are adding the concept of dependent and independent surveillance. To process these inputs, a robust enterprise location engine is needed (Figure 4.1). This location engine will be part of a care traffic control system, which will be considered a core system like the

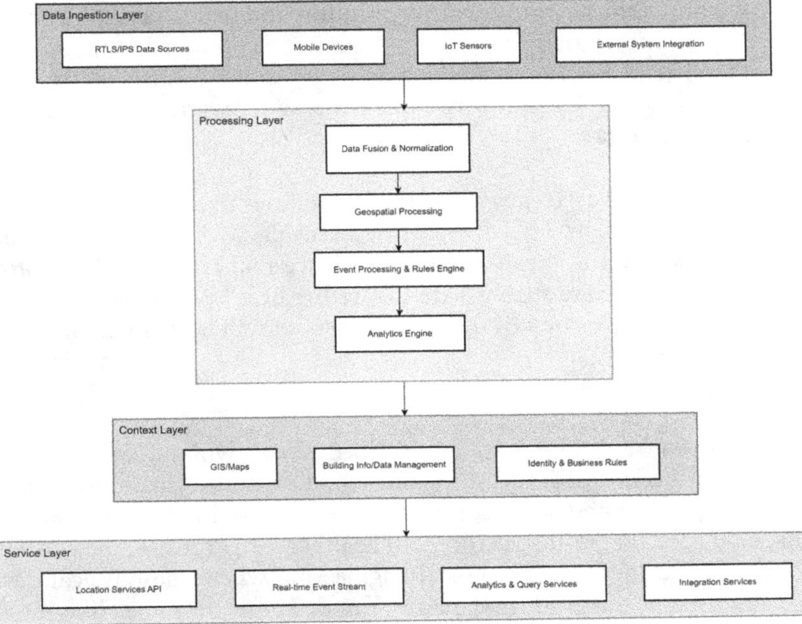

Figure 4.1 Enterprise location engine diagram.

electronic health record (EHR), ERP, or CMMS. It will take in the data from multiple location producing systems, process it, and distribute it where needed. The location-dependent systems and the downstream core systems will get the location information for people and property and access the spatial information from a central data source we are calling "places."

The data ingest process will consider the capabilities and limitations of each of the location sources. Combinations of each of the location source options add to the location fidelity, but only if there is a location engine to process the inputs correctly. This is where centralized geospatial information is important so that there is one source of truth. For example, if the position of a device is described as room "I-328" in one system, it shouldn't appear as "I 328" in another. Department names have the same concern as one might be called "Cardiology" in one system and another it is called "6 West Cardiology".

Traditionally, the focus of location services has been on the position (or location) of people and things. Location engines are built to determine the position of an active (battery-powered) beacon. These beacons can be used to perceive other geospatial parameters that can be used to do many things. The four listed below are the **4Ps** we use in care traffic control.

- Position: The location and identity of an entity using some 3D coordinate system.
- Proximity: The distance from a source entity to a target entity in the x, y plane. Either entity can have position and/or direction, but it is not required for proximity.
- Presence: A Boolean indicating an entity is in a defined space.
- Possession: A Boolean where one entity assumes the position information of another.

The 4Ps create a way to inventory the capabilities that the location sensors provide to the system. They are part of a sensing layer that is used to automate a workflow and create a user experience that is designed to optimize that workflow. Even though we are suggesting BLE beacons, sensor technology that can perceive any of these four items should be evaluated.

IT and OT

The expansion and automation described above will coincide with closing the gap between IT and OT. OT, or operational technology, is defined as "the hardware and software used to monitor and control physical processes, devices, and infrastructure". In healthcare operations, the concept of OT is historically found in clinical engineering where the physical devices that are used at the point of care are found. These are things like Infusion Pumps, Patient Monitoring Systems, and Imaging Systems. There is building automation, laboratory automation, and pharmacy automation that all have systems like this. As IoT and Location-based Services advance, the systems that they support will become part of the OT stack. At the same time, the interconnectedness between all the OT systems will create a need to close the gap between what we call IT and OT.

Whether it comes from an expansion using a multiplicity of point solutions or the strategic implementation of an enterprise solution, that solution will be a digital replica of the building. Such a solution is what is known in the automation industry as a digital twin.

Indoor positioning

Indoor positioning (IPS) is a vital component in Location-based Services 2.0. It is the capability of a mobile device, like an Android or iOS device, to get a latitude, longitude, and vertical position that is usually in the form of a floor number. IPS works like GPS, but it functions indoors. IPS allows the mobile devices to participate in location-aware workflows and be located when necessary. There is a wide array of features we have become familiar with as we have seen the pervasive use of GPS. These features are becoming made available indoors, as well as new features that are unique to the indoor use cases. Way finding, routing, mapping, and tracking are some of the features that can now be done indoors. There are many sensors that are becoming standard equipment on these devices. They are a critical part of the technological ecosystem. There are peripherals like barcode scanning sleds that can be added. Extended life batteries are available for some use cases.

The difference between locating a mobile device and locating a medical device is that the mobile device "knows" where it is, separate from any locator system. The onboard GPS chip and the location system that is part of a smartphone compute its location. The GPS does not know the location of devices that are using the system, but the devices know where they are because of the system. With the medical device, the tracking system knows the location of the medical device because it can find the tag that is fixed to it. The medical devices have no capability to know where they are, nor does the tag that is fixed to them. In LBS 2.0, the mobile devices will know where they are indoors and can use that capability to make workflows location aware.

An example of an IPS that works with Android and iOS is Polestar®. Polestar® is interesting because they have a beacon base system that uses anchor beacons to establish the IPS, and Polestar® has RTLS that needs little additional infrastructure because the RTLS tags use the anchor beacons for their location, instead of needing gateways. This architecture is a good fit for CTC. Increasing the location fidelity is done by adding more anchor beacons, but you get the additional benefit of increasing the location fidelity of the IPS at the same time.

Mobile crowdsensing

Mobile crowdsensing,[1] also known as crowdsensing or participatory sensing, is a technique where a large group of individuals using mobile devices (such as smartphones, tablets, and wearables) collectively share data and extract information. Here are the key points.

1. Data Collection:
   - Participants use their mobile devices to sense and collect data.
   - Sensors in these devices (such as GPS, accelerometer, and microphone) capture information about the environment, movement, and other relevant factors.
2. Common Interest:
   - The collected data aims to measure, map, analyze, estimate, or predict processes of common interest.
   - Examples include monitoring pollution levels, locating potholes, or tracking exercise data within a community.
3. Types:
   - Participatory Crowdsensing: Users voluntarily contribute information.
   - Opportunistic Crowdsensing: Data is sensed, collected, and shared automatically without explicit user intervention.
4. Applications:
   - Environmental Monitoring: Detecting pollution, noise levels, etc.
   - Infrastructure Mapping: Locating potholes, road conditions, etc.
   - Social Context: Tracking community activities, health data, and more.
5. Benefits:
   - Leverages the ubiquity of powerful mobile devices.
   - Enables businesses to collect data without significant investments.
   - Used by companies like Facebook, Google, and Uber for big data services.

The concept of mobile crowdsensing is fundamental to the way the Apple AirTag works. The value of this location-dependent system is widely recognized. The AirTag does not work indoors, but bringing the concept indoors is only a matter of using IPS. Currently, AirTags will not work for RTLS because the AirTag network is restricted to consumers.

An example of a company that has enterprise mobile crowdsensing is Luna XIO. The Luna Locate app can use proximity detection to find RTLS tags or other mobile devices. It has the advantage over an AirTag in that it works indoors and outdoors. It can use the IPS to locate *source* mobile device and detect the *target* object by using its proximity to the *source*. Luna's Software Development Kit (SDK) allows this capability to be built into any app.

Location is a critical part of any type of crowdsensing, and the capability of doing this indoors is game-changing. The concept of crowdsensing is related to the broader category of pervasive computing, where the ubiquity of computing and microprocessors has led to the concept of including more capabilities on those devices. For example, if a mobile device is in the emergency department, why not have it look for a missing wound vac?

In Chapter 1, section "Current technologies", we will go into some depth explaining options for IPS, and in Chapter 1, section "Real-world application: location services in action", we will look at pervasive computing in some detail.

SENSOR FUSION

For locator systems to become more effective and to enable workflow automation, the concept of **sensor fusion**[2] will be needed. This is used now in mobile devices where the device uses an array of sensors to *fuse* the information into a perception of the world that is much more accurate than what a single sensor can produce. One such example of this is being done now in air traffic control, and it is called dependent and independent surveillance.

The concept of dependent and independent surveillance comes from air traffic control. The radar systems that are used to track aircraft do so in two ways. One is independent surveillance, which is done by bouncing RF energy off the airplane and listening for its return. The other is dependent surveillance, which is done by listening for the signals that are sent from a beacon transponder that is located on the airplane. When tracking aircraft, it is important to ensure that a reliable and independent tracking option is available. If a transponder is turned off, the tracking will not work, but independent surveillance will work if the aircraft is in range of the sensor. The radar processes both inputs to get the best location fidelity.

We can see this idea of dependent and independent surveillance realized indoors for LBS2.0. The dependent systems require battery-powered tags that become useless when the battery runs out of charge. Independent surveillance is like the RFID systems that use RF energy to "ring" the small tags that are on the devices that are being tracked. They are not dependent on onboard power to work. Like the strategy used in air traffic control, these technologies complement each other because the system can use either, or both, as options for tracking objects.

Strengths and weaknesses of dependent surveillance

The strength of the dependent surveillance is that the cost of the fixed sensors is less as they are sharing some of the load with the tags and they require less power. Because the tags are powered, the range of the sensors is increased. This means a single sensor can cover more area. Limitations of dependent surveillance are the cost of the tags and the support that is necessary to ensure that they have good batteries. This puts a limit on the number of things that get tracked. The tags are transmitting, so the sensors are mostly listening and sending the information back to a server. Many of these fixed sensors are even able to use battery power instead of needing to be cabled in.

Strengths of Dependent Surveillance:

- The cost of fixed sensors is reduced as they share the load with tags.
- Reduced power requirement for fixed sensors.
- Increased sensor range due to powered tags.
- Improved area coverage by a single sensor.

Limitations of Dependent Surveillance:

- Cost of tags and maintenance of their batteries.
- Limited number of objects that can be tracked.
- Sensors primarily listen and transmit data to a server.
- Some fixed sensors can operate on battery power, reducing wiring needs.

Strengths and weaknesses of independent surveillance

The strength of independent surveillance is that it uses small, inexpensive tags that can be put on many devices. These systems are quite reliable and are relatively easy to maintain. The weakness is that the amount of power that is required to get the tag to "ring" is very high. This means that the range of the sensors is much less than the dependent surveillance. The sensors need to be connected to a power source to get the energy needed to transmit at the higher power required. This means they are typically used in traffic chokepoints and building exits.

Strengths of Independent Surveillance:

- Uses small and inexpensive tags.
- Tags can be attached to many devices.
- Reliable and easier to maintain.

Weaknesses of Independent Surveillance:

- High power requirement for tag activation.
- Reduced range of sensors compared to dependent surveillance.
- Sensors are wired to power, so they require cabling.
- Sensors are used in strategic locations due to power constraints.

Ubiquitous tracking

A key feature of the next generation of LBS2.0 is ubiquity. Restated, ubiquity is the ability to track everything, everywhere. For this discussion, we will talk about tracking property. There are two types of ubiquity that are required for tracking property, like medical devices and supplies. The first is the ubiquitous *geographic* coverage of the tracking capabilities. The second is the *item* coverage for the number of devices or things that are being tracked. The nature of the environment in a hospital means that objects that are being tracked can move almost anywhere in the building. To be effective for the entire enterprise, the geographic coverage needs to be wall-to-wall and top top-to-bottom. Just as important as the geographic coverage is to ensure that as many devices as possible can be tracked. The value in tracking the devices comes not only because of their monetary value but also because of their role in a workflow.

The cost of tracking has generally come down, but the relative costs of dependent and independent surveillance are still the same and will likely remain the same because of the way that they work. There is a cost ceiling that operates between everywhere and everything, and somewhere and some things. Figure 4.2 shows that the cost of tracking everything everywhere is prohibitive for both RFID and RTLS. This is what you normally see in LBS1.0. An enterprise location engine can take in multiple location inputs, which facilitates a new "hybrid" option. This option offers much more coverage than a single tracking option by itself.

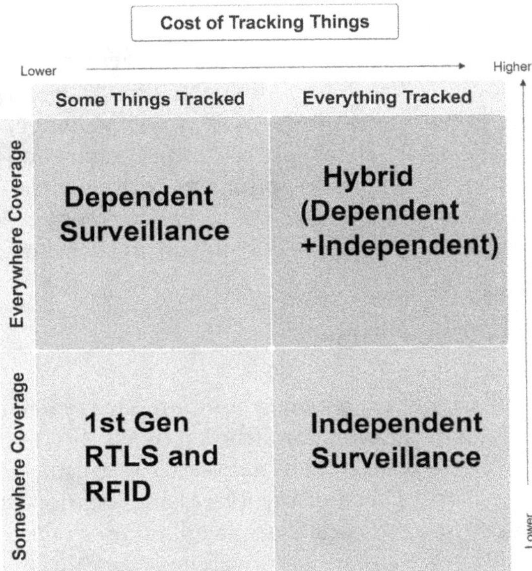

Figure 4.2 Cost of tracking quartile diagram.

RTLS is an example of dependent surveillance. One of the shortcomings of RTLS is that the active (battery powered) tags are expensive enough that it becomes cost prohibitive to tag all devices. This creates a limit on what can be tracked. The advantage of RTLS is that achieving "everywhere" location coverage is possible because the sensors cost less than RFID and the range is higher. So, with RTLS, you get some devices tracked everywhere in the building. Conversely, the example of independent surveillance is RFID. With RFID, the tags are inexpensive, and they are not dependent on power, but the sensors that locate the devices are expensive and have a short range. This means that you get what we could call "tag ubiquity" with the tagged devices, but the location coverage is limited.

Hybrid surveillance

A hybrid design that takes advantage of the best of both, by combining independent and dependent surveillance. RFID's coverage issues can be reinforced with RTLS. RTLS maintainability issues can be mitigated with RFID. For instance, a critical device that has both an RTLS and RFID tag on it might run out of battery power, and the RFID tag will remain to find the device and replace the battery.

The approach is to tag everything with RFID and install sensors at the choke points, points of egress, and storage areas. Then, install the RTLS throughout the building, but tag only the high-dollar and high-value devices. This is one design option that can be used to get the ubiquity we are going for in LBS2.0. There are other options that will present themselves, but the approach is the same. Determine the cost per square ft for tracking geography and the cost per device for device category coverage.

This hybrid approach helps to illuminate why an enterprise location engine is required. Having multiple options is very valuable, but they need to work together. There are other types of both dependent and independent surveillance, and there will be new options in both as ultra-wideband and what is called Ambient IoT mature. Using the concept of dependent and independent surveillance allows for those advances in technology.

DEPARTMENTAL SOLUTIONS

The digital twin will change the way that solutions are created in the location services market. Using the granularity afforded by the 4Ps, opportunities for workflow automation will become numerous. The sensors that are a part of the sensing layer map to each of the 4Ps. Using location technologies to detect arrivals and departures, calculate dwell, establish custody, and measure occupancy will create situational awareness and automation that will be tailored for specific workflows. The logistics concept of track and trace will come indoors. Also, the pattern that is often described as Uberization will be done indoors as well. This is where the location of people who are providing and receiving services are sharing their location with each other to optimize the workflow.

In air traffic control, there are many technologies that participate in the flight of a single aircraft. You have ground control, terminal control, and route control workflows that all use the same types of technologies, but they are designed for the specific needs of their part of the overall workflow. The ground radar rotates at one revolution per second because there is a need for a higher update frequency for the location of the aircraft when it is on the ground. The aircraft are closer together, so the reaction time is sped up. In contrast, the air route surveillance systems rotate at one revolution every 12 seconds where there is more space between aircraft. The systems are all radar, but they operate differently. Our indoor location systems are the same in that there are several locator systems that are participating in controlling a workflow.

For instance, designing a solution to automate an indoor workflow can get as granular as using near-field communication (NFC) to establish the courier's possession of a pathology sample, tracking the location of the courier with IPS, and detecting the arrival of the courier with a BLE beacon. All of this is on board a single iPhone.

This workflow-centric design contrasts with the use case-centric market that is often described as a Swiss Army knife as opposed to LBS2.0, which is a 10-blade scalpel. If you are performing surgery, you will choose the 10 blade. The departments have specific needs that are not one-size-fits-all, so the "10 blade" is what they need. An example is finding equipment in the emergency department. A solution that is used to find equipment for maintenance does not have the use experience that considers the urgent need for finding equipment quickly. Trying to use a location-aware solution that works for clinical engineering might not work for the emergency department because their workflows are so different (Figure 4.3).

SENSING AND CONNECTIVITY

The next generation of location-based systems will use combinations of location tech to create solutions. Those solutions will be tailored to departmental workflows that involve motion. The "4Ps" expose location technologies at a lower level to help ensure that the location information can be used at an enterprise level.

Below is a 4Ps evaluation for different technologies that are on the market now. This is only an example of how to evaluate them, so it is important to understand the capabilities of the particular vendor's offering in the market. For instance, the RTLS user in the hypothetical example below has an option for Passive Infrared (PIR) sensors that are a part of the suite of locating devices that it offers (Tables 4.1–4.5).

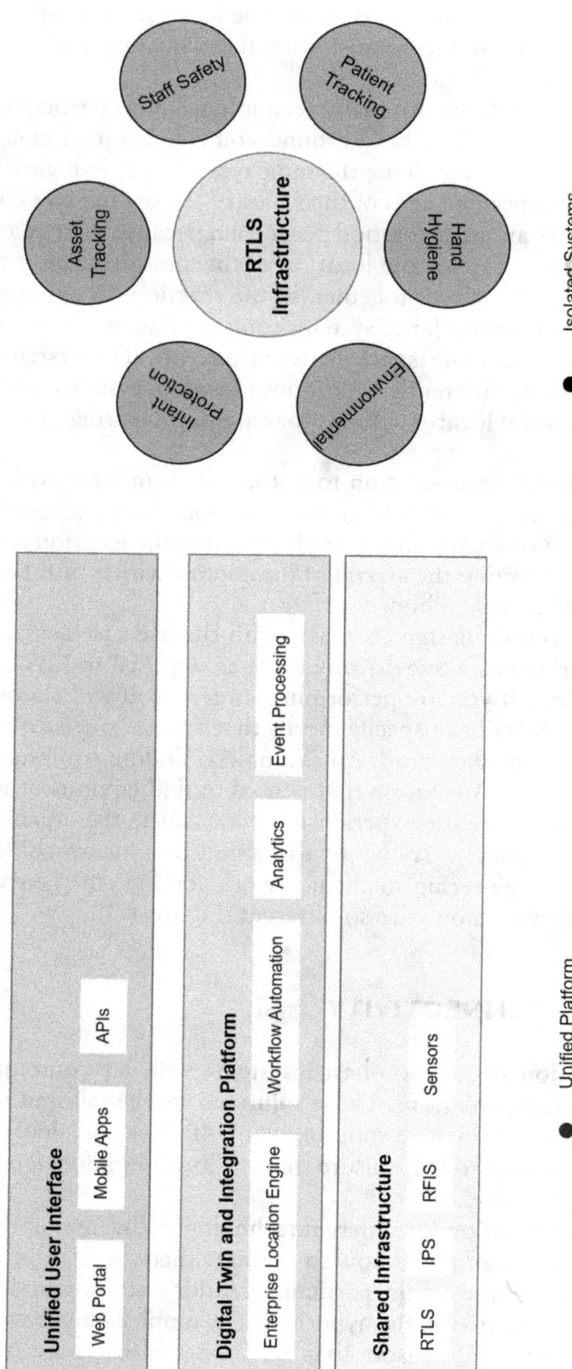

Figure 4.3 Location-based services 1.0 and location-based services 2.0 comparison diagram.

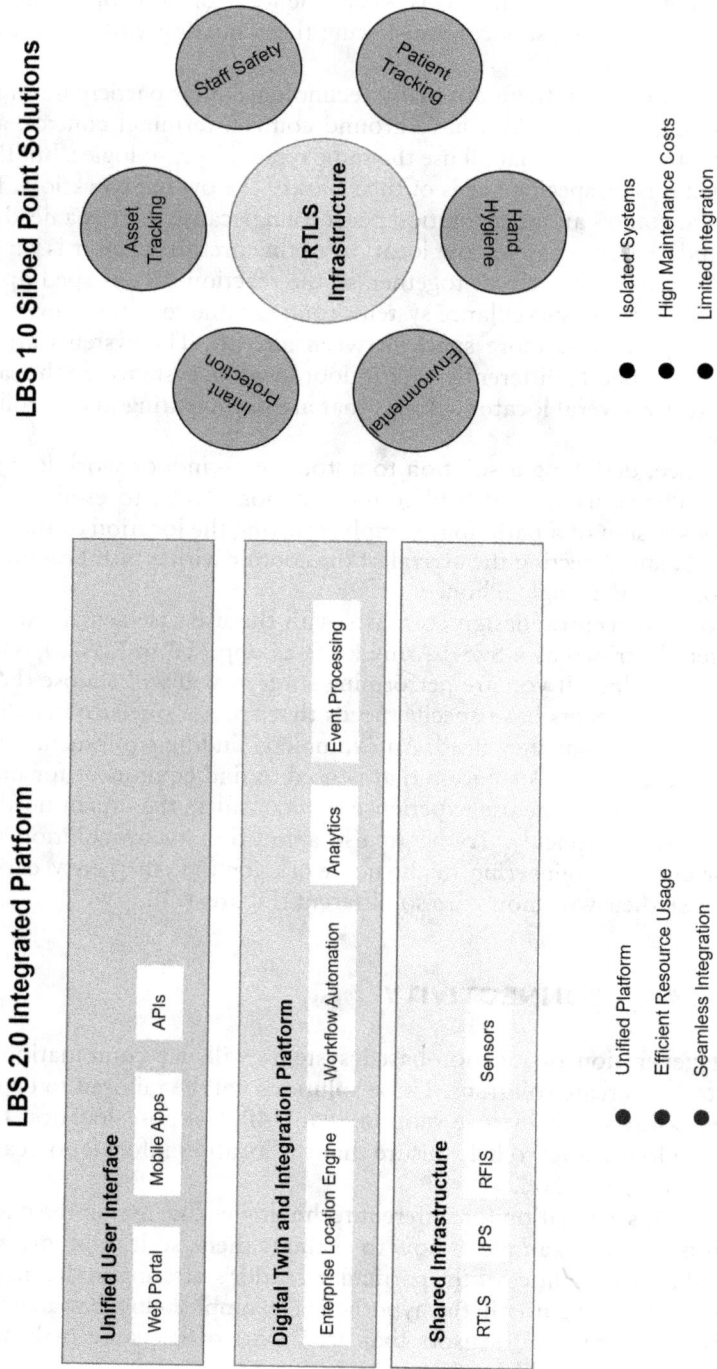

Table 4.1 BLE RTLS: location for BLE beacons

Position	Proximity	Presence	Possession
RTLS returns a room that correlates to the latitude, longitude, and floor of the center of the room.	BLE RTLS uses iBeacons or Eddystone so that mobile devices can determine their proximity to the beacon (ranging).	RTLS has a PIR camera to detect the presence of people in a room.	RTLS proximity can use ranging to infer possession by measuring the continued close proximity of the beacon.

Table 4.2 RFID: location for small RFID tags

Position	Proximity	Presence	Possession
RFID determines if a tag is close to the installed sensor and registers the position of the sensor as the location of the tagged device.	RFID system has scanning sleds that can be used with mobile devices to find the location of tags without the use of the installed sensors.	NA	NA

Table 4.3 IPS: location for mobile device

Position	Proximity	Presence	Possession
Works like an indoor GPS and returns latitude, longitude, and floor of a mobile device.		NA	NA

Table 4.4 Crowdsensing: location for BLE tags (requires IPS)

Position	Proximity	Presence	Possession
IPS establishes the position of the mobile device and the range of the mobile device to the beacon, which infers that the beacon's location is the location of the mobile device.	NA	NA	NA

Table 4.5 NFC: location for NFC tags

Position	Proximity	Presence	Possession
	Mobile device senses the proximity of the near-field communication (NFC) tag	NA	NA

DIGITAL TWIN AS A CORE HIS SYSTEM

When we look at the core healthcare information systems (HIS) that exist in hospitals, we have the EHR, revenue cycle, the ERP, a CMMS, communications tech, and others. These are core systems that require resources to support and advance them. Location-based services will enter a phase where it will become a core HIS that can fuel amazing new features in the other core systems. An enterprise location engine (ELE) will be part of a **Digital Twin**[3] that can track and process geospatial information and package it for any solution that needs it. Location-based services are technologies that are necessary for real-time healthcare (RTHS) and care traffic control. The early advances made in location services led to a plateau in adoption. That plateau has revealed that a body of knowledge is needed for health systems to adopt this new technology domain, but equally and operational framework is needed to fully leverage the capabilities of the systems. This will come with new roles and organizational changes.

Technologies that create real-time contextual information about people, property, and places will create capabilities that are as broad as the imagination. With the Digital Twin and its enterprise location engine, a single source of truth for all location information, the care traffic control vision can become realized. Advanced operations, automation, and orchestration are possible using these technologies at the enterprise level. As these technologies evolve, the healthcare systems can drive new requirements for more advanced and interoperable use cases. This is a phase where the Digital Twin becomes part of what is called OT, or operational technology. This evolution will blur the lines between IT and OT.

THE EDENVALE JOURNEY – DISCOVERING LOCATION-BASED SERVICES 2.0

(cont from Chapter 3)

Derek and Imani went back to Performance Improvement (PI) and asked to get a list of all the initiatives that they had in their queue that were related to flow. At the top of the list was a data analytics project for patient flow. EGH had an improvement team called the LOS team. They were trying to get good length of stay (LOS) data so they could find bottlenecks and decrease the overall LOS. The data that was coming from EHR was suspect because it was not granular enough to find the delays they were looking for. Derek said that it was the perfect place to start.

He explained that the strategy would include the "use what you have" theme. Their implementation of RTLS for the CMMS had enough coverage to do the patient tracking. It would get them the data they needed for the LOS project, and it didn't require a new application because all we wanted was the data at this early stage.

The strategy is to get the focus on patient flow. Start tracking patients with zone level coverage, and the data would be analyzed over weeks and months. It would be correlated with the EHR to show how inaccurate the EHR data was in comparison. That would allow them to "earn the right" to do the next project. All they asked was that if they were able to improve LOS, could they get access to data so they could use it to pitch the next project? The answer was an emphatic yes.

The "LOS" project was funded by PI because all they needed to do was buy patient tags for the RTLS. They bought a 90-day supply to get started while they collected the data. Derek had done this before, and he knew that once they saw the data, they would want to go deeper with the patient tracking to get a closer look at the departmental throughput. This was what Derek and Imani were banking on, so the next project that was put into the strategy was patient transport.

The next project would be to get the real-time data to the bed management team if the location fidelity is good enough for them. It would eventually get there, so this project could push if needed. All that was needed was a real-time user interface for the patient tracking data. Derek had a couple of options he could show them. This would be called the "Capacity Management" project.

The next project was going to be the "IV Pump PAR stocking" project because now we have earned the right to add to the RTLS footprint. The project would be to put the sensors only in the control points where the pumps are supposed to go when the process is being followed correctly. The CMMS already had a module for PAR stocking and although it wasn't perfect, it would work for what they needed. It was a "use what your already have" item in the plan.

There was enough expected ROI in this project to put the entire program back in the black and fund more projects going forward. Derek said that is where we have fixed LBS 1.0, and we will now get into LBS 2.0. He said here, you will notice that the tools we have given the users are observational tools. That is what LBS 1.0 is about: the observation of location information. As we get into LBS 2.0, we are going to use the location information for automating some of the work.

The "Patient Transport" project would use several of the other themes. It would require the maps (everything starts with maps), IPS, workflows (workflows are king), and it was mobile work, so there would be a mobile app (mobile apps for mobile work) that was necessary for the transporters. It would use the User Interface that was being used for the Capacity Management project (use what you already have).

The transporters would be tracked like Uber drivers, but indoors. By tracking them when they were moving patients, the location of the transport would add accuracy to the RTLS data. More precision to get greater insight into throughput. The result of tracking the patient transports meant that they would have the EHR data, the RTLS data, and the IPS tracking data for the patients all for very little investment.

This was the strategy that would be presented to the steering committee. The only cost that was submitted was Derek and Imani's labor cost because PI was picking up the cost of the patient RTLS tags. PI had the data scientist and the data architect do the data work.

The string of projects each ended with a tollgate where the value was measured and calculated. It started with the RTLS and CMMS for clinical engineering. Clinical engineering (CE) made the initial investment in the RTLS, so the value from its integration with the CMMS was credited to CE. That didn't hurt the LBS program because the initial investment for LBS was so small. The entire plan was presented to the steering committee, and they approved the strategy, but most importantly, they liked the themes that were the foundation for the approach. Derek knew this would make this process repeatable for the program far into the future. Now it was time to get to work (Figure 4.4).

Location Services Program – Milestone Plan

1. CMMS/RTLS implementation
    a. RTLS
    b. Map improvements
    c. Filter and send the data to the data lake for the LOS project
2. Maps
    a. Convert the computer-aided design (CAD) to IMDF
    b. Create images and install them in the CMMS
    c. Get all of the prep for Apple indoors done
3. Pervasive Computing
    a. Install the Luna agent on the desktops
    b. Send the location data to the data lake
4. LOS Project – Tracking the location of patients with the RTLS
    a. Add patient tracking tags
    b. Data cleaning and preprocessing
    c. Data analysis for flow
    d. AI agent for deeper insights
5. Capacity Management
    a. Real-time UI for patient location information
    b. Real-time data analysis
6. PAR Stocking IV Pumps
    a. Add RTLS sensors in the PAR stocking locations
    b. Use the CMMS PAR stocking tool
7. Patient Transport
    a. IPS - Do the Apple Indoor Survey
    b. Real-time UI
    c. Implement the iPhones and Fleet Management

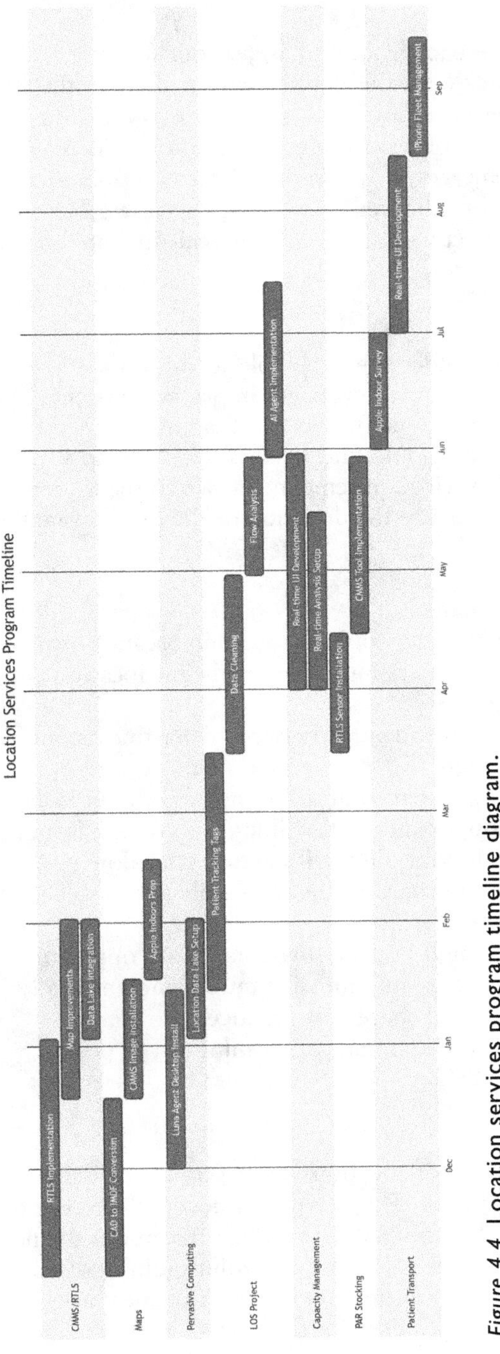

Figure 4.4 Location services program timeline diagram.

PLAYBOOK FOR LOCATION-BASED SERVICES 2.0

We are still in the background phase, so our focus is on learning the foundational concepts. With the digital twin coming to the forefront, the LBS market will need to adapt. That adaptation is one where the focus of the products goes from observation to automation. When a location-based services platform emerges, it will serve all the solutions that can benefit from location instead of a limited number of use cases. The platform fits in the digital twin architecture and creates the real-time updates that are needed.

Improvers

Improvers should understand the role location-based services can play in providing visibility into the process improvements that they are trying to accomplish. There are many good LBS solutions in the market now that can help. Improvers should find what is available now and employ it. They should also make their requirements known to the leaders, who will inform the market and influence the direction of the products and services that are available.

1. Process Assessment
    - Evaluate current workflows to identify location-awareness opportunities
    - Document pain points where real-time location data could improve outcomes
    - Map interdependencies between departments and workflows
2. Solution Design
    - Focus on departmental solutions rather than isolated use cases
    - Identify opportunities to compose solutions from existing features
    - Ensure solutions align with actual workflow needs
    - Create pilot programs that can scale across departments
3. Implementation Strategy
    - Start with high-impact, low-complexity opportunities
    - Build on successful implementations incrementally
    - Document and share best practices
    - Measure and communicate results

Leaders

The next generation of location-based services will be in support of the operational digital twin. This involves a new architecture that is workflow-centric and involves mobile devices. LBS2.0 is about the next generation of services that use location. It is not a revolution in new sensing technologies. There are plenty of good products in the current market that can produce the perception that is required for those services. The revolution comes when there is enough interoperability to leverage the existing sensing technologies to perceive a vast array of conditions in the environment that can be used anywhere that can benefit from them.

1. Strategic Planning
   - Develop an enterprise-wide location services strategy
   - Focus on platform capabilities rather than point solutions
   - Plan for incremental implementation while maintaining vision for comprehensive coverage
   - Establish clear success metrics
2. Resource Allocation
   - Invest in foundational platform components
   - Support training and education initiatives
   - Plan for long-term maintenance and expansion
   - Balance immediate needs with future scalability
3. Change Management
   - Build organizational support through demonstrated value
   - Address privacy and security concerns proactively
   - Foster innovation culture around location services
   - Support cross-departmental collaboration

Creators

Pushing beyond the situational awareness that LBS 1.0 provides requires a paradigm shift from observation to automation. This automation will relieve people who are participating in the workflows from much of the effort that is required to produce the rich array of events and data that will allow dramatic process improvements.

1. Product Development
   - Create modular, composable solutions
   - Support standard protocols and open integration
   - Focus on workflow-centric features
   - Build flexible deployment options
2. Implementation Support
   - Provide comprehensive training programs
   - Develop clear documentation
   - Support proof-of-concept implementations
   - Maintain ongoing technical support
3. Partnership Approach
   - Work closely with healthcare organizations
   - Adapt solutions to specific needs
   - Share industry best practices
   - Contribute to standards development

NOTES

1 https://ieeexplore.ieee.org/document/6069707
2 https://www.mdpi.com/1424-8220/21/6/2140
3 https://www.digitaltwinconsortium.org/glossary/glossary/#digital-twin

Chapter 5

Maps and geospatial science

Paul E. Zieske

MAPS AND GEOSPATIAL SCIENCE

Maps provide much more than just a visual representation of physical spaces. They have spatial data that can be used to compute the spatial relationships between objects. This becomes very powerful as evidenced by the amazing products that are using the maps we see in our consumer products. In this chapter, we are going to provide an overview of maps and Geographic information systems (GIS) and learn how indoor spaces are going to become an important part of the future of the LBS2.0 market. We will look at where they fit into the user experience and the architecture of the enterprise approach to LBS.

GEOGRAPHIC INFORMATION SYSTEMS

GIS introduce something called geospatial science. It is often called "the science of where." GIS bring a rich library of proven software services that are critical for a digital twin. We are singling out the maps to emphasize that geospatial science starts with maps. Accurate building maps are needed to create the digital twin of the building. Those maps will be used in the GIS layer of our enterprise location engine.

To understand GIS, when we use Apple Maps, Google Maps, Waze, or running and fitness apps, we are using GIS. When viewing a GIS map, you can usually see a small logo for the base map that is being used. There are a handful of companies that have created digital maps of the world. It is a massive undertaking with a dramatic history, and one that is very difficult to get right. For the digital twin, we may or may not need anything other than the building, and fortunately, the world maps we work with these days are quite mature and accurate. The building maps can be part of the base map, but most often, they are overlaid on top of the base map.

DOI: 10.1201/9781003625483-6

GIS and the digital twin

The digital twin needs a high-fidelity digital representation of the building to support virtualization. Much like a video game that has a representation of the world that the players operate in, the digital twin needs that virtual world as its foundation. There are tools available to create 3D scenes for digital twins, but they are much more focused on the physical aspects of the twin than the operational aspects. While some workflows might benefit from 3D visualization, most workflows cover large pieces of geography where 2D representation is more practical and easier to work with. This is where GIS come in – offering the right balance of fidelity and simplicity to create a foundation capable of supporting enterprise operations (Figure 5.1).

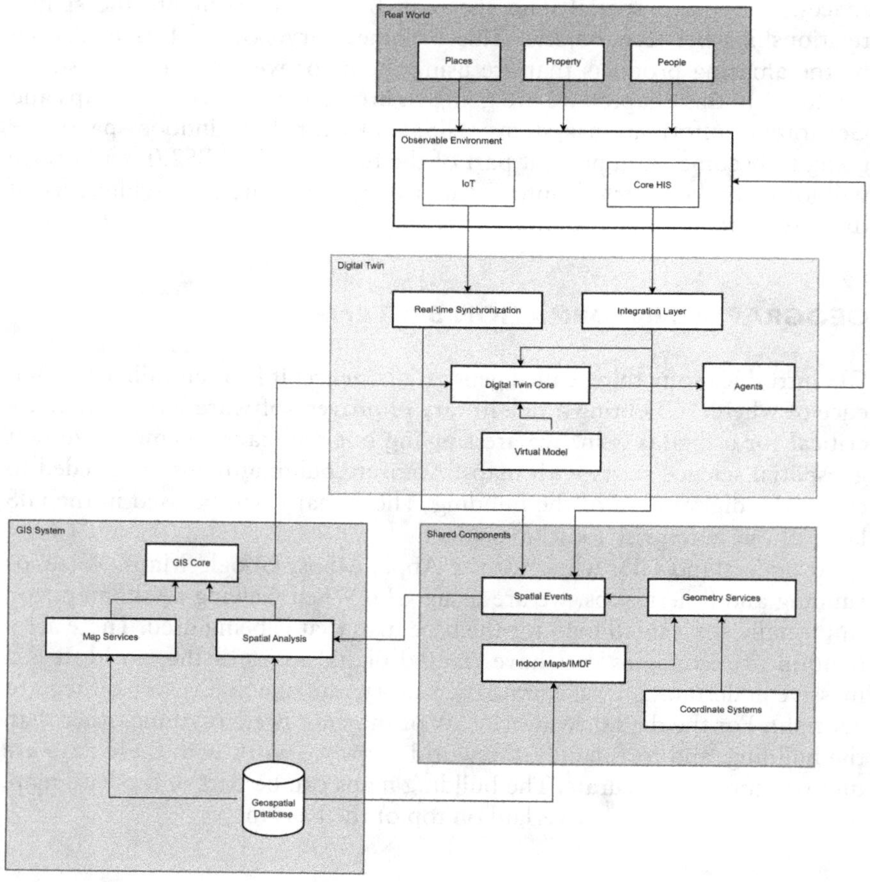

Figure 5.1 Digital twin, system of systems diagram.

LOCATION IS COMING INDOORS

For outdoors, the world is well-represented in digital maps, and GPS provide accurate location data. Our phones show that magical "blue dot" that follows us everywhere we go. But indoors is much different. When you come indoors, your blue dot blooms to show degrading location accuracy and bounces around due to poor GPS performance in indoor environments.

When you look at an outdoor map, you typically see only silhouettes of buildings without interior detail. However, this is changing. Try using Apple Maps on your iPhone or Mac and zoom in to a major airport near you. You'll see detailed interior layouts and even a floor switcher to view different levels. Below is Detroit Metropolitan Wayne County Airport and another image that is zoomed in to the McNamara terminal (Figure 5.2).

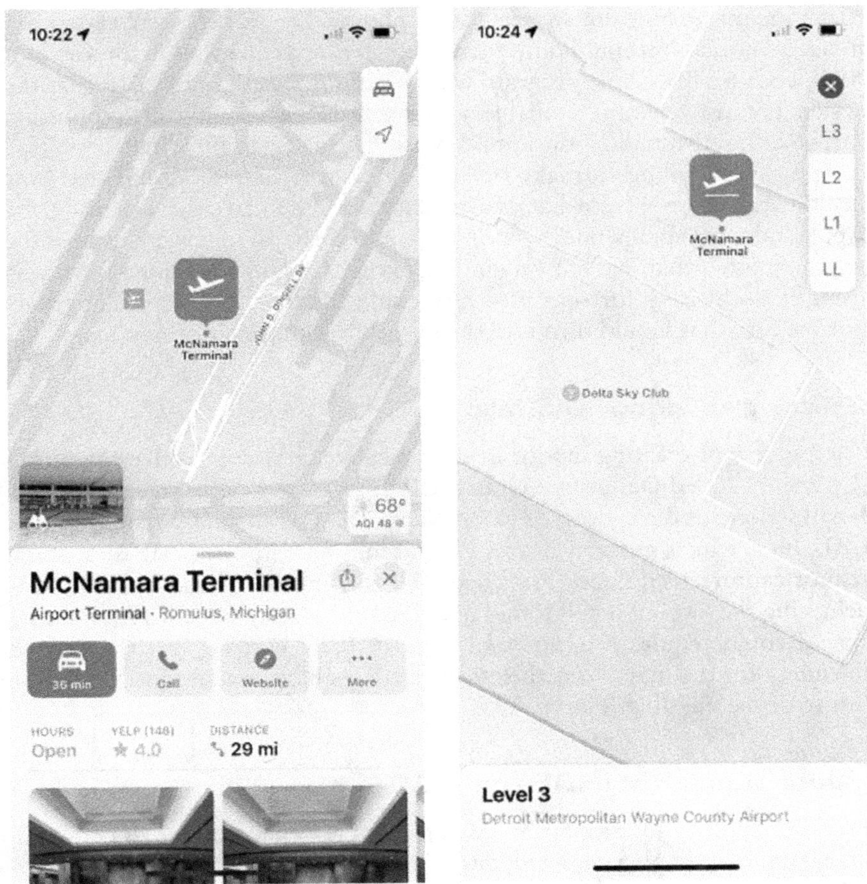

Figure 5.2 Apple maps airport iPhone screenshot.

As you zoom into Concourse A on the map, a floor switcher appears. When we switch to Level 3, we can now see the Delta Sky Club instead of the shops on Level 2. If I am at the airport, I can see my exact location and what floor I am on. At Detroit Metro, your iPhone's location works indoors. Using the Delta Airlines map, I can route from the Delta Sky Club to my gate and see if I can get there quicker by the tram or just walking.

Looking at a little history, we will start with Apple because it started in 2014 when, at their worldwide developer conference, they announced they were "bringing location indoors." They had purchased a company called WiFiSLAM in 2013, and this event was the reveal for the technology they acquired from that transaction. They showed on the stage how you could get an indoor location on an iPhone with no new infrastructure. This launched a flurry of activity in the developer community, trying to figure out how they could get involved. Apple showed how you could use an app that was on the app store, called "Indoor Survey," to capture the WIFI signals and use them to get the magic blue dot we see on our phones. Developers were clamoring to access it, but you could only participate if your venue was an airport or a Mall, because the whole program was in beta. It wasn't until 2019 that the system became generally available, and the developers could start submitting their maps, downloading the app, and using it to survey buildings.

Apple was willing to make one exception to that policy, and that was healthcare. There were a handful of hospital systems that were using the Apple Indoor system while it was in beta, and perhaps none were using it for anything other than patient wayfinding except for Navv Systems. Navv was using it exclusively for operations, tracking the location of patient transporters for what would turn into their workflow automation product.

Creating an indoor GIS map

The process of creating indoor maps typically starts with converting CAD (Computer Aided Design) files into a GIS format. In healthcare, regulations for life safety call for detailed floor plans. These are usually the building's CAD files, which are scaled and very accurate. Without CAD files, some **reality capture** techniques can create 3D geometries of the building, but achieving the level of detail found in a CAD file is very difficult. Annotating spaces could require thousands of lines of hand entry to get the textual metadata for the map. Nonetheless, these maps have immense value for the future of the building (Figure 5.3).

Indoor standards: IMDF and OGC

In 2014, Apple's indoor maps were called Apple Venue Format (AVF). In an unusual move, Apple partnered with Google, ESRI, and Autodesk to establish a mapping standard with the Open Geospatial Consortium (OGC). They changed the name from AVF to indoor mapping data format (IMDF).

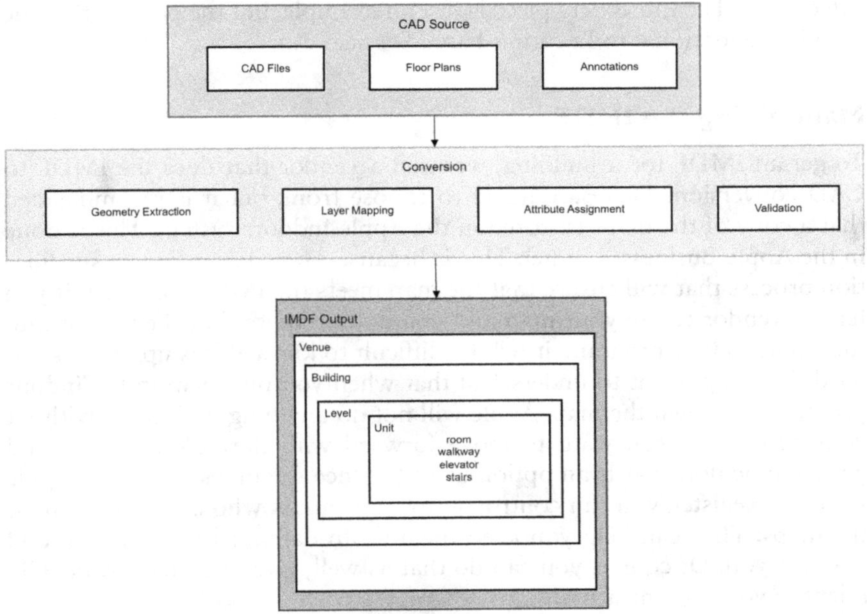

Figure 5.3 CAD to IMDF conversion diagram.

The participating organizations included ESRI and Autodesk, which makes AutoCAD. ESRI makes maps, but Autodesk makes the software that creates the drawings used to build these buildings. To make indoor maps, we need an accurate representation of the building, and there is no better representation than the CAD drawings used to create it. Hospitals are required by The Joint Commission standard LS.01.01.01 EP3 to keep accurate Life Safety Floor Plans, making the transition to GIS maps often straightforward.

Other uses for IMDF

When we create this digital twin, we must add a certain level of detail to adhere to the IMDF standard, but that is only the start of what can be added. We can add whatever attributes are necessary to give more life to our digital twin. We can add access restrictions, ADA (Americans with Disabilities Act) information, life safety information, and capacity, and we can expose those attributes only when needed. We can add geometry, like points of interest for fire extinguishers, fire alarms, and safety equipment like eyewash stations. GIS is a much friendlier format than CAD for this kind of data because that is exactly what it was built for. If we look back to our Joint Commission standards, there is no reason that compliance to that standard could not be done with a map. With a map, instead of just demonstrating that you are compliant and have a plan, you can use the map as a part of executing a safety plan. The Life Safety piece is just an example, but the point is that the map is foundational to Location-based Services 2.0.

Maintaining the IMDF

To get an IMDF for a building, we need a vendor that does the IMDF to CAD conversion. There are many to choose from, but it is recommended that a copy of the maps is stored in the Apple Indoors system. This is done in the Apple Business Register. This is because Apple has a rigorous validation process that will ensure that the map meets the IMDF standard. If you have a vendor create your map and you don't require that they put it into the Apple Indoor program, it will be difficult to know if it is up to the standard. It is important to understand that when you put them in the indoor program, you own the map. Apple will not do anything with them without your consent. If you want to move forward with the indoor survey and get the blue dot, that is an option as well. Once the maps are in the Apple Business Register, you can control access to vendors who can contribute to the maps. They can help you keep them up to date, or they can even add data for you. Of course, you can do that as well, given you have some GIS talent in your organization.

Walkways

No matter how the maps are done, an important thing to think about is corridors, which are also called walkways, in IMDF. The corridors need to be accurately segmented so that they begin and end at a door or opening and the polygons don't carry on indiscriminately. For the IMDF to be a true digital twin, this segmentation will become important for RTLS and other systems that need to know where the doors are. Sometimes, the vendors ignore this because they are used to creating maps that are going to be used for wayfinding only.

Additionally, the walkways should have names that will help people find their way. This is much like a driving app's turn-by-turn directions that might say something like, "continue on Main St for 3 miles and turn right on Atwater." That is the same type of experience we should strive for indoors. Henry Ford's West Bloomfield hospital has walkways that are named after tree species like "Maple," "Beech," and "Oak." Buildings usually have some semantic and schematic composition that will yield something that is easy to understand and consistent. The CAD files usually have strange numbering schemes that mean something to the architect but little to other users.

Maps for location services solutions

Once we have narrowed the list of map vendors, we should consider that a refinement, not a constraint. The maps should be considered master data,

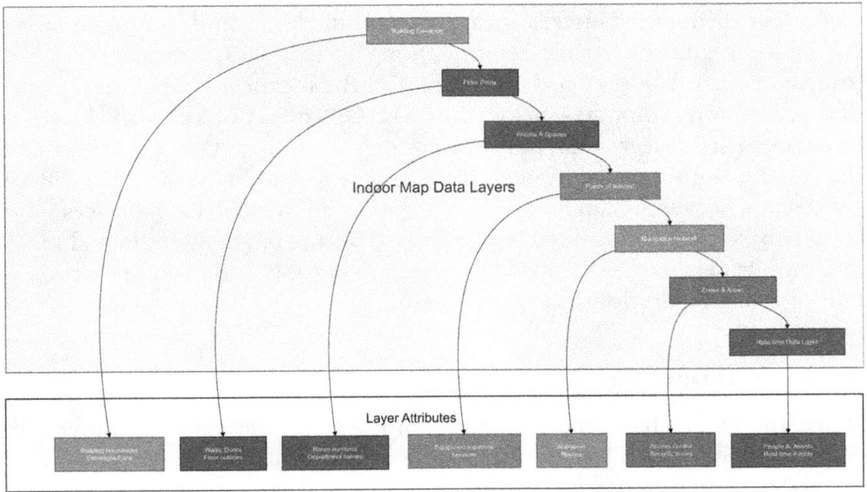

Figure 5.4 Indoor map data layers diagram.

and their reuse is a measure of location services' maturity. There are plenty of location services software solutions that don't use GIS maps, but the maps can be pushed out in any format so that if the software uses png or pdf files, we can still use the IMDF for our source of truth for maps. But if they are starting with maps instead of CAD, at least they will be coming from your "source of truth" for maps. Those solutions will not be able to take advantage of the geospatial technology that the maps provide, however.

Once the IMDF is created, the process continues to align the IMDF feature types with the layers and attributes (Figure 5.4). IMDF is designed to contain many feature types that can be used to render as many details as are needed.

INDOOR POSITIONING

Indoor positioning (IPS) is a vital component in Location-based Services 2.0. It enables mobile devices like Android or iOS devices to get latitude, longitude, and vertical position (usually in the form of a floor number). IPS works like GPS but functions indoors. IPS allows mobile devices to participate in location-aware workflows and enables features we've become familiar with through GPS. These capabilities are now available indoors, along with new features unique to indoor use cases. Wayfinding, routing, mapping, and tracking can now be done indoors. The devices themselves contain many sensors that are becoming standard equipment and are a critical part of the technological ecosystem. Peripherals like barcode scanning sleds can be added, and extended life batteries are available for some use cases.

The key difference between locating a mobile device and locating a medical device is that the mobile device "knows" where it is, separate from any locator system. The onboard GPS chip and the location system that is part of a smartphone computes its location. The GPS does not know the location of devices using the system, but the devices know where they are because of the system. With medical devices, the tracking system knows the location of the devices because it can find the tag that is fixed to it. Medical devices have no capability to know where they are, nor does the tag fixed to them. In LBS 2.0, mobile devices will know where they are indoors and can use that capability to make workflows location aware.

Apple indoors IPS

When the IMDF has been created from the CAD files, we can move forward with enabling IPS with Apple Indoors. This will give us "indoor GPS," or more accurately IPS for indoor positioning. This can be done with no infrastructure other than the WIFI that is already there. This is what all the excitement was about in 2014, and it was released to the public in 2019. Hospitals have an advantage that makes the Apple system perform better than most other venues. This is because the WIFI systems that have been implemented in hospitals have more access points (AP) than the average building. When the indoor survey takes a "fingerprint" of the WIFI parameters, it georeferences them to latitude, longitude, and floor, and more APs means higher location fidelity.

The process starts by registering the venue and sending the IMDF files to Apple. After the IMDF is received and approved, Apple will send an email that the building is "ready for survey." Next, it takes someone with an iPhone and the Apple Indoor Survey mobile app to walk through the building and take the data. The instructions are included in the mobile app. The files are sent to Apple, and a few hours later, every iPhone will get latitude, longitude, and floor when it is using location services on the device (Figure 5.5).

An interesting feature is that when someone calls 911, those coordinates are sent to 911, with the floor. Most emergency services are not even aware that these capabilities exist.

With IPS, the mobile devices "know" where they are at. But there is no tracking that is being done unless the permissions are set accordingly. They will only send their location if the user is aware.

Mobile crowd-sensing

Mobile crowd-sensing (MCS) represents another significant opportunity that comes from adding IPS. The concept of MCS is fundamental to how the Apple AirTag works. The value of this location-dependent system is widely recognized. The AirTag does not work indoors, but bringing the concept

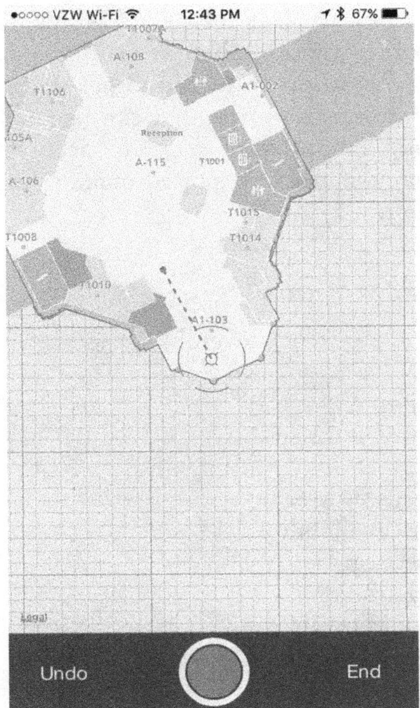

Figure 5.5 Apple indoor survey app image.

indoors is only a matter of using IPS. Currently, AirTags will not work for RTLS because the AirTag network is restricted to consumers.

An example of a company that has enterprise MCS is Luna XIO. The Luna Locate app can use proximity detection to find RTLS tags or other mobile devices. It has the advantage over an AirTag in that it works indoors and outdoors. It can use the IPS to locate the *source* mobile device and detect the *target* object by using its proximity to the *source*. Luna's Software Development Kit (SDK) allows this capability to be built into any app.

Location is a critical part of any type of crowd-sensing, and the capability of doing this indoors is game-changing. The concept of crowd-sensing is related to the broader category of pervasive computing, where the ubiquity of computing and microprocessors has led to the concept of including more capabilities on those devices. For example, if a mobile device is in the emergency department, why not have it look for a missing wound vac?

Emerging technologies

Ultra-Wideband (UWB) represents the likely future of IPS, but its adoption is currently limited to newer mobile devices, and it remains in the early stages of implementation. The technology offers superior accuracy and reliability compared to other solutions, but the ecosystem needs time to mature.

Ultrasonic location detection presents another option, though it requires a more complex device configuration that can be challenging to maintain. While the technology can provide excellent accuracy, its infrastructure requirements and maintenance needs often make it less practical for enterprise-wide deployment.

Integration considerations

When implementing IPS systems, several key factors must be considered:

1. Coverage requirements
   - Building layout and size
   - User density
   - Accuracy needs by area
   - Infrastructure availability
2. Technology selection
   - Device compatibility
   - Accuracy requirements
   - Maintenance considerations
   - Cost implications
3. System management
   - Updates and maintenance
   - Performance monitoring
   - User support
   - System redundancy
4. Privacy and security
   - Handling of location data
   - User consent management
   - Data retention policies
   - Access controls

The selection of an IPS solution should align with both immediate needs and long-term strategic goals for the organization's location services implementation.

IPS with BLE beacons

There are a couple of options that work with Android, but they are not as straightforward as Apple. The first involves stationary BLE beacons. Battery-powered BLE beacons are distributed around the building, and a location vendor will map them into their location engine. The vendor will provide a SDK to allow solution developers to get the same blue dot experience you see with Apple Indoors. There is no way to compare the accuracy of the two, because it depends on the number of beacons, and for Apple, it depends on the WIFI. It is safe to say they are comparable. The big difference is that the Android solution will be more difficult to maintain. The batteries on the beacons should last over two years because they are stationary beacons. The other thing that is very important is to have a beacon system that can be administered remotely. Updates to firmware, settings, and the condition of the beacons need to be monitored to guarantee a quality of service for the IPS.

Another option for Android is geomagnetic deflection. We all have seen how an analog compass behaves indoors, where it is inaccurate and wobbles as you move around. It turns out that the amount of deflection is the same in space. The geomagnetic deflection algorithm uses the magnetometer in the mobile device and fingerprints it. Then, the location engine uses the magnetic field and the other sensors on the device to produce latitude, longitude, and floor. This is a "no-infrastructure" solution, but it is not a no-cost solution as it needs to be licensed from a vendor.

IPS is a key component of Location-based Services 2.0, but the decision about whether to move forward with Apple or Android is a big one. The most important thing is to understand the limitations that come with Android and to bake that into the decision. In either case, IPS is still an important part of our foundation.

There are more IPS technologies, but we did not list them because they are less "native" to what the hardware is already using for location. For instance, the future of IPS is likely to be Ultra-Wideband (UWB), but only the newer mobile devices are able to leverage that, and it is still bleeding edge. Ultrasonic location detection is another option, but it requires a device configuration that is hard to maintain and somewhat fragile.

MAPS CONTENT MANAGEMENT

An important consideration to the mapping capabilities is the ability to manage changes to the geometry data and the metadata for the maps. This spans from the creation of the geometries from nothing but the ground truth to a simple label change for a room.

Hospitals are fortunate to benefit from regulations that require them to have "life safety" drawings to show the details for the life safety equipment and the processes associated with them. This means they have CAD files that are usually accurate and provide a good starting point, but not all buildings have this. This is where tools that can create geometry like photogrammetry and LIDAR (Light Detection and Ranging) are useful. This data needs to be converted into maps, and there are expensive building information management (BIM) and GIS tools that can do this, but each of these requires specialists to do the work.

Mappedin has created a maps content management system (CMS) that makes this much easier and can do the maps management. You can use their tools for adding new buildings, floors, and departments to make simple changes. Their CMS can integrate with other parts of a greater location services architecture, and it can provide many GIS services like wayfinding.

There are more sophisticated tools like ESRI and QGIS (free) that are full-featured GIS suites. These usually require GIS professionals to operate them effectively. Many hospitals have GIS professionals on staff in strategic planning or facilities, so they might be able to help as well. As a last resort, the vendors that maintain the CAD sometimes have their own GIS talent on staff, so it might be a good idea to ask them as well.

THE SCIENCE OF WHERE (CREDIT TO ESRI)

The 2D rendering of an indoor map is an overlay on a Basemap, like Google, Apple, or Open Street Map. Because it is 2D, you need a way to switch floors separate from the zoom feature we are all familiar with. This feature is a floor switcher.

It is important to understand how GIS works. The most important thing to understand is that a map is *data* that is organized hierarchically. The hierarchy starts with vertices that are made up of latitude, longitude, and altitude. A single vertex for Los Angeles might look like (34.0522, -118.2437, 305). If that vertex was indoors, we could swap out altitude and substitute floor, and it would look like (34.0522, -118.2437, 1), where the 1 is the floor.

Then, we use those vertices to make what is called **geometry**. Geometries consist of points, lines, and polygons:

- **Points** are a single vertex
- A **line** is two or more vertices that are connected but not closed
- A **polygon** is three or more vertices that are connected and closed

Everything builds on top of that. In its raw form, a map is data in a database. GIS compute the geometries. There are many software libraries out there that have been developed to do the heavy lifting here.

With our polygons, we can make rooms, walkways, stairs, and elevators. Lines can make doors and openings. Points can be points of interest or markers for anything we want to call out. That is where the IMDF standards become very important, because the combinations of geometry and attributes are endless, so for interoperability of the maps, we need that standard.

With maps, RTLS, and indoor GPS, we can introduce some geospatial science to create solutions. We have already established that maps are, in their simplest form, geospatial data. Geospatial science is, in its simplest form, how to get information out of geospatial data. If we are tracking our wheelchairs and want to know how many wheelchairs are in the main lobby at 8:00 am, we can use a geofence around the main lobby, and our locator system can give us the count. If we want to see how many times in a month we have no wheelchairs in the main lobby at 8:00 am, we can do that too. If we want to see the flow of wheelchairs around the building on any given day, we have everything we need. You can swap anything for wheelchairs, and it is the same process.

Maps as a standard

Once you have the map, you are not restricted to the given vendor's capabilities. If we have the map data, we have access to all the geospatial science and tools that have been around for decades. The IMDF is in a text format called geoJSON. There are open-source tools like QGIS for analyzing GIS data. As we said above, it all boils down to points, lines, and polygons. Maps are a powerful data visualization tool. We see them used outside for crime rate data and weather, and we saw how important they were during COVID-19. By bringing that kind of analysis indoors, analysts can use them to plot the location of things like Hospital-Acquired Infections (HAI), Infectious Diseases, and safety incidents.

Location events

Another important type of data is time-delimited geospatial data. The most obvious example is GPS tracking data, but you can get the same data indoors. Any event that you can capture digitally with its location can be stored and used for analysis. For instance, scanning a patient's wristband with an iPhone gives you the identity of the patient and the time and location of the scan. As popular as barcode scanning is in healthcare, imagine the power of location-aware barcode scanning (Figure 5.6).

WAYFINDING AND PATIENT EXPERIENCE

In aviation, the airlines divide the services that go into each flight as the "above-the-wing" services and "below-the-wing" services. The above-the-wing focuses on customer experience and hospitality services, and the below-the-wing is the flight preparation and operational tasks. We are differentiating wayfinding from patient experience in that patient experience includes situational awareness for the below-the-wing tasks. This benefits both the patient and the operational tasks.

Above-the-wing

Wayfinding is the most obvious use case for IPS, but we are addressing this toward the end for a reason. Wayfinding and patient experience need an abstraction of the "employee grade" maps. The employee grade maps are

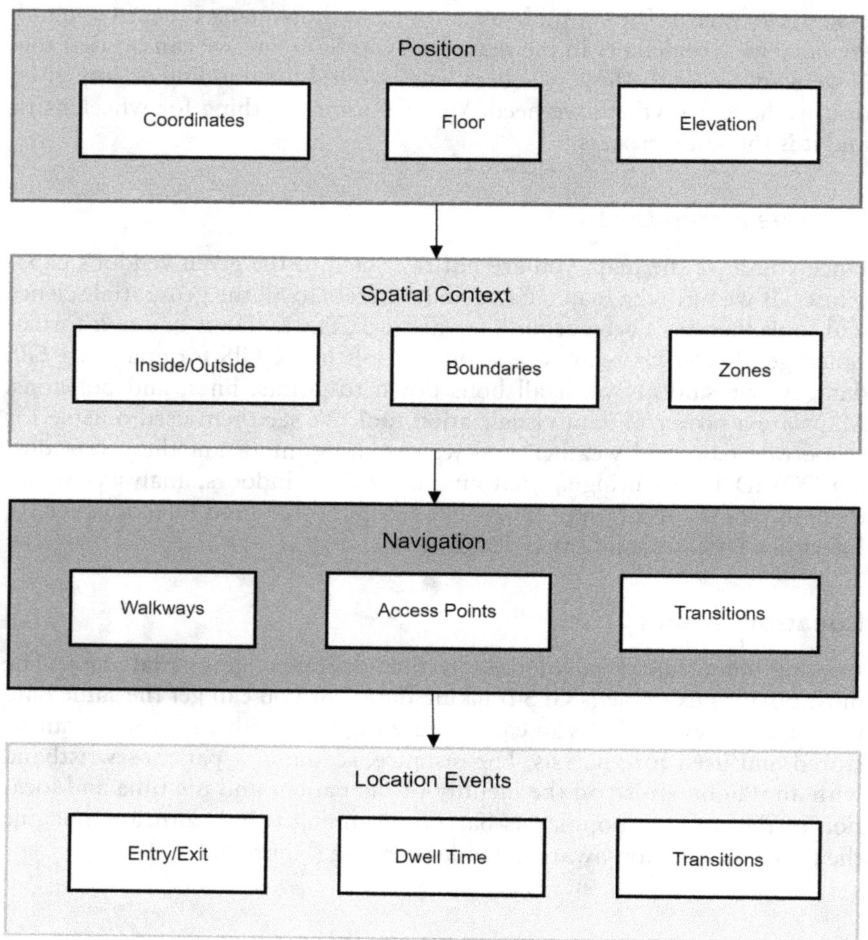

Figure 5.6 **Processing position into events diagram.**

high fidelity when applied to a digital twin, and we need more of a "digital shadow" for wayfinding. Operations needs more detail than is needed for patients and visitors. The patients and visitors are directed to locations where there is someone to receive them. Reception areas, amenities, and information desks are the primary locations. Here, we introduce points of interest (POI) that are simply points on the map that are curated for the target user groups. The vendor should know what the best approach is to getting POIs that offer the best user experience. When working with a wayfinding vendor, they should be able to take the employee grade IMDF and use it to get a wayfinding grade map.

Parking is one of the most important aspects of patient experience because it is important to make the transition from outdoors to indoors as smooth

Figure 5.7 Indoor wayfinding app image.

as possible. These solutions can be sophisticated, with positioning in the individual parking spaces, or they can be a simple indoor–outdoor transition. One thing to note is that IPS can be set up in enclosed parking decks. There is a lot of value in fortifying this part of the experience, so it should be strongly considered (Figure 5.7).

Below-the-wing

When we look at mobile experience from the perspective of above-the-wing and below-the-wing, there are the customer-facing features and services, and there are tasks that support providing the services. What we want to do for situation awareness is provide information to the patient from the below-the-wing services to make them aware and able to be more involved in their care. Conversely, when can get information from the patient that will improve the flow of the operational tasks. This combination of the above-the-wing and below-the-wing will make the entire patient experience better.

Features like appointment notifications with directions to the reception area, real-time appointment updates, auto check-in, and waiting anywhere in the building are some of the amazing features that have become available. These will lead to better HCAHPS (Hospital Consumer Assessment of Healthcare Providers and Systems) scores and reduce late arrivals for appointments. The goal is to empty the waiting rooms. People are either at their appointment or in a pleasant spot in the hospital where they can relax if their appointment is delayed. These are only a few examples to illustrate what we are building toward.

Patient experience

Patient experience is also known as the "digital front door." It is the cyber grand entrance to the organization. It must be done right, and even though wayfinding is a part of every digital engagement model, few have executed it well. This could be because wayfinding and patient experience solutions are attempted too early in the location services' maturity curve. Starting with operations will help the organization learn enough so that when they are ready for patients, it will be able to design an amazing experience. Getting the below-the-wing components right will prepare for the above-the-wing components because, as we have noted above, situational awareness should extend to the patient.

Integration with the Electronic Health Record is the key to moving from wayfinding to the more advanced patient experience features. Wayfinding includes patients and visitors, but patient experience is an integrated, interactive user experience that leverages our context-aware environment. The EHR (Electronic Health Record) is where much of the below-the-wing information lives, but when combined with situational awareness, afforded by a location-aware workflow, the patient experience can be amazing.

ROUTING

We are not including the routing in the wayfinding section for a reason. A "routing engine" is a service that is a part of our digital twin. It is the technology behind the turn-by-turn directions that you get in your favorite mapping app, but in this case, it is indoors. The routing engine will be able to deal with floor transitions, and it should be available to any system that needs to compute a route or calculate an ETA. The routing service should have at least three versions of routes:

1. Employee routes
2. Patient and visitor routes
3. Barrier-free routes for ADA compliance

Another key feature is that it should be "tunable." By saying tunable, we mean it should be able to deal with the complex restrictions you see in a hospital. For instance, if the shortest route to a particular location is through the transplant unit, this is an area that does not want to drive traffic through, so the routes need to be tuned to adhere to those restrictions. The routing engine uses a network of lines to find a single shortest path to the destination. To compensate for the restrictions, a weight is added to make the restrictions less favorable to the algorithm. What makes it complex is that because there are so many different points of origination, a route that works for one point of origination breaks another. That is why having different versions of the routes might be necessary. When all there is to consider is a digital shadow, it is less complex, but a routing network that works for every room in the building requires much more testing.

GEOFENCES

Geofences are the capability that GIS uses to determine if a point is inside or outside of a polygon. The point could be the location of people or property. The polygon could come from the GIS maps or even be generated on the fly. Geofences can be used in workflow automation to determine arrivals, departures, and dwell. A workflow that uses an origin or destination would have all three attributes. There are other ways to detect arrivals with proximity or presence, but geofences are a valuable tool that trigger events that are a part of a mobile workflow.

GIS AND THE OPERATIONAL DIGITAL TWIN

We are building toward describing the digital twin, but it is important to understand, at this point in that journey, that the type of digital twin used by care traffic control is an "operational" digital twin. Location-based services, at their core, are solving spatial data problems. GIS has capabilities to solve spatial problems. These capabilities have been built over many years. The operational digital twin uses GIS Enterprise Location Engine to process inputs from mobile devices and IPS, as well as the dependent and independent surveillance systems.

Events in a mobile workflow

When processing the mobile workflows, it is important to define the parameters that are used to analyze them. Below are the parameters that are used for describing both the temporal and spatial events that are part of a workflow. These use some of the same terminology used in the simulation modeling we will discuss in Chapter 16.

Geospatial events in the workflow

- **Origin:** The starting point of a route or a trace
- **Destination:** The finishing point of a route or a trace

- **Route:** A series of time-sequenced positions that are used to indicate the path to be taken to a destination
- **Trace:** A series of time-sequenced positions that are used to show the actual path that was taken to a destination

Temporal events in the workflow

- **Start:** The event that occurs at the time the activity starts.
- **Finish:** The event that occurs when all the tasks in the activity are completed.
- **Arrival:** An event indicating that the position of the entity is satisfactorily close to the destination.
- **Departure:** An event indicating that the position of the entity is satisfactorily far from the origin
- **Dwell:** The time that the entity has spent in proximity, presence, or possession
- **Velocity:** The rate of the distance traveled based on the position information
- **Task completion:** An event to indicate that a step has been completed

To make use of the data, it is necessary to understand the quality of the data that is being provided. Below are terms that describe the location data quality.

- **Ground truth:** The real-world geospatial situation that is being represented digitally.
- **Accuracy:** The percentage difference in distance between the reported location when compared against the ground truth.
- **Update frequency:** The rate at which the system gets the location reports from the end point.
- **Variability:** The rate of changes in accuracy or update frequency.
- **Certainty:** The probability that the reported location of an entity is correct when compared against the ground truth.

THE EDENVALE JOURNEY – EVERYTHING STARTS WITH THE MAPS

Imani was working from the strategy that she and Derek put together. Derek was gone, and she was going to recover from it. They had a weekly call set up, but she felt confident she could execute the plan. Even before she got into the details, she saw the themes, and she wondered why the maps were so important. Derek told her that when the RTLS goes live, she will see what he meant.

They weren't doing the IPS and the patient transport project until after the initial project to track the patients with the RTLS. The RTLS already had maps, so why might they need them right away? She soon found out.

As the program manager, she was the first person to be trained on the CMMS, and when the integrator showed her the page with the RTLS maps, she saw what he was talking about. The maps were pictures of the CAD files, were unpleasant to look at, and were hard to manipulate to get a good sense of where things were. She pictured something else when she thought of an RTLS map. This was not it.

On her weekly call with Derek, she said, "Ok, I get it about the maps but what can we do about it." Derek explained that the process we are going to use to create the maps will generate maps that are easy to manipulate into very useful maps that we can use for the RTLS and any other application that needs the maps. The first thing is to get the geometries and the data right before we use the maps.

He said, "The most important thing right now is to earn the right to move on from the length of stay project. So, how is that coming?" Imani told him that the patients are being admitted with the RTLS tags attached to their wristbands, and she is already seeing good data.

He said, "Ok get the CAD from the integrator because they must have it from the RTLS project. Derek gave her a contact for the CAD conversion to IMDF and said this company will guide you through the entire process. He said, "Once the IMDF is done, these guys will print you some replacement images for the CAD pictures in the RTLS. You will win friends in Clinical Engineering with that one."

> They will help you get into Apple Indoors and when we are ready for the tollgate for the patient transport project they can start on the maps. We need to know how many iPhones we need for patient transport and where the charging cabinet will go. I will set up the application to stream the data from the phones. The subscription is not much. We can work it into the budget with the phones and the charging cabinet.

We will work on the rest of the plan for the patient transport project next week and be ready for the steering committee at the end of the month."

PLAYBOOK FOR MAPS AND GIS

The playbook for maps and GIS is as simple as saying that everything starts with maps. Getting the geospatial components of the LBS program started is going to start with the indoor maps.

Improver

The goal for the maps is for them to become the single source of truth for all the geospatial information for the buildings and places where work is being done. This includes the naming and labeling of rooms. The sooner these data are cleaned, the better prepared the organization will be for all LBS projects.

1. Map Assessment & Planning
    - Inventory existing floor plans and CAD drawings
    - Inventory existing floor plans and CAD drawings
    - Evaluate current mapping needs across departments
    - Document pain points where improved spatial awareness could help
    - Identify opportunities for integrating location data with maps
2. Data Quality & Standards
    - Establish standards for spatial data collection and maintenance
    - Create processes for keeping maps current
    - Implement quality control procedures for spatial data
    - Ensure consistent naming conventions across systems
3. Implementation Steps
    - Start with high-quality base maps
    - Begin with critical areas first
    - Document map update procedures
    - Create feedback loops for map accuracy
    - Build processes for regular map maintenance

Leader

The field of GIS is new to healthcare, and it is important to understand its value and place in the future of the Digital Transformation. The adoption of location-based solutions hinges on the amazing user experience that is enabled with maps. Leaders should ensure that the market is aware of the importance of a strong user experience to carry these solutions into the future.

1. Strategic Investment
    - Understand the foundational role of maps in location services
    - Prioritize high-quality map data as core infrastructure
    - Plan for ongoing map maintenance resources
    - Invest in GIS expertise development
2. Resource Planning
    - Allocate resources for initial map creation
    - Plan for ongoing map maintenance
    - Consider internal vs. external GIS expertise
    - Budget for mapping software and tools
3. Partnership Development
    - Build relationships with CAD/GIS vendors
    - Engage facilities management teams
    - Coordinate with IT for system integration
    - Develop relationships with mapping expertise providers

Creator

One of the failings of LBS1.0 is the one-size-fits-all approach to use cases. It is a struggle because the infrastructure should be ubiquitous and reusable, but the solutions have different requirements in different departments. This means that an LBS program that is trying to expand into many departments might struggle when the user experience is not what is needed. As an example, a nurse trying to find equipment in the emergency department is typically under more time pressure than a nurse in the ICU.

1. Standards Compliance
   - Support IMDF and other relevant standards
   - Support IMDF and other relevant standards
   - Provide clear documentation of mapping requirements
   - Offer tools for map validation and quality control
   - Enable seamless integration with other systems
2. Implementation Support
   - Provide tools for CAD to GIS conversion
   - Offer map maintenance solutions
   - Support multiple map format outputs
   - Enable easy map updates and versioning
3. Service Development
   - Create tools for map validation
   - Develop solutions for ongoing map maintenance
   - Build integration capabilities with location services
   - Provide training and support resources

Chapter 6

Pervasive and mobile computing

Paul E. Zieske

Pervasive and mobile computing describes the use of computer technologies in everyday things, including their interconnectedness and ubiquity. Unlike traditional computing environments, pervasive computing seamlessly integrates into our surroundings, creating an environment where computing power is available everywhere but often invisible to users.

Key characteristics that define pervasive computing include:

1. **Invisibility:** Computing technologies blend into the background, operating without requiring direct user attention. Users interact with services and applications naturally, often unaware of the underlying technology.
2. **Integration:** Multiple devices and systems work together seamlessly. In healthcare, this might mean patient monitors, mobile devices, and facility systems all sharing data and functionality.
3. **Optimized Interfaces:** Systems adapt their interfaces based on context and user needs, providing the most appropriate way to interact in any given situation.
4. **Online and Offline Operation:** Systems maintain functionality regardless of network connectivity, ensuring critical operations continue even during network disruptions.
5. **Security Measures:** Robust security protects against unauthorized access while maintaining ease of use for authorized users.
6. **Personalization:** Systems adapt to user preferences and patterns without requiring extensive technical knowledge.

In the world of Internet of Things (IoT) and pervasive computing, every endpoint becomes a potential sensor and data collection point. This concept extends beyond traditional computing devices to include environmental sensors, mobile devices, and even building infrastructure. When we examine how these endpoints participate in location-based services, we see opportunities to leverage the existing infrastructure in new ways.

The relationship between pervasive computing and location-based services creates a foundation for more intelligent and responsive healthcare

DOI: 10.1201/9781003625483-7

environments. By understanding how these technologies work together, organizations can build more effective and efficient systems while minimizing the need for additional infrastructure.

This chapter explores how pervasive computing transforms healthcare operations, examining both the technological components and their practical applications in creating more intelligent and responsive healthcare environments.

ENDPOINT COMPUTING IN HEALTHCARE

The healthcare environment presents a unique opportunity for endpoint computing. Through decades of digitization, particularly with electronic health records, healthcare facilities have accumulated a vast network of computing devices. These devices, traditionally viewed as single-purpose workstations, can play a much broader role in a pervasive computing environment.

EVOLUTION OF HEALTHCARE ENDPOINTS

What was once a simple desktop computer used for charting and order entry can now function as a sensing node in a larger network. For example, a nursing station computer not only serves its primary clinical documentation purpose but can also act as a BLE gateway, contributing to the facility's location awareness capabilities. This dual-purpose utilization maximizes the return on existing technology investments.

Types of Endpoints in Healthcare Settings:

1. Clinical and Administrative Workstations
    - Traditional documentation stations
    - Medication dispensing computers
    - Imaging review stations
    - Treatment planning systems
    - Office workstations
2. Mobile Devices
    - Clinical tablets and smartphones
    - Support services tablets and smartphones
    - Patient monitoring devices
    - Portable diagnostic equipment
    - Mobile documentation carts
3. Infrastructure Endpoints
    - Wireless access points
    - Security cameras
    - Environmental controls
    - Building automation systems

4. Smart Medical Devices
   - Connected patient monitors
   - Smart pumps
   - Diagnostic equipment
   - Tracking-enabled mobile equipment

This distributed network of endpoints creates opportunities for enhanced location services without requiring significant additional infrastructure. By leveraging existing devices, healthcare organizations can build robust location-aware systems while minimizing new technology investments.

The key is understanding how these endpoints can contribute to the broader pervasive computing environment while maintaining their primary functions. This dual-purpose approach requires careful consideration of:

- Processing capabilities
- Network bandwidth
- Power requirements
- Security implications
- User impact

PERVASIVE COMPUTING LOCATOR SYSTEM (PCLS)

The PCLS represents a paradigm shift in location tracking, utilizing existing computing infrastructure to create a comprehensive locator system. This "no new infrastructure" or "software-only" approach to RTLS leverages computer endpoints as gateways to establish a BLE sensor network. The system not only tracks IoT devices but also maintains location awareness of the computing endpoints themselves.

Key Components:

1. **Desktop Computers**
   - Function as BLE gateways with simple software installation
   - Provide coverage in administrative and clinical spaces
   - Require minimal configuration and maintenance
2. **Wi-Fi Access Points**
   - Act as location sensors using built-in BLE capabilities
   - Offer broad coverage across the facility
   - Integrate with existing network infrastructure
3. **Mobile Devices**
   - Serve as data collectors and location beacons
   - Enable crowd-sensing capabilities
   - Provide real-time location streaming

The PCLS is a concept that uses pervasive computing to create a locator system that can track the location of BLE tags and all the computing endpoints in the environment where they already exist. The pervasive computing locator system leverages as many computer endpoints as possible and uses them as gateways to establish the BLE sensor network that detects the location of the IoT devices. It also finds the location of all the devices that are a part of the system itself. It still uses BLE gateways and BLE tags, but this architecture recognizes that there are many devices that have all the necessary hardware to do this already and they have the advantage of already being in locations that are being covered. The software that is necessary to make these endpoints serve as gateways is called an agent.

PCLS agents

The PCLS software agent transforms endpoints into active components of the PCLS network.

Core Functions (Figure 6.1 and Table 6.1):

1. Gateway Operation
   - BLE communication with other agents
   - Real-time location data processing
   - Inter-agent coordination
2. Spatial Awareness
   - Geolocation processing
   - RSSI (Received Signal Strength Indicator) fingerprinting
   - Position verification

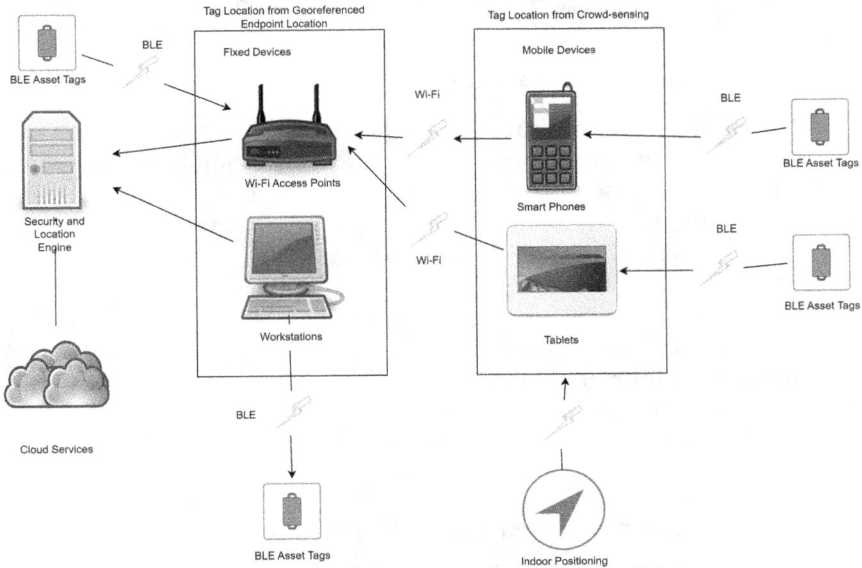

Figure 6.1 PCLS architectural reference diagram.

Table 6.1 Traditional RTLS vs PCLS approach

Feature	*Traditional RTLS*	*PCLS*
Infrastructure	Dedicated hardware	Existing endpoints
Cost	High initial investment	Minimal hardware cost
Coverage	Fixed by design	Dynamically adaptive
Maintenance	Hardware-focused	Software-focused
Scalability	Hardware-dependent	Software-defined
Integration	Often siloed	Inherently integrated

3. System Monitoring
   - Gateway status tracking
   - Performance metrics
   - Position change detection

Dividing these into desktop, access point (AP), mobile, and IoT, we will look at each category for how it participates in location services.

Key feature: disturbance detection

The agent establishes a 3D matrix of RSSI fingerprints across the facility. Changes in this matrix indicate potential movement of gateway devices, enabling automatic detection of unauthorized equipment relocation.

Desktop integration in PCLS

Healthcare's digital transformation, particularly through EHR adoption, has resulted in widespread deployment of desktop computers throughout medical facilities. These existing computers can be repurposed as BLE gateways within the PCLS framework, creating a dense network of location-sensing nodes using already-deployed hardware.

Key Benefits:

- Leverages existing infrastructure
- Reduces additional hardware costs
- Provides comprehensive coverage
- Minimal impact on primary computing functions

Wireless access point integration

Modern wireless APs increasingly ship with built-in BLE capabilities, offering natural integration points for the PCLS network.

Benefits:

- Leverages existing Wi-Fi infrastructure
- Widely dispersed for optimal Wi-Fi coverage
- Dual-purpose utilization of hardware

Considerations:

- AP locations optimized for Wi-Fi coverage may not be ideal for RTLS
- Integration with existing network management systems
- Impact on AP performance and capacity

Best Practice: Use AP-based sensing as a primary layer and add dedicated location sensors to enhance overall system coverage and reliability.

Infrastructure

A standard BLE RTLS can be used to augment the distributed system if the gateway sensors are open enough to see the BLE tags that have been applied to the devices. Not many, if any, of the BLE RTLS vendors are open to the idea of sharing the coverage with this software-only option, but we note this as an option, because it still fits within the concept of a PCLS.

Mobile crowd-sensing

Mobile devices that have access to an IPS (Indoor Positioning System) can act as sensors for locating BLE tags. Using the iPhone as an example, when the BLE tag is within a certain range of the iPhone, it can tell the iPhone to retrieve its location and, with IPS, the latitude, longitude, and floor will be returned. From here we infer the location of the tag to be the location of the iPhone. The inferred location and tag id are sent back to the enterprise location engine for processing. This is the same crowd-sensing concept employed by Apple's AirTag and originally with the Tile. With crowd-sensing only, you lose some certainty and predictability, but you gain coverage and location fidelity. With crowd-sensing as an additional input to the PCLS, you get improved coverage and the ability to sense devices with proximity detection. This is like the find-my feature in the Apple iPhone with the AirTag. This is the concept first described in Chapter 1, "Healthcare adoption".

Definition:

Mobile crowd-sensing leverages the sensing capabilities of mobile devices carried by facility occupants to enhance location awareness and spatial context.

Key Components:

1. Data Collection
   - Device sensors
   - Environmental readings
   - Proximity detection
2. Processing Layer
   - Data aggregation
   - Pattern recognition
   - Privacy protection
3. Application Layer
   - Location services
   - Navigation support
   - Asset tracking

Implementation Considerations:

- Privacy and consent management
- Data quality assurance
- Battery life impact
- User participation incentives

ENTERPRISE LOCATION ENGINE

The enterprise location engine serves as the central nervous system of the PCLS, ingesting and processing location data from multiple sources to create a unified view of location awareness. Unlike traditional location engines that process data from a single type of sensor system, the enterprise location engine is designed to handle diverse inputs and create a more comprehensive understanding of position, proximity, presence, and possession.

Core functions

The enterprise location engine performs several critical tasks:

1. Data Aggregation
   - Collects raw location data from various sensors
   - Normalizes data from different sources
   - Validates incoming data quality
   - Maintains historical records
   - Manages real-time data streams
2. Location Processing
   - Calculates precise positions
   - Determines proximity relationships

- Detects presence in defined zones
- Establishes possession relationships
- Filters and smooths location data

3. Context Integration
   - Combines location data with facility maps
   - Incorporates business rules and policies
   - Adds environmental context
   - Links to workflow systems
   - Maintains relationship models

Data sources

The engine processes input from multiple sources:

- RTLS systems
- Indoor positioning systems
- Mobile device locations
- Crowd-sensing data
- Environmental sensors
- Building automation systems

These diverse inputs create a rich tapestry of location information that can be used to support various use cases and applications (Figure 6.2).

The real power of the enterprise location engine lies in its ability to democratize location data across the organization, making it available to any authorized system or application that could benefit from location awareness.

MOBILE STRATEGY

Mobile devices represent far more than just communication tools in a pervasive computing environment. Think of them as powerful mobile computers that serve as both data collection points and interfaces for location-aware workflows. In healthcare environments, this shift in perspective is particularly important as these devices become integral to care delivery and operational efficiency.

When considering mobile devices in healthcare, we need to move beyond thinking of them merely as phones or tablets that need cellular service. Most use cases can operate effectively with just Wi-Fi connectivity, supporting asynchronous communications like texting and data transfer. The real power lies in their ability to deliver time-sensitive information to staff wherever they are, eliminating the delays associated with finding a workstation or returning to a desk.

Consider how Delta Airlines approaches mobile strategy – they issue what they call an "AirPro" to every above-the-wing employee. These devices are

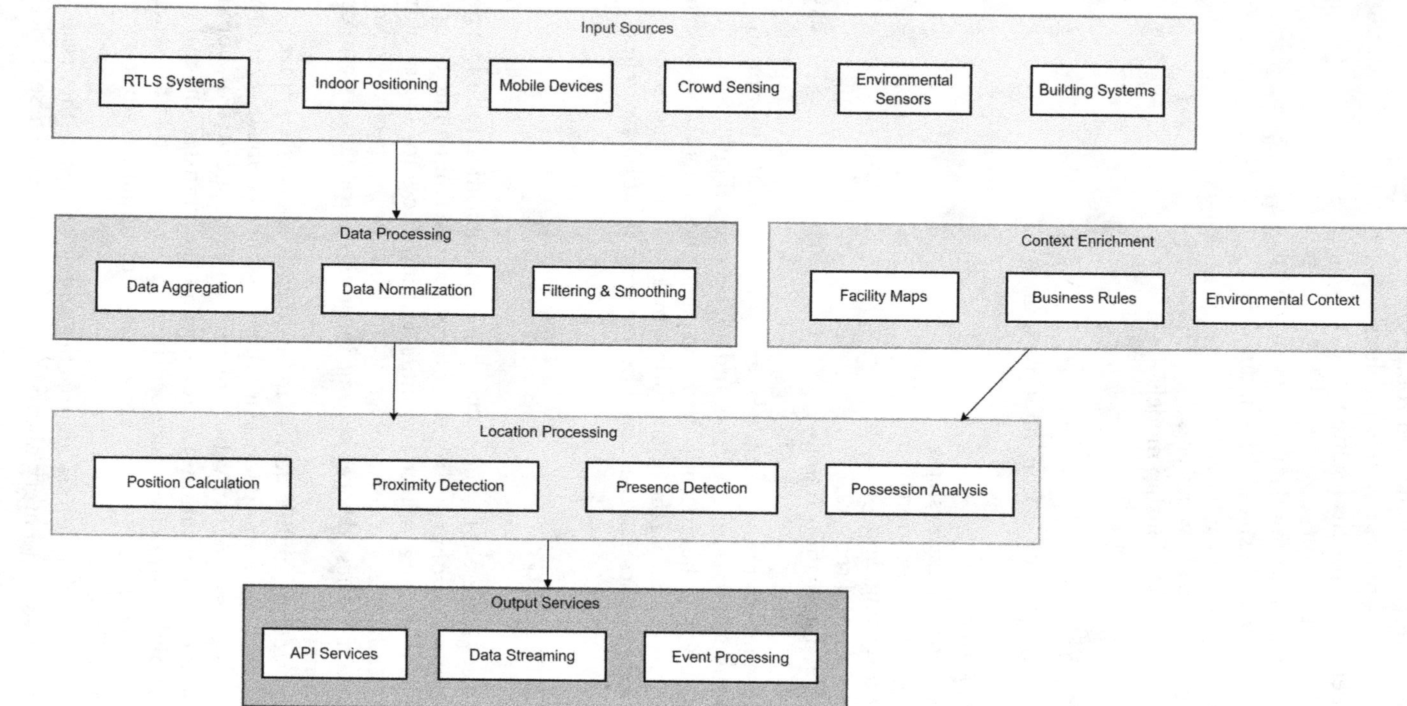

Figure 6.2 **Enterprise location engine logical diagram.**

so crucial to operations that staff cannot work without them. Healthcare could benefit from a similar mindset, where every mobile worker has what we might call a "CarePro" – a device that's essential to their workflow rather than just an optional tool.

Device management approaches

The relationship between devices and the organization typically falls into four categories, each with its own considerations (Table 6.2).

Table 6.2 Device categories and organizational control

Category	*Description*	*Control level*	*Advantages*	*Challenges*
BYOD	Personal devices used for work functions	Limited organizational control	– Lower hardware costs – User familiarity – High adoption rates – Device maintenance by user	– Security concerns – Inconsistent capabilities – Privacy management – Support complexity
Assigned Devices	Organization-owned, personally assigned	Full organizational control	– Consistent configuration – Standardized applications – Clear accountability – Simplified support	– Higher hardware costs – Device replacement cycles – Personal use policies – Lost device liability
Dedicated Devices	Single-purpose, workflow-specific	Maximum control	– Purpose-built configuration – Simplified management – Focused functionality – Optimized performance	– Limited flexibility – Idle time between uses – Single point of failure – Redundancy needs
Shared Devices	Department-owned, multi-user	High organizational control	– Cost-effective utilization – Shift-based optimization – Resource pooling – Flexible deployment	– User transition management – Shared responsibility – Device availability – Authentication complexity

Making devices location-aware

A crucial aspect of any mobile strategy is making devices location-aware within indoor environments. This means implementing indoor positioning systems that allow devices to be located with the same ease as outdoor GPS tracking. The relationship between the device and the organization determines how they are managed and what privacy controls are needed.

Single sign-on: removing friction

Think about how many applications a typical healthcare worker needs to access throughout their shift. Single sign-on becomes critical here – it is not just about convenience, it is about removing barriers to efficient work. When a nurse needs to access patient records, communication tools, and clinical references, they should not have to authenticate multiple times. A robust single sign-on solution ensures security while maintaining workflow efficiency.

This comprehensive approach to mobile strategy supports the broader goals of pervasive computing while addressing the specific needs of healthcare environments. By viewing mobile devices as essential tools rather than accessories, organizations can build more effective and efficient workflows that truly support their staff's needs.

Internet of things (IoT)

The IoT is fundamental to pervasive computing, and we are witnessing an explosion in the IoT market that is transforming healthcare environments. Medical device manufacturers are increasingly incorporating BLE transmitters into their newest equipment, though they are typically not offering complete locator systems. Instead, their strategy tends toward interoperability, allowing their devices to be detected and tracked by existing location infrastructure. This approach reinforces the importance of an enterprise location engine that can aggregate and process data from multiple sources.

Ambient intelligence (AmI)

A particularly exciting development in IoT is the concept of ambient intelligence (AmI), which allows devices to work cooperatively with people performing everyday activities. Think of AmI as creating an environment that is sensitive and responsive to human presence. For example:

- Thermal cameras that can distinguish between different heat sources
- Sound sensors that can detect specific acoustic signatures
- Proximity sensors that can track movement patterns
- Environmental sensors that monitor air quality and occupancy

Real-world applications are already emerging. Some facilities have installed highly sensitive microphones connected directly to wireless APs for security purposes. These systems can detect specific sounds like aggressive voices or even identify different types of security threats based on acoustic signatures.

Clinical applications

The potential for applying AmI in clinical settings is particularly promising. Consider these scenarios:

- A patient room that recognizes when a physician enters and automatically authenticates them to the correct patient record
- Fall detection systems that use multiple sensor types to accurately detect patient falls while minimizing false alarms
- Environmental monitoring that adjusts automatically based on patient conditions and clinical requirements
- Equipment tracking that considers not just location but usage patterns and maintenance needs

Integration considerations

Many RTLS vendors have begun embedding additional sensors in their location hardware, taking advantage of their existing infrastructure footprint. This creates opportunities for:

- Temperature monitoring
- Humidity detection
- Motion sensing
- Occupancy tracking
- Environmental quality assessment

Understanding these sensing capabilities becomes crucial when designing solutions that will remove friction from workflows and personalize user experiences. The key is identifying which sensors are available in your environment and how their data can be leveraged to enhance operations (Figure 6.3).

Internet of things (IoT)

The IoT is fundamental to pervasive computing and there has been an explosion of the IoT market. Many medical device manufacturers are moving forward with BLE transmitters in their newest devices. It is not likely these companies will be offering locator systems, so we should expect interoperability to be their strategy for finding devices. An enterprise location engine would allow these devices to be seen by the system.

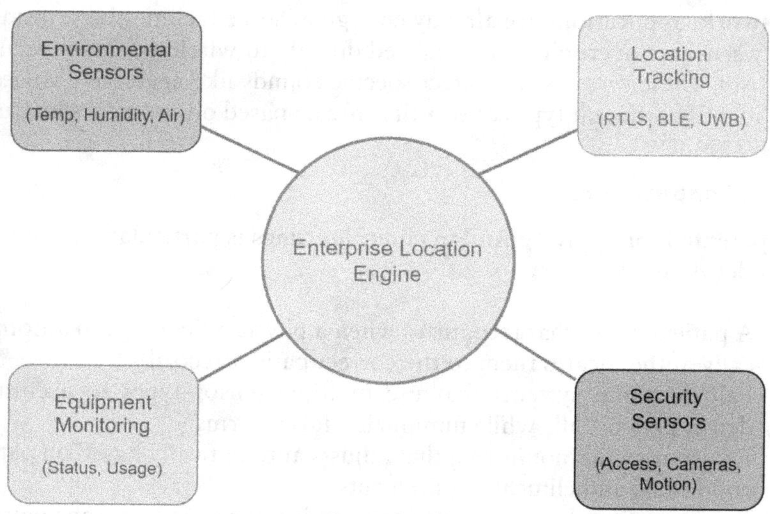

Figure 6.3 Enterprise location engine sensor input diagram.

AmI is a pervasive computing concept that allows devices to work in a coordinated fashion with people who are doing work or other ordinary activities. These ambient sensors could include thermal cameras, IR sensors, sound, BLE proximity sensors, and others. An example of this is where several companies have installed sensitive microphones that connect directly to the wireless AP to detect gunshots in a building. These systems are so sensitive they can tell what kind of weapon and determine if a person is using an aggressive voice.

The ability to apply AmI with clinicians and medical equipment has great potential. A patient room that knows the doctor has entered can authenticate the identity of the doctor, open the medical record with correct patient record. Fall detection could be done with the same suite of sensors and AmI.

Some of the RTLS vendors have loaded their location hardware with sensors that do more than location. They are taking advantage of the footprint they have in the building. Being aware of the sensing that is available in these systems will help drive new solutions that will remove friction from workflows and personalize the user experience.

MANAGING ENDPOINTS

The management of endpoints in a pervasive computing environment poses unique challenges due to their distributed nature and diverse functionality. Yet what might seem like a management burden can become a strategic advantage when approached systematically. Let us explore how organizations can effectively manage their endpoint ecosystem through various tools and approaches.

Unified endpoint management (UEM)

The trend in endpoint management is moving beyond traditional mobile device management (MDM) toward unified endpoint management (UEM). This shift reflects the growing complexity of our computing environment. While MDM traditionally focused on iOS and Android devices, UEM expands this scope to include:

- Desktop computers
- Mobile devices
- IoT sensors
- Medical devices
- Network equipment

This unified approach provides several key benefits:

- Centralized management interface
- Consistent security policies
- Streamlined updates and configurations
- Integrated monitoring and reporting
- Automated compliance management

Remote management capabilities

Modern endpoint management requires robust remote capabilities that allow IT teams to:

- Monitor device health
- Deploy software updates
- Troubleshoot issues
- Manage configurations
- Control security settings
- Track asset location

Organizations must implement remote management that balances security with accessibility, ensuring devices remain both protected and functional.

Security management

Security in a pervasive computing environment requires a multi-layered approach:

1. Endpoint detection and response (EDR)
    - Continuous monitoring
    - Threat detection
    - Automated response

- Incident investigation
- Integration with other security tools

2. Physical Security
   - Device tracking
   - Loss prevention
   - Access control
   - Tamper detection

THE EDENVALE JOURNEY – THE "USE WHAT YOU ALREADY HAVE" PROJECT

Edenvale has their maps, IPS, and soon transport will be using the iPhones. Clinical engineering is using the new RTLS, and the Length of Stay project is getting good data for the movement of patients in the building. The Length of Stay project is focusing on discharges, but the bed management team is seeing the data, and they are talking about how they can improve overall capacity management with what they are seeing.

In the initial phases of the program, the data was analyzed over long planning horizons and used for strategic observations. Now that those projects are moving forward, the patient transport part is trending toward enabling the users with real-time data. The earn-the-right approach has fueled more projects than they had even anticipated. One project they are anxious to move forward is what they are calling the "AirTag" project. This concept uses the iPhones to find any BLE RTLS tag that is in its proximity. It works like the AirTag works but indoors. The company was called Luna, and they can do this with desktops as well. Their BLE RTLS already uses the Wi-Fi APs as gateways, but this will be a nice enhancement to the location fidelity for all of the projects.

This is a big "use what you already have" project because, as it turns out, EGH has wall-mounted workstations in every patient room. They opted for that approach because the CNO(Chief Nursing Officer) did not like the WoW (Workstations on Wheels) carts cluttering the halls and she got dinged for it in a Joint Commission inspection at another hospital. It costs EGH more to put the workstations in the patient rooms and now they can get more value from them as location sensors.

The Luna product will allow any device that has their agent on it to find how close they are to a BLE RTLS tag. It works like the AirTag user experience. The Clinical Engineering team is getting iPhones because the CMMS (Computerized Maintenance Management System) has an app and can assign their jobs to the workers via the phone (the mobile apps for mobile work theme). They want to use the phones to find equipment for preventative maintenance. Patient transport wants to use the concept to verify that the patient transporter has the right patient by using the phone-to-wristband proximity detection.

Derek has been helping them with this pervasive computing project and when they engaged with the vendor he told Imani, "Welcome to Location-based services 2.0." She said, "glad to be here." Imani reflected on how far they had come from the stress and frustration of the first few months when the way forward looked like such a long climb. Derek reminded her they are in pretty good shape with LBS 2.0 but there is a long way to go to get to care traffic control.

PLAYBOOK FOR PERVASIVE AND MOBILE COMPUTING

The playbook provides guidance for different stakeholders in implementing and leveraging pervasive computing within healthcare organizations. The focus is on practical steps and considerations for each group.

Improvers

Performance improvement teams should focus on:

1. Technology Assessment
   - Evaluate existing endpoints for potential sensing capabilities
   - Identify opportunities to leverage current infrastructure
   - Map workflows that could benefit from location awareness
   - Document potential efficiency gains from automation
2. Implementation Strategy
   - Start with high-impact, low-complexity use cases
   - Build on successful implementations
   - Document and share best practices
   - Measure and communicate results
3. Process Integration
   - Align technology implementation with workflow improvements
   - Ensure user adoption through proper training and support
   - Monitor and adjust based on feedback
   - Create sustainable improvement cycles

Leaders

Healthcare leaders should concentrate on:

1. Strategic Planning
   - Develop a comprehensive pervasive computing strategy
   - Align technology investments with organizational goals

- Create a roadmap for implementation
- Establish clear success metrics
2. Resource Allocation
   - Invest in foundational infrastructure
   - Support training and education initiatives
   - Allocate resources for ongoing maintenance
   - Plan for future expansion
3. Change Management
   - Build organizational support
   - Address privacy and security concerns
   - Manage stakeholder expectations
   - Foster innovation culture

Creators

Technology vendors creators should focus on:

1. Solution Development
   - Create interoperable solutions
   - Support standard protocols
   - Provide flexible integration options
   - Develop scalable architectures
2. Implementation Support
   - Offer comprehensive training programs
   - Provide clear documentation
   - Support proof-of-concept implementations
   - Maintain ongoing technical support
3. Innovation Partnership
   - Work closely with healthcare organizations
   - Adapt solutions to specific needs
   - Share industry best practices
   - Contribute to standards development

This structured approach helps ensure successful implementation and adoption of pervasive computing technologies while maintaining focus on organizational objectives and stakeholder needs.

Chapter 7

Artificial intelligence and rational agents

Paul E. Zieske

The study of artificial intelligence (AI) goes back to 1950, and the famous article published by Alan Turing called "Computing Machinery and Intelligence." It is important to note that none of the machinery described in the article was created at that time, nor was the field even called artificial intelligence. That happened in 1956 at a workshop at Dartmouth where John McCarthy from Princeton offered the term, and it stuck.

To study AI, one must first tackle understanding what *intelligence* is. The study of intelligence comes from philosophy. Aristotle (384–322 B.C.) created syllogisms which were informal rules of logic that eventually lead to the formal rules of logic we have now. The mechanics for reasoning were being developed and understood. From there the path winds through many related fields like Mathematics, Economics, Neuroscience, and Psychology before it lands in Computer Science.

AI has quite a few definitions which shows the large scope it has. AI is often simply defined as the study of agents. Britannica says, "AI is the ability of a computer or robot to perform tasks associated with intelligent beings." IBM says, "AI enables computers and machines to simulate human intelligence and problem-solving capabilities." You will find the latter two definitions describe the behavior of agents which solidifies the validity of the simple definition.

When we learn about agents, we see right away that in addition to AI, humans are agents, but so are organizations. The process of creating AI forces us to model these agents and get deeply into how they behave and what success looks like. This modeling gives us a way to look at system dynamics in a way that is different from other types of systems analysis. When we design a system that is using AI, we analyze the problem and we only need to look at *what* needs to be computed, as opposed to conventional software systems where we need to look at *how* to compute it.

Modeling workflows as agents elevates the role of location-based services to serve as the sensing mechanism for the agent. Agents allow us to look at the entire human/machine system and target improvements that will find the correct balance of human and machine in pursuit of the optimal outcome. We evaluate the amount of uncertainty and opportunities to

DOI: 10.1201/9781003625483-8

reduce uncertainty. Uncertainty is the enemy of optimization and good decision-making.

This chapter is going to provide a brief overview of AI and agents that is nowhere near exhaustive. Much of the information is from the excellent book "Artificial Intelligence 3E" by Poole and Mackworth. We need to cover just enough to give us the tools we need to create what is called an agent architecture for the organization. Whether or not targeting the entire enterprise is a worthwhile pursuit is up for debate, but having the tools to get a framework for hierarchical agent architecture is valuable. In later chapters, we will see how to apply these tools to specific problems.

AGENTS

Agents will form the foundation for creating the workflow-centered system that CTC (Care Traffic Control) requires. An agent is simply something that acts in an environment. **Rational agents**[1] come from AI and are defined as "a person or entity that chooses the optimal actions from all possibilities." We will be looking at **bounded rationality**[2] as computational agents operate within their computational limits. At the highest level, these agents receive **stimuli** from the environment, process those stimuli, and perform actions that change the **state** of the environment. The stimuli can be any external information that the controller needs to choose its actions. Rational agents have goals, and as said above, they choose the actions that achieve those goals.

These agents involve a **body** and a **controller** (Figure 7.1). The body is the interface between the environment and the controllers. The body receives

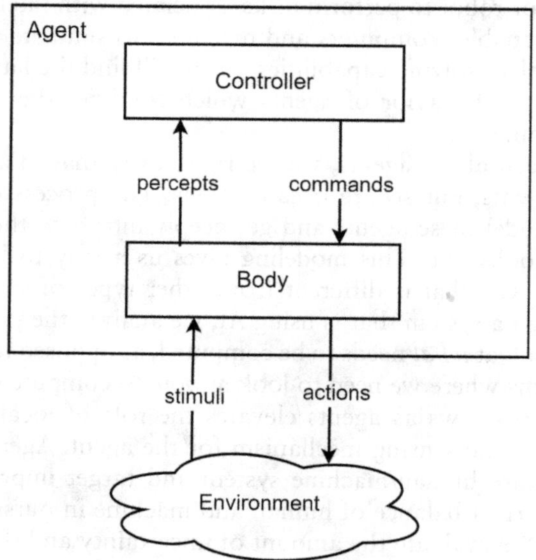

Figure 7.1 Agent, controller, body, environment relationships diagram.

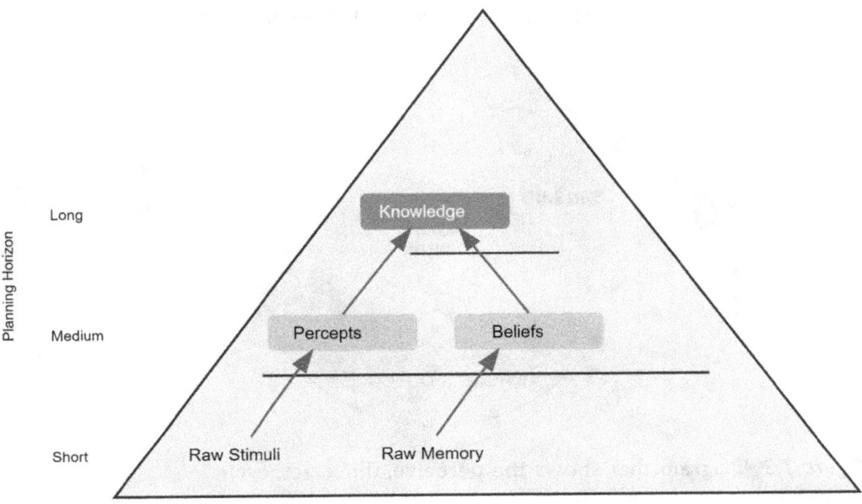

Figure 7.2 Pyramid that shows the planning horizons and the steps that lead to knowledge.

the information from sensors or external systems and processes that information into **percepts** that it sends to the controller. Percepts are how the body perceives the **state** of the environment. The controller uses those percepts to choose the correct action and sends commands to the body to perform the action.

The controller is capable of planning, but it is also capable of learning, and this is where the **memory** is processed into **belief**. Memory is the raw history of the percepts and commands in their time sequence. Belief evaluates how that history has affected the environment in support of the goals for the agent. Memory is to belief as stimuli are to percepts. This is where the raw data is refined into useful information. In our hierarchical architecture, where the planning horizon (think-time) increases as we step up in the layers of hierarchy, we see that what was belief near the bottom is now called **knowledge** near the top. Knowledge is created from an accumulation of beliefs (Figure 7.2).

PEAS

PEAS is a structure that helps us prepare to describe the behavior of "rational agents" in a task environment. PEAS stands for *performance measures, environment, actuators, and sensors*. The emphasis on this type of agent is because, in a task environment, the agent will perform an action that will change the environment to a desired state. Using PEAS allows us to organize the components of the agent to ensure we get the outcomes we want and the maximum reusability from the component of the agents. There will be times when the agents will have to share these capabilities, so structuring the agent in this way will help with organization as well as design.

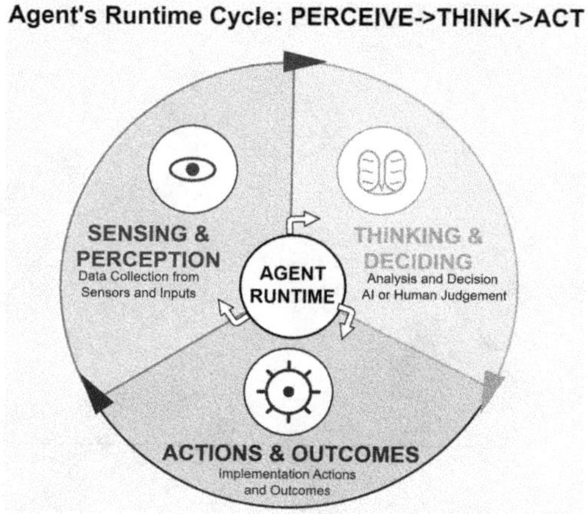

Agent's Runtime Cycle: PERCEIVE->THINK->ACT

Figure 7.3 Diagram that shows the perceive, think, act, cycle.

The agent runs through cycles of perceive → think→ act. Viewing the agent in each of these phases, we can look at the states and the changes in state that drive the behavior of the agent (Figures 7.3 and 7.4).

Performance measures

Performance measures define the success of the rational agent. The performance measures can be a single measure or a set of measures, depending on the agent's goals. The performance measures are also limited to what the agent can perceive from the sensors that are available to it. The success of the agent is represented by the state of the environment.

The generalization in Figure 7.5 describes the lowest level in the PEAS model. Performance measures can be abstracted above this to get to higher-level goals. The purpose of showing this low level of abstraction is that it makes it easier to see how it maps back to the environment, actuators, and sensors.

Environment

The agent and the environment exist in the **world**. The **environment** determines what the agent can perceive about the world. That limitation comes from the stimuli that are available to the agent. Another way of saying it is that outcomes happen in the world but the way that agent perceives those outcomes is the environment. In the LBS domain, we call the world, "ground truth." This can get confusing because the literature on agents will seemingly mix up the world and the environment, so we are not going to try to sort that out here, we merely want to point it out.

Accurate knowledge of the world is critical to the success of the agent, but we can be assured that 100% knowledge of the world is impossible. Even with good stimuli, certainty is limited so we need ways to deal with uncertainty. The stimuli that is available to the body is all that the agent has for knowing

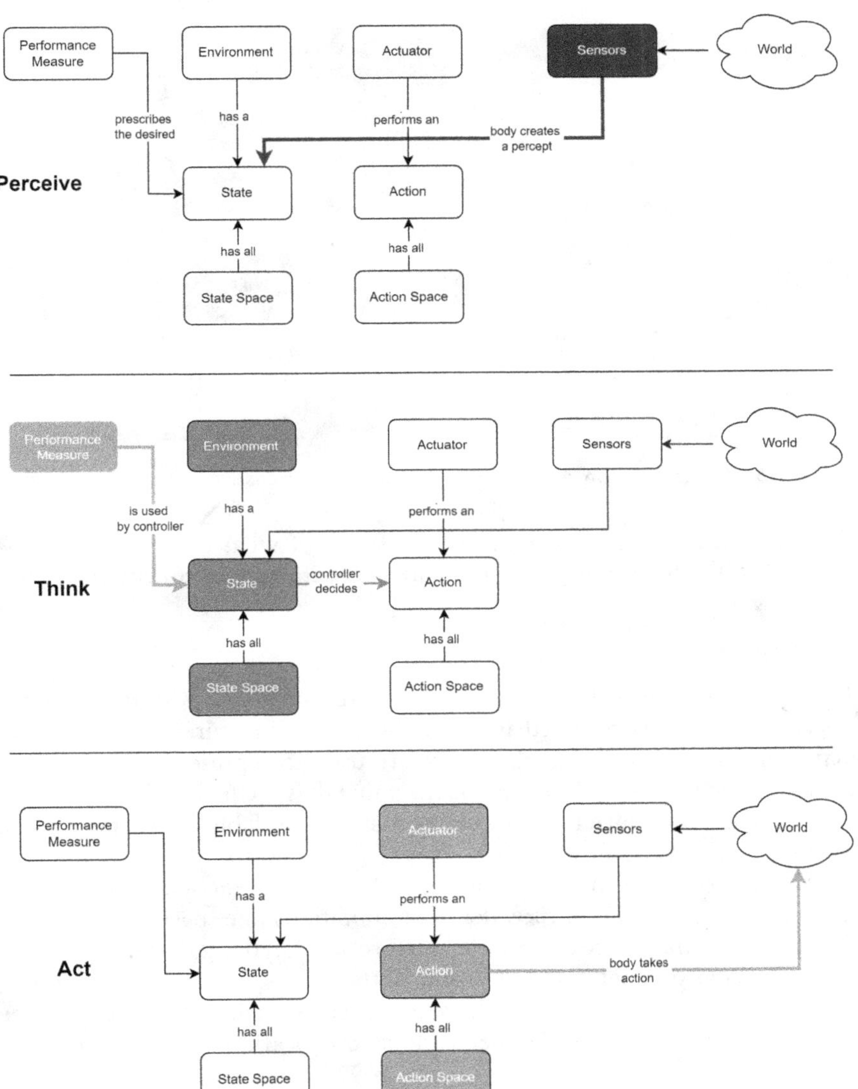

Figure 7.4 Diagram that maps PEAS to the perceive, think, act, cycle.

anything about its environment. The sensors and other contextual information that make up that stimuli are important to how the agent can plan and learn.

The agent's environment can also include other agents which would make it a multi-agent system (MAS). These agents can be a part of a hierarchical system of agents making a hierarchical agent architecture. In this way, entire organizations can be modeled using agents.

The generalization in Figure 7.6 contains a more comprehensive hierarchy of environmental elements than what would normally be included in a

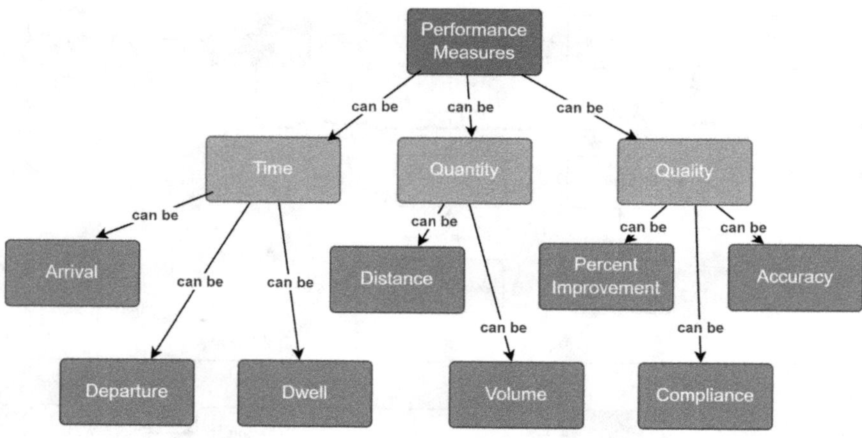

Figure 7.5 Generalization diagram for performance measures.

single agent. It does, however, show the scope of what the agent might be working with when trying to operate in a care traffic control environment.

State Space

The goal of the agent is to change the environment in a way that gets the desired outcome as reflected in the performance measures. Those performance measures use the **features** that are used to represent the **state.** The **features** have values, and the state is the value that the feature has at a point in time. The **state space** is all the states that are available to the agent to be used in its reasoning.

The types of location-based features that we might encounter in the state space are an arrival, departure, delay, or conditions like sensing a room has the light on or that there are people in the room. Anything that we can sense about the environment could be a part of the state space. Contextual information is an important part of the state space as well. The agent could be 50% through the deliveries of medications to a location that is contained in the job it was assigned.

Types of environments

- **Fully Observable vs. Partially Observable**
  - If an agent can perceive or sense everything from the environment it requires to get its desired outcome, it is **fully observable. Partially observable** is anything less than fully observable. Unobservable is where it cannot perceive its environment. It may be that a human could provide the sensing in an unobservable environment.
  - Fully observable environments make automation easier than partially observable.

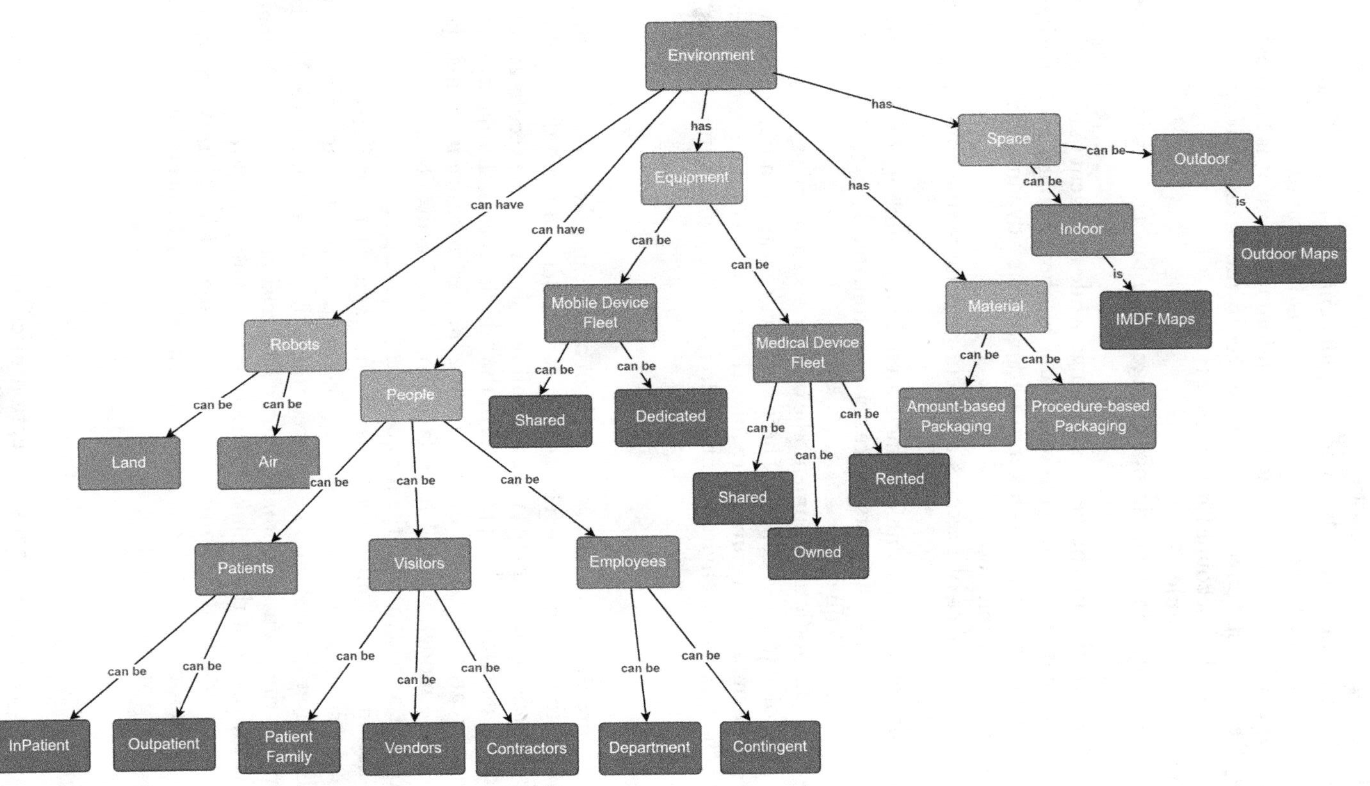

Figure 7.6 Generalization diagram for the environment.

- **Deterministic vs. Stochastic**
  - If the agent can apply an action to its current state and fully determine the next state, the environment is **Deterministic.** If the resultant state of the environment is random in nature, it is **Stochastic.**
  - Deterministic environments are easier to automate as the agent does not need to account for uncertainty.
- **Static vs. Dynamic**
  - **Static** environments do not change while the agent is in the think phase.
  - A **Dynamic** environment can change while the agent is in the think phase and the agent needs to account for these changes in the design.
  - A static environment is easier to automate than a dynamic environment.
- **Discrete vs. Continuous**
  - If the number of percepts and actions is finite, the environment is said to be **Discrete.**
  - **Continuous** environments have an unlimited number of percepts.
  - Discrete environments are easier to automate.
- **Episodic vs. Sequential**
  - In an **Episodic** environment, the outcome is encapsulated in a grouping of states and actions. These episodes repeat for a new outcome.
  - **Sequential** environments require the agent to consider the current changes to the environment for decisions regarding future actions.

Actuators

Actuators are the means through which an agent can take actions to affect the state of the environment. The actions can be derived from the capabilities of humans or machines. Actuators allow the agent to execute actions based on its decision-making process. In the "think" phase, the agent selects actions to create the optimal outcome using the performance measures. For an enterprise model, we will have layers of these agents. This means, we need to have a structure for them to cooperate (Figure 7.7).

The **action space** is all the actions that the agent has available to it to change the state of the environment. The actions that the agent chooses from the action space should be selected to get the optimal outcome. This is what makes the agent a *rational* agent. The decision to select a particular action is the result of the "think" phase that the agent goes through.

Figure 7.7 shows an example of the action space for the task environment. The actions can be a communication, a job, or a sequence of jobs that we are calling an orchestration.

Sensors

Sensors are part of the agent's perception mechanism that allows them to perceive the state of the environment. The sensors provide stimuli that are

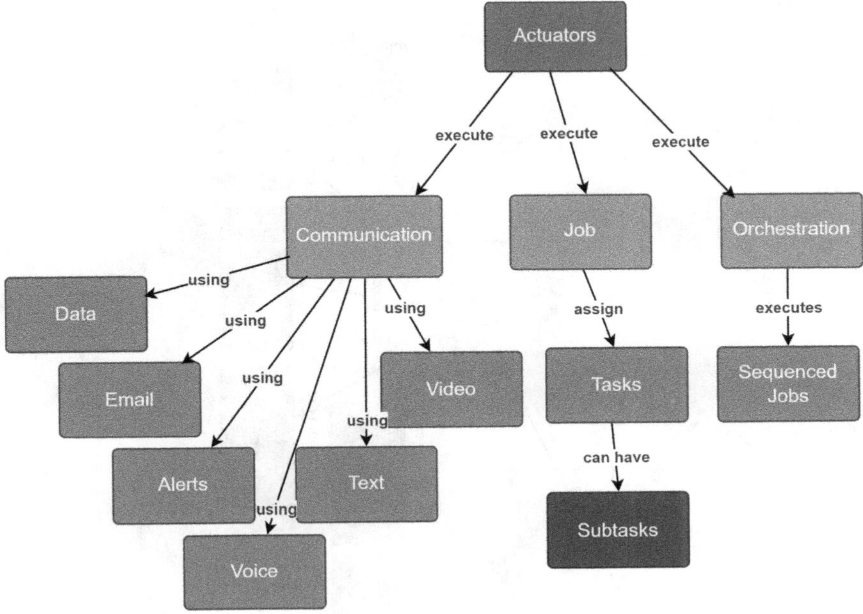

Figure 7.7 Generalization diagram for the actuators.

further processed into what is called a **percept**. Sensors can be physical sensors that capture data from the surroundings, such as IoT devices, cameras, microphones, or virtual sensors that receive data inputs from the software or other agents. Sensors can be the senses of a human in some circumstances. Sensors provide the agent with the necessary input to make informed decisions and take appropriate actions.

Figure 7.8 shows sensors that can gather percepts from data, location, or conditions. These percepts are compared against memories to form beliefs about the state of the environment.

Uncertainty

Uncertainty plays a big role in how AI is used by the agent. The AI is much like a human in that it takes time to gather information that it needs to plan. This think-time is called the **planning horizon.**[3] The planning horizon is a design time constraint that AI is operating in. An AI in a highly uncertain environment might need more time to either gather information, retrieve its memory, or process the information it has.

Removing some of the uncertainty from the environment is helpful to the AI and to the outcomes, in general. By making the environment more observable, deterministic, static, and episodic, we can remove some of the uncertainty and work within shorter planning horizons.

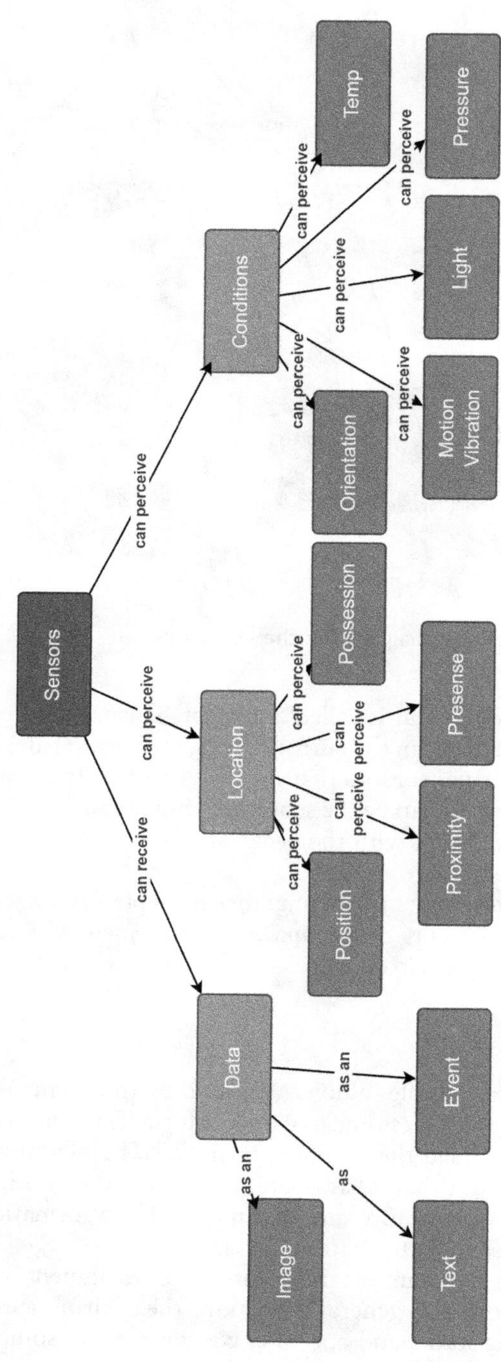

Figure 7.8 Generalization diagram for sensors.

Even though this is an AI architecture, it can function without AI, and it can even function without much automation at all. With the **human-in-the-loop** (HITL) approach, the agent and the human work together to solve problems. This can occur at any point in the flow from perception to action. By architecting it in this way, a foundation is set to allow these agents to become more intelligent and capable over time. We are introducing a modeling technique from AI that can help us compose solutions from the tools we have talked about in previous chapters.

AGENT ARCHITECTURE

For our CTC digital twin, these agents will be hierarchical (Figure 7.9) so the body can be made up of other agents that are processing lower-level actions. They will also be cooperative where and the operational digital twin is structured much like the organizational structure. This MAS is structured so that the higher-level goals of the organization can be positively impacted by the lower-level agents. When there are more human decisions that are a part of the HITL workflows, the hierarchical structure will mirror the roles in the org structure. As AI becomes more involved, the structure of both the agent architecture and the organization will change.

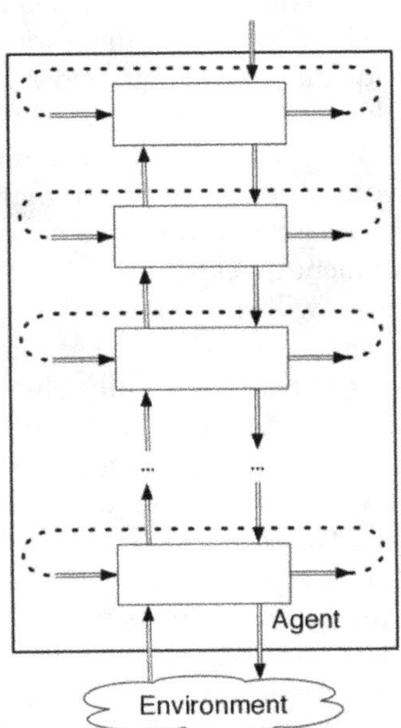

Figure 7.9 Hierarchical agents diagram.

Each layer of the hierarchy operates in its planning horizon that is set to the needs of the workflow. The lower-level workflows are real-time and have a very short planning horizon, and the departmental agent has oversight over these workflows and has a longer planning horizon. The shorter the planning horizon, the less the time that the controller must compute the correct command. This is where we see the advantage we provide by reducing the uncertainty in the environment. More certainty in the environment allows the controller to match the processing with the percepts it has coming in. At higher levels in the hierarchy, there will be more uncertainty, but the planning horizon will be longer, and the controller will have more time to reason.

When we get into a deeper discussion about implementation, we will see that we will have agents to manage the interaction between other agents. These supervisory agents will follow the departmental boundaries and responsibilities as they will likely be assisting humans that are already in roles that follow these boundaries. Layering these rational agents hierarchically is more about the flow of work than it is about organizational structure.

Multi-agent system (MAS)

At the operational level of the workflows, the agents are involved in real-time changes to the environment that are designed to achieve the outcomes prescribed for the agent. This shorter planning horizon requires that the AI process the information quickly so that its work can be accomplished in concert with the rest of the workflow. This means that we want to offer the AI an environment that allows this ease of processing. In reflecting on the types of environments from above, we can see that the more fully observable, deterministic, static, discrete, and episodic, an environment will help the AI process the environment quickly.

The digital twin is how we will create the environment that will allow the agents to use AI to their best advantage. We use maps and IoT to make the geospatial part of the environment more fully observable. The structure of workflows can make the environment more deterministic, and we can assume that the environment will remain static while the agent is in the think phase. The digital twin and its agents will also make the environment more discrete and episodic. This will all set the low-level operational agents up with the best chance of success.

As we described with the hierarchical agents, the operational agents will mirror the roles for the org structure, but at the operational level, the multi-agent architecture becomes very important. These agents must work together so there needs to be a structure for that too.

Figure 7.10 shows the agent operates in the portion of the real world that it has the capability to observe. That is defined as its environment.

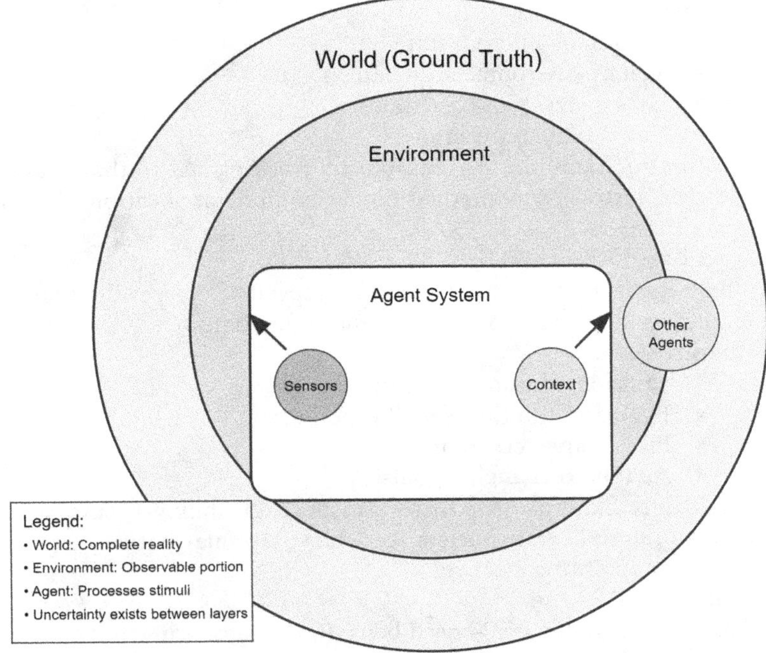

Figure 7.10 Diagram shows the relationship between the real world, the environment, and the agents.

Types of agents in healthcare operations

Healthcare environments require different types of agents depending on the complexity and requirements of specific tasks. Here are the main categories, arranged from simplest to most sophisticated:

1. Simple Reflex Agents
   These agents operate on basic condition-action rules, making them ideal for straightforward, deterministic tasks.
   Characteristics:
   - Operate on if-then rules
   - No internal state or memory
   - Require fully observable environment
   - Best for repetitive, standardized tasks

   Healthcare Example: A patient transport scheduling agent that coordinates multiple transporters to achieve optimal patient flow while meeting appointment times.
2. Model-Based Reflex Agents
   These agents maintain an internal model of their environment, allowing them to handle partially observable conditions.

Characteristics:

- Maintains internal state
- Tracks environmental changes
- Uses memory of past states
- Can handle uncertainty

Healthcare Example: An equipment tracking agent that maintains location history and predicts likely equipment locations based on usage patterns.

3. Goal-Based Agents

   These agents make decisions based on specific goals, evaluating different action sequences to achieve desired outcomes.

   Characteristics:

   - Considers future implications
   - Evaluates multiple possible actions
   - Plans sequences of actions
   - Adapts to changing goals

   Healthcare Example: A patient transport scheduling agent that coordinates multiple transporters to achieve optimal patient flow while meeting appointment times.

4. Utility-Based Agents

   These agents refine goal-based behavior by measuring and optimizing specific performance metrics.

   Characteristics:

   - Quantifies outcomes
   - Balances competing objectives
   - Optimizes resource allocation
   - Measures success metrics

   Healthcare Example: A bed management agent that optimizes bed assignments based on multiple factors like staffing levels, patient acuity, and predicted length of stay.

5. Learning Agents

   These sophisticated agents improve performance through experience and adaptation.

   Components:

   - Learning Element
     - Acquires new knowledge from experiences
     - Updates internal models and rules
     - Identifies successful patterns
   - Critic Element
     - Evaluates performance
     - Provides feedback on decisions
     - Measures success against standards
   - Performance Element
     - Executes learned behaviors
     - Selects actions based on learning
     - Implements improvements

- Problem Generator
    - Creates learning opportunities
    - Tests new strategies
    - Explores alternative solutions

Healthcare Example: A workflow optimization agent that learns from past scheduling decisions to improve resource allocation and reduce wait times across multiple departments (Figure 7.11).

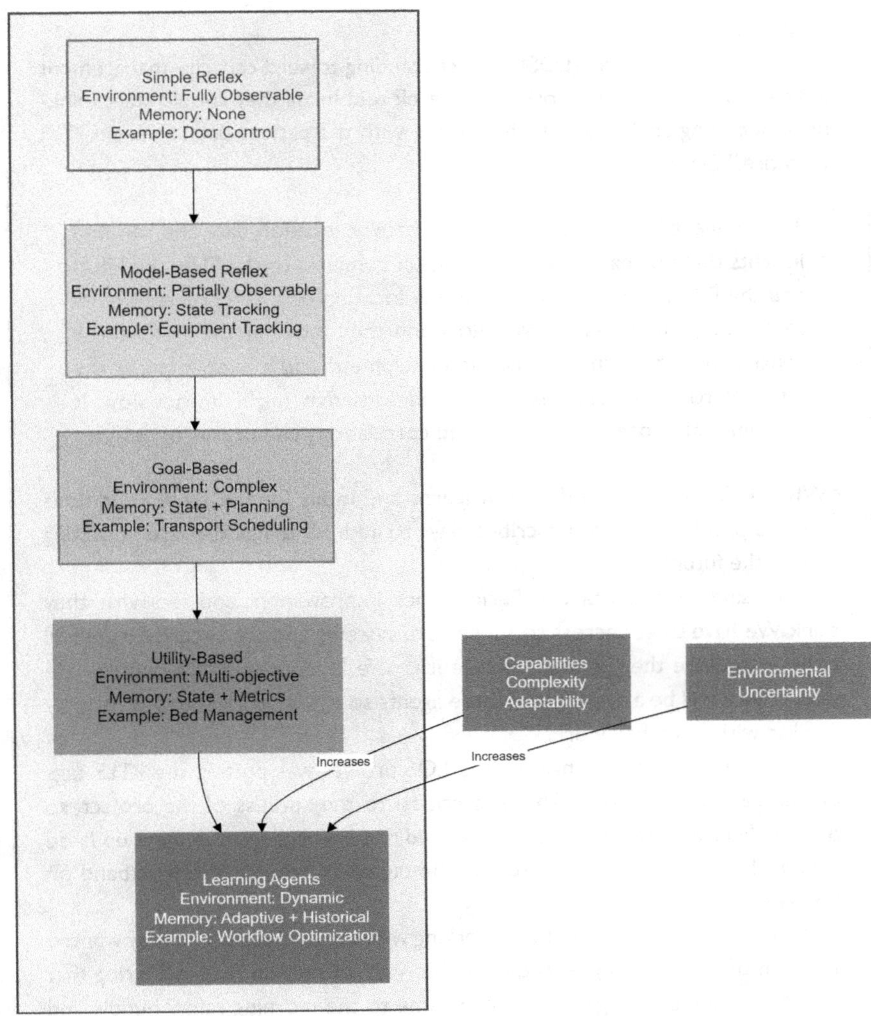

Figure 7.11 Diagram that shows types of agents and how they build on each other.

The choice of agent type depends on factors such as:

- Task complexity
- Environmental predictability
- Available data
- Required autonomy
- Performance requirements
- Integration needs

THE EDENVALE JOURNEY – THE FIRST AGENT

(cont. from Chapter 6)

With the Length of Stay (LOS) project trending toward capacity management and a lot of good data to work with, Derek told Imani they should start thinking about using an AI agent to help them with the patient data. She said, "Tell me more." Derek said,

> The AI agent I have in mind looks at patient location data and can find insights that normal analytics will miss. It connects to the EHR, the HRM and the ERP. It can find the jobs in the location data and creates events from it. It detects issues with flow and then looks at the staffing, the census, the scheduling, supplies and equipment, and it even looks at the Internet to understand external conditions that might impact flow. It combines all those data and can find correlations and causes of delays.

"When it finds these conditions, it learns and looks for the same conditions to make predictions and prescribes ways to address things that are impacting flow in the future."

Imani said, "We can talk to Performance Improvement and see what they think. We have to get access to those core systems and the security team will have to evaluate the agent to be sure it is safe." Derek said, "Of course." He said, "There will be a lot more of these agents so it will be good to get security familiar with how they work."

The only workflow change for the LOS project was putting the RTLS tags on the patient wristbands. This was critical to the success of the project, so the supply chain and HIPAA details needed to be worked out and the updated step in the admission process to add the tag when you put the wristband on the patient.

Performance Improvement was working with the LOS team, and they wanted a month of data to analyze so they had to wait to see the results. During that month, the nurse manager for 6 West came to the morning safety huddle and asked if the CTC system could see if a patient had left the building. The Chief

Nursing Officer, Gail Dawkins, said yes. Nothing else was said. Later, Gail got an email from the nurse manager with an MRN (Medical Record Number) and asked can you tell me if that MRN (patient) left the building? Gail said I will let you know. She forwarded the email to the CTC project manager and asked her to check. She did and she said the patient had left the building and was outside the building for 15 minutes and came back in. She also provided the approximate route that was used.

The next day in the safety huddle, the director for 6 West asked to speak. Gail said, "of course." The director said,

> We have a patient on 6 West who is a COPD patient and has multiple comorbidities. She is not ambulatory, but she won't likely be discharged for a couple weeks. She has been agitated and asking to get out of her room and we set her up in a wheelchair and put her down in the visitor's lounge. She was on two IV drips and oxygen.
>
> When we went to get her, she was gone. We looked around the unit and her room and called security. About 10 mins later they found her near the elevators on 6 West and she said she was on her way back and she hadn't left the floor. A couple hours later I got a call from security, and they got a report from a hospital employee that they saw someone in the off-campus smoking area in a wheelchair smoking a cigarette. This person was on oxygen, smoking, near a bunch of people smoking and 20ft from the boulevard. The only question I have is when can we get this system for our unit?

The CNO said, "It's coming"!

PLAYBOOK FOR ARTIFICIAL INTELLIGENCE AND RATIONAL AGENTS

The playbook for AI in the background phase is to ensure that the concepts around agents are well understood. Later, in future chapters, we will explain the application of these concepts and show how they apply to the task environments that are the subject of this book. The advantage of using the rational agents is the way they use the sensors and perception that is provided by location-based services.

Improvers

Improvers will have a critical role in the development of agents as they are on the front line of process improvement. Processes will receive the assistance of the agents and will need to be articulated in a new way more suited to the creation of the agents.

1. Agent Design Planning
   - Map current workflows to identify opportunities for agent assistance
   - Document decision points and required perception inputs
   - Break down complex processes into agent-compatible components
   - Identify areas where human judgment should be preserved
2. Environment Assessment
   - Evaluate current observability of processes
   - Document sources of uncertainty in workflows
   - Identify opportunities to make environments more deterministic
   - Map available sensors and data sources
3. Implementation Strategy
   - Start with simple reflex agents for well-defined tasks
   - Build gradually toward more complex agent types
   - Document performance measures clearly
   - Create feedback loops for agent improvement
4. Success Metrics
   - Define clear performance measures for each agent
   - Establish baseline metrics before implementation
   - Create monitoring processes for agent effectiveness
   - Document both successes and failures for learning

Leaders

Leaders will guide the development and implementation of agents ensuring that the role of the human in these HITL systems is done to the advantage of everyone involved. These are systems that are augmenting and extending the capabilities of humans, very seldom replacing them.

Investments in sensors for location should have the intention of creating an enterprise system of perception that can be leveraged by multiple systems through standardized means of access.

1. Strategic Planning
   - Understand the role of agents in organizational transformation
   - Plan for incremental adoption of agent technologies
   - Balance automation with human expertise
   - Establish clear governance frameworks
2. Resource Allocation
   - Invest in foundational sensor infrastructure
   - Support training for staff working with agents
   - Plan for ongoing agent maintenance and improvement
   - Allocate resources for agent development

3. Change Management
   - Build understanding of agent capabilities and limitations
   - Foster trust in agent-assisted workflows
   - Support gradual transition to agent-assisted operations
   - Maintain focus on the HITL approach

Vendors

Vendors that align with the vision of an enterprise agent architecture will be well positioned to ride the advancements in AI and sensor technology. If a platform were to emerge, it could create an environment where vendors are able to create agents that can compete head to head to deliver outcomes for specific business problems.

1. Solution Development
   - Create modular agent architectures
   - Support incremental capability growth
   - Build flexible integration options
   - Develop clear agent interfaces
2. Implementation Support
   - Provide comprehensive training programs
   - Develop clear documentation
   - Support proof-of-concept implementations
   - Maintain ongoing technical support
3. Best Practices
   - Share implementation experiences
   - Develop agent design patterns
   - Create reusable agent components
   - Build agent evaluation frameworks

NOTES

1 https://link.springer.com/chapter/10.1007/978-3-031-01543-4_2.
2 https://artint.info/3e/html/ArtInt3e.Ch1.S5.html.
3 https://artint.info/3e/html/ArtInt3e.Ch1.S5.html.

Chapter 8

Digital twin

Paul E. Zieske

> A digital twin is a data-driven virtual representation of real-world entities and processes, synchronized at a specified frequency and fidelity.[1]

The digital twin was introduced by Dr. Michael Grieves in 2002, showing how virtual models can mirror physical systems. It expanded beyond manufacturing in the early 2010s but its alignment with Industry 4.0 strengthened it in manufacturing and product development. Industry 4.0 is called the fourth industrial revolution, and it is blazing a trail by combining cutting-edge technologies into an ecosystem for automation and improvement. In the late 2010s, internet of things (IoT) and artificial intelligence (AI) were advanced enough to fuel expansion to many other industries.

In the concept, the digital twin can virtualize any physical entity. For our purposes, the intent is to model the operations within the enterprise, so more specifically, this is an **operational digital twin.** The physical entity will be the buildings and spaces where the operations are taking place. The processes are the mobile workflows that are part of the operations. Because this is an operational digital twin, the sensors will be used to synchronize the location of people and property with the location in the real world. Rational agents are used to virtualize the operations, and we will go deeper into those in Chapter 2, "Core geospatial concepts".

Healthcare operations are a great candidate for applying the digital twin. Successful operations are largely about successful workflows. As more workflows are connected and interdependent, the ability to examine upstream processes will yield predictive insights that will create huge benefits downstream.

To virtualize the workspaces, we are going to represent them digitally with GIS. The process of creating a digital representation of the building in GIS is called **reality capture.** Because hospitals are required to keep accurate Computer Aided Design (CAD) drawings, the reality capture is done by converting the CAD to GIS.

Situational awareness and automation are the keys to location-based services 2.0. We will use sensors and computational reasoning to make the digital representation context aware. When we use a combination of GIS and

DOI: 10.1201/9781003625483-9

sensing, it opens a new evolution of location-based services to the intelligence we can get with AI and machine learning (ML).

PLATFORM STACK ARCHITECTURE FRAMEWORK

There are many frameworks that have been established for digital twins and the goal here is not to prefer one over the other. There is the IBM Digital Twin Reference Architecture, Microsoft Digital Twin Reference Architecture, AWS Stack, we do, however, want to establish the preferred properties in a framework so that the best framework can be selected for our particular use case. The Digital Twin Consortium (DTC) and Dr. David McKee have authored the Platform Stack Architectural Framework[2] that captures the structure for the system-of-systems approach to the digital twin. This framework is designed to encompass all use cases so we will start with this framework to describe the architectural components of the digital twin (Figure 8.1).

- Security, trust and governance forming a foundation for the Digital Twin.
- The real world from which the digital twin is instantiated and with which it is synchronized.
- The IT/OT platform for implementing a digital twin system.
- The virtual representation of the real world and its context.
- The virtual representation is wrapped in service interfaces for integration and interoperability.
- Applications where the digital twin is used by actors who use the system to provide value.

Trustworthiness

The digital twin is a system-of-systems which means there is a lot of interaction between systems. This puts security, trust and governance as a top priority. When there is a need to integrate systems, each system being integrated must ensure it is not the weak link (Figure 8.2). As defined by the Industrial Internet of Things Consortium trustworthiness is:

> The degree of confidence one has that the system performs as expected. Characteristics include safety, security, privacy, reliability and resilience in the face of environmental disturbances, human errors, system faults and attacks.[3]

These subdomains make up the

- Privacy: The right of individuals to control or influence what information related to them may be collected and stored and by whom and to whom that information may be disclosed. (ISO/TS 17574:2009 2).[4]

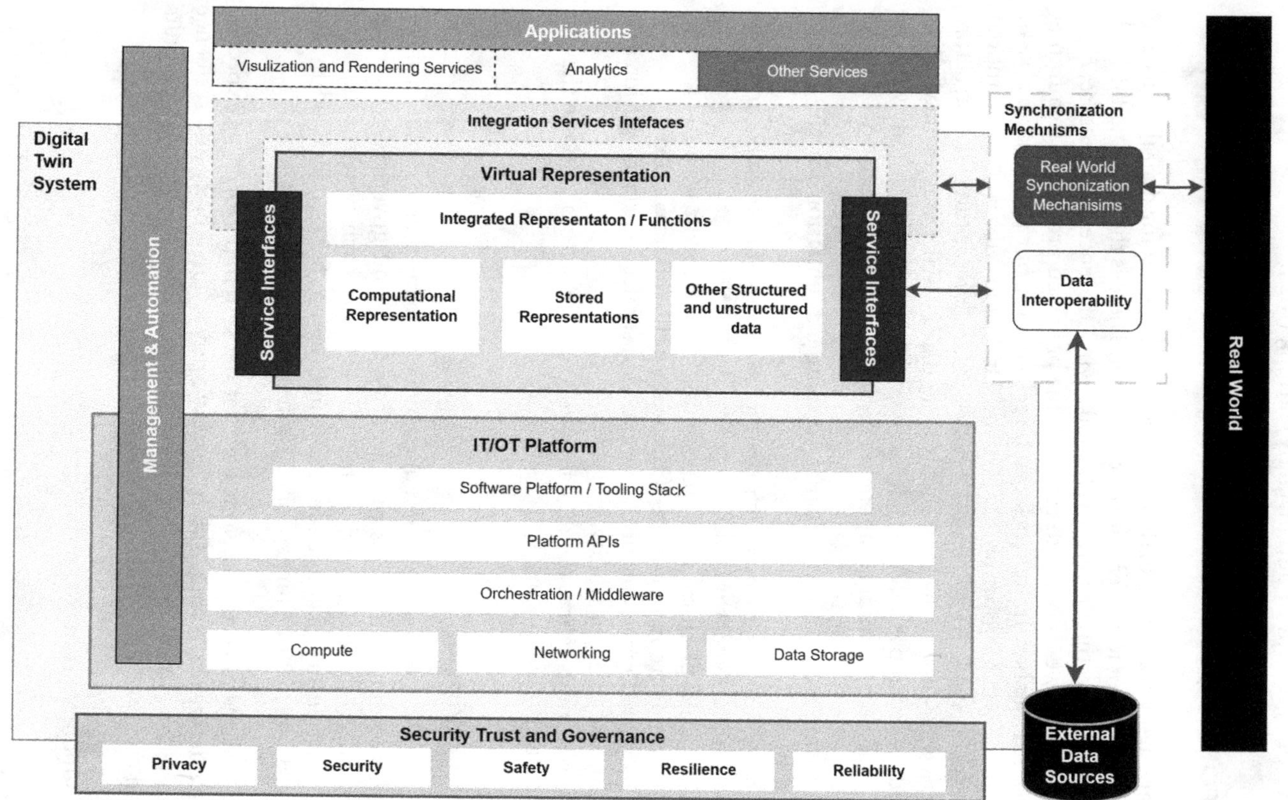

Figure 8.1 DTC platform stack architecture diagram.

credit DTC.

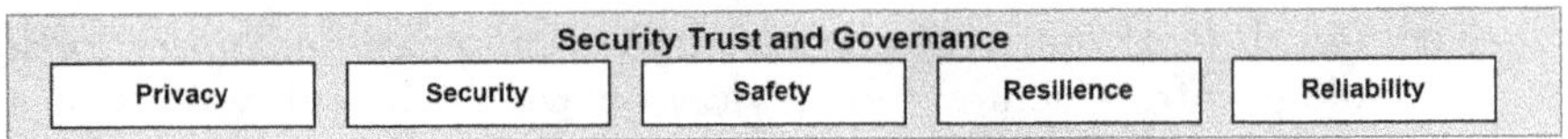

Figure 8.2 Security, trust and governance diagram.

credit DTC.

- Security: The property of being protected from unintended or unauthorized access, change or destruction, ensuring availability, integrity, and confidentiality.
- Safety: The condition of the system operating without causing unacceptable risk of physical injury or damage to the health of people, either directly or indirectly as a result of damage to property or the environment (ISO/IEC Guide 51:2014 3).[5]
- Resilience: Ability of a system or component to maintain an acceptable level of service in the face of disruption.
- Reliability: Ability of a system or component to perform its required functions under stated conditions for a specified period of time. (ISO/IEC 27040:2015 1).

We will talk more about Trustworthiness in Chapter 2.6 in the context of care traffic control.

IT/OT platform

The IT/OT Platform is where the operational technologies (OT) and the information technologies (IT) converge. The context for much of the operation lies in the IT infrastructure, so as automation becomes more advanced, that information is valuable to the operational technology infrastructure. Location-based systems use sensors to provide real-time information to operations (Figure 8.3). Additional sensing and access to core IT systems is critical to successful outcomes.

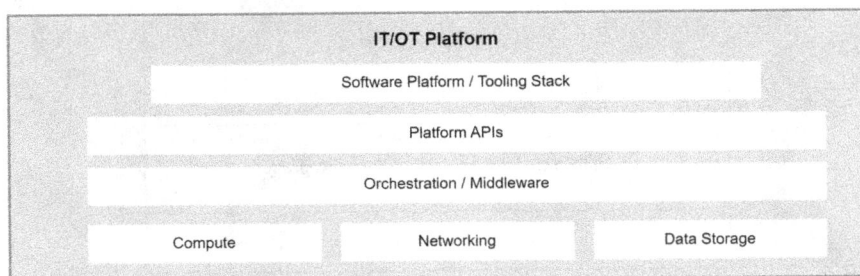

IT/OT Platform

Software Platform / Tooling Stack

Platform APIs

Orchestration / Middleware

Compute | Networking | Data Storage

Figure 8.3 IT/OT platform diagram.

credit DTC.

The IT/OT Platform is the information technology and operational technology infrastructure and services on which the subsystems of a digital twin system are implemented.[6]

- The computing, storage, and networking infrastructure are core and could include the cloud, partially, or entirely. These provide the foundational resources to support the operation of the software necessary for the system to function.
- The Orchestration/Middleware functions as the rules engine and control center for the platform.
- Platform APIs (application program interfaces) that provide access to the platform services and platform management.
- Integration representation/functions, which are primarily for the storage of data for the digital twin and transforming data between various systems.

Virtual representation

Data is the heart of the digital twin. This is encapsulated in the virtual representation. This data could be sourced from many locations, then it is stored, computed, and delivered from the virtual representation (Figure 8.4).

> A complex, cohesive digital representation comprising stored representations, computational representations and supporting data that collectively provide an information-rich "virtual" experience of their subject matter.[7] [8]

Stored representations

The stored representations are where the static and historical data for the digital twin are kept. It can be any kind of database from relational to

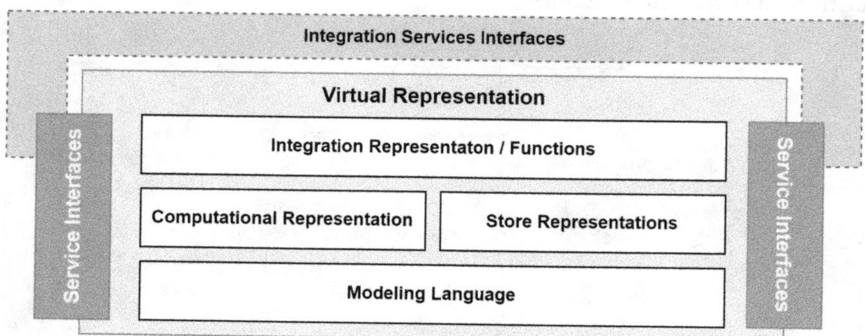

Figure 8.4 Virtual representation and integration services diagram.
credit DTC.

NoSQL or Graph. Things like the historical state, as represented by sensor data from IoT, are stored here. The history can be used for things like simulations, but these data are used to represent the entity in real time as well. The digital representation for the physical entity is necessary for all the spatial processing that goes on. BIM (Building Information Modeling), CAD or GIS is an example of data that might be available here.

Computational representations

The processing of the state information is done in the computational representation. The information come in as inputs and algorithms use additional reference data to compute an output. This is the real-time processing area of the digital twin.

Modeling language

A modeling language is necessary to create a common data model so the digital twin can use a rich array of contextual data. The system-of-systems approach emphasizes integration to gain access to these data.

Integration

Integration is key to increasing the fidelity of the twin, so connecting systems through interfacing is critical. The interfacing adds dimension to the data that is used to create the representations. This means services and processing of the data need to be robust and comprehensive. The service interfaces and integration representation receive and process the data that comes in.

Synchronization

Synchronization is where the sensing, that is in the real world, sends information back to be processed into perception. This is done at a specified interval and fidelity according to the definition of the digital twin. The interval and fidelity are critical for situational awareness but even more critical for automation. Data interoperability has the added challenge of making the data interoperable in real time, if real time is the specified interval (Figure 8.5).

Applications

The value of the digital twin is realized when users can solve problems by accessing its information from applications. Even where automation is applied, there is still a need to report progress to the users, so a user interface is required (Figure 8.6).

Applications are the interactive layer where the digital twin interfaces with human actors. The business logic that is needed to process the data into

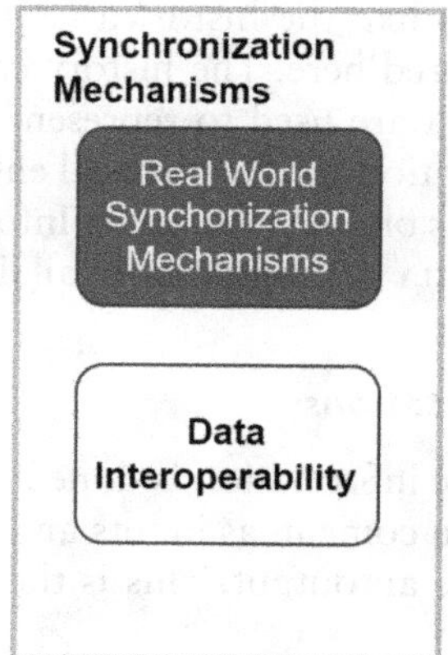

Figure 8.5 Synchronization mechanisms diagram.

credit DTC.

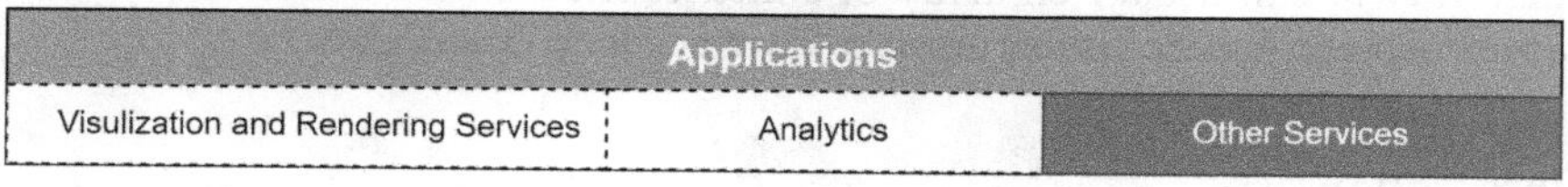

Applications
Visulization and Rendering Services
Analytics
Other Services

Figure 8.6 Applications diagram.

credit DTC.

useful information is in the applications. The digital twin has a rich array of visual data that can be rendered to the users, so visualizations need a rendering service to provide that information to the users.

OPERATIONAL DIGITAL TWIN

The definition of the digital twin does not specify the intentions of the digital twin. The digital twin should have the intention of being a solution to a specified problem. Below are the four types of digital twins that have been commonly recognized.

- Component twins
  - Component twins are virtual representations of individual parts like motors, sensors, switches, and valves. They use real-time and historical performance data to help organizations monitor and adjust component health and performance as needed.
- Asset twins
  - Asset twins are virtual representations of physical assets like buildings, machines, and vehicles. They use real-time data on operational

status, performance, and environmental conditions to help organizations reduce downtime and enhance efficiency.

- System twins
  - System twins are virtual representations of entire systems or processes. They enable organizations to monitor, analyze, and optimize performance, identifying areas for improvement and enhancing operations.
- Process twins
  - Process twins are virtual representations of entire business processes or customer journeys. They use real-time insights into customer interactions to help organizations identify and improve areas of the customer experience.

The properties of each type of digital twin can overlap when we apply them, so we will see the operational digital twin has properties of the asset, system, and process twin. We will define the
operational digital twin by describing its intentions further.

> An **operational digital twin** describes the intentionality of a digital twin to virtualize, monitor, automate and optimize the operations of a physical entity, process or processes.

This definition is an extension of the definition of the digital twin to describe its application to an operational environment. The digital twin synchronizes with the real world, so the definition helps narrow down the real world to the spaces and the processes that comprise the operations within an enterprise. The synchronizing that is done with the real world is done with sensors, and much of what we will talk about are location sensors. This is for locating the people and property that are part of the operations (Figure 8.7).

DIGITAL TWIN – CAPABILITIES PERIODIC TABLE

The DTC has created a tool to help solutions align with the capabilities that are a part of the digital twin concept. This capabilities periodic chart (CPT) shows what the DTC calls level 1 capabilities that are organized into groupings. Grouping the capabilities into categories helps align the capabilities to outcomes. Going the other direction, the CPT helps map the capabilities to the platform stack architecture. The diagrams below show the groupings and the level 1 details. This version of the CPT is unfiltered for its alignment to the operational digital twin. We will discuss that in a later chapter (Figures 8.8 and 8.9).

Table 8.1 shows more detail for each of the level 1 capabilities.

The capabilities of the digital twin are implemented over time which speaks to its composability and incremental value.

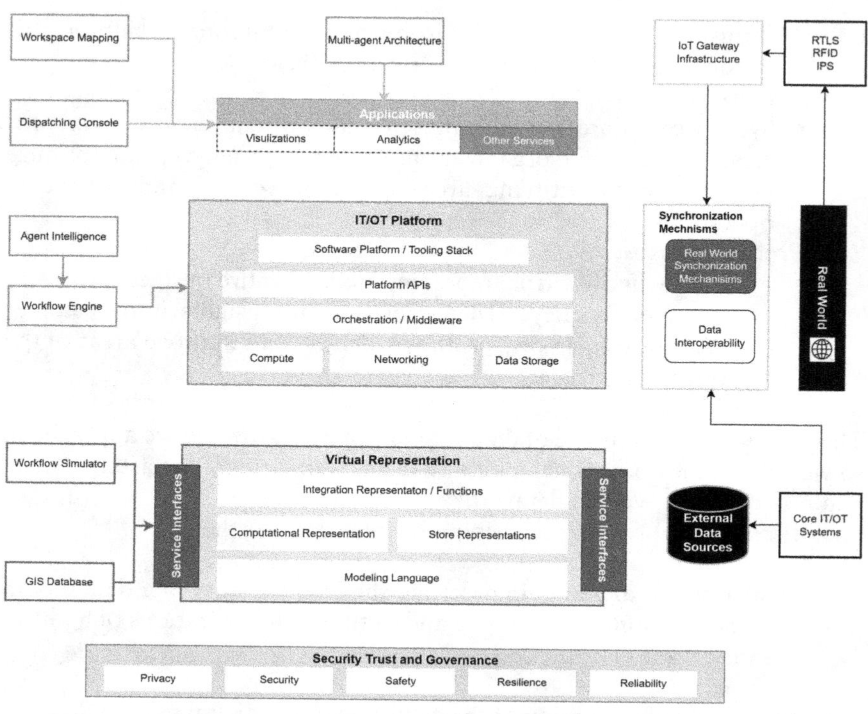

Figure 8.7 Operational digital twin platform stack diagram.
credit DTC.

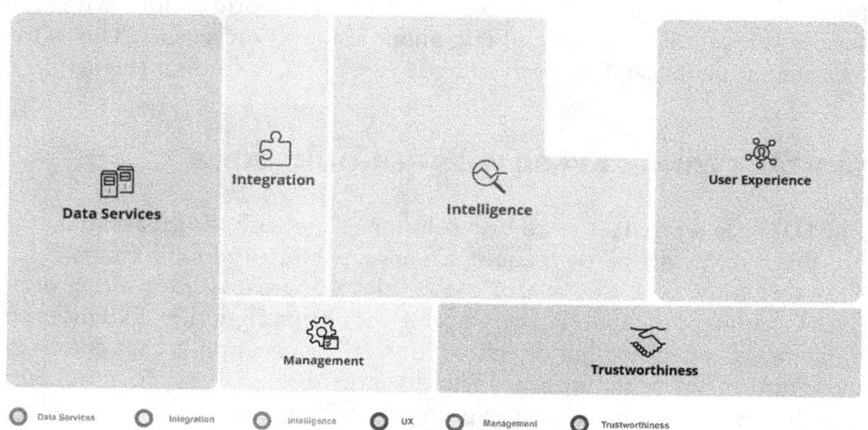

Figure 8.8 DTC capabilities periodic table.
credit DTC.

DS.AI Data Acquisition & Ingestion	**DS.SG** Synthetic Data Generation	IR.ET Enterprise System Integration	IC.SR Search	IC.PR Prediction		**UX.BV** Basic Visualization	**UX.DB** Dashboards
DS.ST Data Streaming	**DS.ON** Ontology Management	IR.EG Eng. System Inegration	IC.CC Command and Control	IC.AI Artificial Intelligence		**UX.AV** Advanced Visualization	**UX.CI** Continuous Intelligence
DS.TR Data Transformation	**DS.RP** Digital Twin Model Repository	IR.IO OT/IoT Twin System Integration	IC.OS Orchestration	IC.PS Prescritive Recommendations		**UX.RM** Real-time Monitoring	**UX.BI** Business Intelligence
DS.CX Data Contextualization	**DS.IR** DT Instance Repository	IR.DT Digital Twin Integration	IC.AL Alerts and Notifications	IC.FL Federated Learning	IC.BR Business Rules	**UX.ER** Entity Relationship Visualization	**UX.BP** BPM & Workflow
DS.BP Batch Processing	**DS.DS** Domain Specific Data Management	IR.CL Collab Platform Integration	IC.RP Reporting	IC.SM Simulation	IC.DL Distributed Ledger & Smart Contracts	**UX.XR** Extended Reality (AR,VR,MR)	**UX.GE** Gaming Engine Visualization
DS.RT Real-time Processing	**DS.SA** Data Storage & Archive Services	IR.AS API Services	IC.AA Data Analysis & Analytics	IC.MA Mathematical Analysis	IC.CS Composition	**UX.GM** Gameification	**UX.3R** 3D Rendering
DS.AS Asynchronous Integration	**DS.SR** Simulation Model Repository	**MG.DM** Device Management	**MG.EL** Event Logging	**TW.EC** Data Encryption	**TW.SC** Security	**TW.SF** Safety	**TW.RP** Responsibility
DS.AG Data Aggregation	**DS.AI** AI Model Repository	**MG.SM** Systems Monitoring	**MG.DG** Data Governance	**TW.DS** Device Security	**TW.PR** Privacy	**TW.RL** Reliability	**TW.RS** Resilience

Data Services · Integration · Intelligence · UX · Management · **Trustworthiness**

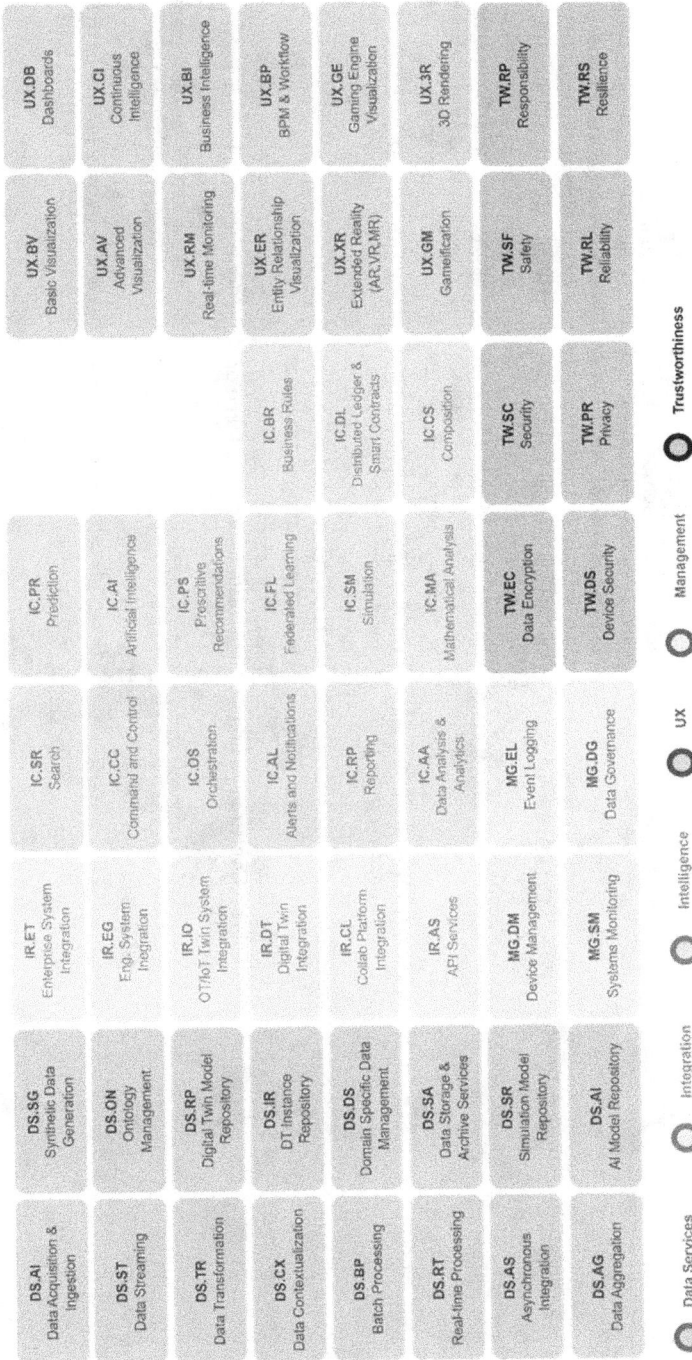

Figure 8.9 DTC capabilities periodic table continue.

credit DTC.

Table 8.1 DTC level 1 capability details

Category	*UID*		*Digital twin capability*	*Ability*	*Purpose*
DS. Data Services	DS.AI	1	Data Acquisition and Ingestion	The ability to configure and acquire data from different data sources, including control system, historians, IoT sensors, smart devices, engineering system, enterprise systems, etc.	The purpose is to acquire data from the physical world, engineering technology systems, and information technology systems to support subsequent processing and insight generation.
DS. Data Services	DS.ST	2	Data Streaming	The ability to transfer large volumes of data continuously and incrementally between a source and a destination without having to access all data simultaneously.	The purpose is to acquire fast continuous packets of information, which is changing at high speed to be able to get near real-time insights.
DS. Data Services	DS.TR	3	Data Transformation and Wrangling	The ability to convert data types and properties through cleaning, structuring, and enriching raw data to make it suitable for further processing and analytics	The purpose is to make data usable in digital twins.
DS. Data Services	DS.CX	4	Data Contextualization	The ability to add language or metadata to enrich real time or transactional data	The purpose is to combine data from different sources such as real time and context to make it suitable for subsequent processing by the digital twin.
DS. Data Services	DS.BP	5	Batch Processing	The ability to execute against previously collected data in bulk form	The purpose is to provide an efficient way of processing high volumes of data in batches or groups.

DS. Data Services	DS.RT	6	Real-time Processing	The ability to manage and act on the captured data with minimal latency	The purpose is to support immediate insights from the data.
DS. Data Services	DS.AS	7	Data PubSub Push	The ability to package filtered data to different services based on publish/subscribe model	The purpose is to provide information to subscribed digital twin consumers.
DS. Data Services	DS.AG	8	Data Aggregation	The ability to gather raw data and express it in a summary form	The purpose is to gather data from multiple sources with the intent of combining these data sources into a summary for data analysis.
DS. Data Services	DS.SG	9	Synthetic Data Generation	The ability to generate synthetic data based on patterns and rules in existing sources	The purpose is to create representative synthetic data that can be used by the digital twin to train and score predictive models.
DS. Data Services	DS.ON	10	Ontology Management	The ability to manage knowledge graphs and ontologies	The purpose is to enable a digital twin to interpret data directly from knowledge graphs and ontologies.
DS. Data Services	DS.RP	11	Digital Twin Model Repository	The ability to store, manage, and retrieve the metadata that describe the digital twin model. The model can include formal data names, comprehensive data definitions, proper data structures, and precise data integrity rules	The purpose is to register and manage a portfolio of digital twin models in a central repository to improve configuration management and model governance.

(*Continued*)

Table 8.1 (Continued)

Category	*UID*		*Digital twin capability*	*Ability*	*Purpose*
DS. Data Services	DS.IR	12	Digital Twin Instance Repository	The ability to store, manage, and retrieve digital twin instance data that conforms to the requirements of the digital twin model	The purpose is to store, manage, and retrieve digital twin instance state data.
DS. Data Services	DS.DS	New	Domain Specific Data Management	The ability to efficiently handle, store, and retrieve data based on the distinct characteristics inherent to specific data types.	The purpose is to store, manage, and retrieve domain-specific data.
DS. Data Services	DS.SA	14	Data Storage and Archive Services	The ability to store, organize, and retrieve data based on how frequently it will be accessed and how long it will be retained.	The purpose is to reduce the cost and effort of managing digital twin data by using hot, cold, and archival data services.
DS. Data Services	DS.SR	15	Simulation Model Repository	The ability to store, manage, and retrieve the algorithmic codebase, business rules, and metadata that describe a simulation model.	The purpose is to register and manage a portfolio of simulation models in a central repository to improve configuration management and model governance.
DS. Data Services	DS.AR	16	AI Model Repository	The ability to store, manage, search, and retrieve the algorithmic codebase that describes an AI model or ML model.	The purpose is to register and manage a portfolio of AI and machine learning models in a central repository to improve configuration management and model governance.

IR. Integration	IR.ET	17	Enterprise System Integration	The ability to integrate the digital twin with existing enterprise, such as ERP, EAM, CRM, and CMMS.	The purpose is to integrate business applications that enable data to flow between digital twin systems with ease.
IR. Integration	IR.EG	18	Engineering Systems integration	The ability to integrate the digital twin with existing engineering systems such as CAD, CAM, BIM, and Historians.	The purpose is to integrate engineering applications that enable model use and data to flow between digital twin systems with ease.
IR. Integration	IR.IO	19	OT/IoT system integration	The ability to integrate directly with control systems and IoT devices/sensors, SCADA.	The purpose is to integrate operation technology (OT) and IoT applications that data to flow between digital twin systems with ease.
IR. Integration	IR.DT	20	Digital Twin Integration	The ability to integrate or access information from existing digital twin instances.	The purpose is to integrate digital twin applications with one another to enable interoperable digital twins.
IR. Integration	IR.CL	21	Collaboration Platform Integration	The ability for the digital twin to interface with platforms like Yammer, Jabber, Teams, and Slack.	The purpose is to integrate collaboration platforms to provide digital twin users with a conversational user interface.
IR. Integration	IR.AS	22	API Services	For the digital twin, the ability to publish APIs to external, partner, and internal developers to access data and services.	The purpose is to simplify digital twin development by allowing digital to integrate with products and services without knowing how they are implemented.

(Continued)

Table 8.1 (Continued)

Category	*UID*		*Digital twin capability*	*Ability*	*Purpose*
IC. Intelligence	IC.SR	New	Search	The ability to efficiently query, locate, and retrieve relevant information or data from a larger dataset or collection.	The purpose is to efficiently query, locate, and retrieve relevant information or data from a larger dataset or collection.
IC. Intelligence	IC.IC	24	Command and Control	The ability to execute upon work instructions without human interaction. Control would be limited to IoT devices and nonplant controls.	The purpose is to support future smart IoT devices with centralized management.
IC. Intelligence	IC.OS	25	Orchestration	The ability to coordinate the automated configuration, management, and coordination of systems, applications, digital twins, and services.	The purpose is to easily manage complex tasks and workflows between different systems, applications, digital twins, or systems of digital twins.
IC. Intelligence	IC.AL	26	Alerts and Notification	The ability to display and manage alerts, messages, message queues, triggers, and notifications.	The purpose is to trigger actions that may require intervention to the ongoing processes.
IC. Intelligence	IC.RP	27	Reporting	The ability to generate configurable and customizable reports to get insights into the data.	The purpose is to get insights into the data that can be useful for various stakeholders in the system as well as for regulatory compliance.

IC. Intelligence	IC.AA	28	Data Analysis and Analytics	The study and presentation of data to create information and knowledge. The ability to analyze data through charts, tables, dashboards, fetch data between dates, and filter data based on various criteria. The analysis of data, typically large sets of business data, using mathematics, statistics, and computer software with the objective to draw conclusions.	The purpose is to understand past trends from historical data.
IC. Intelligence	IC.PR	29	Prediction	The ability to estimate that a specified event will happen in the future or will be a consequence of other events.	The purpose is to use historical data, engineering, and analytical models to predict future events before they occur.
IC. Intelligence	IC.AI	Combined 23, 30, and 31	Artificial Intelligence	The ability for a system to perform actions and take decisions like humans. AI would include machine learning, natural language processing, knowledge modeling and representation, reasoning, inferencing, Generative AI, LLMs, and Edge AI.	The purpose is to enable a digital twin or a digital twin system to take actions and decisions like humans.
IC. Intelligence	IC.FL	32	Federated Learning	The ability to train an algorithm across multiple decentralized digital twin edge devices or servers holding local data samples, without exchanging their data samples.	The purpose is to enable multiple actors to build a common, robust machine learning model without sharing data, thus addressing critical issues such as data privacy, data security, data access rights, and access to heterogeneous data.

(Continued)

Table 8.1 (Continued)

Category	*UID*		*Digital twin capability*	*Ability*	*Purpose*
IC. Intelligence	IC.SM	33	Simulation	The ability to create an approximate imitation of a process or a system using past historical information, physical models, video, audio, and animation, and what-if-scenarios.	The purpose is to imitate the behavior of a physical system in the digital twin before applying to the physical world. Training operations and maintenance teams on simulated digital twins is another purpose of simulation.
IC. Intelligence	IC.MA	34	Mathematical Analytics (Engineering Calculations)	The ability to perform mathematical and statistical calculations to enable physics-based and other mathematical models.	The purpose is to enable the use of physics models and mathematics calculations in digital twin analytics.
IC. Intelligence	IC.PS	35	Prescriptive Recommendations	The ability to create prescriptive recommendations based on business rules and AI logic to suggest the best next actions to take when a predetermined event happens.	The purpose is to enable digital twins to provide guidance based on a combination of analytics, business rules and workflow to create actions and deliver business outcomes.
IC. Intelligence	IC.BR	36	Business Rules	The ability to create, manage, and use business rules that influence the digital twin behavior throughout its lifecycle.	

IC. Intelligence	IC.DL	37	Distributed Ledger and Smart Contracts	The ability to use distributed ledgers for digital twin applications that require immutable data for digital twin instances, transactions, and automation (smart contracts).	The purpose is to enable digital twins to interact in an automated, trustworthy, and responsible manner with systems that support smart contracts and provide a full, immutable transaction record.
IC. Intelligence	IC.CS	38	Composition	The ability to use a modular digital twin application development approach to rapidly compose and recompose digital twin services that deliver use case specific outcomes.	The purpose is to compose or recompose digital twins from a set of packaged, reusable business capabilities (PBCs) to reduce time to value, duplication, and support citizen development of digital twins.
UX. User Experience	UX.BV	39	Basic Visualization	The ability to graphically or parametrically (that is, through parameters and values) visualize data through simple charts, graphs, simple dashboards, tables, hierarchical and basic 3D views of the as sets.	The purpose is to help people understand the significance of data by placing it in a visual context.
UX. User Experience	UX.AV	40	Advanced Visualization	The ability to graphically or parametrically (that is, through parameters and values), visualize data through complex charts and graphs, dashboards fetching raw, and process data from multiple systems, complex 3D models, and animations, visualizations with overlaid data from different systems.	The purpose is to help people understand the significance of data by placing it in a visual context.

(Continued)

Table 8.1 *(Continued)*

Category	*UID*		*Digital twin capability*	*Ability*	*Purpose*
UX. User Experience	UX.RM	41	Real-time Monitoring	The ability to present and interact with continuously updated information streaming at zero or low latency.	The purpose is to help make decisions that are of consequence to real time.
UX. User Experience	UX.ER	42	Entity Relationship Visualization	The ability to present digital twin entities and their hierarchical or graph-based relationships interactively.	The purpose is to help business users navigate and interact with complex entity (asset) hierarchies in a user-friendly manner.
UX. User Experience	UX.XR	Combined 43 and 44	Extended Reality (XR)	The ability to provide an interactive experience of a real-world environment where the objects that reside in the real world are enhanced by computer-generated perceptual information such as visual, auditory, haptic environment.	The purpose is to realize an improved, immersive, and interactive experience for the user around simulating the physical world in a virtual environment.
UX. User Experience	UX.DB	45	Dashboards	The ability to provide a graphical user interface that provides at-a-glance views of key performance indicators relevant to a particular objective or business process.	The purpose is to enable various personas in operations, technology, and business to visually understand the current or past state of a system.
UX. User Experience	UX.CI	46	Continuous Intelligence	The ability to analyze data in flight (signals) to derive insights and actions in a business user-focused visual interface.	The purpose is to have various personas in operations, technology, and business to make informed real-time decisions.

UX. User Experience	UX.BI	47	Business Intelligence	The ability to analyze stored data (records) to derive insights and actions in a business user-focused visual interface.	The purpose is to have various personas in operations, technology, and business to make informed real-time decisions.
UX. User Experience	UX.BP	48	Business Process Management and Workflow	The ability to execute a sequence of actions as a process flow to achieve specific business outcomes.	The purpose is to have effective, repeatable actions that deliver the business outcomes of the digital twin.
UX. User Experience	UX.GE	49	Gaming Engine Visualization	The ability to create immersive virtual worlds and interactive experiences with gaming engine technology.	The purpose is to enable digital twins in a digital metaverse where users interact with the digital twin in a highly interactive manner.
UX. User Experience	UX.3R	50	3D Rendering	The ability to render 3D visualizations from point cloud data sets generated by LiDAR and other scanning technologies.	The purpose is to interact with large point cloud and 3D datasets in a user-friendly manner.
UX. User Experience	UX.GM	51	Gamification	The ability to enable typical elements of game playing in digital twin interaction.	The purpose is to facilitate the use of gamification elements such as points scoring, badges, and competition in the user experience and interactive engagement of a digital twin.
MG. Management	MG.DM	52	Device Management	The ability to provide, authenticate, configure, maintain, monitor, and diagnose connected IoT devices operating as part of digital twin environment.	The purpose of (IoT) device management is to provide and support the whole spectrum of functional capabilities of the devices and sensors.

(Continued)

Table 8.1 (Continued)

Category	*UID*		*Digital twin capability*	*Ability*	*Purpose*
MG. Management	MG.SM	53	System Monitoring and Alerting	The ability to observe digital twin systems, applications, and services by collecting, analyzing, and acting on their health data to maximize their availability and performance.	
MG. Management	MG.EL	54	Logging	The ability to record events, transactions, access data of users, and transactions to understand and trace the activities occurring in a digital twin system.	
MG. Management	MG.DG	55	Data Governance	The ability to manage the availability, usability, integrity, and security of the data in digital twin systems, based on internal data standards and policies that also control data usage.	The purpose is to ensure that data is consistent and trustworthy and does not get misused.
TW. Trustworthiness	TW.EX	56	Data Encryption	The ability to convert digital twin data from a readable format into an encoded format that can be used to transfer data securely. It also includes the ability to decrypt the data to read or process the data once it reaches its destination.	

TW.Trustworthiness	TW.DS	57	Device Security	The ability to enforce authenticated and authorized access to IoT device data through identity management, role-based access, encryption, and policies.	The purpose is to control access to device data by having the appropriate privileges and enforcement framework for users and programs.
TW.Trustworthiness	TW.SC	58	Security	The ability to protect digital twins from unintended or unauthorized access, change or destruction. Security concerns equipment, systems and information, ensuring availability, integrity, and confidentiality of information.	
TW.Trustworthiness	TW.PR	59	Privacy	The ability to enable the rights of individuals that interact with digital twins to control or influence what information related to them may be collected and stored and by whom and to whom that information may be disclosed.	
TW.Trustworthiness	TW.SF	60	Safety	The ability to operate digital twins without causing unacceptable risk of physical injury or damage to the health of people, either directly, or indirectly as a result of damage to property or the environment.	

(Continued)

Table 8.1 (Continued)

Category	*UID*		*Digital twin capability*	*Ability*	*Purpose*
TW.Trustworthiness	TW.RL	61	Reliability	The ability of a digital twin system or component to perform its required functions under stated conditions for a specified period of time. This includes expected levels of performance, QoS, functional availability and accuracy.	
TW.Trustworthiness	TW.RS	62	Resilience	The ability of a digital twin system or component to maintain an acceptable level of service in the face of disruption. This includes the ability to recover lost capacity on time (using a more or less automated procedure), or to reassign workloads and functions.	
TW.Trustworthiness	TW.PR	New	Responsibility	The ability to ensure digital twins are designed and utilized in a manner that upholds ethical standards, promotes transparency and accountability in decision-making, actively prevents biases, and considers long-term societal and environmental impacts, without compromising the trust and welfare of stakeholders.	The purpose is to guarantee that the systems operate within a framework of ethical guidelines, ensuring that they not only perform their intended functions but also do so in a way that aligns with societal values and norms.

THE EDENVALE JOURNEY – PAR STOCKING IV PUMPS

The LOS (Length of Stay) project (aka patient tracking project) was helping leadership make decisions that would improve the flow of patients.Throughput at the various clinics and services was being evaluated over the long planning horizon. Bed management had real-time data for capacity management.

The PAR stocking project

Edenvale's IV pumps go through the sterile processing cycle which is the responsibility of the sterile processing and distribution (SPD) team.They have the challenge of distributing clean pumps where and when needed.The problem was, without monitoring the locations of the device in the cycle, it was inefficient and difficult to control the availability of devices coming into the cycle. They decided to introduce the concept of PAR (periodic automatic replenishment) stocking. Central to the concept is the ability to guarantee a clean pump can be found at a designated PAR location, at any time.This is a supply chain concept that uses the principles of supply and demand as well as control loops to manage the supply.This is done by using real-time data to maintain what are called PAR levels or the amount that is necessary to ensure that there is never what is called a "stock-out."

The IV pumps had RTLS tags on them by clinical engineering so the project would start with installing the RTLS sensors needed to monitor the PAR levels and location of the pumps in the sites that were a part of the cycle.The patient rooms already had sensors that used the wall-mounted workstations as hardware.This was part of the pervasive computing project (Figure 8.10).

The implementation team proposed an automated process that looks like this.

- Install RTLS sensors that can count the pumps in:
  - Soiled utility closets
  - Cleaning station in SPD
  - Storage location for the supply
  - The clean utility closets
- Use the existing CMMS (Computerized Maintenance Management System) par stocking features
  - Shows the PAR levels at each location
  - Shows the count of pumps at each location
  - Identifies which clean utilities have dropped below PAR
  - Identifies the soiled utilities where pumps need to be retrieved
  - Assigns a restocking job to an SPD technician
  - Assigns a retrieval job to an SPD technician

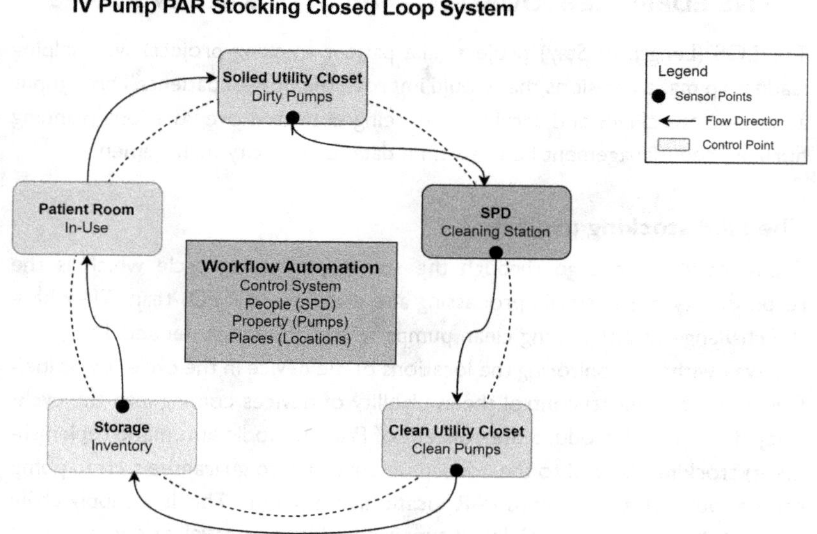

Figure 8.10 IV Pump PAR stocking closed loop system diagram.

- Three times per day a job is assigned that has:
  - A list of locations where the devices have dropped below the PAR level
  - The required number of devices to restore the closet to PAR
  - The total number of devices necessary for the job
- Morning and late afternoon a job is assigned that has:
  - The soiled utility closets where devices need to be retrieved
  - The total number of devices expected to be retrieved

The agent would create a report for clinical engineering, supply chain, and nursing.

- Devices and their last known location
- Devices that had a last known location (LKL) that exceeded the utilization threshold
- Soiled utility closets that were not getting dirty pumps based on a threshold
- Any locations that experienced a stock-out
- Supply and demand trends.

That condition was caused by the nurses hoarding the pumps and the system could tell which units were offending because those units weren't putting dirty pumps into the soiled utilities. Of course, sometimes there were valid reasons why the units didn't have dirty pumps, but tracking was so tight that it was difficult not to stand out if there was hoarding going on.

Gail had a standing agenda item on her nurse manager meetings for discussing the data for the PAR stocking project. She wanted to see it expanded to other types of equipment and she believed in the concept. In one of the meetings, the manager for four central said they had no issues with the pumps but they wanted to know if the project could help them find other equipment like vitals machines and WoundVacs. Gail said, "Denise is on the steering committee for these projects, Denise, can you answer the question?" Denise Henry said, "The patient tracking and equipment tracking are coming, but the work they are doing now is building the foundation for that." Denise said, "Gail, can we talk about the orderly?"

Just looking around the room, you could see the curiosity when they heard the work orderly. Gail said,

> We don't want to get out in front of our skis here, and no promises in anything I am about to say. We don't want nurses to be spending time in yet another computer system, so it has been proposed that we create a new role called the orderly. This person would be able to find equipment for you, help with supply issues and basically make sure that everything is in order and easy to find. I am oversimplifying it but you get what I mean.

The manager for 6 West said, "Could the orderly find my patient that left the building to have a smoke?" Gail smiled and said, "100% yes. Even better, the orderly could help make sure that patient never left the building in the first place."

PLAYBOOK FOR THE DIGITAL TWIN

The play for the digital twin is the need to understand that the digital twin is a system-of-systems, and it can be a single platform or an ecosystem. For care traffic control it will be an ecosystem. This doesn't mean there is no integration and to the contrary, integration will be the key to applying for contextual awareness to the enterprise. The digital twin is an architectural strategy that allows the organization to chart a course toward care traffic control.

Improvers

Performance improvement professionals play a critical role in realizing the value of the digital twin across the organization. Here are key areas of focus:

- Process analysis and optimization
  - Map current processes and identify areas where digital twin capabilities can drive improvement

  - Use digital twin data to identify bottlenecks and inefficiencies
  - Create baseline measurements to quantify improvements
  - Design new workflows that leverage digital twin capabilities
- Use case development
  - Identify high-impact opportunities that align with organizational priorities
  - Work with stakeholders to document specific requirements and success criteria
  - Develop pilot programs to test and refine digital twin applications
  - Create standardized methodologies for measuring and reporting outcomes
- Change management
  - Partner with operational leaders to implement new workflows
  - Develop training programs that help staff understand and utilize digital twin capabilities
  - Create feedback loops to continuously improve digital twin applications
  - Document and share best practices across the organization
- Data utilization
  - Define key performance indicators (KPIs) that align with improvement goals
  - Design dashboards and reports that provide actionable insights
  - Establish processes for regular review and analysis of digital twin data
  - Create mechanisms for turning insights into action
- Cross-functional collaboration
  - Work with IT teams to ensure technical capabilities align with improvement needs
  - Partner with operational leaders to prioritize improvement initiatives
  - Coordinate with clinical teams to ensure improvements support patient care
  - Facilitate communication between technical and operational teams
- ROI analysis
  - Develop methodologies for measuring both tangible and intangible benefits
  - Create business cases for digital twin investments
  - Track and report on realized benefits
  - Identify opportunities for expanding successful implementations.

Leaders

Leaders should understand that implementing a digital twin is a transformational journey, not just a technology implementation. The digital twin will become a core system that enables real-time operations and decision-making. Key considerations include:

- Strategic planning
  - Align digital twin initiatives with broader organizational goals
  - Plan for incremental implementation that delivers early wins while building toward comprehensive capabilities
  - Consider both short-term operational improvements and long-term strategic advantages
- Investment priorities
  - Focus initial investments on foundational components like data infrastructure and integration capabilities
  - Prioritize use cases that demonstrate clear ROI and operational improvements
  - Balance investment between technology infrastructure and organizational change management
- Organizational readiness
  - Assess current technological and operational maturity
  - Identify gaps in skills and capabilities needed for digital twin implementation
  - Create a roadmap for developing internal expertise and capabilities.

Creators

Vendors and solution creators play a crucial role in shaping the digital twin ecosystem. Focus areas should include:

- Interoperability
  - Design solutions that integrate with existing healthcare systems and workflows
  - Adopt standard protocols and data formats to ensure seamless integration
  - Create flexible APIs that enable custom integration with various systems
- Healthcare-specific requirements
  - Build solutions that address specific healthcare operational challenges
  - Ensure compliance with healthcare regulations and privacy requirements
  - Design for the unique needs of healthcare workflows and processes
- Platform development
  - Create modular solutions that can scale with organizational needs
  - Develop clear upgrade paths that protect customer investments
  - Provide robust security features that meet healthcare standards
- Implementation support
  - Offer comprehensive training and support programs
  - Provide clear documentation and implementation guides
  - Develop tools and methodologies for measuring success and ROI.

These additions provide strategic guidance for both leadership and vendor audiences, focusing on their specific roles in successful digital twin implementation. Would you like me to expand on any of these points or add additional sections?

NOTES

1 https://www.digitaltwinconsortium.org/glossary/glossary/#digital-twin.
2 https://digitaltwinconsortium.org.
3 https://www.iiconsortium.org/pdf/Trustworthiness_Framework_Foundations.pdf.
4 https://www.iiconsortium.org/wp-content/uploads/sites/2/2022/04/Industry-IoT-Vocabulary.pdf.
5 https://www.iso.org/standard/53940.html.
6 https://www.iiconsortium.org/wp-content/uploads/sites/2/2022/04/Industry-IoT-Vocabulary.pdf.
7 https://www.digitaltwinconsortium.org/glossary/glossary/#itot-platform.
8 https://www.digitaltwinconsortium.org/glossary/glossary/#virtual-representation.

Section II

Care traffic control

Section 2 defines and explores the concept of care traffic control (CTC), drawing parallels with the proven reliability and efficiency of air traffic control systems. This section demonstrates how modern location-based technologies, combined with thoughtful system architecture and operational processes, can revolutionize healthcare operations. Building on the foundational concepts from Section 1, we examine the components, implementation considerations, and security requirements necessary for successful CTC deployment.

Chapter 9 – Care Traffic Control introduces the fundamental concept and definition of care traffic control, explaining how it aligns with established practices from aviation while addressing healthcare's unique challenges. This chapter outlines how CTC combines situational awareness and automation to optimize mobile workflows across the enterprise.

Chapter 10 – Care Traffic Control Ecosystem presents the comprehensive platform architecture required for CTC implementation. This chapter examines how various technologies, systems, and processes work together to create a cohesive operational environment, detailing the interactions between mobile platforms, IoT devices, clinical systems, and support services.

Chapter 11 – Agents: Perception and Observability explores the critical first phase of the agent cycle – perception. This chapter examines how different sensing technologies and data sources can be combined to create comprehensive situational awareness, detailing how agents observe and interpret their environment.

Chapter 12 – Agents: Thinking and Decisions delves into how agents process information and make decisions. This chapter explores the role of context-aware computing and various decision-making frameworks, showing how agents can effectively support both human and automated decision-making processes.

Chapter 13 – Agents: Actions and Outcomes addresses the final phase of the agent cycle, examining how decisions are translated into actions that create meaningful changes in the environment. This chapter explores different types of actions and how they contribute to achieving desired outcomes.

DOI: 10.1201/9781003625483-10

Chapter 14 – Privacy and Security tackles the critical considerations of data protection and security in a CTC environment. This chapter examines both how to secure CTC systems and how CTC can enhance overall operational security, while ensuring compliance with healthcare privacy requirements.

Chapter 9

Care traffic control

Paul E. Zieske

DEFINITION AND CORE CONCEPTS

Care traffic control (CTC) is a systematic approach to healthcare operations that uses situational awareness and automation to optimize mobile workflows across the enterprise. At its core, CTC can be defined simply as:

> Care traffic control is using situational awareness and automation to optimize mobile workflows across the enterprise.

This operational paradigm draws inspiration from aviation and air traffic control systems, where complex motion and coordination challenges were handled through technology and carefully designed processes. While healthcare presents unique challenges, the principles that have made air traffic control highly reliable and efficient can be adapted to transform healthcare operations.

THE BALANCE OF HUMAN AND MACHINE

Like aviation, CTC recognizes that complete automation isn't always desirable or practical. Instead, it seeks to strike an intelligent balance between automated systems and human expertise. In aviation, a Boeing 747 has the technical capability to take off and land automatically, yet takeoffs are always performed manually due to the complex variables involved and potential risks like bird strikes. Similarly, CTC aims to automate appropriate processes while maintaining human oversight for complex decision-making and unexpected situations.

The role of automation in CTC is primarily to:

- Reduce cognitive load on healthcare workers
- Enable staff to work at the "top of their license"
- Provide real-time situational awareness
- Handle routine tasks and monitoring
- Support informed decision-making.

DOI: 10.1201/9781003625483-11

CTC TECHNOLOGY

The CTC technology stack is a workflow-centric, platform-oriented, enterprise architecture that ensures all the contextual data necessary to create situational awareness and automation is used in as many workflows as possible. It is a combination of the digital twin and communication technologies, which are the two main components of a real-time platform. The digital twin platform exists in an ecosystem of technologies that are required for situational awareness and automation.

The CTC technology stack consists of three primary components that work together to create a comprehensive operational platform:

1. **Digital twin**
   - Virtual representation of physical spaces and operations
   - Real-time synchronization with the physical environment
   - Integration with existing healthcare information systems
   - Process modeling and simulation capabilities
2. **Communication systems**
   - Real-time messaging and alerts
   - Voice communication infrastructure
   - Mobile device integration
   - Emergency notification systems
3. **Workflow automation**
   - Task management and routing
   - Process orchestration
   - Resource optimization
   - Performance monitoring and analytics.

The CTC platform is a core healthcare information system (HIS) system that makes location and contextual data available across the enterprise to create situational awareness and automation (Figure 9.1).

The platform contrasts with the islands of technology as we see in LBS1.0. Because these systems have no bridge to the rest of the enterprise, they linger as point solutions that become difficult to support and maintain. Instead of focusing on use cases, the CTC platform offers modularity and presents the autonomous features that were a part of the use cases as we saw in LBS1.0. The composable nature of the platform means that solutions can be created that conform to the specific needs of a department. What were previously viewed as use cases in LBS1.0 are now delivered as features of departmental solutions as described by LBS2.0 in Chapter 1, "Healthcare adoption" (Figure 9.2).

A CTC ecosystem is realized with the digital twin providing composable departmental solutions that are context aware. In LBS1.0, we saw the RTLS in the center with the use cases surrounding it, and little consideration for

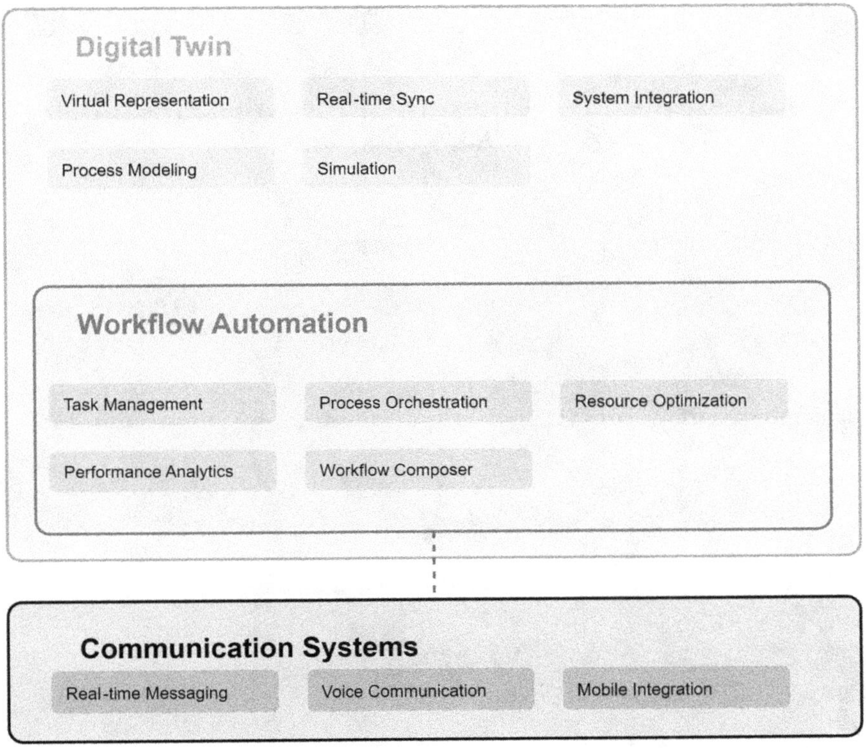

Figure 9.1 CTC Platform structure diagram.

the workflows they support. With CTC, the workflows can interact with each other, and the hub can orchestrate the location aware workflows that are the spokes. The spokes contain the features that are necessary for the solution. The use cases are still there, but if a department needs, for instance, employee duress, it is delivered as a feature of a departmental solution. If the department's workflows need equipment location, the RTLS can provide that as a feature of workflow automation. The CTC architecture allows a department, like bed management, to know exactly when the patient left the room from the patient transport department.

The digital twin requires a strategic approach to location services to open the real-time data to the entire enterprise. The constraints of the LBS1.0 limit healthcare delivery organizations (HDO) to being reactive because the architecture doesn't support departmental solutions very well. A common scenario is where a department has some adverse event that causes them to look at location tech. They buy a use case that can hopefully solve their problem, but the other departments that could benefit are not considered. Employee duress is a common example where, when a high-risk department, like the

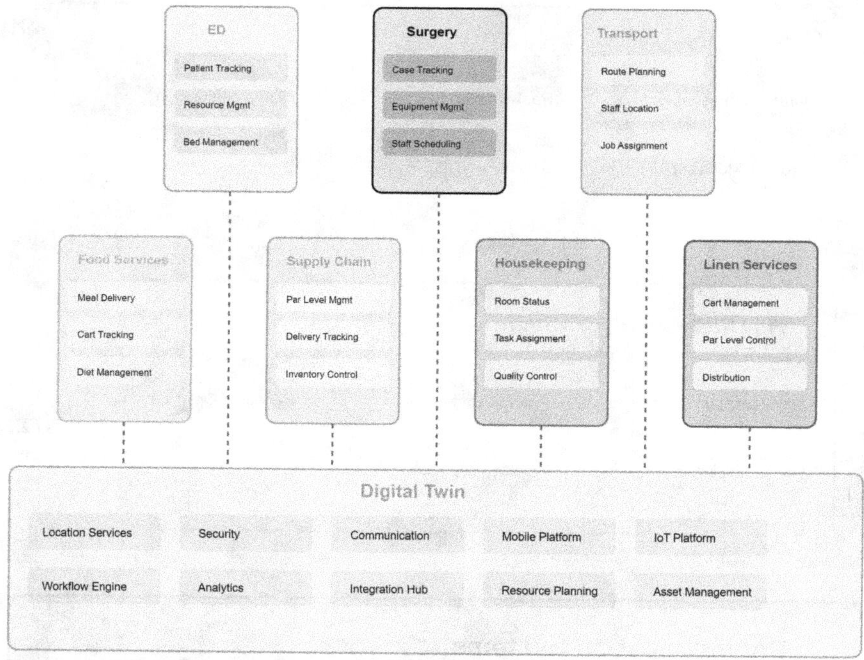

Figure 9.2 CTC ecosystem diagram.

emergency department, has an incident, a solution gets purchased and the other departments don't benefit. Granted the cost considerations are a key factor but with an enterprise strategy much more can be done. With LBS1.0 each use case is a one-size-fits-all point solution that may work well for one department but not another. With CTC, these use cases are features of a departmental solution that takes only what is needed from the LBS1.0 use case.

Digital twin's impact on solutions development

The digital twin will fundamentally transform how solutions are developed in the location services market. By leveraging the granularity provided by the 4Ps (position, proximity, presence, and possession), organizations can identify numerous opportunities for workflow automation.

The sensing layer, comprised various sensors and technologies, maps directly to these 4Ps, enabling:

- Detection of arrivals and departures
- Calculation of dwell time
- Establishment of custody chains
- Measurement of space occupancy.

This comprehensive sensing capability creates both situational awareness and automation opportunities that can be precisely tailored to specific workflows. Just as track-and-trace revolutionized outdoor logistics, these capabilities are now moving indoors. The "Uberization" of services – providing real-time visibility and control – will become standard for indoor operations as well.

Communications: structured and reliable information exchange

Effective communication is the cornerstone of any complex operational system, and CTC is no exception. Drawing inspiration from air traffic control, where precise and unambiguous communication can mean the difference between safety and disaster, CTC implements a sophisticated communication framework that balances immediacy with reliability.

In healthcare settings, we already see examples of structured communication through standardized code systems. When a "Code Blue" is announced, it triggers an immediate, coordinated response from specific team members – much like how air traffic controllers use precise phraseology to ensure clear understanding and appropriate actions. CTC builds upon this foundation, expanding it to encompass both emergency and routine operational communications.

The system employs two distinct but complementary communication methods: synchronous and asynchronous. Each serves specific purposes and offers unique advantages in different situations.

Synchronous communication

Real-time voice communication remains essential for situations requiring immediate interaction and decision-making. Like an air traffic controller speaking directly to a pilot, **synchronous communication** enables instant clarification and confirmation. This immediate exchange is crucial during time-sensitive situations or when complex information needs to be conveyed quickly.

Asynchronous communication

The system also heavily utilizes **asynchronous communication**, primarily through text messages and alerts. This approach offers several significant advantages over voice-only communication. Every message is automatically documented, creating an audit trail that shows not just what was communicated, but when. This documentation proves invaluable for process improvement, training, and accountability. Unlike verbal instructions that rely on memory, text-based communications provide a permanent record that can be referenced and verified.

Mobile device integration

At the heart of this communication system lies the mobile device infrastructure. Every staff in the CTC ecosystem carries a mobile device, ensuring they're always connected to the communication network. However, this reliance on mobile devices introduces important considerations that must be carefully managed.

Alert management becomes crucial – notifications must be properly configured to ensure important messages aren't missed while avoiding alert fatigue. The system employs sophisticated alert prioritization, ensuring that critical communications break through while less urgent messages don't become disruptive.

One of the most powerful features of the mobile platform is the ability to use standardized or "canned" messages. These preformatted communications, similar to the standard phraseology used in air traffic control, serve multiple purposes. They speed up routine communications, ensure consistency across different shifts and departments, and reduce the possibility of misunderstanding. For example, a simple "PT Ready" message might indicate that a patient is prepared and waiting for transport, triggering a specific series of actions from the transport team.

The success of this communication system depends on careful balance – between immediate and delayed communication, between standardization and flexibility, and between the need for awareness and the risk of overwhelming staff with information. Through thoughtful implementation and continuous refinement, CTC creates a communication environment that enhances both efficiency and safety.

DEPARTMENTAL SOLUTIONS

Each department may have workflows that can be identified as candidates for the CTC system. The amount of motion and the value of optimizing the workflow will dictate if there is a departmental solution that should be created. These solutions will take the form of agents that are part of the operational digital twin.

The agents assist with nominal processes and help detect and correct anomalies. The **nominal** flow is the desired or normal flow. The **anomalies** are off-normal occurrences. Anomalies are often addressed with communications, but when they are detected digitally, they could become a part of the workflow automation. When the department and its workflows are represented as rational agents, this would constitute a departmental solution.

Departmental agents need to work together because each department structures the services they provide differently. This is done to optimize the throughput for their department. The flow of surgery is highly planned and structured so when anomalies occur in an episode, also known as a case, there is a ripple effect that needs to be accounted for. Clinic flows are highly planned to remove uncertainty. The emergency department operates with uncertainty caused by random arrivals.

CARE TRAFFIC CONTROL OPERATIONS

CTC operations are about creating flow. CTC combines the people and technology that are required to find and eliminate delay. That delay could be from the lowest level of the workflow up to the organizational level. The technology that the users interact with is the operational digital twin and its agents. The agents assist the users by using their ability to perceive the environment to remove delay. That could be as low level as eliminating a button press on a mobile app or as high-level as adjusting a staffing plan.

Figure 9.3 shows the dynamics at play in the command center environment. This is not comprehensive, but it does give a sense of the amount of activity that is going on in the hospital operations.

The technology

The CTC system is an operational digital twin. The CTC system is designed for a new operational paradigm that takes from the best of what we see in air traffic control. Healthcare workflows usually operate with uncertainty, so part of the agents' goals is to adapt to that uncertainty. Uncertainty in air traffic control is addressed by using situational awareness and automation to minimize the impact caused by random changes. Anomalies can cause delays and a corrective response to an anomaly is ineffective if there is a delay in recognizing the anomaly. Real-time data improves recognition and helps this situation by detecting the anomaly quickly and allowing a response to occur.

Air traffic control is rife with real-time information coming in from networked sensors. Real-time information is only useful if it is actionable, and it is only actionable, if it is received by someone who can act. In air traffic control, the action is taken by the air traffic controller. The controllers are trained to use real-time data and other tools to make decisions and act in real time.

The goal of CTC technology is to provide the actors (people who can act) with the information they need; at the time they need it. That is the role of situational awareness. The role of automation is to remove effort, monitor nominal flow, optimize the process, and detect anomalies.

The people

In healthcare the role of the dispatcher is someone who takes real-time inputs from phone calls and computer systems and makes assignments to

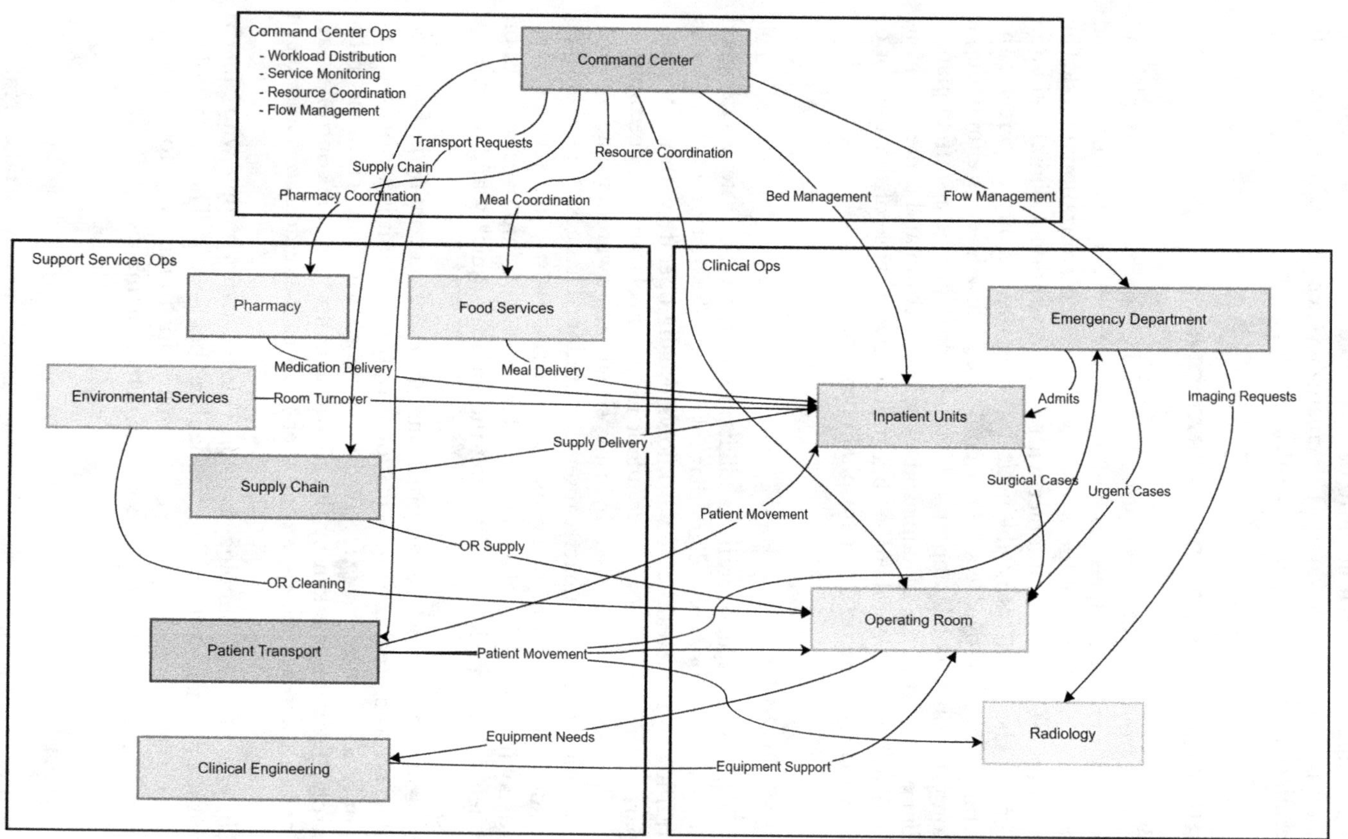

Figure 9.3 CTC command center and department relationships.

workers who can act. Only certain workflows are afforded the benefits of dispatching because, either the data is not available or the expense will not yield the return. A CTC system reduces that expense and opens many new workflows to the benefits of a role like a dispatcher. With CTC this is a dynamic that cascades into adding more workflows and more automation. Dispatching is the type of role that will evolve as the organization evolves in its CTC journey. As CTC matures within the organization, dispatching will grow to resemble the role of the air traffic controller.

The controller is different from a dispatcher. The dispatcher only has responsibilities for flow within the scope of their department. The controller, however, must also manage the handoffs between departments. The controller is a problem solver, but they also use continuous improvement techniques to help their customers avoid problems. The controllers work as a team with each other and have enterprise goals alongside their departmental goals. Certain controllers will have above-the-wing and below-the-wing situational awareness to help patients participate in their care.

The command center

As departments grow to have controllers that represent their part of the operational flow, it will make sense to have the dispatchers and controllers collocated so that even more delay can be removed at an enterprise level. This collocation will facilitate the interaction of the departments to solve problems and remove delays. This collocation occurs in air traffic control in the terminal and air route centers that are responsible for the safe transitions of aircraft through the phases of a flight. Establishing a CTC command center will collocate the people who act on real-time information and allow orchestration based on situational awareness.

As the capabilities of AI improve, automation will allow the controllers to process more inputs and reduce the cognitive load on the controllers. The AI will have the combined knowledge of all the agents that are a part of the system. This will allow the controller's roles to evolve to problem solver and oversight (Figure 9.4).

Simulations

Although we have included an entire chapter on simulation in Chapter 16, we wanted to include an introduction here as it is one of the more important features of the digital twin. Simulators and simulation modeling are an important part of aviation, from airplane simulators to air traffic control simulators. Because both are based on systems with real-time data, simulations can be used for training, and actual data can be used to determine the root cause for anomalies. With a CTC system and a digital twin, this real-time data will allow simulation models to be created for hospitals and clinics. These can be used to simulate anything that we can produce real-time

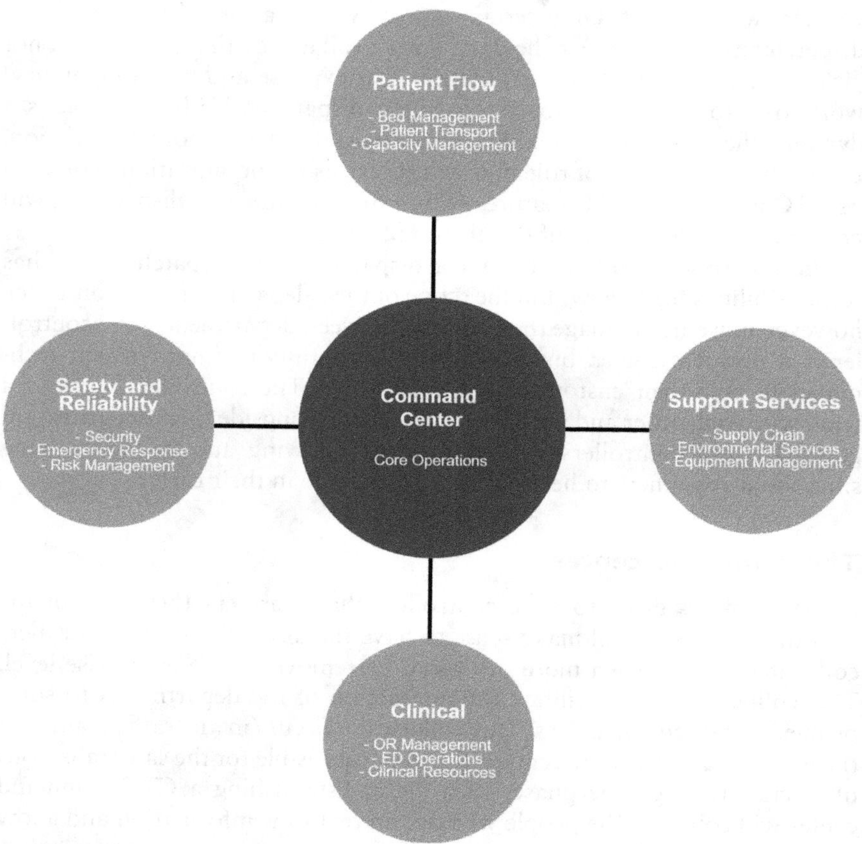

Figure 9.4 **Command center organizational structure diagram.**

data for. The process of creating situation awareness and the automation will generate these models as byproducts. The controllers described above will be able to use these simulations to prepare for situations that can cause impact to flow and even emergencies preparedness.

An example of a simulated flow problem might be what is called a "bed emergency." A bed emergency usually causes what is called "boarding" in the emergency department (ED). This means there is no place to put patients, so they must wait in a hallway. This could cause what is called a code black where no more patients can be taken into the ED. This is a major problem for a hospital that could mean life or death for some patients. The goal for reacting to a bed emergency is to find out where the grid lock is and fix it. This could mean housekeeping needs to clean a room or a discharge needs to be escalated. Several patients could be moved to make room for new patients. There are many possibilities that are in play.

Simulators used in training

Training a user on software systems can be done by showing the user how the system operates but getting a user to solve actual problems with the system is more difficult. Real-time systems are more challenging because they create situational awareness and without an actual situation to present to the user the training is limited. But, with a simulator, the actual tools and simulation data can be used to perform a scenario-based training. We see this in aviation with flight simulators that allow a pilot to experience the cognitive load that comes from the scenario. The same approach of using a simulator can be used to train dispatchers to solve problems with the real-time information that comes from the digital twin.

For example, a CTC system that includes an RTLS will sense the real-time location of every patient and nearly the exact second that a patient got moved. A housekeeping and patient transport department solution could show the exact time a room was ready and when a transporter was enroute to move a patient. With all this real-time capability comes the ability to simulate a real-time scenario. In Chapter 16 we will see more details on simulation modeling.

Simulations for continuous improvement

Simulations are different from simulators because they are used to visualize process improvements and the operations of new systems to predict how they might perform. There are simulation modeling tools that allow a flow to be created and a representation of the environment to be presented visually. These tools can be fed inputs, and the tool allows the entire flow to be viewed. This becomes very useful risk mitigation for changes to workflows. These tools can be used to model new systems as well for feedback on their effectiveness.

THE EDENVALE JOURNEY – PATIENT TRANSPORT

Edenvale General Hospital (EGH) had cleaned up their LBS program and was just getting started with the CTC journey. The initial projects were showing Return on Investment (ROI) and they were starting on the last project in that first phase of the program. That was the Patient Transport project.

They weren't saying much about CTC outside of the steering committee, but the steering committee was preparing a pitch to the Hospital Executive Committee about it. They knew CTC would be transformational to the hospital operations, but it would take organizational change and require executive sponsorship.

Patient transport was the first of these projects to fall into the category of CTC because it was, in its essence, a workflow automation project. It would require an agent that would not need any AI, but the agentic design would allow AI to be added later.

LOS and patient transport project benefit each other

The LOS project benefits from seeing the flow of patients when in transport. Also, when correlated with the RTLS data and ADT (admit, transfer, and discharge) data, the patient transport project benefits from the LOS project. The reason Patient Transport liked the RTLS was that when the patients were being moved by nurses there was no transport data. With the RTLS there was transport data so now they had a complete picture of all patient transports.

The LOS project data had pointed out something the patient transport manager had been saying all along. The time to pick up a patient was a big source of delay. Often the patients weren't ready and the nurses needed for the transition were unavailable when the transporter showed up. The transporter would be asked why the delays were occurring, and at times it would turn into finger pointing. The patient transport project would provide data that would stop the negative behavior.

The patient transport project

They implemented Apple Indoor (IPS) in the beginning of the project, and it was much easier because the vendor that converted the CAD helped them through the entire Apple process. The hospital owned an expanding fleet of iPhones. The IPS was accurate everywhere on the campus. This meant that patient transport could stream their location back through their streaming service to the same UI (User Interface) that capacity management was using. Capacity management was using the RTLS for patient location, so there was some real-time data analytics to make the correlation, so both could complement each other. The iPhones required no cellular subscription and an inexpensive app was used to stream the location. Apple Indoor system required only the cost of implementation. For EGH Transport would need 30 iPhones.

There was also a feature on the app that worked like contact tracing where the patient's NFC/BLE RTLS tag would be detected by the phone's BLE and/or NFC (Near Field Communications) sensor when it was close to the patient. This made the data very accurate when the transporters had the patients, and it confirmed the patient's identity for the transport job. It would be used for a chain of custody for the patients. The nurses were wearing NFC/BLE RTLS badges. Now they had real data that showed an arrival time, and the scans would confirm that the nurse and the transporter had connected (Figure 9.5).

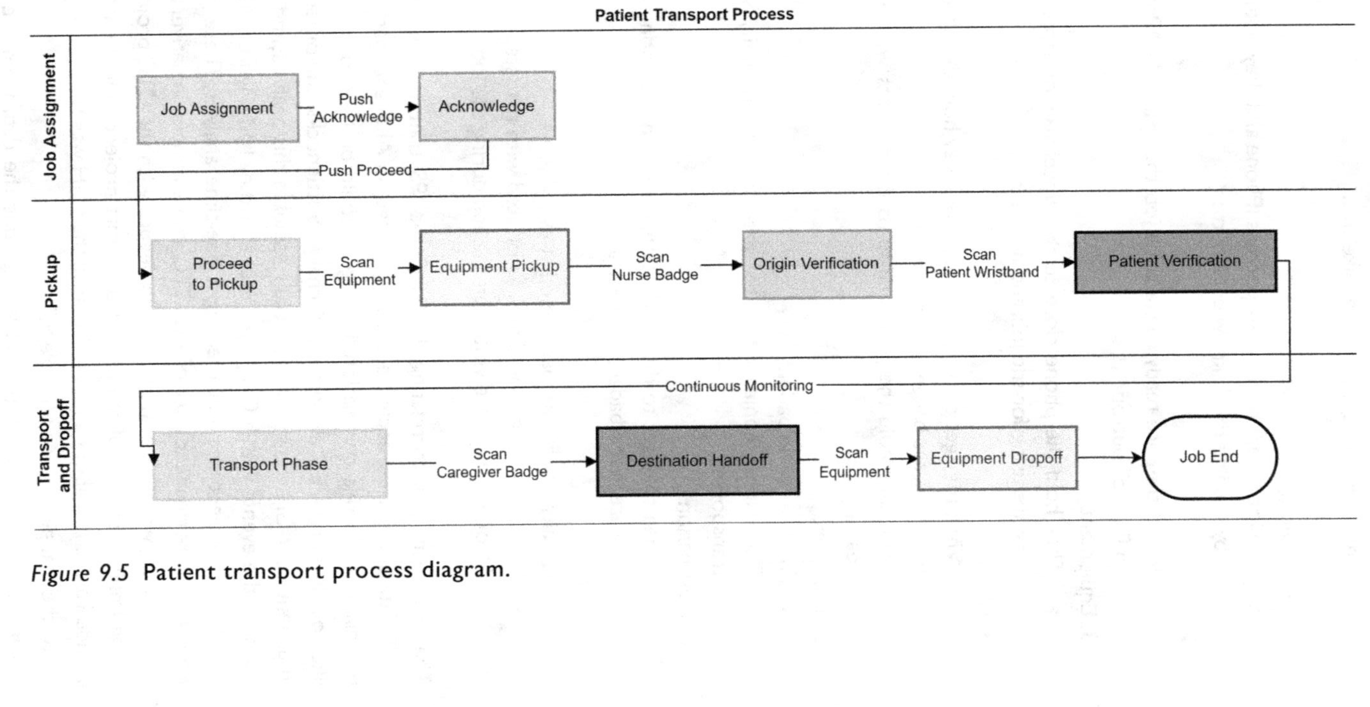

Figure 9.5 Patient transport process diagram.

The patient transport agent worked like this:

1. Acknowledge
   a. The job is sent to the transporter's iPhone and they acknowledge it by pushing the Acknowledge button
2. Pickup
   a. When they are ready to start the job, they push the "Proceeding to Pickup" button
3. Equipment
   a. They hold the phone close to the wheelchair or stretcher that they are using for the job, and hear a beep
4. Origin
   a. When they get to the pickup location, they hold the phone close to the nurses badge, and hear a beep
   b. Then they hold the phone close to the patients wristband, and hear a beep
5. Transport
   a. Transport the patient
   b. The phone monitors that the patient is in proximity with the transporter
6. Destination
   a. When they get to the destination, they hold the phone close to the caregiver's badge, and hear a beep
7. Notes
   a. Quality checks are performed at every scan
   b. Each beep has a tone that is associated with that step
   c. All of the steps are visible on the app during the job.

The LOS team was correlating the RTLS, the IPS, transport orders, and the ADT data and getting accurate data. They used an AI agent that was trained especially to do this correlation. This agent could be told to look for things like boarding in the ED, elopement, discharge bottlenecks, and other anomalies in patient flow. GIS tools were especially useful in this analysis, and they could playback the events with a GIS player tool that they had (Figure 9.6).

The LOS project was not creating a one-time analysis. These dashboards were now a permanent part of the CTC improvement initiative, and it also showed them where they wanted to go deeper with the CTC projects.

The implementation of the patient transport project took 4 months, which included a delay of about a month because the EGH was slow getting the CAD file to the mapping vendor (Figure 9.7).

The hardest part of the project was getting the data from the electronic medical record. This was being done as a business intelligence project and

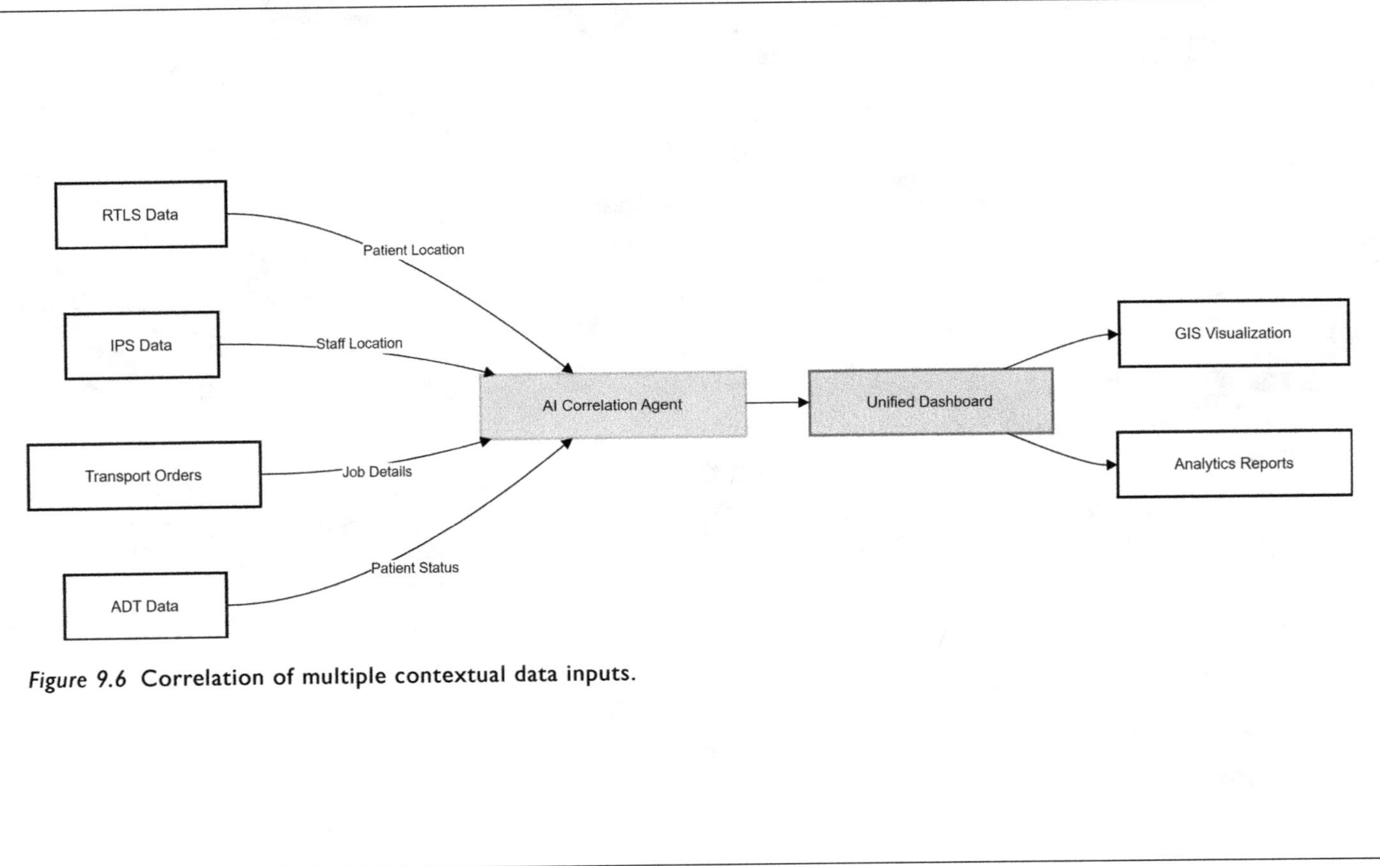

Figure 9.6 Correlation of multiple contextual data inputs.

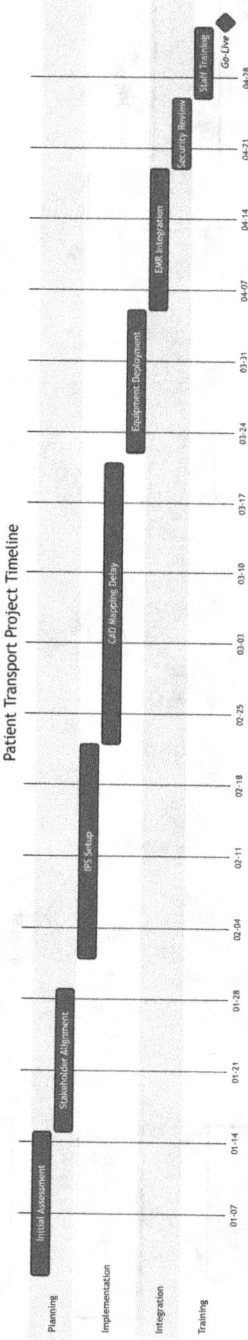

Figure 9.7 **Patient transport project timeline.**

all the software was approved, but the privacy and security team needed to review everything before the data could be linked up.

Derek, Imani, and Suresh were meeting to discuss the preparation for Suresh's pitch to the Hospital Executive Committee. Suresh said,

> I have Bruce (VP Support Services) and Roni (COO) on board. I have a lot of good data to show the committee, and we have a solid methodology. The ROI numbers are good, but we are asking for some significant changes with this command center. Gail is going to talk about the orderly role, and she has savings numbers to support a new job description. It is great to have Gail there to show we have nursing's support. I am confident they will like CTC as a concept, but I think the concern is going to be about the amount of change.

Derek said,

> In my experience, it comes down to how long the changes are spread out over. Spreading it out diminishes the returns and sometimes they want the returns more than they resist the change. I can't tell you how they will respond, but that is what I have experienced. If you can get them into a discussion about that then you will have your CTC project and only the timing is the issue.

Johnathon said,

> I am confident about this phase, but you all realize that Patricia (CEO) will have to present the entire, 5 year program, to the board. This is an operational change that I know Roni wants, but it uses more technology than I think she realizes. We will have to prove the stability of these systems because we will be more dependent on them than ever before. I guess I am just saying let's be sure we do our homework and be completely transparent.

Everyone agreed.

PLAYBOOK FOR CTC

CTC, when adopted, offers a long-term strategy for reducing delays and improving quality and safety. Its success is a direct function of the situational awareness and automation that is created with the digital twin. CTC is a framework to apply those technologies to make significant improvements in operational efficiency. This is possible when the organization recognizes the opportunities these new capabilities present and is open to changing accordingly.

Adopting CTC as an operational transformation can set in motion coherent people-and-process changes that can proceed in lockstep with the technology. Pairing healthcare experts with industrial engineers and location services architects to create a strategy of coordinated steps to CTC maturity shows a commitment to this kind of change. The rest of this section will describe what some of those steps might look like.

Improvers

Improvers can use the CTC implementation methodology to find delays and any anomalies that can benefit from additional technology. Finding opportunities to use communications is a great place to start. Early on, there are good solutions for many departments that will make up the workflows that comprise the digital twin. Later we will build the specifications for the department solutions. Improvers are critical to that process.

1. Assessment and planning
   - Document current workflow pain points and bottlenecks
   - Map existing communication patterns and gaps
   - Identify opportunities for improved situational awareness
   - Evaluate current automation capabilities and needs
2. Implementation framework
   - Start with observation before automation
   - Build foundation for situational awareness
   - Document critical information flows
   - Create measurement systems for outcomes
3. Process design
   - Focus on workflow optimization opportunities
   - Design for both normal operations and exceptions
   - Create clear escalation paths
   - Build feedback loops for continuous improvement
4. Metrics development
   - Define key performance indicators
   - Establish baseline measurements
   - Create monitoring systems
   - Design outcome evaluation methods

Leaders

Leaders will see the technology needs for CTC lean toward situational awareness as automation is going to be a longer journey. The composability of the platform is a challenge but one that will bring the most value and allow it to become a core system.

Situational awareness is best enabled with mobile communication technologies like smartphones. As Wi-Fi 6.0 and private 5G become more prevalent, voice communications will not require accounts with cellular carriers.

Voice is a synchronous communication medium, and text is a valuable asynchronous medium that requires only basic Wi-Fi connectivity.

1. Strategic vision
   - Understand CTC's role in organizational transformation
   - Develop clear goals and objectives
   - Create roadmap for implementation
   - Build support across departments
2. Resource planning
   - Assess technology infrastructure needs
   - Plan for staffing requirements
   - Allocate resources for training
   - Budget for ongoing support
3. Organizational change
   - Develop communication strategy
   - Build cross-functional teams
   - Create new roles where needed
   - Foster culture of continuous improvement
4. Risk management
   - Identify potential implementation risks
   - Develop mitigation strategies
   - Create contingency plans
   - Monitor progress and adjust as needed

Creators

The technology platform for CTC is likely to be enabled by the creation of standards when it comes to IoT and the operational digital twin. There are organizations like the Digital Twin Consortium that are sources for information regarding the operational digital twin.

1. Solution architecture
   - Design for enterprise scalability
   - Build modular components
   - Support standard integrations
   - Enable customization for specific needs
2. Implementation support
   - Provide comprehensive training
   - Offer implementation guidance
   - Support system optimization
   - Maintain ongoing technical support
3. Development focus
   - Create workflow-centric solutions
   - Build flexible integration capabilities
   - Support real-time operations
   - Enable progressive automation

Chapter 10

Care traffic control ecosystem

Paul E. Zieske

The evolution of healthcare operations has led us to a critical understanding: no single system can effectively manage the complex interactions and workflows within a modern healthcare environment. Air traffic control integrates multiple systems to manage flight operations safely and efficiently. Care traffic control also requires a comprehensive ecosystem of interconnected platforms and technologies.

EVOLUTION OF LOCATION SERVICES IN HEALTHCARE

The journey from basic location tracking to comprehensive operational awareness illustrates how healthcare technology has matured to meet increasingly complex demands. This evolution provides valuable insights into why an ecosystem approach has become essential for modern healthcare operations.

Traditional approach: location-based services 1.0

Early implementations of location services in healthcare followed a pattern familiar to many technology adoptions – solving individual problems with individual solutions. Organizations would identify a specific need, such as tracking mobile medical equipment, and implement a standalone system to address that need. As new requirements emerged, additional systems would be added, each operating independently.

This approach led to a proliferation of point solutions with specific capabilities:

Point Solutions:

- Asset tracking for equipment management
- Staff duress systems for security
- Patient tracking for safety
- Environmental monitoring systems

DOI: 10.1201/9781003625483-12

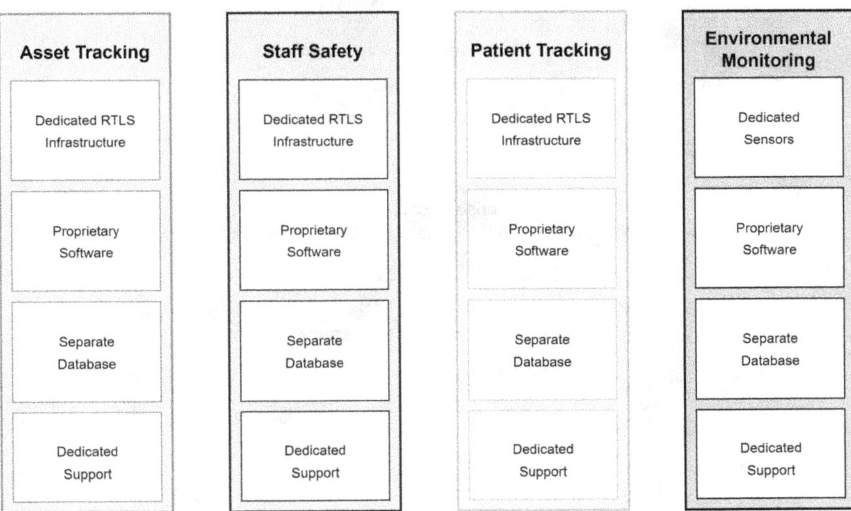

Figure 10.1 LBS siloed architecture.

While these solutions could effectively address their targeted use cases, they created significant operational challenges. Each new system required its own infrastructure, training program, and maintenance schedule. The burden of managing multiple independent systems often outweighed their individual benefits (Figure 10.1).

Healthcare organizations found themselves facing mounting challenges.

Implementation Challenges:

- Each solution required its own infrastructure
- High costs per use case
- Limited integration between systems
- Difficult to scale across the enterprise

The financial impact was particularly significant. Each new use case required its own business justification, infrastructure investment, and ongoing support costs. The inability to share components or infrastructure between systems meant that the total cost of ownership continued to climb with each new implementation.

Modern approach: location-based services 2.0

The evolution to LBS 2.0 represents a fundamental shift in how healthcare organizations approach location services. Rather than implementing individual solutions, organizations now focus on building a comprehensive

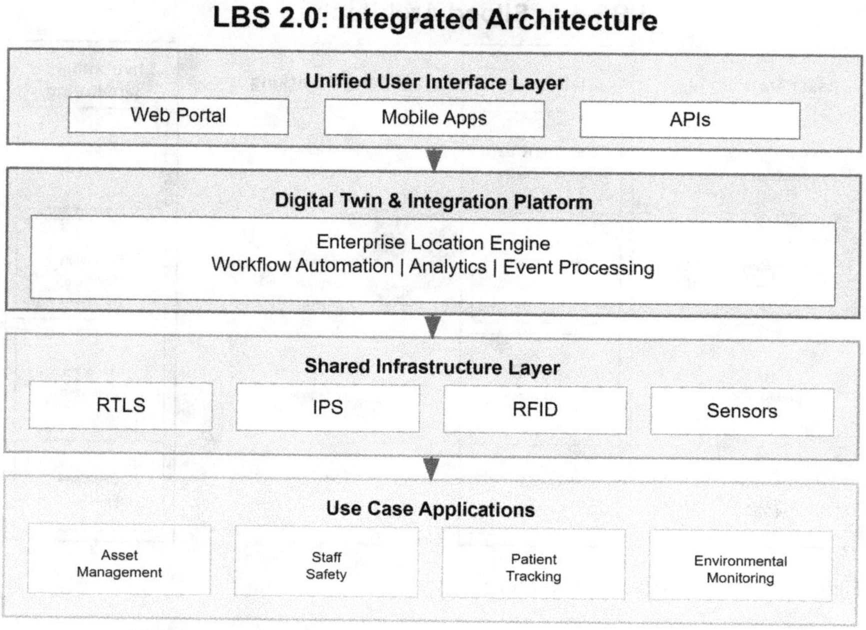

LBS 2.0: Integrated Architecture

Unified User Interface Layer

Web Portal | Mobile Apps | APIs

Digital Twin & Integration Platform

Enterprise Location Engine
Workflow Automation | Analytics | Event Processing

Shared Infrastructure Layer

RTLS | IPS | RFID | Sensors

Use Case Applications

Asset Management | Staff Safety | Patient Tracking | Environmental Monitoring

Figure 10.2 LBS 2.0 integrated architecture.

platform that can support multiple use cases through shared infrastructure and services.

This modern approach emphasizes integration and scalability through:
Platform Architecture:

- Enterprise-wide infrastructure
- Shared location services
- Common data model
- Standardized APIs
- Unified security model

The benefits of this approach extend far beyond simple cost savings (Figure 10.2). By creating a unified platform, organizations can rapidly deploy new capabilities, enhance existing workflows, and create interactions between previously isolated systems. This integration enables new levels of operational efficiency and care delivery optimization.

CARE TRAFFIC CONTROL ECOSYSTEM

The care traffic control ecosystem builds upon the foundation of LBS 2.0, creating a framework that enables complex healthcare operations to function with the precision and reliability seen in air traffic control. Just as

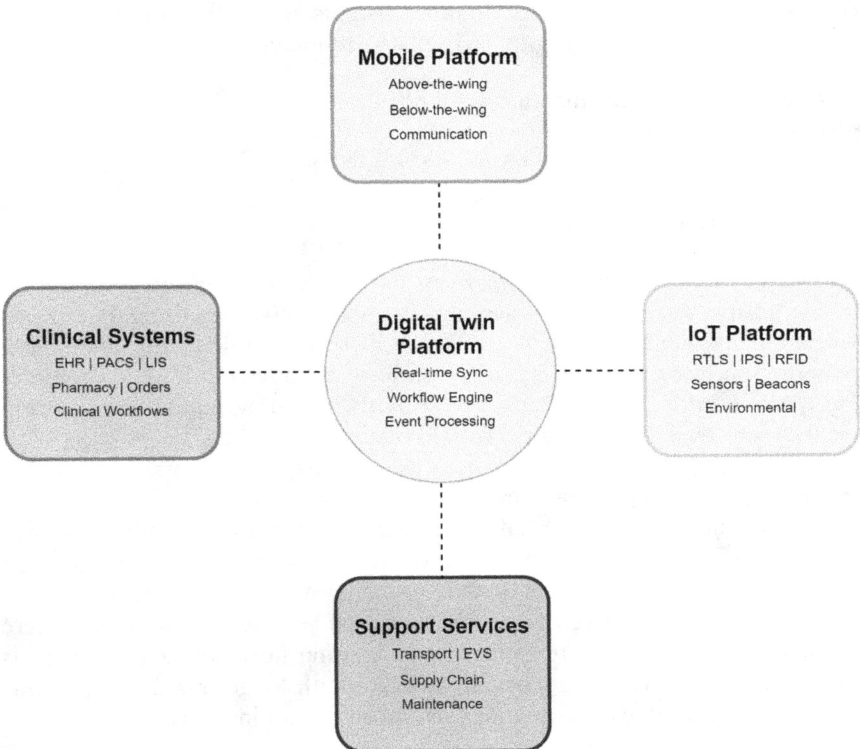

Figure 10.3 Care traffic control and the operational digital twin.

aviation systems must coordinate boarding gates, ground control, terminal operations, and support services, healthcare requires seamless integration of multiple operational domains (Figure 10.3).

This integration is achieved through five core platforms, each playing a vital role in the overall ecosystem:

- Digital Twin Platform
- Mobile Platform
- IoT Platform
- Clinical Systems Platform
- Support Services Platform

Digital twin platform

At the heart of the CTC ecosystem lies the digital twin – a virtual representation of the physical healthcare environment that serves as the central nervous system for operations. Unlike traditional monitoring systems, the digital twin goes beyond simply displaying information; it processes and contextualizes data to create actionable insights and enable automation.

Key capabilities of the digital twin platform include:

- Real-time synchronization with physical spaces
- GIS-based spatial representation
- Agent-based workflow modeling
- Event processing and analytics
- Integration broker services

The digital twin's power comes from its ability to integrate information from multiple sources and present it in a context-aware manner. For example, when a patient needs to be transported for an imaging study, the digital twin doesn't just show the patient's location – it understands and automates the entire context of the transport request, including equipment requirements, staff availability, and potential scheduling conflicts.

The digital twin is presented to the users as assistive agents. These HITL (Human in the Loop) agents interact with each other in a multi-agent framework, and they are hierarchical. The agents are hierarchical, meaning they have control relationships up and down the hierarchy. These relationships mostly mirror the organizational structure. They are also multi-agents, meaning they have cooperative relationships at each level of the hierarchy. There are workflows that operate at different planning horizons at each level as well. The higher-level agents usually operate with longer-planning horizons and the lower-level agents operate with shorter-planning horizons.

Mobile platform

Healthcare operations are inherently mobile, with staff constantly moving throughout the facility. The mobile platform recognizes this reality by providing both "above-the-wing" and "below-the-wing" capabilities – terms borrowed from aviation to distinguish between patient-facing and operational functions.

Above-the-wing features focus on enhancing the patient and visitor experience:

- Wayfinding and navigation
- Appointment management
- Service status updates
- Communication tools

Below-the-wing capabilities support staff operations:

- Workflow management
- Resource location

- Team communication
- Task automation
- Safety and security features

This dual approach ensures that both care delivery and operational efficiency are optimized. For instance, a nurse receiving a patient call can simultaneously view the patient's location, needed equipment locations, and available support staff – all through a single interface.

IoT platform

The IoT platform serves as the sensory system for the CTC ecosystem, gathering real-time data about the state of the environment, assets, and operations. This platform extends far beyond simple location tracking, creating a rich tapestry of environmental awareness.

The platform incorporates various sensing technologies:

- Real-time location services (RTLS)
- Environmental sensors
- Asset tracking systems
- Security monitoring
- Condition monitoring

Clinical systems platform

The clinical systems platform bridges the gap between care delivery and operational efficiency. While electronic health records (EHR) and other clinical systems excel at managing patient information and care documentation, they often lack real-time operational awareness. The CTC ecosystem enriches these systems with location context and real-time operational data.

This integration manifests in several critical ways:

- Patient Flow Management
  - Real-time location awareness enhances the ADT processes
  - Automated updates to patient status and location
  - Streamlined bed management and capacity planning
- Clinical Workflow Support
  - Location-aware clinical documentation
  - Equipment and supply chain integration
  - Staff coordination and task management

The real power of this integration becomes apparent in daily operations. For example, when a physician orders an imaging study, the system doesn't just schedule the procedure – it coordinates all related activities, from patient transport to equipment preparation, ensuring optimal resource utilization and minimal delays.

Support services platform

Support services form the operational backbone of healthcare delivery, yet they often operate with limited real-time information about the environment they serve. The CTC ecosystem changes this by providing contextual awareness and automated coordination capabilities.

Key areas of support service integration include:

- Environmental Services
  - Room turnover coordination
  - Real-time cleaning requests
  - Resource allocation optimization
- Materials Management
  - Just-in-time supply delivery
  - PAR level management
  - Equipment distribution
- Facilities Management
  - Preventive maintenance scheduling
  - Emergency response coordination
  - Resource utilization tracking

These services benefit from the ecosystem's ability to provide real-time context. For instance, environmental services staff receive automatic notifications when rooms become available for cleaning, complete with information about specific cleaning requirements and priority levels.

Communications layer

The ecosystem's effectiveness depends heavily on its ability to facilitate both synchronous and asynchronous communication among all participants. This dual-mode communication approach ensures that information flows efficiently while maintaining operational flexibility.

Synchronous Communications:

- Voice communications for immediate coordination
- Real-time alerts and notifications
- Emergency response coordination

Asynchronous Communications:

- Task assignments and updates
- Status changes and notifications
- Documentation and reporting

The communication layer adapts to user needs and operational requirements, ensuring that critical information reaches the right people at the right time, in the most appropriate format.

Integration and orchestration

The true value of the CTC ecosystem emerges through the orchestration of these platforms working in concert. This orchestration enables:

- Automated workflow coordination
- Resource optimization
- Predictive operations management
- Real-time problem resolution
- Continuous process improvement

For example, when a patient is scheduled for discharge, the ecosystem coordinates multiple activities simultaneously:

- Notifies transport services
- Alerts environmental services for room cleaning
- Updates bed management systems
- Coordinates medication delivery
- Triggers support service workflows

This level of coordination would be impossible with traditional point solutions or manual processes.

THE CONTROL LOOP

Care traffic control is, fundamentally, a control system. There are two main types of control systems: open-loop and closed-loop feedback systems. While automated control systems require closed feedback loops, both types play important roles in operational environments.

Open vs. closed-loop systems

In an open-loop system, there is no automatic feedback mechanism to correct deviations from desired outcomes. These systems rely on human observation and intervention to make corrections. While open-loop systems are common, the measurements and corrections typically occur at a higher level in the organization and over longer-planning horizons. This restricts the speed and effectiveness of corrective actions.

Closed-loop systems, by contrast, incorporate automatic feedback mechanisms that enable rapid detection and correction of deviations. The system continuously monitors outcomes against desired states and automatically implements corrective actions when needed. This enables much faster response times and more precise control.

Workflow analysis and control loops

When analyzing a workflow for potential automation, it's critical to:

1. Ensure all elements necessary for desired outcomes are included
2. Identify existing feedback loops that maintain system stability
3. Evaluate the value proposition for adding new control loops

By decomposing the workflow into three key components – people, property, and places – we can thoroughly map the control environment (Figure 10.4). This decomposition helps reveal opportunities for implementing effective control loops:

- **People:** Includes employees, visitors, and patients who participate in or are affected by the workflow
- **Property:** Encompasses equipment, tools, supplies and other physical resources required
- **Places:** Involves the physical spaces and geography where the work occurs

The level of closed-loop control implemented should align with the value it provides. Some workflows may operate adequately with open-loop control and periodic human oversight. Others may require tight closed-loop control to achieve desired outcomes. The key is evaluating each situation to determine the appropriate control architecture.

Building control loops

When implementing new control loops, consider starting with:

1. Clear definition of desired outcomes and acceptable tolerances
2. Identification of key variables that need to be monitored
3. Selection of appropriate sensors and measurement approaches
4. Design of control algorithms and corrective actions
5. Implementation of automated response mechanisms
6. Verification of control loop effectiveness

By taking a systematic approach to control loop implementation, organizations can gradually enhance their operational control capabilities while maintaining focus on value creation.

People

People are involved in the workflow in some way. They could be performing the work, or they could be receiving the services. In healthcare, there

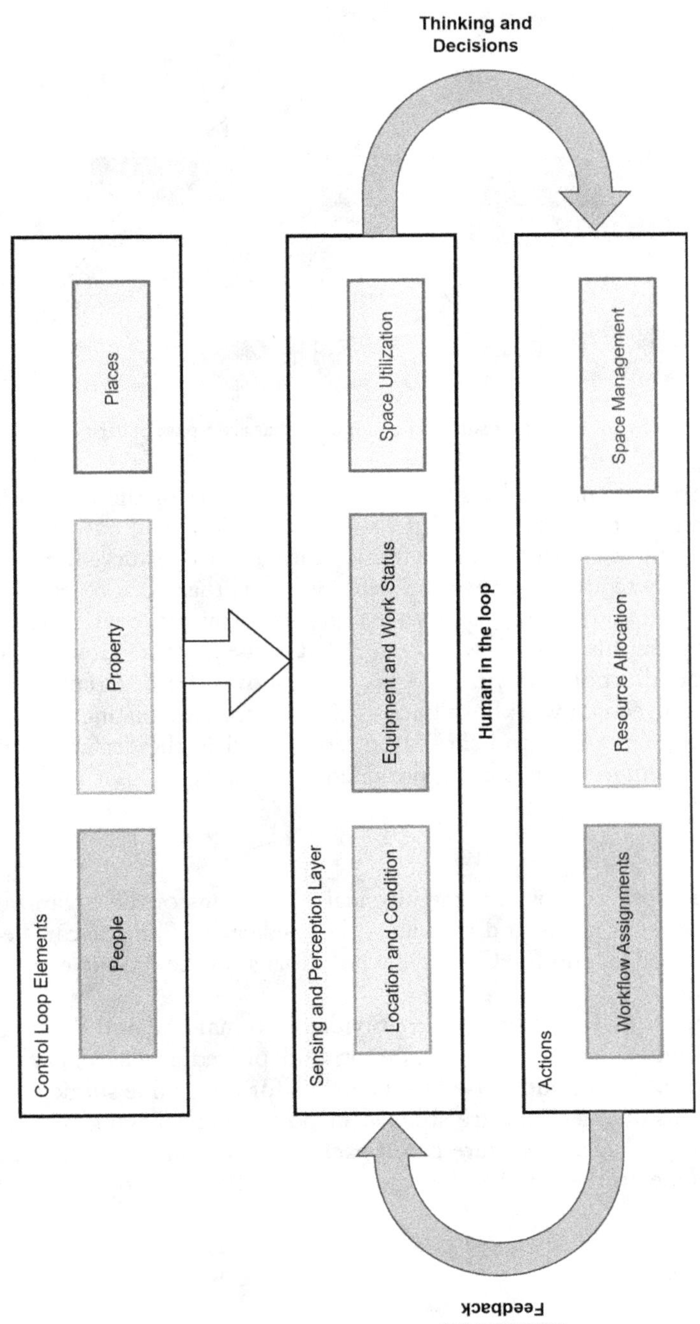

Figure 10.4 Diagram that shows control loops.

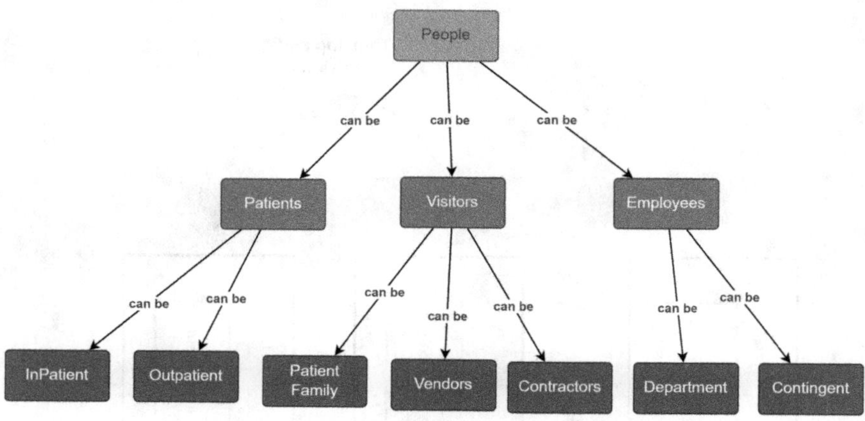

Figure 10.5 Generalization that shows the personas that are a part of care traffic control.

are workers, patients, and visitors that are all a part of the environment. Understanding the personas and the work being done can ensure that the design is done with all the contextual information considered. For some workflows, there are the above-the-wing personas that need to be listed as well as the below-the-wing personas that are performing the services. Listing the personas in this way allows a design that will ensure we close the loop.

The generalization shown in Figure 10.5 shows the different personas that are involved in a workflow. Each of the personas are distinctly different actors in the workflow and should be represented in the design to ensure that the maximum value is being provided.

Property

Property, for our purposes, is the physical possessions of the organization, like medical equipment and supplies. The medical equipment can be stationary or mobile, and for CTC, we would focus on the mobile equipment (Figure 10.6).

The supplies and consumables are divided into material and the material is divided into amount-based packaging and procedure-based packaging (Figure 10.7). The amount-based packaging is for things like surgical gloves or other consumables that are stocked in boxes or packaging with many items in the package. Procedure-based packaging is connected to a patient's case which means they are handled and stocked differently from other types of supplies.

Places

The geographic spaces that are a part of the workflow are important to understand. It is not just the GIS representation of the building that needs

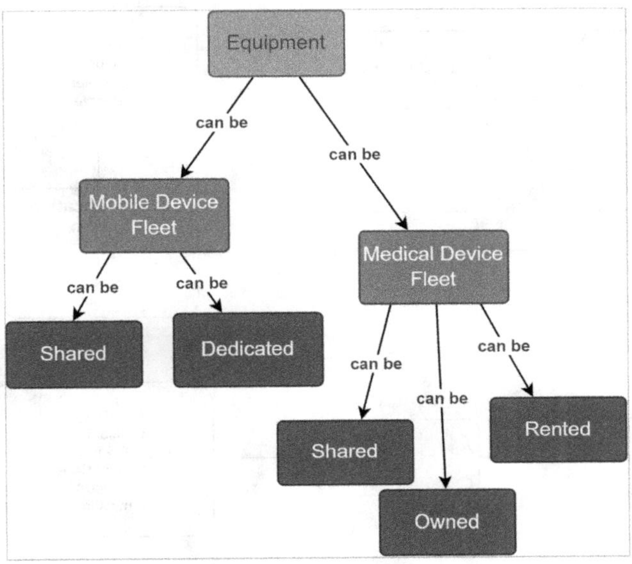

Figure 10.6 Generalization that shows the equipment.

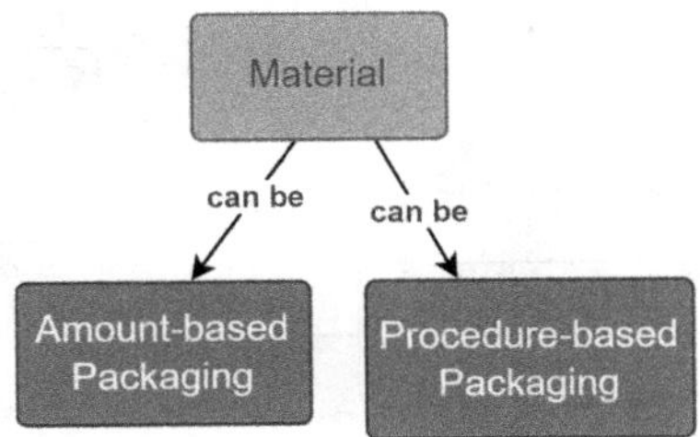

Figure 10.7 Generalization the show material.

to be understood, and it is the organizational hierarchical components, as well. The venue, floors, departments, and rooms are all important to understand. Knowing when a courier is done with a department or a floor is helpful. Also, in the process of locating places, much like we do outdoors, it is important to have a hierarchy in the address. The floor changes are also important to understand because vertical transversals have their own complexity with elevators and stairs.

The origins and destinations that are a part of the mobile workflows are necessary for assigning work. They are also required for arrivals and departures. We have talked about geofences, routing, and tracing, which have value in automation (Figure 10.8).

Management and utilization of places is a critical component of the digital twin and ties back to the events the feed into the occupancy of the room.

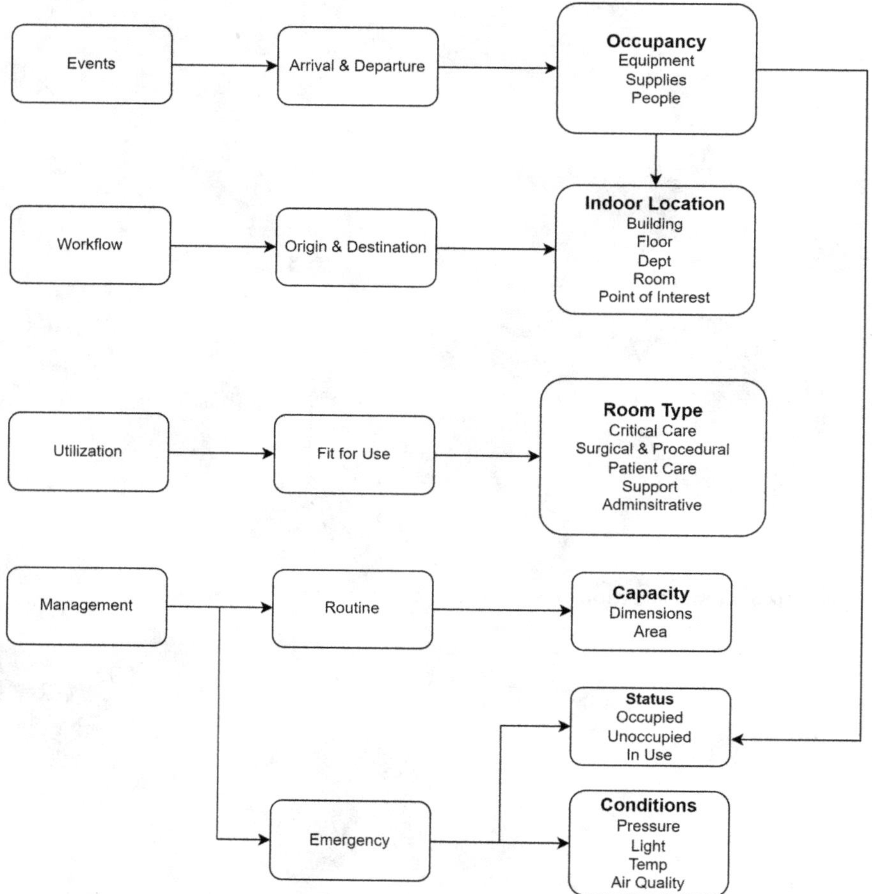

Figure 10.8 Events, workflow, utilization and management of places.

THE EDENVALE JOURNEY – CARE TRAFFIC CONTROL

Suresh, Johnathon, and Gail showed the Hospital Executive Committee the data the LOS project collected. They showed how data identified where the bottlenecks were. Then they showed the methodology, which used the care traffic control sensing to evaluate operational flow at a high level first and then drill down when the data revealed places where they should focus.

In the meeting, Suresh showed the specific instance of patient transport. Everyone knew there was much more to LOS than just patient transport, but the LBS committee agreed that the path to care traffic control would go through support services. They would ease into the clinical workflows by starting with the services that support patient care and then direct patient care. He explained that it was a change management strategy they felt would work best.

They presented data that showed the patient transport dwell at the pickup locations in the nursing units. Gail said the nurses would start something after they placed the transport order and make the transporter wait if they were not done. Because they could get a good ETA, the nurses were trying to be efficient with their own time not thinking about the impact of transport. Transport is a shared resource, and delays affect everyone who uses the service.

Gail said the data allowed her to talk to the nurses about a new way of reducing the delays at these transitions. With the patient transport project operational, the nurses were participating in the new workflow with the badge scans. Just like the PAR Stocking project, the data helped change behaviors. The results, after only two months, showed the time from the order to arrival went from 15 to 7 minutes. Suresh showed that the time for patient transport jobs had improved from 22 to 15 minutes and the number of postponements and cancels had been dramatically reduced.

They were not in the meeting to represent the LOS project, but it was obvious everyone saw the correlation. The LOS project was on the radar of the executive team, and they had seen the improvement numbers. Patient transport and the CTC methodology were more about seeing how the improvements were being made. They saw this as a repeatable cycle that they should invest in. The executive committee approved the next phase of the project and wanted to hear more about the technology and change management in the next meeting. They were interested in the AI strategy, and they heard Suresh use the word "pioneering" when he mentioned agents. They said they could discuss the financials and the timeline then.

After the executive committee meeting the three of them gathered in Johnathon's office and the discussion seemed to focus on the comment about "pioneering." They all knew that Edenvale had a reputation for pioneering new and promising concepts, so it wasn't taken negatively, but they knew they had been successful with being a pioneer by managing risk. Suresh said, "We have the methodology, we have the toll gates, and we have "earn the right." I think if we emphasize those three things we are in good shape."

Johnathon said,

> We are two years into this. In this next meeting we are presenting the entire Care Traffic Control 5-year plan. It includes the command center, the technical team, the operational changes, the methodology, the technology and a ton of assumptions. Assumptions come with any long-term plan, but assumptions are where you get the most questions so lets be ready for those questions.

The team pitched the 5-year plan, and it was like they thought. The questions came with the things they had to assume. The biggest assumption was the pace of the technology improvements. Since the previous Exec Committee meeting, Edenvale's work with the digital twin got the attention of one of their core technology partners. Big-tech company had been working on some technology that they thought would be a great fit so they decided to move forward with a joint venture (JV) to build it at Edenvale. Big-tech company wanted to make it a case study for their operational digital twin product. It had been done in other industries and they knew it had a good chance of success in healthcare. The biggest reason they were confident was because of two things: composability and agentic design. These concepts were what was being pioneered even more than the solutions that come from them.

Sharing some of the technical risks with Big-tech company was a big positive, and the committee had questions about both the composability and when they heard agentic design, they thought agents, and they were savvy enough to have heard of AI agents. They were keeping a close look at the AI strategy not only at Edenvale but in healthcare overall.

Care traffic control had become a big initiative, and Johnathon had become the champion because its size needed someone from the c-suite. Johnathon explained that composability meant they could create reusable modules that would operate autonomously. Roni asked about what autonomy meant specifically. Johnathon explained that autonomy only meant that the modules had a certain level of automation. Composability is not a black-and-white thing, and there is a gradient in the amount of modularity and automation that would evolve.

That is exactly why composability is paired with agentic design. Agentic design is not to be confused with AI agents. AI agents can be an output of agentic design, but agentic design allows us to design our workflows as agents without AI to get started, and that enables the amount of automation or AI to evolve over time. That means the Edenvale employees who are impacted by these changes can adapt because the technology can adapt. Roni said, "human in the loop." Johnathon said, "exactly." Roni said, "We are calling these agents our 'superpowers' and that appears to be getting people to keep an open mind about the changes. From some of what I am seeing, that isn't over selling it."

It had become clear that Edenvale had strong executive support for their care traffic control program. Investments were being made in the digital twin, the program, and there was a lot of talk about a command center. The workflow automation was doing a good job, but delays would still show up when anomalies would occur. The command center would help address these issues in a timely manner.

Agents

It had been a year into the program; they were in the early-middle stages of their CTC journey, and all five parts of the CTC ecosystem were involved. They were just getting started with agents, so the agents started at the department leadership level. Edenvale's digital twin uses GIS to spatially represent the building and its contents. The location of people and property can be displayed on beautiful digital maps.

The integration layer was connected to some of the clinical systems and some of the support services systems. These systems were sending job information to the digital twin. This was matched to the location information that is streaming in both the IPS and the RTLS. This allowed the jobs to be shown maps where the delays were easy to see.

It is still early, so the strategy is to provide AI agents at the department level that are used to monitor the workflow. This is done at a longer-planning horizon to prepare for further automation closer to the operations of individual workflows. The departmental agents use the IPS and RTLS for their perception, condition/action for decisions, and humans for the workflow actions (i.e., there are no robots yet).

In the departments, the care traffic control agents are used by dispatchers and managers. This strategy allows the CTC system to be implemented incrementally and keeps the focus on automation. By removing effort from their workflows, the workers can focus on their jobs and agents can measure workflows, not people.

The iPhones are being used by many of the mobile workflows, but the iPhones are used for voice communications for only the workflows that need synchronous communications. Johnathon is looking at private 5G as the fleet starts to grow so everyone can have voice and data while in the building.

The location streaming from the iPhones is being done for patient transport, food services, inpatient pharmacy and supply chain. There is some workflow automation for patient transport and inpatient pharmacy. Nurses are using the RTLS for an employee use case and the location of patients. Nurses don't have iPhones yet.

Imani showed Gail a demo of the nursing agent they were testing. Imani mirrored the iPhone on the monitor in the conference room and said, "Here is an MRN for a patient in 6 West." Imani had heard the story of the smoking patient, so she picked 6 West for all of her nursing demos. She said,

> Here in 'History' I can see the exact time meals showed up, any transports for this patient and when the medications arrived from the pharmacy. Here in 'Schedule', the patient has a pending transport for 3pm and this

phone will get an alert when the transport is on its way, and it will show up like an Uber on the app. Also in alerts, it looks like there are meds for this patient in the medications alcove. The app has things like equipment and patient location, and it works with the nurse call system so that every time the nurse enters the room the agent can register and display it back. This agent was designed by Denise and several other nurses.

Gail said,

That is great and even more functionality than I thought we would get on the first nursing agent. I am working on getting the entire nursing staff their iPhones. Denise said she tested the Fleet Management system, and it worked well. Let's continue testing it and roll it out when the phones come in.

Gail said, "You had a name for the phones but I forgot what it was." Imani said, "Yes, they are going to be called CarePro's."

PLAYBOOK FOR A CARE TRAFFIC CONTROL ECOSYSTEM

The operational digital twin uses events and other context from many "systems of record" to complement its IoT and sensing capabilities. The workflows involve actors who need real-time information that might not be available digitally so communications like voice and text are part of the ecosystem. This part of the playbook looks outside the digital twin to complete the ecosystem.

Improvers

Improvers should find these systems of record and ensure that they understand the needs of the agents so that they can enumerate the events and data that will make the agents successful.

1. Ecosystem Assessment
    - Map current system interconnections
    - Identify integration gaps and opportunities
    - Document data flows between systems
    - Evaluate communication patterns
2. Platform Integration
    - Identify core systems requiring integration
    - Document API requirements and capabilities
    - Map data exchange requirements
    - Create integration test plans

3. Implementation Strategy
    - Build ecosystem components incrementally
    - Start with high-value integrations
    - Create validation processes
    - Establish monitoring systems
4. Performance Optimization
    - Define ecosystem performance metrics
    - Monitor system interactions
    - Identify bottlenecks and constraints
    - Implement improvement cycles

Leaders

Leaders can drive the integration strategy toward kind of interoperability for a care traffic control ecosystem. Securely connecting these domains to the digital twin will fuel the automation strategy.

1. Strategic Planning
    - Develop comprehensive ecosystem vision
    - Set integration priorities
    - Establish governance frameworks
    - Create investment roadmap
2. Partnership Development
    - Identify key technology partners
    - Build vendor relationships
    - Create collaboration frameworks
    - Establish service level agreements
3. Risk Management
    - Assess ecosystem vulnerabilities
    - Create redundancy plans
    - Develop contingency strategies
    - Monitor system dependencies
4. Resource Allocation
    - Plan for infrastructure needs
    - Budget for ongoing maintenance
    - Allocate integration resources
    - Support training initiatives

Creators

Creators who build these connectors will see their systems occupy a higher place in the digital structure of the organization. Integrations that supply context to the kind of intelligence that the digital twin provides will become core systems for automation.

1. Integration Development
   - Build standard interfaces
   - Support common protocols
   - Create flexible APIs
   - Enable secure data exchange
2. Ecosystem Support
   - Provide integration documentation
   - Offer technical assistance
   - Support troubleshooting
   - Maintain update processes
3. Innovation Focus
   - Develop new capabilities
   - Enhance existing features
   - Support emerging standards
   - Enable future expansion

Chapter 11

Agents: Perception and observability

Paul E. Zieske

John Locke (1632–1704): "Nothing is in the understanding, which was not first in the senses."

The care traffic control ecosystem shows the digital twin in the center, with the contributing platforms forming the periphery. The digital twin's rational agents are executing and optimizing the operations for the organization. In these next three chapters, we are going to look at the agents and what is required to make them successful. Their success is facilitated by the performance measures that are part of the PEAS structure. The PEAS structure is for agents that are task-oriented.

In this chapter, we will use our knowledge of rational agents to describe the agent down to the specific percepts necessary for the success of the agent. We will create the agent to be a representation of the workflow that it is modeling. To do that, we cannot ignore the other parts of the agent's structure because everything needs to work together to get the outcomes we want from the agent.

Strong levels of perception reduce the uncertainty in the system which, in turn, allows AI to work in shorter planning horizons. This has many benefits in a hierarchical MAS (Multi-Agent System). The reduction in think-time limits the amount of time for processing by an AI but providing the AI with a more deterministic environment, coupled with strong perception, allows greater speed of processing. The ability to process the sensor data quickly trends toward continuous intelligence.

PERCEPTION AND OBSERVABILITY

In Chapter 7, we said the rational agents go through cycles of perceive→think→act. This comes from robotics and AI. Because artificial intelligence is an artificial representation of human intelligence, it is modeling the way that humans interact with their environment.

During the perception phase the agent is gathering stimuli from sensors. The goal of this phase is to get an accurate representation of the state of the environment. Just like our senses, the stimuli need to be processed into

DOI: 10.1201/9781003625483-13

meaningful information in the body of the agent. In the human brain that processing is done against sensory memory that adds meaning to what is coming in through the senses. The agent does the same thing to process the raw sensor data along with context and memory into percepts.

The digital twin has GIS maps that provide a virtual world for the agents. The quality of the maps and sensing creates the observability that we want to achieve in the environment. The agent uses those maps and the sensors to process the stimuli into percepts. The observability will decrease the uncertainty which will make the application of AI much easier.

In this chapter, we want to understand the process to compile the specific sensor requirements for a workflow and the agent representing that workflow. We will use the states and the state space to look for blind spots where perception is lacking. From there, the value of filling the blind spots can be assessed.

PEAS IN THE PERCEIVE PHASE

The PEAS structure for rational agents, as described in Chapter 7, is used in a task environment. We saw the easiest environment to automate is a fully observable and deterministic environment. We are using the digital twin to create as much observability and certainty as possible.

When the agent runs through a cycle of perceive think act, it starts with sensors receiving stimuli that are processed into percepts. Those percepts will be used in the "think" phase to decide what actions are necessary. The workflow determines what the agent does with these changes in state (Figure 11.1).

The percepts most relevant to the mobile workflows are divided into two categories. First, *location percepts* allow the rational agent to manage everything related to location and motion in the workflow. They provide the geospatial feedback that the agent needs to optimize the mobile components of the workflow. Second, the *condition percepts* are how the agent perceives the condition of places in the environment.

Location percepts

For automating mobile workflows, we have four types of location percepts. Position, proximity, presence, and possession are all types of percepts that come from location sensors. First introduced in Chapter 2, we are calling these the 4Ps of location. As a reminder, position is a location in some coordinate system. Proximity is the distance and maybe the direction from a source to a target. Presence indicates an entity is within some space. Possession is proximity used to establish a custodial relationship with an object. We can automate any workflow with these four percepts.

The sensing stimuli that can yield these percepts can come from many sources. When we are using conventional location-based services, these percepts are usually produced by the system that is managing the sensors.

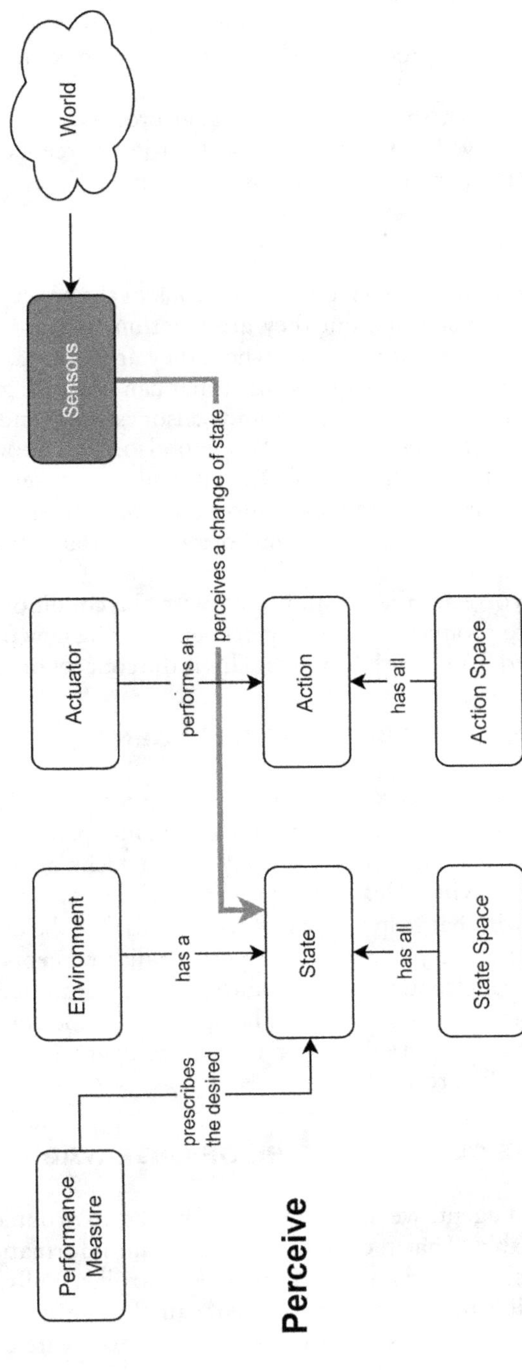

Figure 11.1 Perceive phase and PEAS diagram.

That could be an RTLS, RFID, IPS, GPS, cameras, or another LBS that is not mentioned. These systems usually offer some SaaS-based location engine. This will add additional processing to these data and make them ready for further automation.

In the "think" phase, these percepts can be processed into events like arrival, departure, dwell, and delay. These location percepts can also be correlated with other percepts to many other events.

Condition percepts

We also have sensors that perceive the conditions in the space they occupy. They are not location sensors, but they are location-based services. These sensors are only interesting if we know where they are located. As an example, in Chapter 6, we talked about a system that can perceive gunshots and even aggressive voices. In this case, a sound sensor is used, and the percept is the gunshot or the aggressive voice. You can also have doors, elevators, light, pressure, fire, smoke, humidity, CO_2, and temperature sensors that can provide stimuli that can be processed into percepts. Cameras allow computer vision to process visual stimuli into percepts so that it can recognize objects in these spaces.

Perception can correlate the location data with the condition data in the body of the agent to produce even more percepts. Creating new percepts from the stimuli absorbed from multiple inputs. This is the concept of **sensor fusion.**

PERCEPTION AND THE BODY OF THE AGENT

Perception is necessary before the agent can think or act. The sensors are only one of the ingredients that are necessary to yield quality perception. Context from the CTC ecosystem can help the body of the agent understand more about what it is perceiving. This is information from systems that are external to the digital twin that help it in its effort to virtualize the environment.

Giving the agent more percepts and higher quality percepts is going to ensure the state is represented more accurately. An accurate representation of the state will lead to quality decisions being made by the controller. That is why evaluating the observability of the environment is critical to the design of the agent (Figure 11.2).

INVENTORY THE CURRENT LEVEL OF OBSERVABILITY

When we create an agent, we are trying to make the environment for that agent fully observable. That means that all the state information that the agent needs for its success is available to the controller. Fully observable doesn't mean that it is necessary that the agent can observe everything in the environment. The emphasis is on what is necessary to create certainty for what the agent is trying to accomplish.

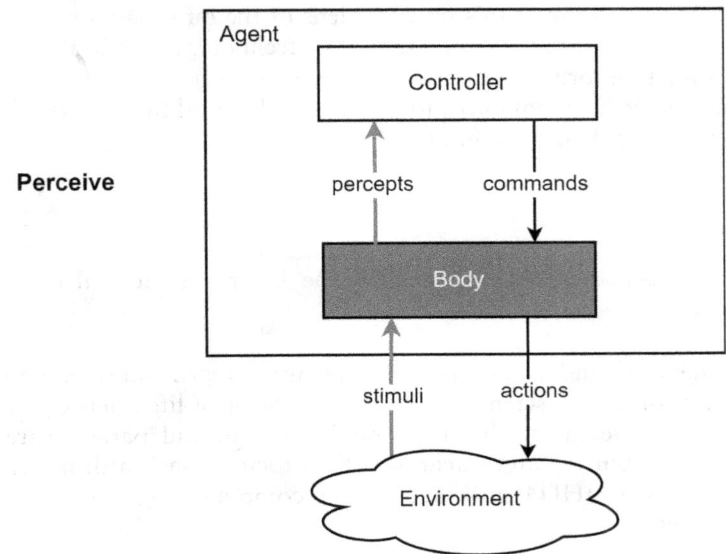

Figure 11.2 Perceive phase and agent processing.

The percepts are derived from the sensory input and for care traffic control that could mean the sensors that are installed in a hospital. Even the average hospital has many more of these sensors than most people know. They are hiding various systems that have a single use case. It is important to have these sensors accounted for and having them on a map helps the staff, who are responsible for location services, ensure they can visualize the coverage. We said the digital twin is not a map, but a map is an important part of the digital twin. Knowing where they are, what they are and how they can be accessed is a great first step.

MODEL THE AGENTS – PERCEPTION

The process of modeling the workflow gets down to the specific sensors and percepts that are necessary for the success of the agent. This means we need to have access to the best practices when it comes to the processes that are embedded in the workflows. Even with the best technology, the most important part of automation and improvement is domain knowledge. Bill Gates famously said,

> The first rule of any technology used in a business is that automation applied to an efficient operation will magnify the efficiency. The second is that automation applied to an inefficient operation will magnify the inefficiency.

We are going to look at this from the lens of the informaticist. The health informaticist thrives at the intersection of technology and healthcare process. Using an informatics approach we will deconstruct the workflows, so we can reconstruct them into a format that will reveal the opportunities for improvement and automation.

Informatics

What is Informatics? As described by the American Medical Informatics Association,

> Biomedical and health informatics applies principles of computer and information science to the advancement of life sciences research, health professions education, public health, and patient care. This multidisciplinary and integrative field focuses on health information technologies (HIT), and involves the computer, cognitive, and social sciences.

These three characteristics of informatics make it the perfect fit for the development of agents.

Agentic process design

The health informaticist would look at agents from the perspective of the people and services that are using technology. Using the agent constructs for process design ensures that there is a cohesive framework established for HITL and creates a modularity that allows human perception, thinking, or actions to be represented in the process and eventually replaced with machine perception, think, and actions. This also creates transparency around design and the roles of humans and machines. This transparency can also be used to show where the human is operating on a "higher plane" when assisted by the agent.

Automation is the process of removing human effort from the workflow without sacrificing quality. Once the workflow is understood, the improvement can be made iteratively to ensure that the improvements are delivering accretive value. Designing processes as agents sets up a holistic approach to improvement where the tech and people are viewed as components that are teamed up to create outcomes.

Later we will look at how we can use the agentic design in simulations that can be used to observe the possible outcomes from the automation. This simulation modeling uses time series data to add dynamic animation to the model. The sensors that are part of the automation provide events that can be simulated to show how the agent should behave in the real world.

THE EDENVALE JOURNEY – TRAINING THE TEAM

As a part of the joint venture, Big-tech company was training both the PI team and the location services engineers on how to build agents. Gwen Franks was the PI engineer and Sam Strickland was a LBS architect that was scheduled for the training. These agents would eventually become much more composable but to get started they needed to get down to a low level in the workflow. There was no coding needed but the agentic design would be used heavily. Big-tech company had plans to reuse the agents that were created at Edenvale so that was all a part of the JV.

Kirk Simon was the architect assigned to Edenvale by Big-tech. He was going to be the trainer. To do the training, Kirk used a rather simple feature of the agent called nurse call cancel. He used it to illustrate the process and how it emphasized only adding automation where there was demonstrated value. This was a hands-on exercise and they even had a room they would use for the training.

The agent for training was for the Labor and Delivery (L&D) department, and this agent was called the "Mother Ship." It was going to have several features, but the training was focused only on the call cancel system and how that feeds the greater workflow. It was going to be integrated with their nurse call system, and luckily, Kirk had worked with that system before, so he knew how it worked.

The "call cancel" is a workflow automation feature that removes the manual effort of pushing a button to cancel the call from the patient. At Edenvale the nurse call system was managed by the Clinical Engineering Department. They were working with nursing and the system's vendor to get a design created that would integrate the cancel system with the rest of the nursing agent.

Current state

Room A-111 was the room that was selected for the training.

Observability assessment

Before they got started with the design of this component, they needed to know the current level of observability in the environment they were working with. Below is a portion of the table that was created for the inventory of sensors and percepts for their Labor and Delivery department.

Table 11.1 shows that the RTLS is able to show the location of medical equipment and patients in Patient Rooms A-111 and A-112, the utility closets used in the PAR stocking project, and the breakroom. However likely or unlikely it might be for either patients or equipment to be in these locations, it is, nonetheless, possible for the RTLS to find them there. There are some unused percepts in the two patient rooms.

Table 11.1 Level of RTLS Observability

Floor	*Dept*	*Room*	*Room type*	*Percepts*	*Sensors*	*Features*	*Agents*
First	L&D	A4	Soiled Utility	• Position of Medical Equipment • Position of the Patient • IPS Position of Mobile	RTLS IPS	PAR Stocking	Clinical Engineering CSPD Capacity Mgmt
First	L&D	A-102	Clean Utility Closet	• Position of Medical Equipment • Position of the Patient • IPS Position of Mobile	RTLS IPS	PAR Stocking	Clinical Engineering CSPD Capacity Mgmt
First	L&D	A-151	Break Rm	• Position of Medical Equipment • Position of the Patient • IPS Position of Mobile	RTLS IPS	PAR Stocking Patient Location	Clinical Engineering CSPD Capacity Mgmt
First	L&D	A-111	Patient Rm	• Position of Medical Equipment • Position of the Patient • IPS Position of Mobile	RTLS IPS	PAR Stocking Patient Location	Clinical Engineering CSPD Capacity Mgmt
First	L&D	A-112	Patient Rm	• Position of Medical Equipment • Position of the Patient • IPS Position of Mobile	RTLS IPS	PAR Stocking Patient Location	Clinical Engineering CSPD Capacity Mgmt
First	L&D	A-111 A-112	Patient Rm	• Presence • Temp • Light	RTLS	NA	Unused

After the inventory, they moved on to preparing the functional description, problem statement, and a description of the automation and added it to the design.

Function of the nurse call system

Patient Alerts – The call is initiated with a handheld device, by the patient (Mom).

Staff Communications – The agent already allows nurses and staff to communicate with each other as a part of the response to a call.

Emergency Signal – The systems can prioritize some calls for emergencies

Location Tracking – RTLS is not being to locate people as a part of a call

Call Cancel – Presently the call needs to be canceled manually by a nurse after they enter the room. This is the target of this design.

The business problem

Problem Statement: Patients sometimes wait longer than they expect, and nurses can be delayed in answering. There can be simultaneous calls, prioritization issues, and frequent calls that all contribute to a chaotic environment. When the nurse enters the room, they are supposed to push a button to cancel the call, but often, the button is not pushed when they enter the room, and it leads to data inaccuracies that can become problematic.

Proposed solution

Automation Description: After automation, the call is automatically canceled when the nurse enters the room. The data for the response to the call is captured so that the time that the nurse is with the patient is accurately recorded. This feature is related to rounding, but because it is in response to a call, it is listed separately. The time that the nurse leaves the patient's room is also recorded to calculate the event duration.

Benefits: Increased patient satisfaction, increased safety, accurate call data

As-Is Workflow: The existing nurse call system is in room A-111. There is no call cancel automation in place, and the nurse presses the button to cancel the call. The nurse could press the button at any time so the time that the system shows as the response to the call can vary from the time when the nurse entered the room (Figure 11.3).

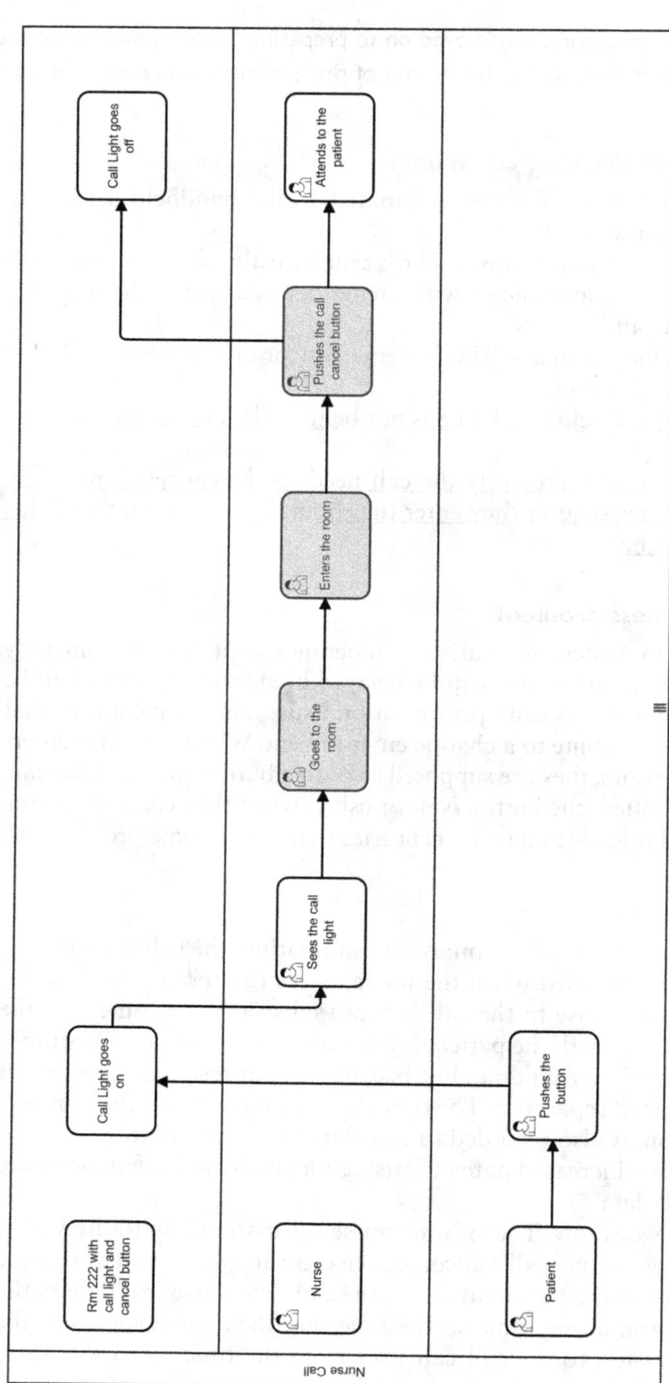

Figure 11.3 Nurse call BPMN diagram.

Agentic design – perception

Nurse call cancel percepts

The team worked together and determined that even though the IPS is quite accurate it was deemed not accurate enough for nurse call cancel. The RTLS has badges that can be worn to detect the location of the nurses. The rooms have sensors that have shown they can accurately detect the location of medical equipment, so the RTLS badges will be used for the design. The badges will be tested to ensure they can reliably create the percepts that are needed to cancel the calls. The inventory of percepts showed that there are presence, light, and temp sensors in the room that are part of the RTLS. Although there is some opportunity to use the presence sensors to add to the perception, it will be considered for future iterations.

They connected to the API for the RTLS and looked at the data to test the response to entries and exits from the room, and the response time was averaging about 15 seconds, and it was reliable and stable. It was time to move on to the next part of the agent's cycle: thinking and decisions.

PLAYBOOK FOR AGENTS: PERCEPTION AND OBSERVABILITY

We should be able to understand what percepts are available in the systems that exist within the building that we are twinning.

At this stage, it is important to have a good understanding of the workflows that can benefit from automation and situational awareness. Creating a list of departments and mapping out each of their workflows that involve motion would go a long way toward preparing for future opportunities. It starts with listing the environment data according to people, property and places, then using PEAS to map it to the process and finally using the 4Ps to get down to the requirements for sensory input.

Improvers

Improvers should understand the level of perception that is available to them when constructing the next generation of workflows. This goes beyond the existing sensor systems in their specific workplace, to understanding the capabilities of solutions that are in the market.

Performance improvement teams or consultants that connect the outcomes to value will be able to prepare business cases for projects to create the digital twin and its agents. This can start a virtuous cycle around the creation of agents that support care traffic control.

1. Perception Assessment
   - Create inventory of current sensing capabilities
   - Document sensing blind spots
   - Map perception needs to workflow requirements
   - Identify opportunities for sensor fusion
2. Observability Planning
   - Define required observability levels for each workflow
   - Document perception quality requirements
   - Map perception to specific outcomes
   - Create validation processes
3. Implementation Strategy
   - Prioritize high-value perception points
   - Build sensor coverage incrementally
   - Establish perception quality metrics
   - Create feedback loops for perception accuracy
4. Quality Management
   - Define perception accuracy standards
   - Establish validation processes
   - Create monitoring systems
   - Document calibration procedures

Leaders

Leaders who are looking for solutions and technologies that fit into care traffic control this is the start of that journey. Close collaboration with performance improvement teams will help itemize the needs of the specific departments.

The location services architect will be the role that is needed to connect it all together. This role will be able to execute the crawl, walk, run, and help with the organizational change that will be required.

1. Strategic Investment
   - Understand the role of perception in automation
   - Plan sensor infrastructure investment
   - Support perception capability development
   - Allocate resources for ongoing maintenance
2. Quality Assurance
   - Establish perception quality standards
   - Create validation frameworks
   - Support monitoring systems
   - Ensure regulatory compliance
3. Organizational Support
   - Build understanding of perception importance
   - Support training initiatives
   - Foster culture of perception quality
   - Enable cross-functional collaboration

4. Risk Management
   - Identify perception vulnerabilities
   - Create redundancy strategies
   - Develop backup systems
   - Monitor perception quality

Creators

Products that support the design of an operational digital twin will be of value far into the future. The interoperability around the sensor's systems that provide the perception to the digital twin will be an asset as well. Understanding how to correlate sensor data to derive more and more percepts might open new opportunities in the market.

As the customers come to understand perception they will care less about the specific sensors and more about the quality of the percepts that are being provided.

1. Solution Development
   - Create robust sensing capabilities
   - Build flexible perception systems
   - Support multiple sensing modalities
   - Enable perception fusion
2. Quality Support
   - Provide perception validation tools
   - Offer calibration support
   - Support troubleshooting
   - Maintain documentation
3. Innovation Focus
   - Develop new sensing capabilities
   - Enhance perception accuracy
   - Support emerging standards
   - Enable future expansion

Chapter 12

Agents: Thinking and decisions

Paul E. Zieske

Care traffic control is using the digital twin and its rational agents to optimize mobile workflows. The rationality of the agents dictates that they are making informed decisions to get the optimal outcomes. The importance of the CTC ecosystem is visible in this phase of the agent's operation. Gathering all the external contextual information to match the sensory information is key to the advanced automation that is possible with agent architecture. We will use the concept of context-aware computing to add structure and further processing to the vast amount of data that is being sourced.

In this phase, the agent's output is the decision for which action to take. In a complex environment, these decisions are equally complex, so simplifying the environment is important to the implementation. A big part of simplifying the environment is accomplished by making it more observable and more deterministic.

In this chapter, we are going to look at both human decision-making processes and machine decision-making. In introducing context-aware computing here, we are not negating the influence that context has on the perception phase. We emphasize that the connections to the CTC ecosystem are vital to ensure that we can virtualize the operations.

THINK AND DECIDE

After the agent has created the percepts from the sensing data, memory and context, the *think* phase will determine the state of the environment. That state will be matched against the performance measures to decide on which action to select from the action space. This is done in the controller portion of the agent.

PEAS IN THE THINK PHASE

In the think phase, the percepts have been sent to the controller and the state of the environment is computed by referencing the state space. The performance measures are compared to the state and the controller decides

DOI: 10.1201/9781003625483-14

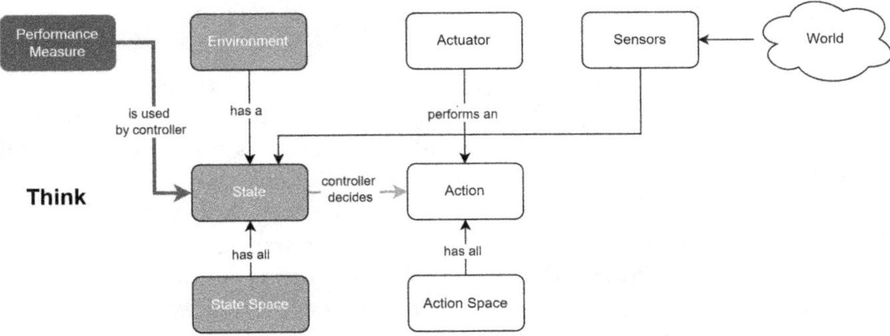

Figure 12.1 Thinking phase and PEAS diagram.

if an action is necessary. If an action is necessary, the command is sent by the controller to the body (Figure 12.1).

CONTROLLER

The controller is where a more observable and deterministic environment will have the most benefit. A more observable and certain environment will mean the controller can decide the correct action in a shorter planning horizon. This will mean the types of computation we can apply will be less complex and less based on learning. This also means they will be easier to implement because we will need less of the historical data that is required for learning (Figure 12.2).

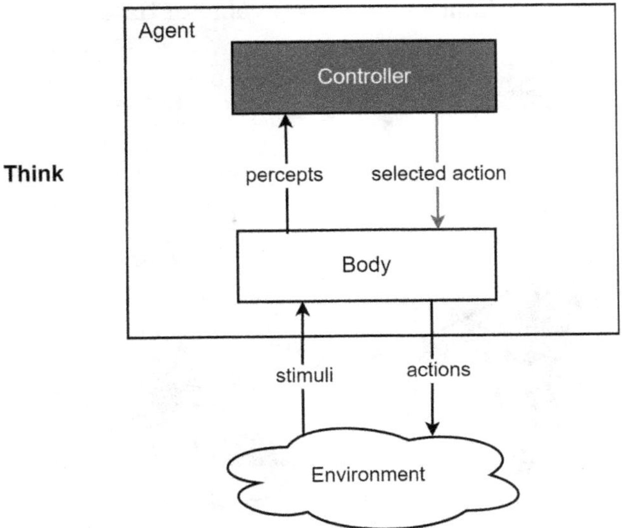

Figure 12.2 Perceive phase agent diagram.

HUMAN DECISIONS

For human decision-making, the planning horizon determines how much time there is to decide. When evaluating the workflow it is important to know how "time-critical" the decision-making process is to the success of the workflow (Figure 12.3).

The cognitive impact of time-critical decisions affects design in many ways. The user interface needs to be made for visual scanning and operating with limited info and that info needs to be actionable. The importance of each piece of contextual info needs to factor into where things are placed and how they are displayed. This is what you see when you look at a cockpit or even a control room in a nuclear power plant. The process of decision-making is different for time-critical decisions versus the reactive and historical (Figure 12.4).

Time-critical decisions can be made using a process called OODA loops: observe, orient, decide, and act. This was created by an Air Force Colonel, John Boyd, and has become a noteworthy standard for making time-critical decisions. In healthcare, there are the obvious emergent decisions, but there are many time-critical decisions that are far less emergent but add up to something important. Removing large amounts of delay can be attributed to summing many small, time-critical, decisions.

Decisions that are not time-critical can use PDCA: plan, do, check, and act. PDCA was originated by Edward Deming and adopted by lean in the continuous improvement process known as Kaizen. The most notable difference is that planning is something you don't have time to do in time-critical decisions (Figure 12.5).

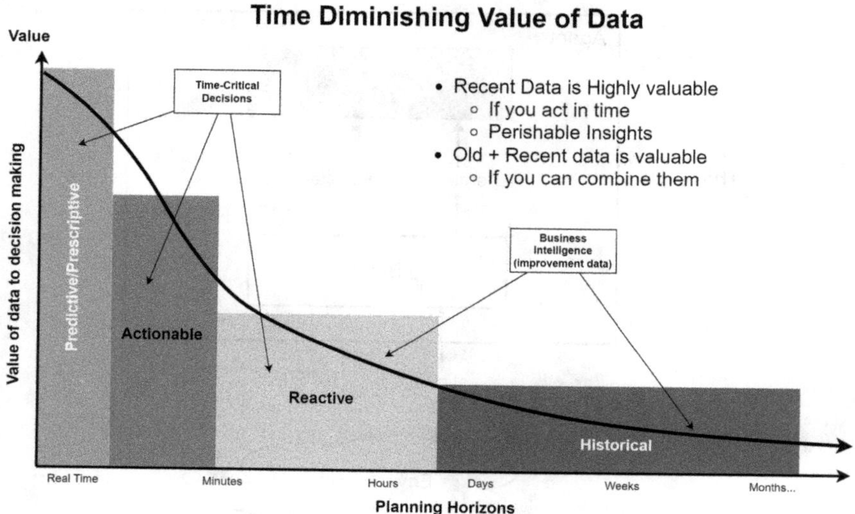

Figure 12.3 Time diminishing value of data.

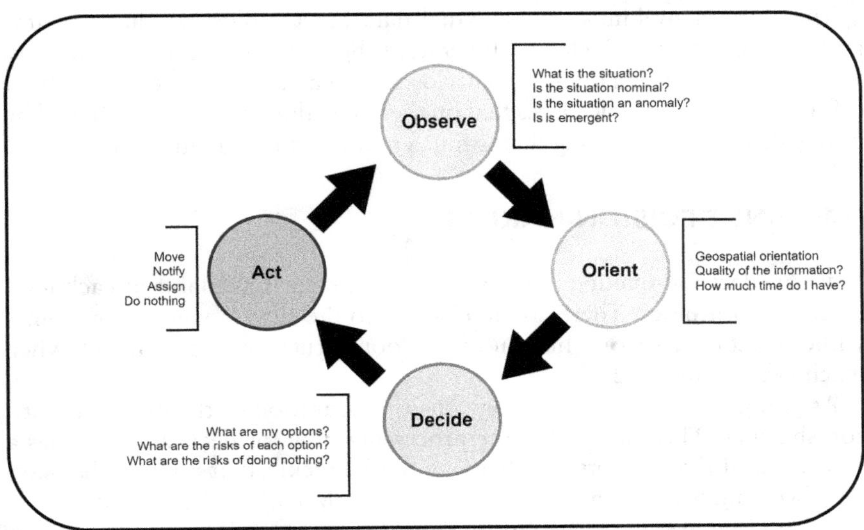

Figure 12.4 Observer, orient, decide, and act cycle.

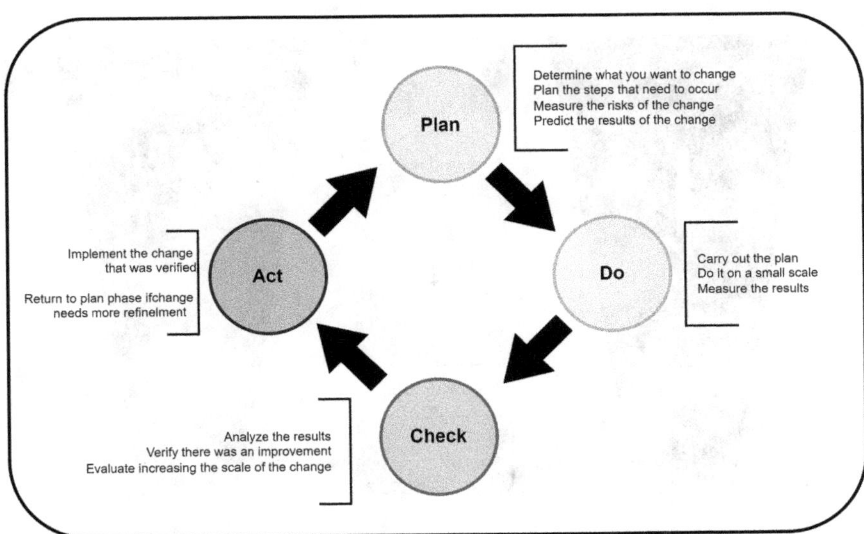

Figure 12.5 Plan, do, check, and act cycle.

In healthcare, many decisions are deferred for lack of contextual data. When you are waiting for something with no ETA you cannot replan the tasks you have in front of you, so you wait. In emergency situations, delays could have grave consequences. Situational awareness is vital in time-critical decisions and the key to situational awareness is context.

There are many kinds of contextual data but the most prevalent is time and location. Others include temperature, light, humidity, and conditions. Conditions include if a door is open, closed, or if a piece of equipment is on or off. These become puzzle pieces that on their own don't mean much, but when fit together show something that is much more meaningful and complete.

MACHINE DECISION-MAKING

Machine decision-making in the task environment is available at each level in the task ontology. There are no changes to the environment or outcomes without actions, so our human-in-the-loop structure is still intact when machines are involved.

As you go down in the ontology, the time duration of the planning horizon shortens. This means that the processing time for decisions becomes a constraint. If the percepts are changing more quickly, that impacts the planning horizon. Rules engines are extremely fast but when the environment is more random, we would like to rely on AI more. AI will be impacted more by shorter planning horizons than a rules engine, so paying close attention to the planning horizon is important (Figure 12.6).

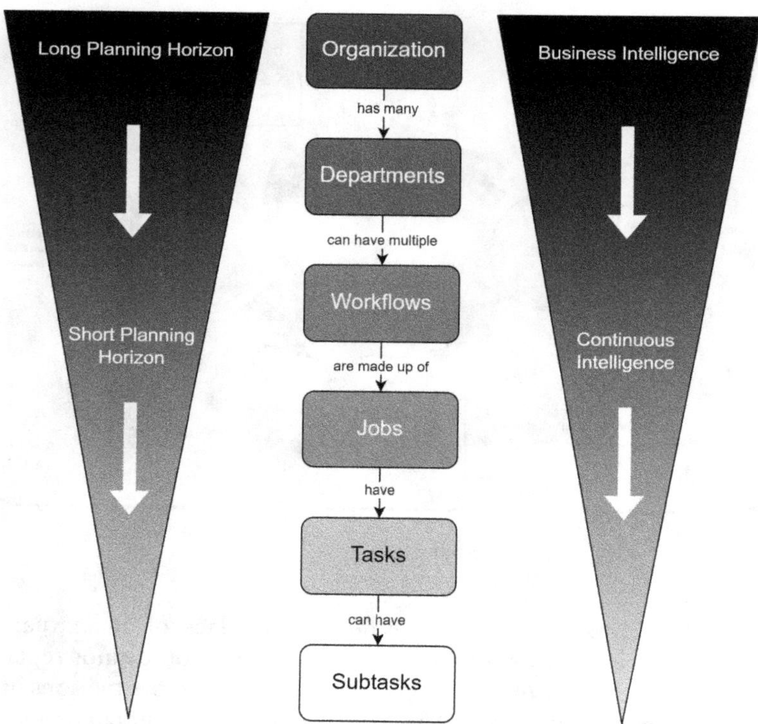

Figure 12.6 Planning horizons enhanced generalization.

Context-aware decisions

Context-aware computing takes percepts from the body of the agent and combines them with other contextual data from the care traffic control ecosystem. It will establish the state of the environment and use performance measures to decide the action to be taken. Then it runs it through a series of steps that allow those decisions to be made. These steps will consider the planning horizon we talked about in the previous chapter, and we will expand on that here.

Because this is a human-in-the-loop design the actors in the workflow will be a part of the model. The situational awareness that is necessary for humans to be a part of the thinking and decisions means that how and when the information is presented to them is critical. That means we will look at how humans make decisions as well as how machines can make decisions.

Contextual information for the rational agent

Dispatching is common for patient transport, housekeeping, facilities, security, and departments that are needed in a timely manner. But delays are found everywhere, and contextual data enables expanding the scope of dispatching services or providing the information directly to the person who needs it at the time that they need it. If an IV Pump is needed, knowing that one is in the clean utility saves time and effort. If a stat pickup for a lab sample comes in, knowing that a courier is close to the pickup location removes delay. If a wound vac has gone down the trash chute, there is only a certain amount of time before it is irrecoverable. If the temperature of the OR is high there are regulations that are in play, so it needs to be corrected immediately. Creating the capability for awareness is different from creating awareness. The system cannot ignore identifying who or what is going to act on the information.

A robust and well-architected network of distributed sensors exposes an endless array of these perishable insights, but it is easy to miss opportunities unless intentionality is applied in the design of the system. For example, the same sensor network that can sense if a nurse has responded to a call in a patient room could show if a PCA pump has been brought to the room. Additionally, that same sensor could tell if the patient has left the room to be taken to surgery.

Distributed context-aware systems

In defining the digital twin, we said to create a *virtual* representation of the physical entity. The virtualization is realized in the rational agents that are described by PEAS. The percepts that are part of the agent make the agent aware of its environment. Sensing alone is not enough, so it is necessary to process the percepts to use the awareness to make decisions. The agent decides what actions will affect the environment to get a new state that described/describes the desired outcome.

The digital twin does this using a class of computing systems called distributed context-aware systems. They are systems that are designed to gather and utilize contextual information from various sources that are distributed geographically. They gather data to understand the user's environment, preferences, and needs to provide personalized and relevant services or information.

Here context refers to any information that can be used to characterize the situation of an entity, such as a user, device, or location. It can include data such as the user's location, time of day, activity, social context, device capabilities, and preferences. By collecting and analyzing this contextual data, distributed context-aware systems can adapt their behavior and provide tailored services or responses.

The distributed aspect of these systems means that they are deployed across multiple nodes or devices that collaborate to collect, process, and share contextual information. Each node may have sensors, such as GPS, BLE receiver, accelerometer, or microphone, to gather context from its surroundings. Additionally, these nodes may communicate with each other to exchange contextual data or coordinate their actions.

The agents use the digital twin and its distributed context-aware system to make intelligent decisions. Using the distributed context-aware system to model the processing leverages all sources of real-time information, from all locations to give the agents the best chance to succeed in the planning horizon they operate in (Figure 12.7).

Context acquisition

Context Acquisition involves collecting contextual data from various sources, such as sensors, user input, or external services. Examples include GPS or IPS coordinates, temperature readings, or user preferences. This is where the percepts are presented to the controller.

Context Acquisition pulls in the raw data that is necessary for the processing being done downstream. It is important to fully understand the nature of the data and its accuracy because any mistakes made at this stage will only be exacerbated moving forward. Things like the inaccuracy and variability of location data can become amplified if applied to the wrong solution. The data doesn't have to be perfect to be useful so doing some analysis here will provide benefits later.

Example – Medication Delivery: A context-aware location delivery solution acquires the location of the courier from an Indoor Positioning System. The job information comes from a work order management system and detects arrivals, departures, and dwell from the location engine. The work order management system is part of the Clinical Platform that is a key component of the CTC ecosystem.

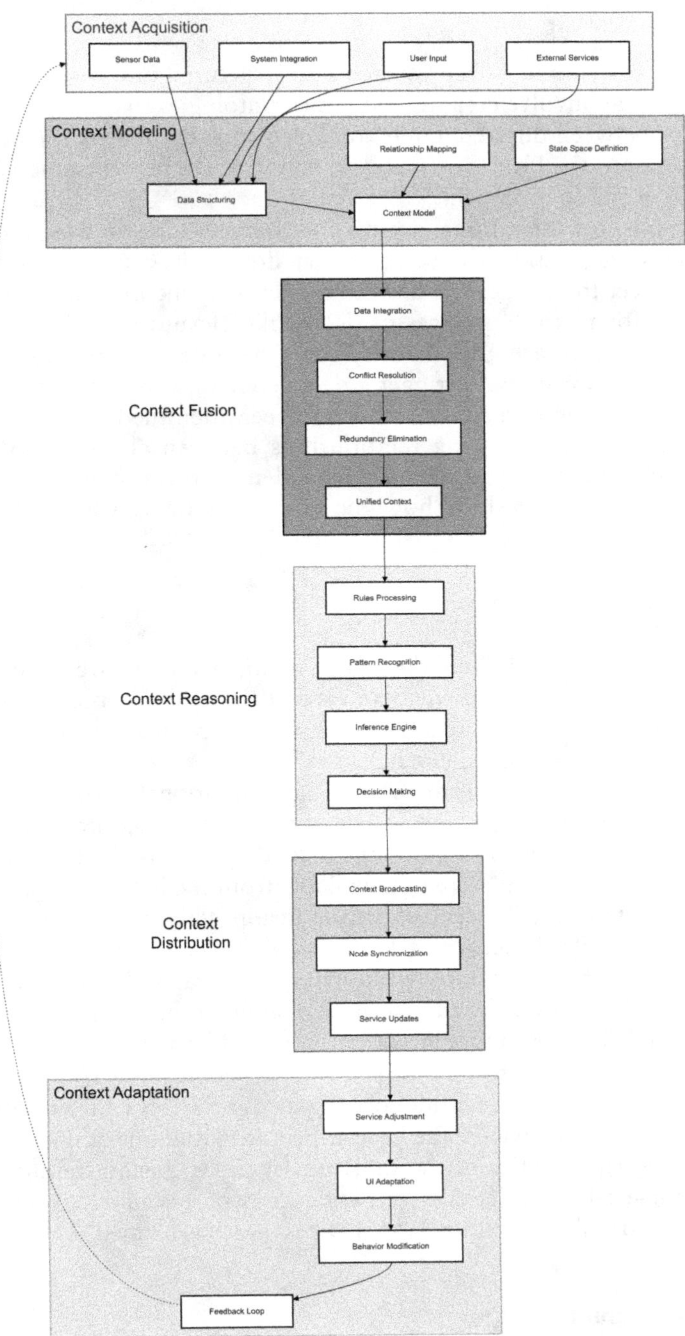

Figure 12.7 Context-aware processing diagram.

Context modeling

The collected context is represented and structured into a meaningful format. This may involve creating models or ontologies that describe the relationships between different contextual elements. By putting the process, or processes, into the PEAS structure, we can map the percepts and context to the state of the environment.

The model for the rational agent's environment is the state space.

In this stage, the data is being modeled to solve a particular problem. For instance, the model for detecting delays might include location and geofences for possible sources of delay, like elevators. In a stat delivery, one job will have a higher priority than the other. A large dwell time in front of an elevator could trigger a delay code or a reroute. At the modeling stage, the contextual data that has been identified for acquisition is shown in a model showing relationships between elements so that the effect of changes in any of the interdependent elements can be understood. Also, the model will show how the context is being used in the larger solution.

Context fusion

Different types of contextual data from multiple sources are combined and integrated to form a comprehensive view of the actor's context. This fusion process aims to eliminate redundancies, resolve conflicts, and create a unified representation of the context.

The data that comes from sensors has limitations as described by the specifications of the sensor. The other systems that are contributing data to the solution have limits as well. When these data are fused together, they can create new insights that were not available from the individual parts.

To understand the concept of sensor fusion when you use location services on a mobile device, the GPS, cellular, gyroscope, accelerometer, and magnetometer all contribute to the navigation capabilities of the device. Each individual sensor provides a piece of context, but each has limitations on its own. When fused together, a lot more can be accomplished.

In a patient room, detecting the presence of people in the room and counting the individual people while looking at door swings for entrances and exits from the room, we see the flow of people in and out of the room without needing the identity of the individual people. Fusing the information from a nurse call, food services, or patient transport would allow even more context about the exact time these services were performed.

Context reasoning

Once the context is fused, reasoning techniques are applied to extract meaningful insights or derive higher-level context from the collected data. This can involve applying rule-based systems, machine learning algorithms, or statistical analysis to make sense of the context. The fusion makes the data ready for further processing that can use descriptive, predictive, or prescriptive analytic methods.

As we recall from Chapter 11, the rational agent makes decisions that are going to get to the optimal outcome. The context reasoning step is where those decisions are made to perform an action that is going to change the state of the environment in a way to get that optimal outcome.

A rules-based system, like a condition-action sequence, can use contextual data to detect a condition and apply an action. In addition to executing a task, the action could be detecting another condition as these rules can be nested in a way to gain deeper insights. Machine learning algorithms can be applied to data to find patterns and make predictions that can be acted upon. Adding the intelligence to decide on the optimal actions enters the area of prescriptive analytics.

The type of reasoning technique that is selected for the reasoning is based on the amount of uncertainty and the amount of planning. The more random or uncertain the input, the more we will lean on AI. Additionally, where there is planning and uncertainty either a human will decide or we will need a reliable AI. When we get to AI, the AI will select the rules that need to be applied instead of trying to solve the task itself. The human-in-the-loop AI will respond to an instruction like "find the best way to get all of the specimens to the lab promptly" or "create the best staffing schedule for the team this week."

Context distribution

Contextual information is shared among the distributed nodes to enable collaboration and coordination. This allows nodes to make informed decisions or adapt their behavior based on the context collected by other nodes.

A distributed system has nodes that contribute to the overall system, making it a system of systems. These nodes form a topology that has endpoints and some of those endpoints are participating in the processing. In the case of an RTLS or PCLS, the active tags are small computers that can adjust the rate of transmissions based on whether the tags are moving. This is an example of the collaboration and coordination that is part of the distributed system.

Context-aware adaptation

Based on the analyzed context, the distributed system can dynamically adapt its services or behavior to better suit the user's needs. This enters the area of ambient intelligence. This may involve personalizing the user interface, adjusting system settings, or recommending relevant content.

Applications of distributed context-aware systems can be found in various domains, such as pervasive computing, smart buildings, healthcare, transportation, and mobile applications. These systems enable personalized experiences, efficient resource utilization, and improved decision-making by leveraging the rich contextual information available in the environment.

THE EDENVALE JOURNEY – INTRODUCING AGENTIC DESIGN

Kirk was the trainer/architect for the agentic design of agents for the Edenvale care traffic control program. He was training some Edenvale resources to use agentic design for agents that would be used in their multi-agent system. They were using a nursing agent to do the hands-on training that everyone felt would get things off to a good start.

Kirk explained that the idea of "Mother Ship" Labor and Delivery nursing agent was demonstrating part of Edenvale's implementation strategy. That strategy called for starting with agents that operate at a higher-level planning horizon. The lowest level agent would be the one that is used directly by the nurses. The Mother Ship has a "servant leader" role to provide automation and simplify workflows, where possible. This was the hierarchical design and the lower-level agents were the multi-agent part of the system. The Mother Ship data showed that nurse call cancel would help with some of the issues that had been revealed.

Assess the environment

The team used the 3Ps of people, property, and places to ensure that everything was included to describe the state of the environment. In this simple automation, there was only the patient, the nurse, and the room (Table 12.1).

The next step is to determine the states that are going to be available to help the controller to decide on what action to choose. For the training, they identified the Calling Patient Room would be A-112, the Other Patient Room was A-112, and the Breakroom was A-151. Then they created the table for all the states that would be used in the rules engine.

State space

The PEAS representation of the workflow starts with the problem statement which is to address the inconsistent data associated with nurses answering the calls from patients. In this round of automation, the goal is to create accurate data for the response to the call (Tables 12.2 and 12.3).

Table 12.1 3Ps: Nurse call cancel

People	*Property*	*Places*
• L&D Nurse • L&D Patient	NA	L&D Patient Rooms

Table 12.2 Features and descriptions of states

Features to describe states	*States*
L&D Nurse's Location – NLoc	Nurse Station – nstatn Other Patient Room – oproom Calling Patient Room – cproom Walkway – walkwy Breakroom – brk Idle – idle
L&D Patient's Location – PLoc	Patient Room – proom
L&D Patient Room – LDRoom	Button Pushed – bpushd Call Light On – lighton Call Light Off – lightoff

Table 12.3 PEAS: Nurse call cancel

Problem	*Performance measures*	*Environment*	*Actuators*	*Sensors*
There is inconsistent data associated with canceling calls which makes improvement difficult	Nurse arrival time Nurse departure time Nurse dwell time	Patient Room Nurse Patient Nurse Call System	Agent cancels the call and records the arrival, departure, and dwell the light goes off	RTLS and Wearable Nurse's Eyes

Environment: Fully observable, deterministic, static, episodic, discrete

Now it was time to see what sensing technology was required to make an accurate determination of the nurse entering and exiting the room. This is done by using the 4Ps to determine what percepts are necessary to provide an accurate cancellation of the call. Here we will list every idea we have for the types of location sensors that might help get the necessary percepts.

Like it was currently done for patients and equipment, the RTLS will give the position of the nurse's badge in the patient room where the call occurred. This required a high certainty for the room-level coverage provided by the RTLS. This certainty was demonstrated in the perception phase. The team talked about other ideas as well.

Sam said,

> If the nurses are going to have iPhones the BLE sensor can determine if the nurse was in close proximity to the patient after the call was made and before it was canceled. The patients are wearing the BLE RTLS wristband for the LOS project. The phone is the source, and the wristband is the target.

Table 12.4 Sensors – 4Ps: Nurse call cancel

Position	*Proximity*	*Presence*	*Possession*
RTLS identifies the position of the wearable badge and it is determined the badge is in the room where the call occurred.	If the patient had a beacon location tag and the nurse had a mobile device the proximity from the mobile device to the beacon could be used to help accurately cancel the call.	Occupancy detection could see a net increase and decrease in occupants correlated with the RTLS data	NA

Gwen said, "We could use that same proximity percept for other new features that involve proximity to the patient. Patient transport is doing that now for custody (possession) of the patient."

Sam said, "The occupancy detection sensors are not being used and they can count the number of people entering and exiting the room. We could add a presence percept that could be correlated with the other two percepts."

Kirk said,

> This is great discussion, and it shows you how this needs to work. We can already see the Percept Inventory changing just from this discussion. You can see how iterative these designs are. It also shows that we should do one percept at a time to be see if we can get what we need with a simple approach. These correlations are powerful, but they can be complex as well. We might want some help from AI when we get there.

The team agreed that the design for this simple workflow automation would use a condition/action sequence. It sees the condition where the light is on (LDRoom = lighton) AND the nurse's location is A-111 (NLoc = cproom) AND the patient's location is A-111 (PLoc = proom). When the agent sees this condition, it sends a command to the body to execute the action (Table 12.4).

The percepts that are available from the RTLS will be used in this first iteration. It will be tested and if it is unstable or unreliable, they have a good list of additional percepts to work with.

PLAYBOOK FOR THINKING AND DECISIONS

The playbook for thinking and decision is to understand individual and low-complexity agents so that the iterations of improvement can be small but effective. The digital twin's model of the operations of an organization will be a multi-agent and hierarchical agent architecture. These agents will be making decisions that might conflict with each other so the modeling that can be done for the low-level agents will be the starting point to be ready when the agents accumulate horizontally and vertically.

Improvers

When working with the workflow subject matter experts, it is important to understand thought processes. The "5 Whys" approach to understanding the decision-making process is a good way to get to the root of the decision.

Understanding the decisions that make the best outcomes is critical to the success of the agent no matter much or how little machines are involved. Knowing the planning horizons that are involved helps ensure that the agents have the time and information to make the best decisions.

Each pass-through PEAS modeling exercise should coincide with visiting the context processing steps listed earlier.

Evaluating the quality of the percepts that come from the sensors is important to each individual agent.

1. Decision Analysis
   - Map current decision points in workflows
   - Document decision criteria and constraints
   - Identify required contextual information
   - Evaluate decision quality requirements
   - Create decision-validation processes
2. Context Assessment
   - Inventory available contextual data
   - Document context gaps
   - Map context requirements to decisions
   - Establish context quality metrics
3. Implementation Strategy
   - Start with simple decision frameworks
   - Build toward more complex decisions
   - Create decision-validation processes
   - Establish feedback loops
   - Document decision outcomes
4. Quality Management
   - Define decision quality metrics
   - Create validation frameworks
   - Establish monitoring systems
   - Document improvement processes

Leaders

The agent's ability to make the right decision to get the optimal outcome is going to be a combination of human and machine. The outcomes are the most important factor in optimization so ensuring they are clearly defined is critical.

Ensuring that the digital twin has access to the best contextual data will make the agent as effective as possible.

1. Strategic Planning
   - Understand the role of automated decisions
   - Balance human and machine decisions
   - Plan for incremental automation
   - Support decision quality initiatives
2. Resource Management
   - Invest in decision support systems
   - Allocate resources for context acquisition
   - Support training initiatives
   - Plan for ongoing improvement
3. Risk Management
   - Identify critical decision points
   - Create fallback procedures
   - Establish oversight mechanisms
   - Monitor decision quality
   - Develop contingency plans
4. Change Management
   - Build trust in automated decisions
   - Support gradual transition
   - Foster culture of continuous improvement
   - Enable cross-functional collaboration

Creators

The cycle of context acquisition, modeling, fusion, reasoning, distribution, and adaptation will need to be represented in a systems architecture for the digital twin. This pattern offers creators a way to leverage the vast amount of data that is available in the enterprise instead of trying to create it in a single product.

1. Strategic Planning
   - Understand role of automated decisions
   - Balance human and machine decisions
   - Plan for incremental automation
   - Support decision quality initiatives
2. Resource Management
   - Invest in decision support systems
   - Allocate resources for context acquisition
   - Support training initiatives
   - Plan for ongoing improvement
3. Risk Management
   - Identify critical decision points

- Create fallback procedures
- Establish oversight mechanisms
- Monitor decision quality
- Develop contingency plans

4. Change Management
   - Build trust in automated decisions
   - Support gradual transition
   - Foster culture of continuous improvement
   - Enable cross-functional collaboration

Chapter 13

Agents: Actions and outcomes

Paul E. Zieske

Care traffic control is optimizing mobile workflows across the enterprise. Optimizing the workflows means getting the best possible outcome from the workflow. For the rational agents, this means applying the correct action to change the state of the environment to the desired state. Most of the agents involved in CTC are human-in-the-loop and most often the human is applying the action.

Understanding those actions is critical to the design of the entire agent. That starts with understanding the desired outcome so the iterative process we have been using is just as important here as it was in the beginning. There may be constraints on the actions when the environment is in a specific state, so accurately capturing that state in the perception phase is important.

The amount of granularity that goes into defining the states and actions is set by the level of automation we want to apply. If humans are executing the actions, then less detail is needed to describe the actions and the expected outcome but perceiving the changes in the environment is still very important for the agent to be able to help the actor get the outcome. For instance, you don't need to describe the action of grasping a lab sample from the pickup location if a human is going to be performing the action. Simply stating "pickup sample" is sufficient.

ACTIONS AND OUTCOMES

In the act phase, the agent is changing the state of the environment in a way that gets the optimal outcome. The action space is the set of all the actions available to the agent. We need the best actions to be available to the agent for it to be successful. We should assign a great deal of importance to action space because it is directly connected to the outcomes. Even if humans are executing the actions, it is important they are represented as a part of the action space. This allows for future automation and presents a more complete representation of the agent.

When the agent has executed an action that changes the environment, that change in state needs to be perceived by the agent so the agent can

DOI: 10.1201/9781003625483-15

know what effect the change had on the outcome. This is a feedback cycle that is fundamental to control systems. Below are the steps for designing the agent from the outcome down to the sensing.

1. Determine the desired outcome
2. Determine what actions will achieve that outcome
3. Describe the conditions for the actions to take place
4. Identify the state of the environment that represents those conditions
5. Ensure that the controller will select the action based on the conditions and state
6. Ensure the body has the percepts that are required to detect the states
7. Ensure the sensors are in place to create those percepts

PEAS IN THE ACTION PHASE

The act phase starts when the command to execute the action has been received by the body from the controller in the perceive phase (Figure 13.1). The action is then carried out by a human or a machine in the world. The action space represents all the actions and the events that are available to the agent.

The action space

In a complex environment, the actions exist in a hierarchy because of the sequencing and interactions that are necessary. For instance, if we want to automate patient transport the actor would be the transporter. There would be sequenced actions like, acknowledge the job, get a wheelchair, move to the pickup location, and several more until the drop-off. The transporter would need to interact with the nurse at the pickup location and someone at the drop-off location. Those are all actions that would need to be considered by the agent. The exercise is to determine if the state space has all of the states that are necessary to ensure that the agent decides on the correct action (Figure 13.2).

In AI, the **action space** refers to the set of all possible actions that are available to the agent in a given situation. A situation is a state or sequence of states that the agent could encounter or create. The action space includes all the possible moves, decisions, or operations that the agent can execute to interact with its environment and achieve its goals. The action space is typically defined based on the specific problem that the agent is trying to solve and the constraints of the environment.

For example, in a game-playing AI agent, the action space might include different moves that the agent can make on the game board. In a robotic AI agent, the action space might include commands for different motor actions or movements. By exploring and evaluating different actions within the

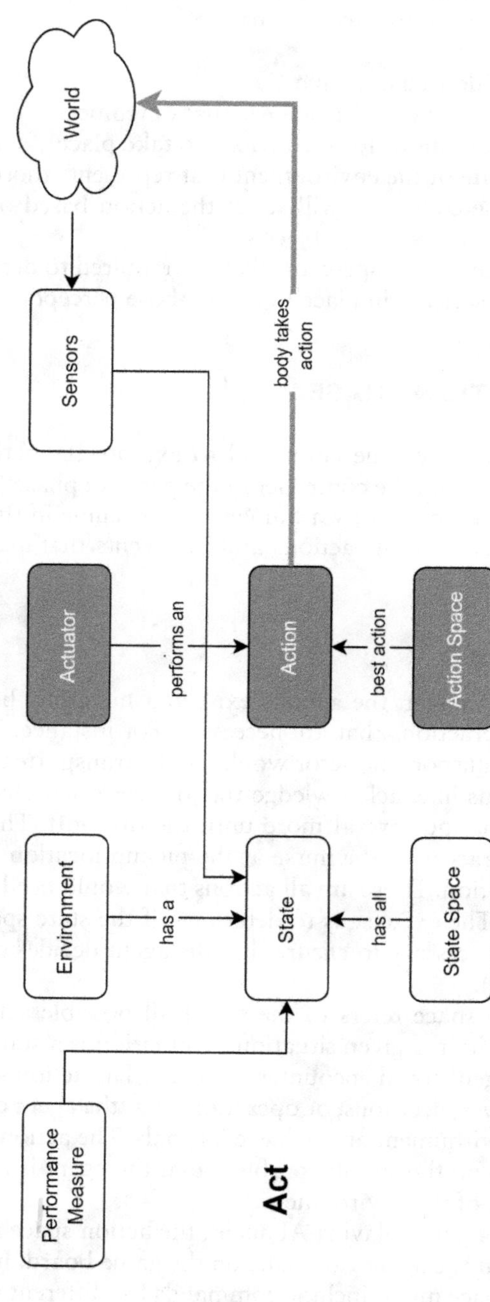

Figure 13.1 PEAS in the action phase diagram.

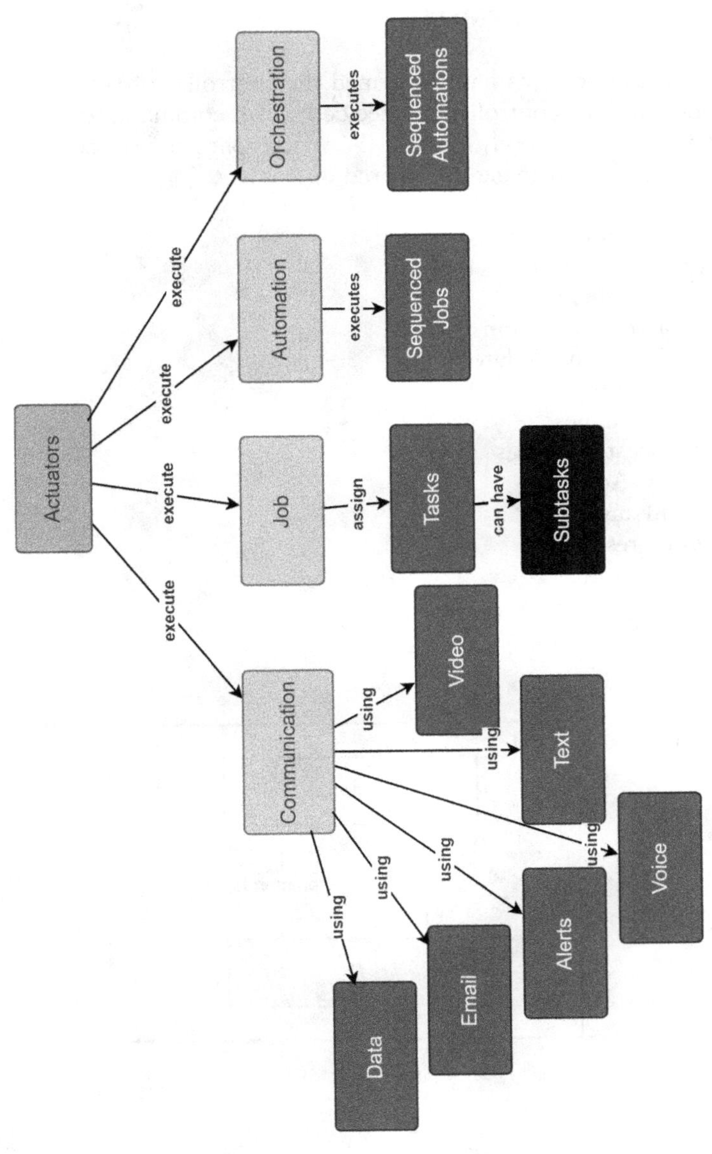

Figure 13.2 Agent in the action phase diagram.

action space, the agent can determine the best course of action to take in order to maximize its performance and achieve its objectives.

THE BODY IN THE ACT PHASE

In this phase, the percepts have informed the controller of the state of the environment, and the controller has decided which command to send to the body (Figure 13.3). The body looks at the action space and selects the action or actions that are best to get the desired outcome.

1. Communication Actions
   - Send notifications/alerts
   - Issue commands
   - Request information
   - Provide status updates
   - Generate reports
   - Escalate issues
   - Broadcast messages
2. Workflow Actions
   - Initiate tasks
   - Assign resources
   - Update status
   - Cancel/modify assignments
   - Schedule activities

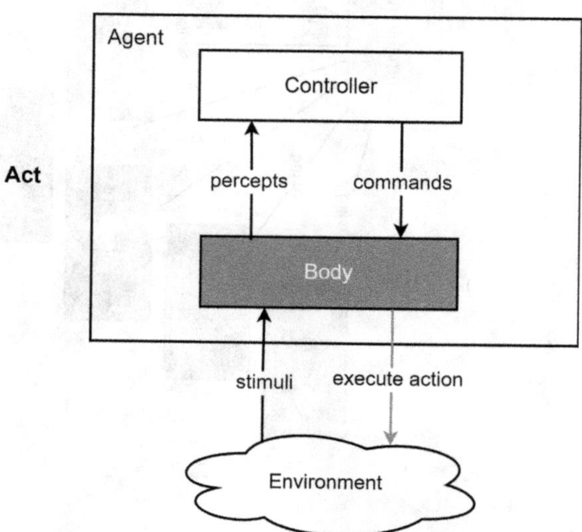

Figure 13.3 The body in the act phase diagram.

- Coordinate handoffs
- Track progress
- Close/complete tasks

3. Automation Actions
   - Activate/deactivate equipment
   - Control access systems
   - Adjust environmental controls
   - Manage device settings
   - Execute predefined procedures
   - Control robotic systems
   - Manage queue priorities
4. Decision Support Actions
   - Generate recommendations
   - Present options
   - Provide analytics
   - Show relevant context
   - Calculate projections
   - Identify patterns
   - Suggest alternatives
5. Physical Actions
   - Transport people or property
   - Take possession of people or property
   - Go to a physical location (locomotion)
   - Observe the environment at a physical location
   - Perform a task that requires dexterity
6. Control Actions
   - Set boundaries/limits
   - Enforce policies
   - Monitor thresholds
   - Apply rules
   - Maintain compliance
   - Regulate flow
   - Manage capacity

All of these actions are designed to change the state of the environment. Some are computational, some are physical, some are performed by humans, and some machines.

EDENVALE'S CTC JOURNEY

Kirk was pleased with the way that Sam and Gwen were working through the design. The training was going well. This was the way the process was supposed to work. Because each hospital is a different environment, the implementation of these agents needs to be done with a configuration exercise like this. This part of the process is called "composing agents." If things go well here, they should go well for the many agents they want to build.

Something as seemingly simple as notifying the Nurse Call system and turning the light off demonstrates that the perception required to recognize the state of the environment is one of the most complex parts of building powerful agents. The agent's ability to decide is based on its ability to perceive. The action space in this case is a combination of actions that are performed by humans and actions that are performed by machines. In this case, when the condition is recognized. That condition is that the patient and the nurse are in the same location and that location is the patient's room. Primary to this is the condition that the call light is on. It is then the command is sent to send the signal back to the Nurse Call system telling it to turn off the light.

Action space (Table 13.1)

Table 13.1 Nurse initiated and automated actions

Actions	
Nurse's actions	**Automated actions**
Push Button – pushb	Turn light off – turnlightoff
Go to room – gotoroom	

The final product

Automated Workflow: The automated workflow introduces a call-cancel system as a part of the nurse's rational agent. The agent uses sensors to perceive that the nurse is in the room and the actuator will cancel the call. The nurse wears an RTLS badge that is assigned to them, and there are sensors in the room to recognize that the badge is in the room. The patient pushes the call button, and the nurse is alerted that the room has a call at the nurse station. The light on the outside of the room goes on. The badge recognizes the entry to the room, and the light goes off, and the call is canceled. The performance measures are time of arrival, departure, and dwell time in the room (Figure 13.4).

When the improvers have the ability to compose agents, the pace of the project will proceed much faster. The Big-tech knew this and a lot was riding on the composability of these agents. The EGH leadership knew that the small incremental changes were what was going to ensure adoption and sustainability.

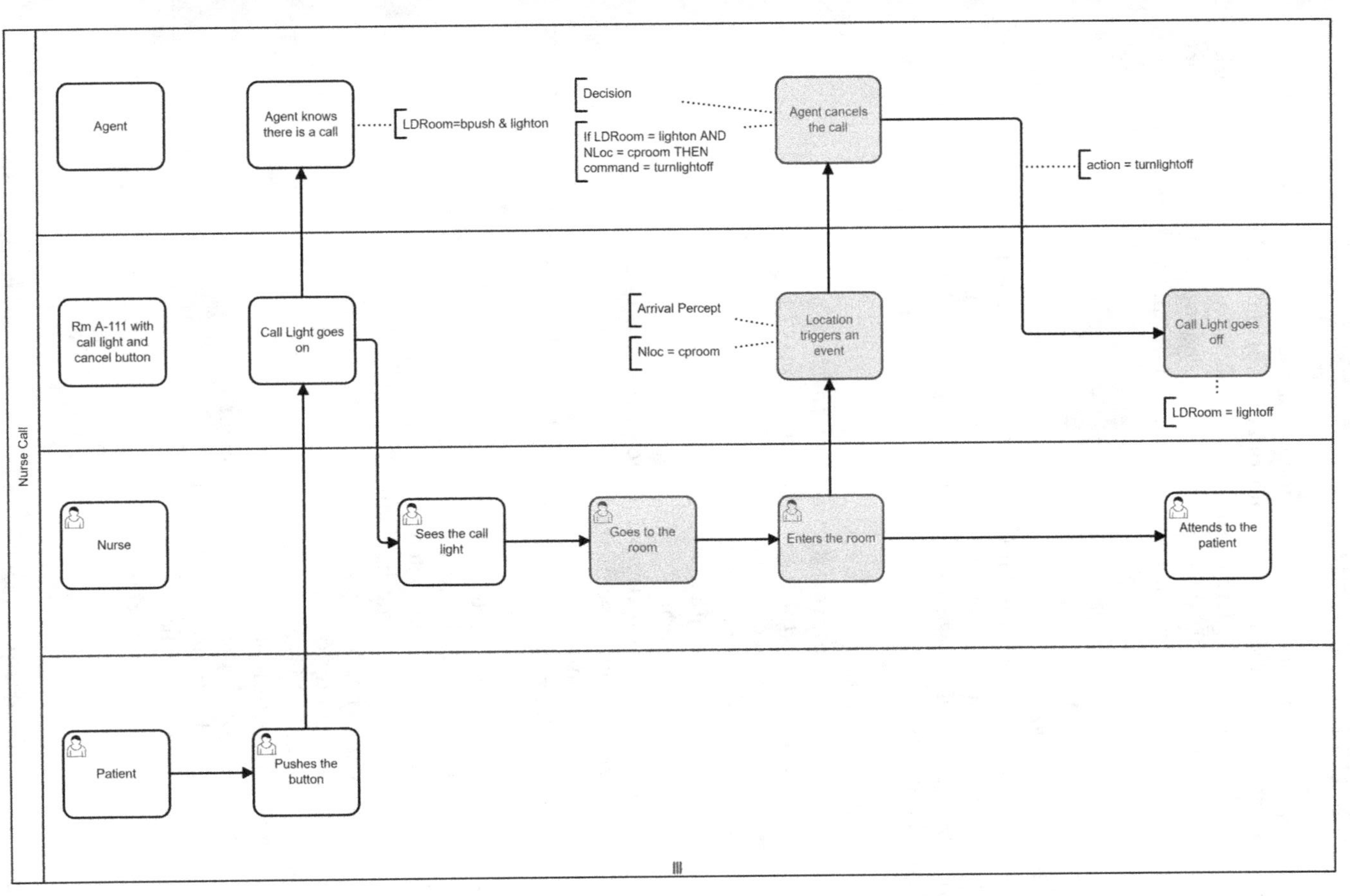

Figure 13.4 BPMN of nurse call-cancel system.

PLAYBOOK FOR ACTIONS AND OUTCOMES

It is important to understand and document the actions that actors undertake to create the outcomes we want from the workflows. This completes the cycle and allows a complete picture for evaluating how effective the workflow is. Actions are where the most effort is applied in the perceive>think>act cycle so it also offers the most automation and optimization potential.

Improvers

Often, in analyzing processes, the actions that are performed by humans are assumed. This is because information systems design can often obscure the outcomes in favor of providing information that is required for tasks or jobs. In agentic design, we are creating a closed loop that concludes with the desired outcomes.

1. Action Analysis
   - Catalog current workflow actions and outcomes
   - Document dependencies between actions
   - Map action success criteria
   - Identify opportunities for automation
   - Create action validation frameworks
2. Outcome Assessment
   - Define desired outcomes for each workflow
   - Document outcome metrics
   - Create measurement systems
   - Establish baseline performance
   - Identify improvement opportunities
3. Implementation Strategy
   - Start with low-risk actions
   - Build validation into action execution
   - Create feedback mechanisms
   - Document success patterns
   - Establish improvement cycles
4. Performance Management
   - Define action quality metrics
   - Create outcome-monitoring systems
   - Establish performance baselines
   - Track improvement trends
   - Document best practices

Leaders

Actions often involve people who are executing tasks, so this is the portion of the cycle where change management is engaged. Sometimes the outcome of the agentic design is the removal of actions and others it can be adding actions that involve some additional monitoring that is necessary to provide structure to the workflow. It is important to look at the "net" amount of automation that is occurring and ensure that the outcomes are measured.

Something like asking a nurse to scan an IV Pump when infusing a patient might add a task to the workflow, but the utilization data is invaluable to the organization.

1. Strategic Planning
    - Align actions with organizational goals
    - Balance automation with human capability
    - Plan for progressive implementation
    - Support continuous improvement
    - Establish governance frameworks
2. Resource Allocation
    - Invest in action automation tools
    - Support training initiatives
    - Plan for ongoing optimization
    - Allocate monitoring resources
    - Enable technology adoption
3. Risk Management
    - Identify critical actions
    - Ensure designs include fallback procedures
    - Establish oversight mechanisms
    - Monitor execution quality
    - Develop contingency plans

Creators

Actions are important for creators to consider because often the users don't articulate the actions they perform to create outcomes. They will talk about what helps them do their jobs, but the details of actions they are performing are often unknown to systems developers. Using agentic design can deepen the discussion to find details where new opportunities for automation lie.

1. Solution Development
    - Build flexible action frameworks
    - Enable outcome tracking
    - Support multiple automation levels
    - Create validation tools
    - Enable integration capabilities
2. Implementation Support
    - Provide action validation tools
    - Offer implementation guidance
    - Support system optimization

- Maintain documentation
- Enable performance monitoring

3. Innovation Focus
    - Develop new automation capabilities
    - Enhance action reliability
    - Support emerging standards
    - Enable future expansion
    - Build adaptive systems

Chapter 14

Privacy and security

Ali Youssef

One can argue that healthcare has gone high-tech especially after Covid, and location services are at the forefront of this revolution. From tracking medical equipment in real time to coordinating emergency response teams, location-based technologies are revolutionizing how healthcare is delivered and managed.

As we dive into this brave new world of location-based healthcare, we're facing a whole new set of challenges when it comes to keeping sensitive data under wraps. We're not just talking about complying with regulations (though that's certainly part of it). We're talking about fundamental issues of patient trust, data ownership, and the ethical use of information that could, in the wrong hands, reveal more about a person than they'd ever want known.

This chapter delves deep into the critical intersection of location services and cybersecurity in healthcare. We will explore the fundamental principles of the CIA triad and their application to location data, examine the pressing privacy and security concerns that arise from the use of these technologies, and investigate the cybersecurity frameworks and standards that guide best practices in the industry.

We will also provide practical guidance, discussing strategies for implementing robust security measures, educating users (because let's be honest, sometimes humans are the weakest link in the security chain), and leveraging cutting-edge tech to keep our data safe. And because all of this fancy tech is useless if no one uses it, we'll tackle the crucial issue of user adoption head-on.

The world of healthcare cybersecurity is constantly changing. New threats are popping up daily, regulations continue to evolve, and technological advancements are a double-edged sword, offering both new protections and new vulnerabilities. That's why this chapter isn't just about providing a snapshot of where we are now. It's about equipping you with the knowledge and critical thinking skills to adapt for the future.

So, whether you're a healthcare pro, an IT specialist, or a policymaker, by the time you finish this chapter, you'll have a solid grasp on the cybersecurity

DOI: 10.1201/9781003625483-16

considerations surrounding location services in healthcare. You'll be better prepared to implement secure systems, protect patient privacy, and harness the full potential of location-based technologies to improve healthcare delivery and outcomes.

UNDERSTANDING THE CIA TRIAD IN THE CONTEXT OF LOCATION SERVICES

The CIA (confidentiality, integrity, availability) triad is a widely adopted security model focused on three universal objectives corresponding to protection of unauthorized access, guarding against improper data changes, and resilience to denial-of-service, respectively. Originally formalized across US government computer security policies like the Department of Defense's "Trusted Computer System Evaluation Criteria" in the 1980s, CIA offers a technology-neutral approach to dealing with vulnerabilities across people, process, and tech controls.

The model is highly pertinent when exploring LBS data protection strategies for hospitals. Hospitals are managing extremely sensitive patient health records, mission-critical assets like MRI machines, safety-focused staff coordination workflows, and regulatory penalties if location-driven systems enabling all these functions are compromised. This chapter will analyze the confidentiality, integrity, and availability dimensions around securing hospital LBS through this CIA lens – along with specific technical and administrative safeguards.

Confidentiality

Confidentiality is all about ensuring that sensitive information, like patient location data, is only accessible to the right people. In healthcare, this equates to complying with laws like Health Insurance Portability and Accountability Act (HIPAA) in the United States and General Data Protection Regulation (GDPR) in Europe.

Location data is always changing and can reveal more about a person than you might think. Imagine if someone could see that a patient visits an oncology clinic every week – suddenly, very private health information becomes not so private.

One effective approach is the use of end-to-end encryption in mobile applications and communication channels. This ensures that location information remains confidential even if intercepted during transmission. For example, a hospital might implement a secure messaging system for staff that includes encrypted location sharing, allowing care teams to coordinate efficiently without compromising patient privacy.

Additionally, healthcare providers should implement strict access controls and auditing mechanisms to monitor and restrict access to location data.

This might involve role-based access control (RBAC) systems that grant location data access only to personnel who require it for their specific job functions.

Integrity

Integrity is all about making sure our data stays accurate and trustworthy. In the world of healthcare location services, data integrity can literally be a matter of life and death. Imagine an ambulance being sent to the wrong address or a medical device being delivered to the wrong patient because someone tampered with the location data.

To mitigate integrity risks, healthcare providers implement various data validation processes and cryptographic techniques. Digital signatures, for example, can be used to verify the authenticity and integrity of location data transmitted between devices and systems. Hash functions can detect any unauthorized modifications to stored location data.

Blockchain technology has emerged as a promising solution for ensuring data integrity in healthcare. By creating an immutable, distributed ledger of location data transactions, blockchain can provide a tamper-proof record of equipment and patient movements. This not only enhances data integrity but also improves traceability and accountability.

Another approach to maintaining integrity is the use of redundant data storage and cross-validation mechanisms. By storing critical location data across multiple secure systems and regularly cross-checking for discrepancies, healthcare organizations can quickly identify and rectify any integrity issues.

Furthermore, integrity checks should be incorporated into the data lifecycle management process. This includes validating data at the point of collection, during transmission, and upon storage or retrieval. Regular data audits and integrity testing should be conducted to ensure the ongoing accuracy and reliability of location information.

Availability

Last but not least, we have availability. This is the "always-on" principle of the CIA triad. In healthcare, timing is everything, and having access to accurate location information can mean the difference between life and death (Figure 14.1).

Location services can be vulnerable to disruptions. That's why healthcare organizations are getting creative with redundancy measures and disaster recovery plans. Some cloud-based location service providers are even spreading their data centers across the globe, like a high-tech game of risk, to ensure that if one goes down, the others can pick up the slack.

But it's not all smooth sailing. Denial-of-service attacks targeting location servers during critical patient transports have shown just how vital it is to

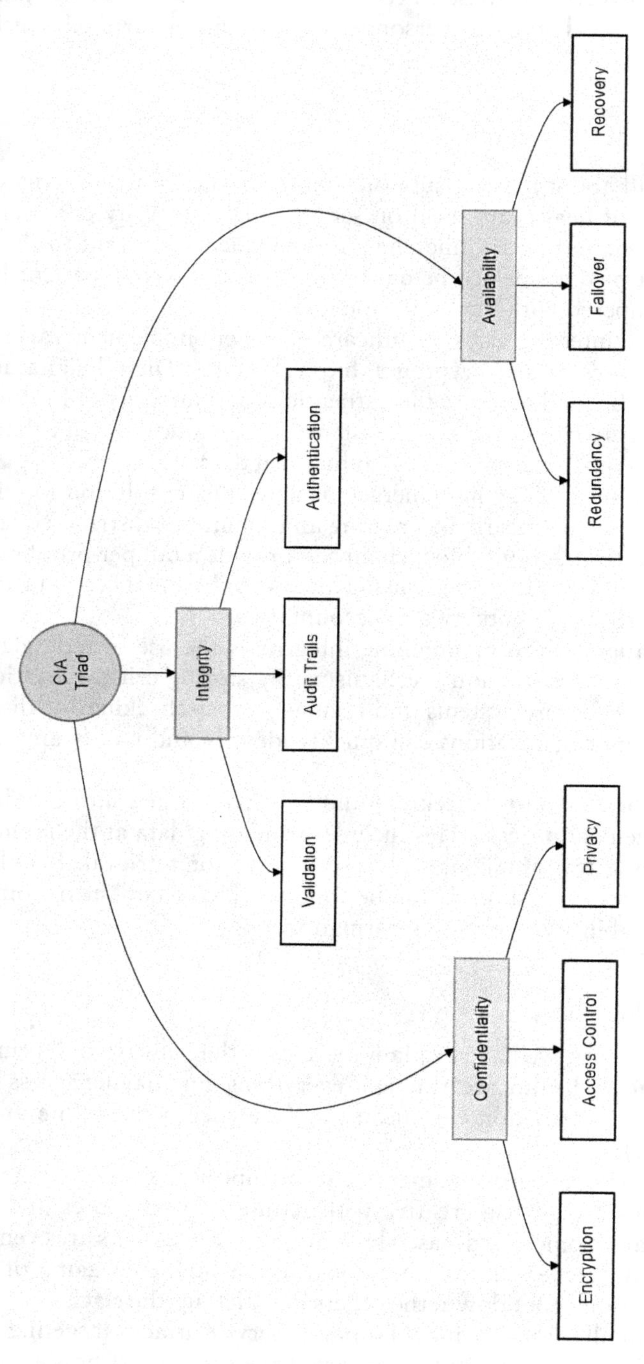

Figure 14.1 CIA triad diagram.

keep these systems up and running. It's like playing whack-a-mole with cyber threats, but the stakes are much higher.

In the next sections, we'll dive deeper into the privacy and security concerns that keep healthcare IT professionals up at night and explore the frameworks and best practices that can help us sleep a little easier. Stay tuned!

PRIVACY AND SECURITY CONCERNS IN LOCATION SERVICES

As location services become increasingly integral to healthcare operations, the industry must grapple with a host of privacy and security concerns. These issues extend beyond mere regulatory compliance, touching on fundamental questions of patient rights, data ownership, and the ethical use of sensitive information.

Privacy concerns

Privacy concerns in healthcare location services stem from the highly personal nature of the data being collected and the potential for its misuse. Patient location information, if not properly protected, can reveal sensitive details about an individual's health status, personal habits, and social interactions.

One of the primary privacy risks is the potential for unauthorized surveillance. If location data falls into the wrong hands, it could be used to track patients' movements, potentially exposing them to stalking, harassment, or discrimination. This risk is particularly acute for vulnerable populations, such as individuals seeking treatment for mental health issues or victims of domestic violence.

Another significant concern is the potential for data aggregation and inference. Even if individual data points are seemingly innocuous, the aggregation of location data over time can reveal detailed patterns of behavior. This could lead to unintended disclosures of sensitive information, such as regular visits to a specialized clinic that might indicate a particular health condition.

Legal frameworks such as the GDPR in Europe and the California Consumer Privacy Act (CCPA) in the United States mandate stringent data protection measures for location data. These regulations require organizations to implement robust consent mechanisms, allowing patients to have greater control over how their location data is collected, used, and shared.

Healthcare providers must also navigate the complex landscape of data sharing and third-party access. While sharing location data with other healthcare providers or researchers can lead to improved care coordination and valuable insights, it also increases the risk of privacy breaches. Clear policies and secure data-sharing protocols are essential to balance the benefits of data collaboration with the imperative of patient privacy.

To address these privacy concerns, healthcare organizations are implementing a range of technical and procedural safeguards. These include:

1. Data minimization: Collecting only the location data that is absolutely necessary for the intended healthcare purpose.
2. Anonymization and pseudonymization techniques: Removing or encoding identifying information to protect individual privacy while still allowing for data analysis.
3. User-controlled privacy settings: Empowering patients to decide when and how their location data is shared.
4. Regular privacy impact assessments: Systematically analyzing the potential privacy risks associated with new location-based services or changes to existing systems.
5. Privacy-by-design principles: Integrating privacy considerations into the development process of location-based healthcare technologies from the outset.
6. Transparent privacy policies: Clearly communicating to patients how their location data will be collected, used, and protected.
7. Secure data deletion processes: Ensuring that location data is permanently and securely erased when it is no longer needed or when requested by the patient.

Security concerns

While privacy concerns focus on the appropriate use and protection of location data, security concerns encompass the broader spectrum of threats targeting healthcare location services. These range from malware infections and data breaches to sophisticated cyberattacks aimed at disrupting critical healthcare operations. If privacy is a group of mosquitos pestering you during a picnic, security is the hungry bear eying your lunch.

One of the primary security challenges is protecting the vast network of devices and sensors that make up a healthcare organization's location services infrastructure. This includes mobile devices used by healthcare professionals, patient wearables, asset tracking tags, and the servers and networks that process and store location data. Each of these components represents a potential entry point for cyber attackers.

Malware and ransomware pose significant threats to healthcare location services. A successful ransomware attack could encrypt critical location data, rendering it inaccessible and potentially disrupting patient care. In 2022, a major healthcare provider experienced a ransomware attack that encrypted critical location data servers, disrupting patient care coordination and emergency response operations. This incident prompted industry-wide collaboration on cybersecurity best practices and the adoption of advanced threat detection technologies.

Data breaches represent another major security concern. The theft of location data could lead to identity theft, financial fraud, or the exposure of sensitive patient information. Healthcare organizations must implement robust access controls, encryption, and monitoring systems to protect against both external threats and insider risks.

Man-in-the-middle attacks are particularly relevant to location services, as they could allow attackers to intercept and potentially alter location data in transit. This could have severe consequences in scenarios where accurate location information is critical, such as emergency response or patient tracking in large hospital complexes (Figure 14.2).

To address these security concerns, healthcare organizations are implementing a multi-layered approach to cybersecurity:

1. Network segmentation: Isolating location services systems from other parts of the network to limit the potential spread of security breaches.
2. Advanced encryption: Implementing strong encryption for data at rest and in transit, using protocols such as TLS 1.3 for secure communication.

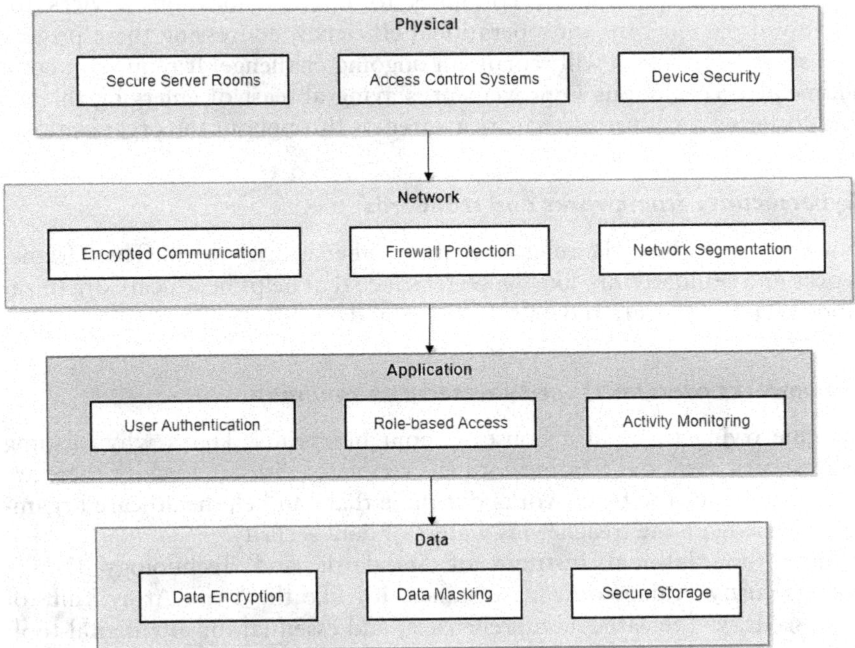

Figure 14.2 Layers of cyber security diagram.

3. Intrusion detection and prevention systems (IDPS): Deploying AI-powered systems to identify and block potential security threats in real time.
4. Regular security audits and penetration testing: Proactively identifying and addressing vulnerabilities in location services systems.
5. Endpoint protection: Securing all devices that interact with location services, including mobile devices and IoT sensors.
6. Security information and event management (SIEM) systems: Centralizing the collection and analysis of security logs to detect and respond to threats more effectively.
7. Incident response planning: Developing and regularly testing comprehensive plans for responding to various security incidents.
8. Secure software development practices: Implementing secure coding standards and regular security reviews in the development of location-based healthcare applications.
9. Vendor security assessments: Carefully evaluating the security practices of third-party location service providers and ensuring they meet stringent security standards.
10. Continuous security training: Keeping staff updated on the latest security threats and best practices for protecting location data.

As the healthcare industry continues to leverage location services for improved patient care and operational efficiency, addressing these privacy and security concerns will remain an ongoing challenge. It requires a commitment to continuous improvement, staying abreast of emerging threats, and fostering a culture of security awareness throughout the organization.

Cybersecurity frameworks and standards

Now, let's talk about the rulebooks of the cybersecurity world. These frameworks and standards are like the secret sauce that helps healthcare organizations keep their location data safe and sound.

Frameworks overview: Your cybersecurity roadmap

Imagine trying to build a house without blueprints. That's why tackling cybersecurity without a framework is a recipe for disaster. Luckily, there are some tried-and-true frameworks out there that can help healthcare organizations navigate the treacherous waters of data security.

Take the National Institute of Standards and Technology (NIST) Cybersecurity Framework, for instance. It's like the Swiss Army knife of cybersecurity – versatile, comprehensive, and essential for any digital toolbox. It breaks down cybersecurity into five core functions: Identify, Protect, Detect, Respond, and Recover. It's like a step-by-step guide to not getting your digital lunch money stolen.

Then there's ISO/IEC 27001, the international gold standard for information security management. It's more prescriptive than NIST, laying out specific requirements for an information security management system. Think of it as the strict parent of the cybersecurity world – it tells you exactly what you need to do to keep your digital house in order.

And let's not forget about the HITRUST CSF (Common Security Framework). This one's tailor-made for healthcare, combining requirements from multiple regulations into one comprehensive framework. It's like having a cybersecurity chef create a custom menu just for healthcare organizations.

Compliance and regulations: Jumping through legal hoops

If cybersecurity frameworks are the carrot, regulatory compliance is the stick. The healthcare industry is subject to a laundry list of regulations, with HIPAA leading the pack when it comes to protecting electronic protected health information (ePHI), including all that sensitive location data.

Non-compliance isn't just a slap on the wrist – it comes with hefty fines, reputation damage, and legal consequences that could make even the most battle-hardened healthcare executive lose sleep. It's like playing a high-stakes game of regulatory Jenga, where one wrong move could bring the whole tower crashing down.

But it's not just HIPAA we need to worry about. For healthcare organizations operating internationally or handling data from patients in multiple countries, compliance becomes even more complex. The GDPR in the European Union, for instance, has stringent requirements for the processing of personal data, including location information.

Navigating the maze of cybersecurity frameworks and regulations isn't easy, but it's essential for protecting patient data and avoiding regulatory nightmares. It requires a commitment to continuous improvement, staying abreast of changing requirements, and fostering a culture of security awareness throughout the organization. It's a tough job, but somebody's got to do it – and in healthcare, that somebody is all of us

Implementing robust security measures is crucial for protecting sensitive location data in healthcare settings. Here are some best practices that healthcare organizations should consider.

Security measures

Encryption: Implement strong encryption protocols for location data both at rest and in transit. Use industry-standard encryption algorithms like AES-256 for data at rest and TLS 1.3 for data in transit.

Access controls: Implement RBAC to ensure that only authorized personnel can access sensitive location information. This should be based on the principle of least privilege, granting access only to those who need it for their specific job functions.

Multi-factor authentication (MFA): Require MFA for accessing systems that handle location data. This adds an extra layer of security beyond just passwords, significantly reducing the risk of unauthorized access.

Secure API management: If location services are accessed via APIs, implement robust API security measures such as rate limiting, token-based authentication, and input validation to prevent attacks like API injections.

Data masking and anonymization: Where possible, use data masking techniques to hide sensitive parts of location data and implement anonymization processes for data used in analytics or research.

Regular security assessments: Conduct periodic vulnerability assessments and penetration testing of location service systems to identify and address potential security weaknesses.

Secure development practices: Implement secure coding practices in the development of location-based applications, including regular code reviews and security testing throughout the development lifecycle.

Physical security: Ensure physical security measures are in place to protect servers and devices that store or process location data.

User education and training: Teaching old dogs new tricks

Let's face it – sometimes the weakest link in our security chain is sitting right in front of the computer. That's why user education is crucial:

1. Security awareness training: We're not talking about boring PowerPoint presentations that put everyone to sleep. Think interactive workshops, simulated phishing exercises, and even cybersecurity escape rooms. Make it fun, make it engaging, and maybe – just maybe – people will stop using "password123" as their password.
2. Role-specific training: One size doesn't fit all when it comes to security training. Tailor your programs to different roles within the organization. Your IT folks need different training than your nurses, who need different training than your admin staff.
3. Continuous learning: Cyber threats evolve faster than fashion trends. Keep your staff up-to-date with regular refresher courses, security newsletters, and maybe even a "Cybersecurity Tip of the Day" screensaver (hey, every little bit helps!).

Technological solutions: Embracing the future

Emerging technologies offer innovative solutions to enhance the security posture of healthcare location services:

Blockchain: Implement blockchain technology to create immutable, transparent records of location data access and usage. This can enhance data integrity and provide a tamper-proof audit trail.

Artificial intelligence and machine learning: Deploy AI-powered analytics platforms to detect anomalies in location data patterns that may indicate potential security breaches or unauthorized access attempts.

Edge computing: Utilize edge computing for processing location data closer to the source, reducing the amount of sensitive data transmitted over networks and potentially reducing attack surfaces.

Homomorphic encryption: Explore the use of homomorphic encryption techniques that allow computations on encrypted data without decrypting it, enabling secure analysis of location data while preserving privacy.

Zero trust architecture: Implement a zero trust security model that requires strict identity verification for every person and device trying to access resources in the network, regardless of whether they are inside or outside the network perimeter.

Secure enclaves: Use hardware-based secure enclaves (such as Intel SGX or ARM TrustZone) for processing highly sensitive location data, providing an additional layer of protection against software-based attacks.

Quantum-resistant cryptography: Begin planning for the integration of quantum-resistant cryptographic algorithms to protect against future threats from quantum computing.

In conclusion, securing location services in healthcare is no small feat. It requires a delicate balance of robust security measures, user-friendly design, and clear communication of benefits. But with patient lives on the line and cyber threats lurking around every digital corner, it's a challenge we must rise to meet. After all, in the world of healthcare cybersecurity, we're not just protecting data – we're protecting lives.

EDENVALE'S SECURITY JOURNEY: BALANCING ACCESS AND PRIVACY

When Edenvale implemented their Care Traffic Control system, they encountered a security incident that would ultimately strengthen their privacy and security protocols. The incident revolved around their employee safety system, which highlighted the delicate balance between providing immediate access to critical location data while maintaining privacy and security.

One evening, Frank McDermid, the shift sergeant for Security, received an alert through his CarePro device about a potential security threat on the 11th floor of the clinic building. The system showed the location with reduced accuracy (indicated by a yellow halo on the map), suggesting some limitations in the location tracking coverage for that area. Frank could see the name of the potential victim, their department, and could track his responding officer's location in real time.

Through the secure messaging system, Frank communicated with his officer without using voice communications that might escalate the situation. The system's privacy controls automatically limited the location data access to only essential security personnel, while still maintaining a complete audit trail of the response team's movements.

A housekeeper had activated her duress alert when she noticed a suspicious individual watching her. She was working alone on a closed clinic floor, a situation that the Care Traffic Control system had flagged as a potential risk. When security arrived, they found the individual had an outstanding warrant for a violent crime.

The incident highlighted several key security and privacy elements of Edenvale's system.

Layered access control

- Only authorized security personnel could see detailed location data
- The system limited data visibility based on role and situation
- Audit trails captured all system access and responses

Privacy protection

- The housekeeper's historical location data was protected
- Only real-time location information was available during the incident
- System alerts were discrete to prevent escalation

Data integrity

- The system accurately tracked response team locations
- Location accuracy indicators (yellow halo) provided confidence levels
- Integration with security protocols maintained data reliability

System availability

- Multiple communication channels ensured constant contact
- Backup location tracking methods provided redundancy
- System remained responsive during the critical incident

In the post-incident review, several privacy and security improvements were identified:

- Enhanced location coverage in low-traffic areas
- Implementation of automated battery level monitoring for mobile devices
- Refined access controls for different security response levels
- Additional privacy training for security personnel

The incident demonstrated both the value of their privacy and security measures and areas for improvement. Edenvale used this experience to enhance their security protocols while maintaining strong privacy protections. The Care Traffic Control system proved its worth not just in managing the immediate security threat, but in doing so while protecting sensitive location data and maintaining system integrity.

PLAYBOOK FOR PRIVACY AND SECURITY

The implementation of location-based services in healthcare requires a delicate balance between operational efficiency and the protection of sensitive information. As healthcare organizations advance through their Care Traffic Control journey, privacy, and security considerations must be woven into every aspect of the implementation. This playbook provides guidance for maintaining this balance while maximizing the value of location-based technologies.

Improvers

1. Security Assessment
   - Conduct privacy impact assessments
   - Map data flows and identify sensitive information
   - Document current security controls
   - Identify vulnerabilities in workflows
   - Create risk mitigation strategies
2. Implementation Framework
   - Build security into process design
   - Implement privacy-by-design principles
   - Create audit trails for sensitive operations
   - Establish incident response procedures
   - Define access control requirements
3. Monitoring and Compliance
   - Develop security metrics
   - Create compliance checklists
   - Establish monitoring protocols
   - Document audit procedures
   - Track security incidents
4. Continuous Improvement
   - Regular security assessments
   - Update security controls
   - Refine privacy protections
   - Enhance monitoring capabilities
   - Improve response procedures

Leaders

1. Strategic Planning
   - Establish security governance framework
   - Define privacy policies
   - Allocate security resources
   - Plan for security investments
   - Create compliance roadmap
2. Risk Management
   - Assess organizational risk tolerance
   - Develop mitigation strategies
   - Create incident response plans
   - Establish business continuity procedures
   - Define recovery objectives
3. Culture Development
   - Build security awareness
   - Foster privacy-conscious culture
   - Support training initiatives
   - Encourage incident reporting
   - Promote continuous improvement
4. Compliance Management
   - Ensure regulatory compliance
   - Maintain security certifications
   - Monitor legal requirements
   - Document compliance efforts
   - Prepare for audits

Creators

1. Security Development
   - Build secure solutions
   - Implement encryption
   - Create audit capabilities
   - Enable privacy controls
   - Support compliance requirements
2. Implementation Support
   - Provide security documentation
   - Offer security training
   - Support incident response
   - Enable security monitoring
   - Maintain security updates
3. Innovation Focus
   - Develop new security features
   - Enhance privacy protections
   - Support emerging standards
   - Enable future compliance
   - Build resilient systems

Section III

Implementation and sustainment

This section provides practical guidance for implementing and sustaining care traffic control (CTC) in healthcare environments. Building on the theoretical foundations and system architecture discussed in previous sections, we now focus on the concrete steps, methodologies, and best practices for successful deployment and long-term operation.

Chapter 15 – Performance Improvement delves into methodologies and tools for improving operational efficiency and effectiveness. It introduces key concepts from lean, Six Sigma, and other improvement frameworks specifically adapted for CTC implementations.

Chapter 16 – Simulations explores how simulation modeling can be used to validate designs, test scenarios, and optimize workflows before implementation. This chapter demonstrates both technical and operational simulation approaches.

Chapter 17 – Digital Twin Implementation provides a structured approach to implementing the operational digital twin, including technical architecture, data requirements, and integration considerations.

Chapter 18 – Systems Management focuses on the operational aspects of maintaining and evolving CTC systems, including monitoring, maintenance, upgrades, and support.

Chapter 19 – Operational Roadmap lays out a strategic approach to implementing CTC, including organizational change management, training, and adoption strategies.

Chapter 20 – Care Traffic Control Services models a starting point for CTC centered on the support services and transport mechanisms in the hospital. These enabling services start the progress toward more advanced and complex clinical structures.

Chapter 21 – Care Traffic Control Capabilities Maturity Model introduces a framework for assessing and advancing organizational capabilities in CTC implementation and operation.

Reading Guide: While the chapters build upon each other, they are designed to be relatively self-contained for readers focusing on specific

DOI: 10.1201/9781003625483-17

aspects of implementation. Cross-references guide readers to related content in other chapters when deeper understanding of particular topics may be helpful.

Expected Outcomes: After completing this section, readers should:

- Understand the key elements of successful CTC implementation
- Be able to assess their organization's readiness
- Know how to plan and execute implementation phases
- Understand how to measure and improve performance
- Be able to maintain and evolve CTC capabilities
- Know how to build sustainable operational practices

Chapter 15

Performance improvement

Paul E. Zieske

The sustained success of aviation and air traffic control stems largely from the industry's unwavering commitment to continuous improvement. This commitment manifests through dedicated resources, structured methodologies, and a culture that embraces change. From the quality revolution of the mid-1970s to modern Lean and Six Sigma approaches, aviation has consistently led the way in operational excellence.

Healthcare operations share remarkable similarities with aviation when it comes to opportunities for improvement:

- Both operate in safety-critical environments where errors can have severe consequences.
- Human factors play a central role in daily operations and decision-making.
- Complex, interconnected systems require careful orchestration.
- Technology integration is crucial for operational success.
- Real-time decision-making impacts outcomes.
- Continuous learning and adaptation are essential.
- Strict regulatory compliance governs operations.

In this chapter, we explore how these parallels inform the implementation of care traffic control and its performance improvement strategy. We'll examine proven methodologies from both industries and demonstrate how they can be adapted for healthcare operations. The goal is to establish a foundation for continuous improvement that leverages real-time data, enhances situational awareness, and supports intelligent automation.

Understanding performance improvement in the context of Care Traffic Control is crucial because of the following:

- It provides the framework for identifying and eliminating operational inefficiencies.
- It establishes methods for measuring and validating improvements.
- It creates sustainable processes for long-term success.
- It helps balance human and technological capabilities.
- It supports the cultural transformation necessary for digital transformation.

DOI: 10.1201/9781003625483-18

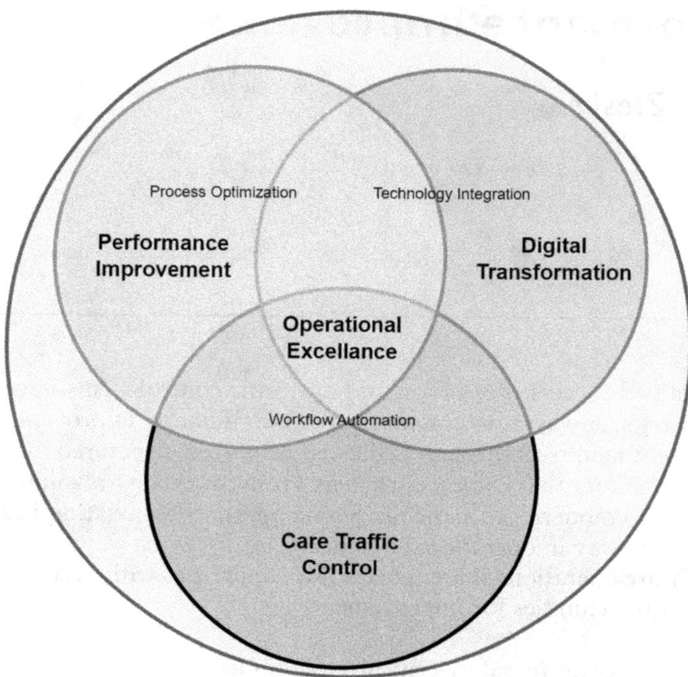

Figure 15.1 Operational excellence Venn diagram.

As we proceed, we will explore specific tools, techniques, and methodologies that support this journey, illustrated with real-world examples from healthcare organizations that have successfully implemented these approaches (Figure 15.1).

HEALTHCARE AND AVIATION: A PERFORMANCE IMPROVEMENT COMPARISON

The parallels between healthcare and air traffic control offer valuable insights for performance improvement strategies. While these industries operate in distinct environments, their shared characteristics – particularly regarding safety, complexity, and real-time decision-making – create opportunities for learning and adaptation.

Safety-critical environment

Both healthcare and aviation operate in environments where safety is paramount, and errors can have severe consequences. In healthcare, patient safety drives protocols and procedures, with multiple checkpoints and verifications built into daily operations. Similarly, aviation has developed robust safety systems with zero tolerance for critical errors.

Key safety elements in both industries include the following:

- Multiple layers of safety protocols
- Rigorous documentation requirements
- Structured handoff procedures
- Continuous monitoring and assessment

Human factors

The human element plays a crucial role in both sectors, though with notable differences in application. Air traffic controllers manage multiple aircraft simultaneously, making split-second decisions based on standardized protocols and clear communication channels. Healthcare professionals face similar cognitive demands but often deal with more variables and less standardized conditions (Figure 15.2).

Critical human factors include the following:

- Cognitive load management.
- Decision-making under pressure.
- Team coordination.
- Communication clarity.

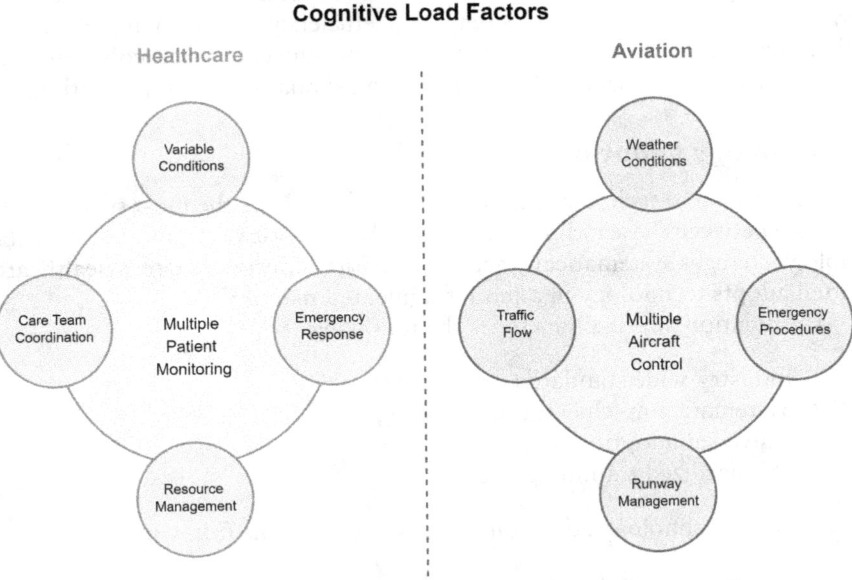

Figure 15.2 Cognitive load comparison between air traffic control and care traffic control diagram.

The fundamental difference lies in how these factors are managed. Aviation has developed highly standardized protocols and communication methods, whereas healthcare must often adapt to individual patient needs and varying conditions.

Complex systems integration

Complex systems in both industries require careful orchestration, though their approaches differ significantly. Consider how a typical day unfolds in each environment:

In aviation, a controller manages the following:

- Multiple aircraft movements
- Weather conditions
- Runway availability
- Crew scheduling

Whereas in healthcare, teams coordinate the following:

- Patient care plans
- Resource allocation
- Emergency responses
- Staff scheduling.

This complexity requires robust systems capable of handling multiple variables while maintaining safety and efficiency. Aviation has achieved this through centralized control systems and universal protocols, whereas healthcare is still working toward achieving similar levels of integration.

Technology adoption

The approach to technology adoption reveals perhaps the most striking difference between these industries. Aviation has historically implemented technology changes systematically across the entire industry, whereas healthcare often adopts technology in a more fragmented manner.

The aviation approach includes the following:

1. Industry-wide standards development
2. Systematic implementation planning
3. Universal adoption requirements
4. Standardized training protocols

Healthcare technology adoption typically involves the following:

1. Department-by-department implementation
2. Variable vendor solutions
3. Complex integration requirements
4. Diverse training approaches

Understanding these differences helps inform how healthcare can adapt successful aviation practices while acknowledging its unique challenges. The key is not to replicate aviation's systems exactly, but to learn from its successful approaches to standardization, communication, and safety protocols.

PERFORMANCE IMPROVEMENT RESOURCES IN HEALTHCARE

Healthcare organizations are increasingly recognizing the importance of dedicated resources for performance improvement initiatives. The evolution from sporadic improvement projects to sustained, systematic approaches requires a careful orchestration of internal capabilities, external expertise, and supporting technologies.

Internal resources

At the heart of successful performance improvement efforts are multidisciplinary teams that combine clinical expertise with improvement science. These teams typically emerge from a deliberate strategy to build internal capabilities, rather than relying solely on external consultants.

A modern healthcare performance improvement team includes several key roles as follows:

- Industrial Engineers who bring process improvement expertise
- Clinical Informaticists who bridge technology and healthcare operations
- Data Analysts who provide insights from operational metrics
- Clinical Experts who ensure solutions align with patient care needs

The power of these internal teams lies in their ability to combine deep organizational knowledge with improvement methodologies. They understand the nuances of their organization's culture, workflows, and challenges, making them uniquely positioned to drive sustainable change.

Training and development

The journey toward performance excellence requires ongoing investment in staff development. Many organizations have adopted structured approaches to building improvement capabilities across all levels of the organization.

Critical elements of a training program include the following:

1. Tiered certification levels
2. Hands-on project experience
3. Mentorship opportunities
4. Continuous skill development

External partners

While internal capabilities are crucial, external partners bring valuable perspectives and specialized expertise. The key is finding the right balance between internal and external resources to create sustainable improvement capabilities.

External partners typically contribute in the following three main areas:

- Methodology expertise
- Technology implementation
- Change management

The most successful organizations use external partners strategically, focusing on knowledge transfer and capability-building, rather than creating dependency (Figure 15.3).

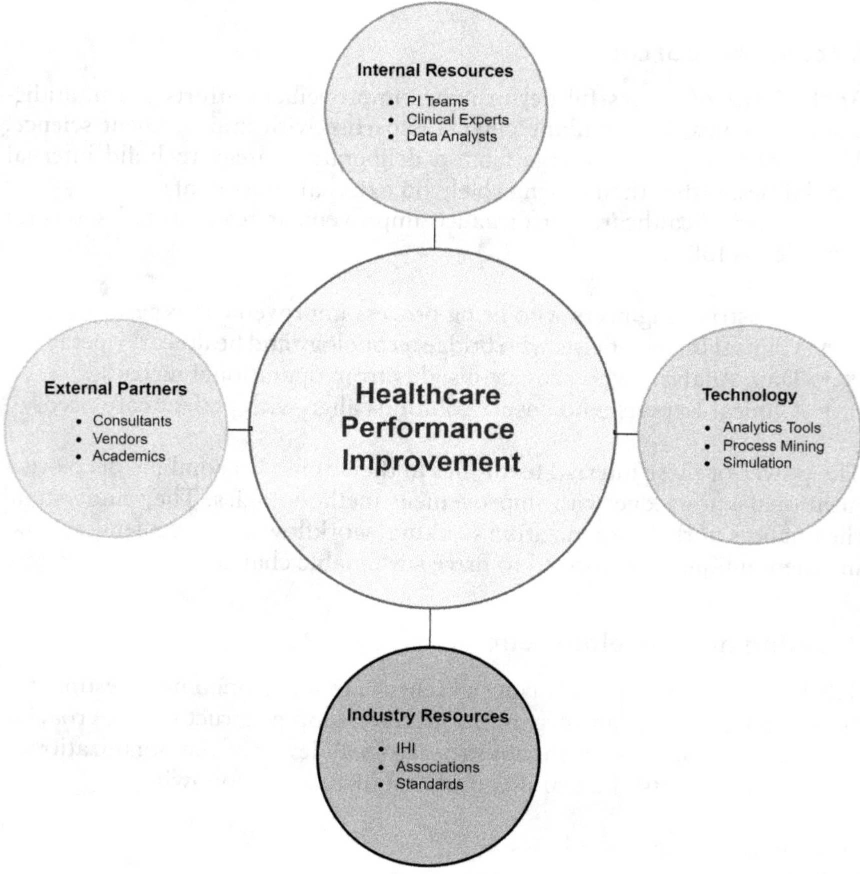

Figure 15.3 Healthcare performance improvement components.

Technology support

Modern performance improvement relies heavily on technology tools that enable data-driven decision-making. The technology stack for performance improvement has evolved significantly, moving from basic data collection to sophisticated real-time analytics.

Key technology components include the following:

- Process mining tools for workflow analysis
- Simulation software for scenario testing
- Analytics platforms for data visualization
- Real-time monitoring systems for immediate feedback

These tools work together to create a comprehensive improvement platform that supports both strategic planning and day-to-day operations.

Industry resources

Healthcare organizations benefit from a rich ecosystem of industry resources that support performance improvement efforts. These resources provide frameworks, best practices, and networking opportunities that accelerate improvement efforts.

The Institute for Healthcare Improvement (IHI) serves as a central knowledge hub, offering the following:

- Evidence-based methodologies
- Implementation guides
- Educational resources
- Networking opportunities

Professional associations complement these resources by providing the following:

- Specialty-specific guidance
- Peer networking platforms
- Professional development
- Standards development

Alignment with care traffic control

The ultimate success of performance improvement resources depends on their alignment with care traffic control initiatives. This alignment ensures that improvements support the broader goals of operational excellence and patient care quality.

Key considerations for alignment include the following:

1. Resource allocation based on strategic priorities
2. Integration of improvement methodologies with existing workflows
3. Measurement systems that track meaningful outcomes
4. Feedback mechanisms that support continuous learning

PERFORMANCE IMPROVEMENT METHODOLOGIES

The successful implementation of care traffic control relies heavily on proven performance improvement methodologies. While healthcare has traditionally borrowed methodologies from manufacturing and other industries, these approaches need careful adaptation to work effectively in the healthcare environment. The key is understanding how each methodology contributes to the overall improvement strategy while maintaining patient care quality and safety.

Lean in healthcare

Lean methodology has found particular resonance in healthcare operations because of its focus on eliminating waste and improving flow. Unlike manufacturing, where Lean originated, healthcare must adapt these principles to account for the variability inherent in patient care. In the context of care traffic control, Lean principles become especially significant when applied to mobile workflows.

Value Stream Mapping becomes especially powerful when enhanced with real-time location data. Traditional mapping relies on manual observation and historical data, often missing the nuances of daily workflow variations. When enhanced with location-based services, value stream maps become dynamic tools that reveal patterns and opportunities for improvement in real time. For example, tracking the movement of medical equipment through a hospital can reveal unnecessary transport patterns that traditional observation might miss.

The 5S methodology (sort, set in order, shine, standardize, and sustain) takes on new meaning when applied to mobile resources. Rather than organizing static workspaces, care traffic control allows organizations to maintain order in dynamic environments. For instance, mobile medical devices can be tracked to ensure that they return to designated locations after use, maintaining organization without constant manual oversight.

Six sigma integration

Six Sigma methodology provides the statistical rigor needed to measure and improve process performance. In healthcare, where variation can mean the difference between good and poor outcomes, Six Sigma's focus on reducing variance becomes crucial. When combined with care traffic control, it creates a powerful system for process improvement.

The DMAIC cycle (define, measure, analyze, improve, and control) takes on new dimensions when applied to location-aware workflows. In the Define phase, real-time location data help identify the true scope of process problems. The Measure phase benefits from automated data collection, providing more accurate and comprehensive metrics than manual observation. Analysis becomes more sophisticated with the ability to correlate location data with other process variables. Improvement actions can be more precisely targeted, and control measures can be automated through location-aware systems.

Theory of constraints

Theory of Constraints (TOC) offers a systematic approach to identifying and managing bottlenecks in operational flow. In healthcare, where resources are often shared across departments and services, understanding constraints becomes critical to improving overall system performance. Care Traffic Control enhances TOC by providing real-time visibility into how constraints impact workflows.

Consider an emergency department where patient flow depends on multiple interconnected processes. Traditional TOC might identify bed availability as a constraint, but care traffic control can reveal how porter availability, cleaning services, and equipment location all contribute to the constraint. This deeper understanding allows for more effective solutions that address the root causes of bottlenecks rather than just their symptoms (Figure 15.4).

Continuous improvement cycles

The PDCA (plan-do-check-act) cycle remains fundamental to performance improvement but takes on new dimensions with real-time data. Instead of relying on periodic reviews and historical data, organizations can now monitor improvement efforts as they happen, making adjustments in real time.

In the Planning phase, historical location data help identify patterns and opportunities that might not be visible through traditional observation. The Do phase benefits from immediate feedback on how changes impact workflow. Checking becomes more precise with real-time metrics, and Acting can be more targeted and timely. This accelerated improvement cycle helps organizations achieve and sustain improvements more effectively.

Agile methodologies

Healthcare organizations are increasingly adopting Agile principles for improvement work, recognizing that traditional project management approaches may

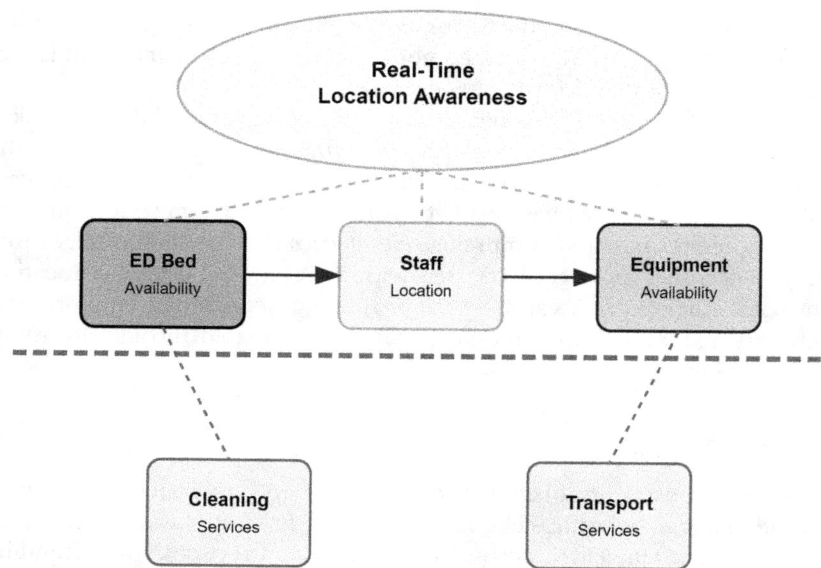

Figure 15.4 The location awareness for the ED bed availability constraint.

not suit the dynamic nature of healthcare operations. Agile's emphasis on iterative development and frequent stakeholder feedback aligns well with the incremental nature of care traffic control implementation.

The Agile approach allows organizations to start small, perhaps with a single department or workflow, and gradually expand based on lessons learned and demonstrated success. This reduces risk and allows for adjustment based on real-world experience rather than theoretical planning.

THE EDENVALE JOURNEY – THE ROLE OF PI

In the Middle Stages of implementation, Edenvale has a Patient Flow agent that is used by Bed Management to ensure that they can stay ahead of issues with patient flow. The Patient Flow agent works with the Patient Transport Dispatching agent to streamline transporter assignments. The digital twin is connected to the EHR, so all of this is coordinated with the EHR (admit, discharge, transfer – ADT). The Patient Flow agent is also connected to the EVS (Environmental services) agent so that Bed Management can see exactly when the room is ready and to reprioritize room cleans to stay ahead of any bottlenecks.

The transporters and housekeepers are carrying iPhones with agents loaded on them. The patient transporter's agent is tracking all the tasks in the workflow including the handoffs at the pickup and drop off locations. These handoffs are done with the assistance of the agents that the nurses carry. The wheelchairs and stretchers are easily located by the transporter's agent because the equipment has the BLE RTLS tags. The routes for the transports are optimized and the transport agent helps with the routes. The housekeeper's agent tracks the room cleans and knows when they are done with a triggering task. When they are cleaning the room, the phone stays in their pocket, but when they are done, they just have to remember to hold the phone close to the Edenvale logo on their cart. The logo has an NFC tag that will trigger the completion of the job. Then, the next job will pop up on the phone.

Edenvale's Performance Improvement team plays a key role in the implementation of care traffic control. They are skilled in composing agents and have done a great job iterating and improving the agents with more effective automation. They were able to work with the transporters and housekeepers to compose the agents for both transport and housekeeping. They are also actively working on improving the courier services that move many of the items that need to get distributed around the hospital.

Edenvale's performance improvement team has been working with finance to ensure that ROI numbers are being captured and they found that the project broke even in the early stages and they have seen exponential ROI as they have moved forward. This was attributed to the precise implementation of the sensors and tying the sensing directly to the workflows.

PLAYBOOK FOR PERFORMANCE IMPROVEMENT

A review of the definition of CTC is important here. "Care Traffic Control is using situational awareness and automation to optimize mobile workflows across the enterprise." The role of performance improvement in CTC is embedded in the phrase "optimizing mobile workflows." If CTC is a journey, performance improvement is the path that we will follow.

Improvers

Improvers are leading the performance improvement efforts. If a foundation has been built by modeling the workflows as rational agents, the path to success should focus on execution rather than discovery.

1. Assessment Framework
    - Document current state processes.
    - Identify improvement opportunities.
    - Create performance baselines.
    - Map value streams.
    - Define measurement systems.

2. Implementation Strategy
    - Use data-driven decision-making.
    - Start with pilot projects.
    - Build improvement cycles.
    - Document best practices.
    - Create feedback loops.
3. Project Management
    - Define project scope.
    - Set clear objectives.
    - Create timeline and milestones.
    - Establish resource requirements.
    - Monitor progress.
4. Success Measurement
    - Define key metrics.
    - Create measurement systems.
    - Document improvements.
    - Track ROI.
    - Share success stories.

Leaders

Leaders will be needed to show commitment to the organizational change initiatives that are necessary for CTC to be successful. Establishing well-defined selection criteria for making the investment in these initiatives is a good way to get that commitment. Project champions and high-level sponsors are also necessary.

1. Strategic Planning
    - Align improvements with organizational goals.
    - Create improvement roadmap.
    - Allocate resources.
    - Support cultural change.
    - Enable cross-functional collaboration.
2. Resource Support
    - Invest in improvement tools.
    - Provide staff training.
    - Allocate project resources.
    - Support technology adoption.
    - Enable data collection.
3. Culture Development
    - Foster improvement mindset.
    - Support experimentation.
    - Encourage innovation.
    - Recognize achievements.
    - Share lessons learned.

4. Sustainability Planning
    - Ensure long-term success.
    - Create sustainability plans.
    - Monitor ongoing performance.
    - Adjust strategies as needed.
    - Build continuous improvement cycles.

Creators

Vendors providing products that support CTC should pay attention to the direction that performance improvement takes. Engaging with improvers is a way for creators to see the methodology that is used for improvement and how new products can help. Improvers, in turn, can learn about the technology from creators and contribute ideas that align with improvement.

1. Solution Development
    - Create improvement tools.
    - Enable data collection.
    - Support measurement systems.
    - Build analysis capabilities.
    - Enable reporting functions.
2. Implementation Support
    - Provide implementation guidance.
    - Offer training programs.
    - Support system optimization.
    - Maintain documentation.
    - Enable performance tracking.
3. Innovation Focus
    - Develop new capabilities.
    - Enhance existing tools.
    - Support emerging methodologies.
    - Enable future expansion.
    - Build adaptive systems.

Chapter 16

Simulations

Paul E. Zieske

Aviation and air traffic control are famous for their use of simulations. From flight simulators installed in everything from desktop computers to full-size aircraft mockups, to sophisticated air traffic control scenario training, simulation plays a vital role in training, improvement, and safety. Healthcare organizations can similarly benefit from simulation approaches, though the applications and implementations may differ.

In this chapter, we examine simulations from two distinct perspectives. First, we explore operations simulators – test instances of real-world systems used by people who are part of daily operations. These simulators allow staff to practice scenarios and build competency without risking actual operations. Second, we delve into simulation modeling – systems used by improvement teams to model processes and test changes before implementation.

For care traffic control (CTC), the operational digital twin enables powerful simulation capabilities by providing real-time data that can emulate actual conditions. This means training scenarios can closely mirror real-world situations, allowing staff to develop skills and confidence in a safe environment. When implementing new workflows or testing process changes, simulations provide valuable insights into potential impacts before making changes are made in the live environment.

Just as air traffic controllers use simulators to practice complex traffic scenarios and emergency procedures, healthcare staff can use simulations to prepare for various situations they might encounter. These range from routine workflow optimization to crisis response preparation. The key difference in healthcare is that while aviation simulations often focus on individual pilot or controller skills, healthcare simulations must account for complex team interactions and varied patient scenarios.

Simulation modeling takes a different approach, using software tools to analyze how processes might perform under different conditions. This approach helps improvement teams understand bottlenecks, resource utilization, and potential impacts of changes before implementation. By combining both operations simulators and simulation modeling, healthcare organizations can build

DOI: 10.1201/9781003625483-19

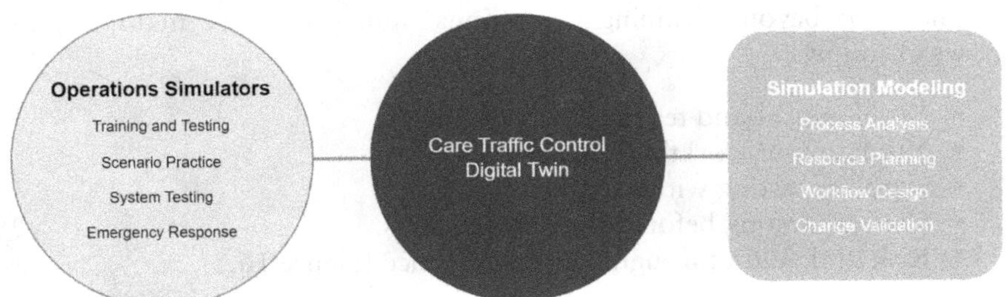

Figure 16.1 Comparison diagram of simulator and simulations with the digital twin in the middle.

comprehensive improvement programs that balance staff training needs with process optimization goals (Figure 16.1).

OPERATIONS SIMULATOR

For CTC, the operational digital twin can be used to create a realistic training environment. An operations simulator is essentially a replica of the digital twin used to emulate scenarios that might occur. Just as airlines and aircraft manufacturers use flight simulators to train pilots, healthcare organizations can use simulators to prepare staff for various operational situations.

Consider a typical scenario: The digital twin is being used by Central Equipment dispatchers to monitor the flow of medical equipment throughout the hospital, ensuring that PAR (Periodic Automatic Replenishment) levels are maintained and preventing stockouts. If we create a replica of this system and feed it simulated data that mimics real-world situations like stockouts or equipment bottlenecks, we have a powerful training tool. This simulator provides the same interface and functionality as the live system, but in a safe, controlled environment.

Key Components of an Operations Simulator are as follows:

1. Digital Twin Replication
   - Complete copy of the production environment interface.
   - Real-time data simulation capability.
   - Full functionality without impact on live operations.
2. Communication Systems
   - Integration with standard communication tools.
   - Ability to simulate various communication scenarios.
   - Practice of protocols and procedures.
3. Console Configurations
   - Replica workstations matching production environment.
   - Additional displays for instructor oversight.
   - Recording and playback capabilities for review.

Applications beyond Training Operations simulators serve multiple purposes as follows:

- Development and testing of new features.
- Validation of workflow changes.
- Usability testing with actual end users.
- Concept testing before major investments.
- Risk mitigation through scenario practice (Figure 16.2).

Consider a bed management scenario: The simulator can replicate a situation where the emergency department is experiencing high patient volumes, while several inpatient units are undergoing cleaning procedures. This creates a complex bed management challenge that staff can practice resolving without impacting actual patient care. The simulator provides real-time data feeds, communication channels, and system responses that mirror the production environment.

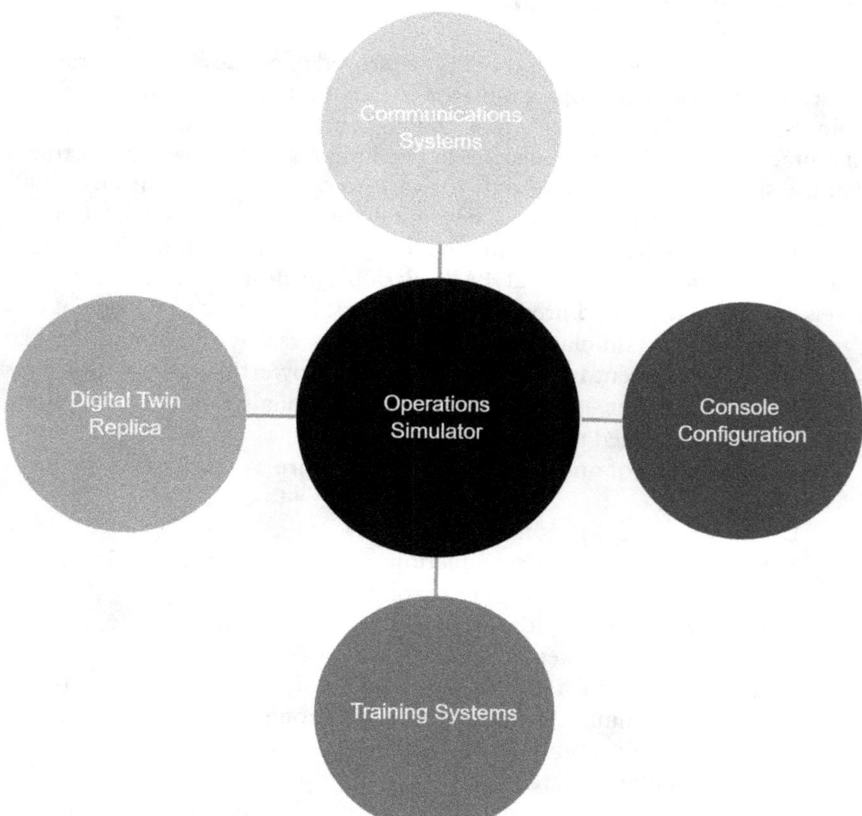

Figure 16.2 Components of a digital twin simulator.

The value of operations simulators extends beyond individual training. They serve as risk mitigation tools by allowing organizations to do the following:

- Test new procedures before implementation.
- Practice emergency responses.
- Validate system changes.
- Train teams in a safe environment.

SIMULATION MODELING

While operations simulators provide hands-on training environments, simulation modeling offers powerful analytical capabilities for understanding and improving healthcare processes. These models help organizations test changes and optimize workflows before implementation, thereby reducing risk and improving outcomes.

Two key approaches to simulation modeling are particularly valuable for healthcare: discrete event simulation (DES) and agent-based modeling (ABM). Each serves different purposes, and many situations benefit from combining both approaches.

Discrete event simulation

DES excels at analyzing workflows that can be broken down into distinct events occurring over time. Consider a patient transport workflow: Each transport request creates a sequence of events – the initial request, assigning a transporter, equipment preparation, patient pickup, transport time, and drop-off. DES allows us to model these sequences and understand how variations in timing, resources, or procedures affect overall performance.

For example, a hospital seeking to improve transport response times might use DES to analyze the following:

- How different staffing levels affect wait times?
- The impact of equipment availability on transport completion.
- Queue formation during peak demand periods.
- Resource utilization patterns throughout the day.
- The effect of prioritization rules on overall efficiency.

The power of DES lies in its ability to model complex sequences while accounting for variability and resource constraints. Organizations can test different scenarios without disrupting actual operations, leading to more confident decision-making about process changes (Figures 16.3 and 16.4).

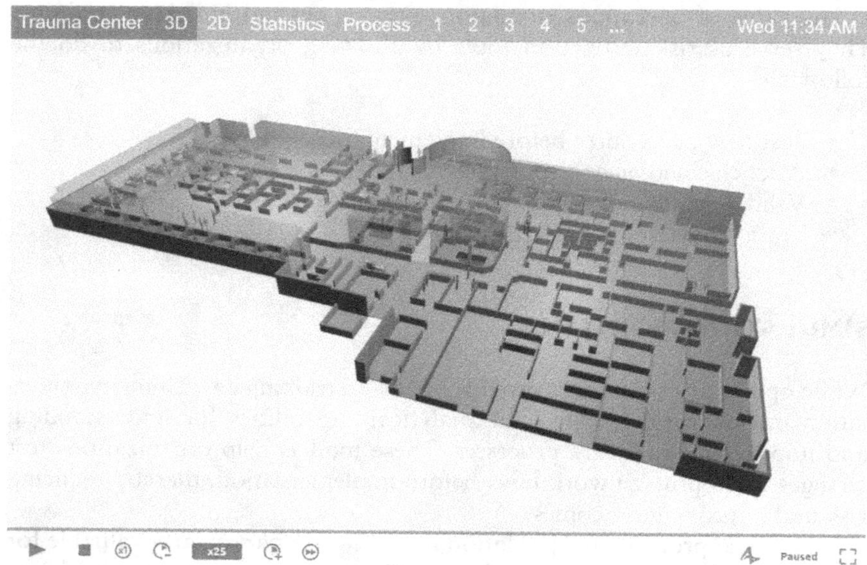

Figure 16.3 Image of the AnyLogic simulation modeling tool single floor. **credit AnyLogic.**

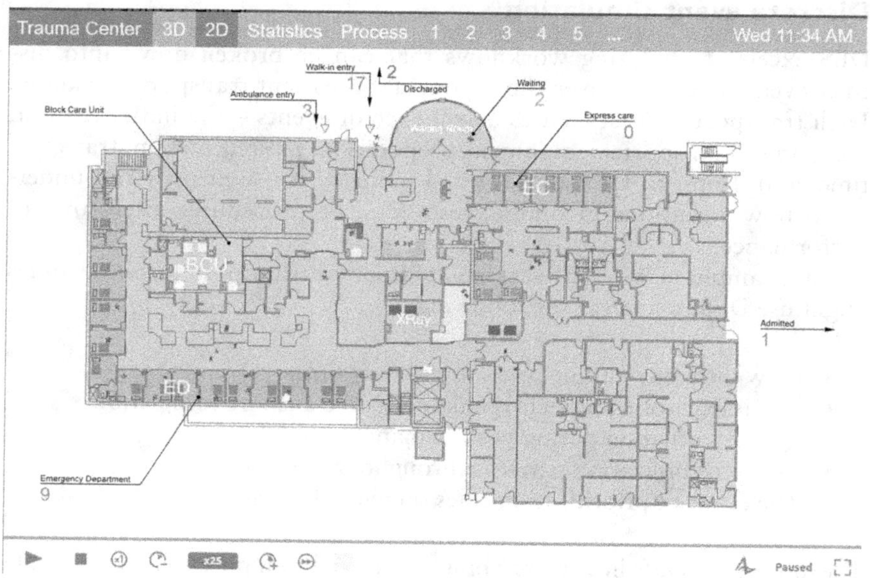

Figure 16.4 Image of the AnyLogic simulation modeling tool multifloor floor. **credit AnyLogic.**

The above two figures show the geospatial representation of the building where the simulation is taking place (credit to AnyLogic). Capturing the geospatial characteristics of a workflow allows a better representation of the real world and more accurate simulations.

Agent-based modeling

Where DES focuses on process flows, ABM examines how individual behaviors and interactions create system-level outcomes. In healthcare, agents might include staff members, patients, equipment, or even departments. Each agent follows its own rules and behaviors, creating complex patterns through their interactions.

Consider a busy emergency department: Nurses, doctors, patients, and equipment all move and interact based on their own priorities and needs. An ABM might reveal the following:

- How staff movement patterns affect response times?
- Where equipment tends to accumulate?
- How different triage rules impact patient flow?
- Which layout changes might improve efficiency?
- How communication patterns affect care delivery?

The strength of ABM lies in its ability to reveal emergent behaviors – patterns that arise from individual actions but might not be obvious when looking at the system as a whole. These insights can be particularly valuable when considering organizational changes or new procedures.

Hybrid approaches

Many healthcare situations benefit from combining DES and ABM approaches. For example, modeling a surgical department might use:

- DES to model the sequence of pre-op, surgery, and recovery.
- ABM to understand how staff and resource movements affect these processes.
- Combined analysis to optimize the entire system.

The key is matching the modeling approach to the problem at hand. Some questions require understanding precise sequences (DES), while others need insights into behavior patterns (ABM). The most powerful solutions often use both, providing complementary perspectives on complex healthcare operations.

Implementation considerations

Success with simulation modeling requires careful attention to several factors:

Data Quality: Models are only as good as their input data. Organizations need accurate information about process times, resource availability, and behavioral patterns to create meaningful simulations.

Validation: Models must be validated against real-world observations to ensure that they accurately represent the system being studied. This often involves iterative refinement based on stakeholder feedback and operational data.

Clear Objectives: Having specific questions or goals helps guide model development and ensures that the results provide actionable insights.

Stakeholder Engagement: Involving key stakeholders throughout the modeling process improves accuracy and increases buy-in for any recommended changes.

SIMULATIONS AND THE DIGITAL TWIN

Often, the primary use of a digital twin is to simulate physical entities or processes. This is a prototyping exercise that can reduce the time it takes to get a product to market or change implemented. This is valuable but it lacks access to real-world stimuli. That is why the operational digital twin and its access to conditions in the real world are so exciting. The ability to do both the prototyping for new processes as well as simulate those processes using data from the real world is game changing. Often the biggest challenge with innovation is the behavioral changes that are necessary for adapting to new technologies. When the stakeholders can see simulations of the changes, it is more likely that they will buy in.

Combining the simulation modeling tools that are described above and a digital twin that can create its own simulations will offer a staged approach to these improvements. This matches up well with the small incremental changes we want from our PDCA cycles.

EDENVALE'S CTC JOURNEY

Edenvale wanted to consolidate the transport of several different items to a single courier service. This initiative was part of their CTC strategy to standardize transport. Standard work is a Lean Six Sigma concept that improves service delivery and reduces costs. They knew this would be a big change that would impact all the departments involved. The items they were going to include were lab specimens, medications, medical gases, medical equipment, and supply chain items. Because this was such a big change, they wanted to run it through a simulation model.

They already had a simulation environment set up with the IMDF maps for the entire building. They have used this simulation before to model the flow of patients, so some of the setup work was already done. There were agents that are currently tracking most of these transports. That makes the data available that can show the current flow of these transports, so the model can be very accurate. Consolidating them into a single courier service will require some sophisticated coordination that will benefit from the modeling exercise.

The performance improvement team uses modeling to understand how to compose the agents. The model shows that the dispatch agent can put a number of different items into a scheduled round of deliveries. It balances the capacity of the transport with the frequency of the deliveries. The existing data show the demand rates for each of the items. There is variance in the demand rates because the measurements at the point of use are still imprecise. The modeling showed where creating more accurate demand measurements can create value.

Edenvale's Command Center was using simulators to create scenarios that were presented to the controllers on the Desktop Agents. These were mostly anomalies that would occur that the controller would need to react to. This helped them practice in preparation for participating as a controller on the floor of the command center. These would range from mass casualty events to scheduling issues that would delay department workflows.

In one simulation, the emergence of a new virus was indicating a possible pandemic, and the simulation was for a supply chain controller. The rest of the controllers that participated in the scenario were simulations, and the controller was put in the situation of dealing with expected shortages and rationing scenarios for PPE (Personal Protective Equipment) and other supplies. This was an airborne virus and the need for contact tracing was high.

Because Edenvale had the orderlies in all the units, the traffic in and out of the units was lowered and there was less human-to-human contact. The challenge in this scenario was to optimize the deliveries of supplies to the units to limit the number of trips while ensuring the correct supply and demand rates. Edenvale was used to just-in-time deliveries, which created the challenge. Also, the hospital had reconfigured several units into "infection disease units," so that changed the supply chain. The controller needed to deal with that as well.

The simulation considered the impact of staff shortages because many had fallen ill. We reallocated some people to different roles because the operations changed when clinics were operating on new schedules caused by the pandemic. The CTC agents were especially useful in a case like this because the agent could assist someone who had been thrust into a new role with limited training. That agent's workflow automation would provide the needed assistance and allow the command center to help by monitoring the workflow in real time.

Supply chain used indoor track and trace so not only could they track the flow of the supplies, but by tracking the movement of people who moved the supplies, they could trace the movement of these possible carriers of the virus. This traffic data was all a part of the analysis and predictions they would rely on to keep the hospital as safe as possible.

The configuration of the command center remained intact in this pandemic scenario, but some procedures were emphasized over others. The command center director wanted as many of these emergency scenarios as possible to keep people sharp. Up to now, they have not had to execute them outside of a drill, but everyone hoped it would stay that way.

In addition to the simulators, Edenvale had live drills that they would conduct in the actual command center. They did not have a full mockup of the command center to do live drills otherwise. The simulators made these drills go quite smoothly because the controllers were sharp from the training done in the simulators and they knew their roles well.

PLAYBOOK FOR SIMULATIONS

The most exciting, impactful, and challenging phase of CTC journey occurs when the automation advances to the point that the workflows must adapt. Simulation modeling is an effective tool for demonstrating the benefits of a workflow change, before the change happens. When CTC is a part of the organization, the workflows are prepared in a way that makes this much easier. The mapping of the flow to the appropriate modeling tools starts out as more of a data entry exercise than starting from scratch.

Improvers

Improvers who learn the skills necessary for creating simulation models will be on the front lines of improvement in any industry they are in. Healthcare improvers are in a unique position as there has never been more emphasis on the need for healthcare to become more efficient.

Many consultants are acquiring simulation modeling skills, but there are specialty services that offer simulation modeling services. These simulations are a deliverable that can be used after the engagement is over.

1. Simulation Planning
   - Identify simulation opportunities.
   - Define simulation objectives.
   - Document simulation requirements.

   - Map required data inputs.
   - Create validation criteria.
2. Model Development
   - Choose appropriate simulation type.
     - Discrete event simulation.
     - Agent-based modeling.
     - Hybrid approaches.
   - Gather baseline data.
   - Build initial models.
   - Validate model accuracy.
   - Refine simulation parameters.
3. Implementation Strategy
   - Start with simple models.
   - Build complexity gradually.
   - Create validation processes.
   - Establish feedback loops.
   - Document simulation results.
4. Analysis Framework
   - Define success metrics.
   - Create analysis protocols.
   - Document findings.
   - Share insights.
   - Track improvements.

Leaders

There are vendors who can create simulations as a service and many who have significant healthcare experience. Vendors are a great place to start with simulation modeling and leaders with good baseline knowledge of simulation modeling will be able to see which projects can benefit the most from the service.

Simulators are a much newer concept and there is very little in the market right now to get started with simulators. The emergence of the digital twin is likely to change that as simulations are a key component of their prototyping capabilities.

1. Strategic Investment
   - Understand simulation value.
   - Plan simulation infrastructure.
   - Support modeling expertise development.
   - Allocate resources.
   - Enable cross-functional use.
2. Resource Management
   - Invest in simulation tools.
   - Support training initiatives.
   - Plan for ongoing development.

- Enable data collection.
- Maintain simulation capabilities.

3. Cultural Integration
   - Foster simulation adoption.
   - Support data-driven decisions.
   - Encourage model use.
   - Share simulation insights.
   - Build analytical culture.
4. Risk Management
   - Validate simulation accuracy.
   - Ensure data quality.
   - Monitor model performance.
   - Create backup plans.
   - Maintain model integrity.

Vendors

Simulators can help customers understand the systems the vendors are selling. They can be used in training and be used as demos as well. A self-serve demo is a wonderful way to present a product when a customer is just trying to get "the feel" of it. The benefits go well beyond sales and business development as customers will want a product that can be used to simulate their real-world problems.

Simulations will allow vendors to prototype and "proof" their hypothesis before coding occurs. Being able to model the upstream and downstream processes for a product will allow some of the guess work to be removed.

1. Solution Development
   - Create flexible simulation tools.
   - Support multiple modeling approaches.
   - Enable data integration.
   - Build visualization capabilities.
   - Provide analysis tools.
2. Implementation Support
   - Provide modeling guidance.
   - Offer training programs.
   - Support model validation.
   - Maintain documentation.
   - Enable results sharing.
3. Innovation Focus
   - Develop new simulation capabilities.
   - Enhance existing models.
   - Support emerging standards.
   - Enable future expansion.
   - Build adaptive systems.

Chapter 17

Digital twin implementation

Paul E. Zieske

Implementing an operational digital twin represents one of the most transformative yet challenging technology initiatives a healthcare organization can undertake. The journey demands both technological innovation and operational transformation, carefully orchestrated to deliver value at each step. While the full implementation spans years rather than months, success depends on building momentum through early wins and demonstrable benefits that secure ongoing organizational commitment.

The implementation journey in healthcare differs markedly from the air traffic control systems that inspired it. Air traffic control benefits from government mandates and funding that support decade-long modernization initiatives. The Federal Aviation Administration can take a long view, methodically rolling out new capabilities across the national airspace system. Healthcare organizations, in contrast, must demonstrate returns much more quickly to justify continued investment. They operate in a market-driven environment where capital competes across many worthy initiatives.

Yet healthcare enjoys one significant advantage over air traffic control – the ability to implement composable systems rather than monolithic architectures. Where air traffic control systems typically require all-or-nothing implementations of tightly coupled components, healthcare digital twins can be built from autonomous components that deliver incremental value. This composability allows organizations to start small, prove value, and scale gradually while maintaining flexibility for future innovation.

The timing for digital twin implementation has never been better. Location tracking technologies have matured beyond simple asset tracking to enable sophisticated workflow optimization. Mobile devices have become ubiquitous tools for healthcare workers. Internet of Things platforms provide robust infrastructure for collecting and analyzing sensor data. Cloud computing offers elastic resources for processing complex scenarios. Artificial intelligence (AI) and machine learning create new possibilities for automation and optimization. Perhaps most importantly, standards for interoperability are emerging that allow these technologies to work together effectively (Figure 17.1).

Success requires carefully balancing several strategic imperatives. The implementation must deliver enough early value to maintain organizational

DOI: 10.1201/9781003625483-20

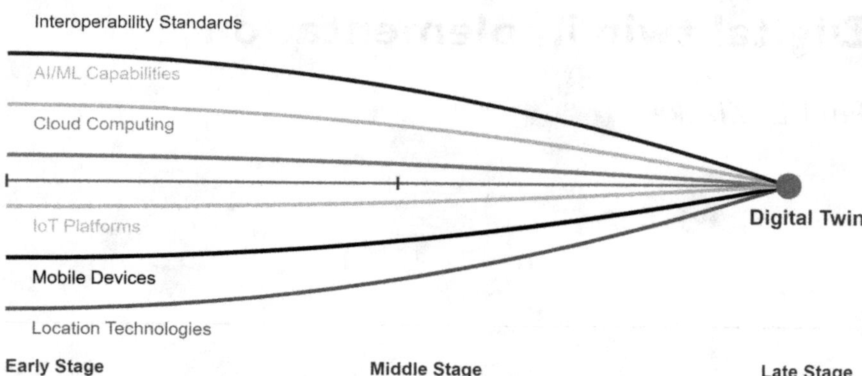

Figure 17.1 **Diagram that shows how systems converge into the digital twin over time.**

commitment while building toward long-term transformation. It needs to manage risk by starting with proven technologies while maintaining flexibility to adopt emerging capabilities. Change management demands sensitivity to organizational culture and user acceptance while steadily advancing new workflows and capabilities. Technology choices must avoid technical debt while supporting innovation (Figure 17.2).

The digital twin implementation framework addresses these imperatives through three integrated elements. First, an agent architecture mirrors the

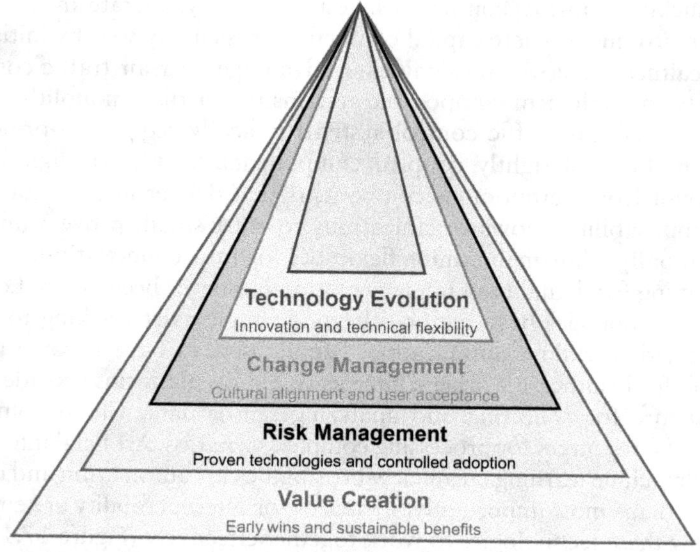

Figure 17.2 **Diagram showing the digital twin implementation and all of its greater parts.**

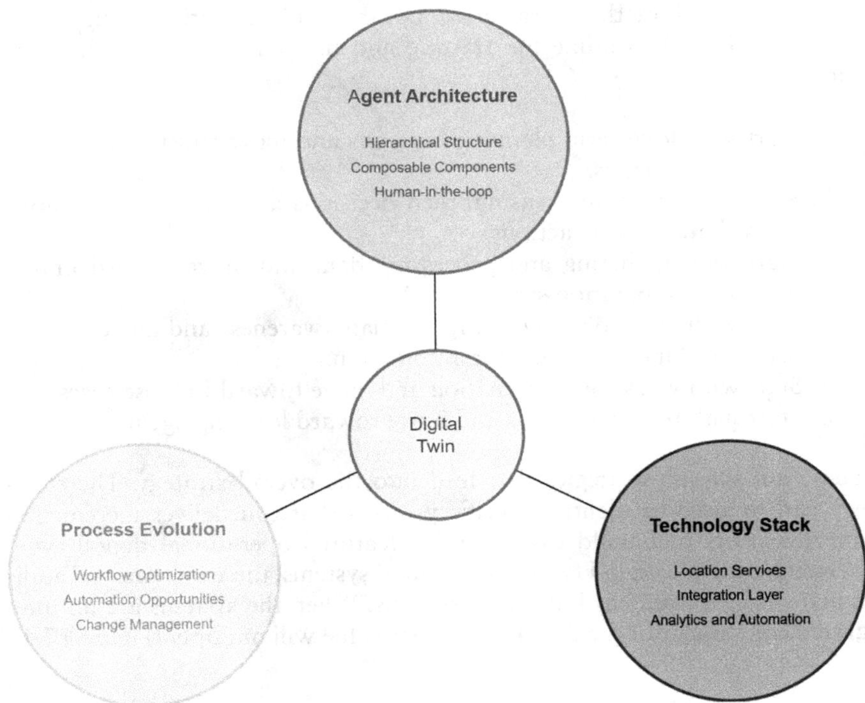

Figure 17.3 Diagram that shows the three parts of the implementation that evolve together.

organization's structure through composable components and human-in-the-loop (HITL) design. Second, a flexible technology stack combines location services infrastructure, integration capabilities, analytics, automation, and user interfaces. Finally, a process evolution approach optimizes workflows and introduces automation opportunities at a pace the organization can absorb (Figure 17.3).

This strategic framework provides the foundation for implementing a digital twin that delivers sustainable value. The following sections detail specific strategies and methodologies for bringing this vision to life. Like the digital twin itself, successful implementation requires maintaining a clear sight of both the destination and the next step in the journey.

IMPLEMENTATION STRATEGY

Because we want the incremental advances that we can tie to economic benefits, we will structure the implementation to ensure the maximum ROI. What are the incremental investments in the operational digital twin that we can make that yield the greatest return? To understand this approach better, we will show the characteristics of the implementation along a continuum. Below, we outline the starting and finishing points for these six sub-strategies.

1. Start with long-term planning horizons and move toward short-term planning horizons.
2. Start with installing sensing, then decisions and thinking and move toward automating actions.
3. Start with gathering and processing data and move toward implementing computation systems.
4. Start with using observation for human awareness and move toward using machine awareness for automation.
5. Start with workflow automation and move toward LBS use cases.
6. Start with reflexive agents and move toward learning agents.

These are six sub-strategies that feed into the overall strategy. The strategy can be used to identify specific projects that can deliver incremental improvements that build toward a full featured operational digital twin. Remembering the digital twin is a system of systems, these incremental additions will have value as individual systems. When the systems are an integrated component of the digital twin, that value will multiply (Figure 17.4).

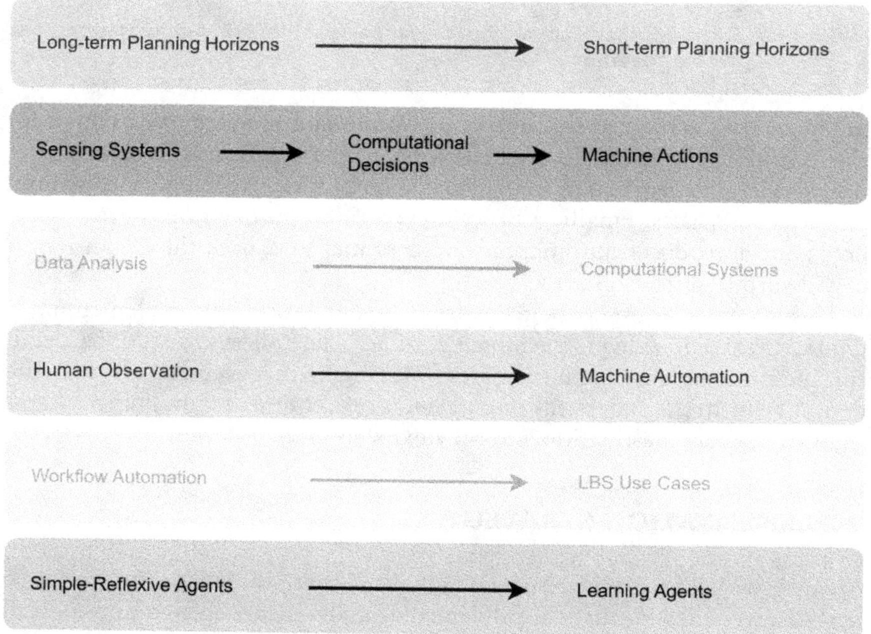

Figure 17.4 Diagram that shows how the strategy evolves based on sub-strategies.

Long-term to short-term planning horizons

The planning horizon is a term that applies equally to our study of AI as it does the organizational time frames. As a reminder, the planning horizon is the "think-time" necessary for decisions to be made. The long-term planning horizon maps to the higher levels in the organizational structure where the tactical and strategic decisions are made over a period of months and even years. The short-term planning horizons pertain to decisions that are made in the lower levels down to the workflow or even tasks.

Starting with a long-term planning horizon has the effect of creating a top-down approach early in the journey. This allows a bottom-up approach later, when details matter more, and operational agents are being created. In this case, the decisions are pertaining to the outcomes for workflows. These are data-driven decisions that come from the instrumentation that is provided by sensing and sensors. The sensing and sensors provide precision data gathered over a longer period. This ensures that the system is ready when we eventually need real-time data for the workflows we are optimizing.

This approach will not impact the operations at the beginning of the journey because it is intended to provide management with the means to observe the performance of the workflows over a longer period.

Benefits of starting with long-term planning horizons are as follows:

- Creates sustained visibility for leadership.
- Less complex because it is sensing-only.
- Less change management early in the journey.
- Analytics are established early to validate the outcomes.
- Lower fidelity tracking needed up front (e.g., RTLS).
- Lower cost in the beginning.
- Introducing AI is easier with longer planning horizons.

Sensing then thinking then actions

When implementing the digital twin, its system-of-systems design creates autonomy for the component systems. This autonomy allows the implementation of a system of sensors before the need for transactional intelligence that is needed with real-time processing. Starting with sensing, then thinking and decisions, and finally moving toward actions is a stepwise approach to implementation. It allows the sensing to be tested in the environment to see the perception it creates. Fully understanding this perception allows us to understand the ability of the agent to make decisions and eventually act. We have discussed that agents use cycles of perceive>think>act to create outcomes in the environment. Automation comes from adding technology to the agent to remove human effort at each stage of the cycle. Implementing the sensing for the selected workflows can be done for the higher level agents before moving down to the operational agents.

Implementing the sensors first creates data from real-world workflows. This allows the agents to be created with a more complete understanding of the perception that is possible. It also informs iterations of the sensing in support of the workflow improvements.

Benefits of starting with sensing are as follows:

- Analytics are applied to real-time data.
- Percepts are created from the analytics.
- Agents are using a robust perception scheme.
- Decisions are made using a better understanding of the environment.
- Actions are performed from better decisions.

Data analysis before computation systems

Starting with data gathering and analysis before moving toward computation systems is a strategy that is somewhat unique to systems that involve sensing. Most systems need their computational features before they can produce valuable data, but big-data producers like IoT are able to create data as they observe the environment. When the data are matched to the workflow, events are created, and those events can be analyzed. Entire processes can be viewed and evaluated before the computation features are used to create automation. The data are of the quality that can be used to train AI. This will support automation and the creation of the agent architecture.

Benefits of the data to computation strategy are as follows:

- Supports first the top-down approach and later the bottom-up approach.
- Collects good data for training future AI.
- Find bottlenecks early, and use computational techniques to remove them later.

Observation before automation

Initially, the agents will observe the environment through the sensing that was implemented and later that sensing will allow automation to remove some of the human effort. Starting with observation and moving toward automation considers the HITL continuum of automation. Observation is the phase where humans use the information that is provided by the sensors to make decisions. Automation occurs when the sensors provide the information to machines that use the information to make changes in the environment. Automation uses the computation features of the system to make the changes.

Benefits of an observation to automation strategy are as follows:

- Creating observation first allows visibility into where the automation should be applied.
- Leverages the sensing in the shorter planning horizon (real-time).

Workflows before use cases

Starting with workflows before moving toward use cases is a strategy that keeps the scope of the digital twin focused on care traffic control (CTC). Location-based services use cases are the solutions that are currently in the market designed to solve a problem, but they are discrete solutions that are difficult to integrate into the workflow. Using the CTC definition like a mission statement: "CTC is using situation awareness and automation to optimize mobile workflows across the enterprise," means we are considering the outcomes of the overarching workflows. Starting with the workflows is the path toward being able to optimize them.

The LBS use cases are still of value, but only in the context of the workflow. Our goal is to eventually embed the use cases into the workflow, so we need to wait until the workflows are ready to move forward with that part of the strategy. For example, consider an RTLS use case like employee duress. If we examine the workflow and create some workflow automation, we might find that parts of the employee duress use case are already a part of the workflow automation that was created.

Benefits of the "workflows to use cases" strategy are as follows:

- Focus on the most valuable workflows first.
- Understand the requirements for the workflow before selecting use cases.
- Create the requirements for the use cases based on the workflows.
- Build a foundation for future use cases.

Simple-reflexive before learning agents

Simple-reflexive agents are rules oriented, have no memory, and do not think ahead. They are useful in the early stages because they are predictable and thrive in a highly observable and deterministic environment. They will do well with long-planning horizons and use sensors to observe the environment. Because they do not have a memory, they do not need lots of stored data to perform well. These could be used to recognize patterns in the data and reveal insights for process improvement and they could be used for the initial iterations of workflow automation.

Model-based agents are gathering state information, as well as state transitions, to understand more about how the world works. Initially, we gather sensor and context data that can be used later to establish the model that these agents will use to gain that understanding. The agent will use this understanding to make better decisions that are based on predictions. With these agents, understanding is based on the model, but the model itself only improves if it is periodically retrained. As the sensors are gathering data and there are more sensors added, the model will improve. Context from external systems is important here as well.

Goal-based agents use the model to go beyond the predictions and plan toward a goal. This could be something simple, like routing to a destination in a building, or more complex, like optimizing the delivery of items in a supply chain.

Learning agents can update the model based on experiences and reduce or eliminate the need for retraining. They adapt to new information and can cooperate with other agents well. However, because they are learning, it is important to ensure that the model is updated regularly, because the agents could conflict. Therefore, hierarchical control is important when these highly capable agents are expected to cooperate and collaborate.

IMPLEMENTATION STAGES

The implementation of a digital twin progresses through distinct stages, each building on previous capabilities while preparing for future advancement. Understanding these stages helps organizations to plan their journey and set appropriate expectations for each phase of development (Figure 17.5).

Early stage: Laying the foundation

In the early stages, organizations focus on establishing basic visibility and understanding. The digital twin begins with observation and data collection, creating a baseline understanding of operations. This emphasis on observation before action allows organizations to validate their approach while building essential capabilities.

For example, implementing patient tracking starts with simply collecting movement data. This information, gathered over time, reveals actual patient flow patterns and variations from expected processes. While the technology infrastructure is being established, teams analyze this data to identify opportunities for improvement and validate system capabilities.

During this stage, analysis focuses on longer planning horizons – weekly and monthly patterns rather than real-time optimization. This measured approach allows both technical systems and users to develop competency with basic functions before taking on more time-sensitive operations.

Early middle stage: Building capabilities

As the foundation stabilizes, organizations begin expanding both the scope and sophistication of their digital twin implementations. Data collection

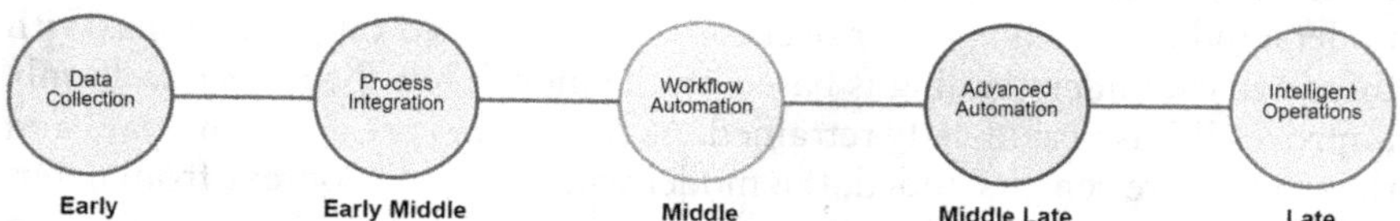

Figure 17.5 Implementation stages.

becomes more comprehensive, and basic tracking evolves into understanding of process flows and interdependencies.

Initial integration between departments begins during this stage. Patient movement data starts to connect with staff scheduling, room cleaning, and equipment availability. The digital twin provides visibility into not just individual processes, but also into how they affect each other.

Real-time monitoring capabilities emerge, though primarily for awareness rather than action. Teams can view current conditions, building understanding and trust while identifying opportunities for future automation.

Middle stage: Deepening integration

The middle stage marks a transition as the digital twin moves from primarily observing to actively supporting operations. The system begins providing decision support based on established patterns and rules.

Workflow automation demonstrates increasing value. For example, patient transport management starts incorporating multiple factors for scheduling and routing optimization. Equipment tracking expands to support preventive maintenance scheduling and par level management.

Integration between systems increases, with the digital twin serving as a central point for operational data. Information flows more efficiently between departments, supporting more coordinated operations across units (Figure 17.6).

Middle-late stage: Advancing automation

With established trust and capabilities, the digital twin takes on more active roles in daily operations. The system handles routine decisions while maintaining human oversight for complex situations.

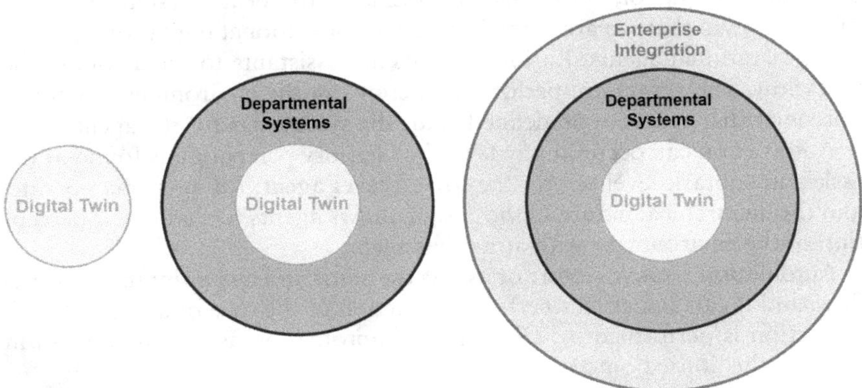

Figure 17.6 Diagram shows the expanding scope of the digital twin.

Automation capabilities expand, managing standard processes while escalating unusual cases for human attention. This balanced approach allows staff to focus on complex decisions while ensuring reliable execution of routine operations.

Late stage: Optimizing operations

In its mature state, the digital twin becomes a core system for operational management. It coordinates complex workflows across departments while optimizing resource utilization in real-time. Predictive capabilities help prevent problems before they occur, while continuing to adapt to new requirements.

This stage focuses on continuous improvement rather than being an endpoint. Organizations continue refining and expanding capabilities based on operational needs and emerging technologies.

PLATFORM STACK ARCHITECTURAL FRAMEWORK

We are returning to where we left off in Chapter 8, with the Platform Stack Architectural Framework that was created by the DTC (Digital Twin Consortium). It offers the high-level abstraction that we need to add some more specifics pertaining to our version of the operational digital twin (Figure 17.7).

AGENTIC ARCHITECTURE

The approach to automation that is used by CTC starts with the digital twin that was first described in Chapter 4. This is a virtual representation of the environment where the automation is targeted. It could be a department, an entire building, or, in the case of CTC, an entire health system. The type of digital twin that we are using is called an operational digital twin, and it involves rational agents. Rational agents are assistants to the actors in the workflow. The actors are performing actions in the environment to create outcomes that are from predefined goals the system has for the agent.

Automation can occur at any level, but sensory perception is found at the task and subtask level within the lowest-level agent. All agents cooperate, and the hierarchical nature of the design allows agents to share their perception of the environment with any other agent.

Automation removes effort or assists the actor and any point in the workflow, and it can sometimes perform the action in the case of a robot. When the action is performed by a human, the automation assists the human in creating the desired outcome.

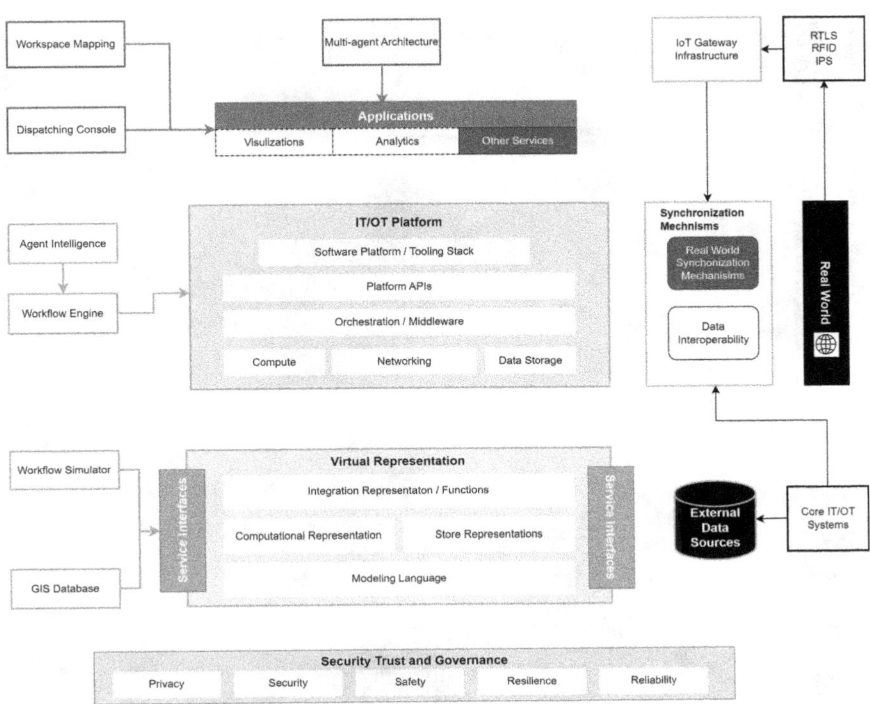

Figure 17.7 Platform stack architecture for the operational digital twin diagram.

Starting with an agentic design that follows the organization structure allows the hierarchical and multi-agent structure to progress incrementally from using little automation and AI toward increasing amounts of automation. The agentic design, which follows the HITL principle, recognizes the role of the human at each step of the perceive think act cycle.

The case of Figure 17.8 the Transport actor is accessing three different agents depending on the assignment that comes from the dispatcher. The dispatcher agent accesses the sensing and perception that comes from the lower-level agents.

For instance, with the agentic design, we would model the tasks in the workflow and how their accomplishment is perceived, whether that perception is human or machine perception. In the case where a patient transport agent is perceiving the arrival of the patient at the destination. Initially, that might be done with a patient transporter calling the dispatcher with a house phone. That phone call would be modeled in the agentic design as perception. Later, when the arrival is done with a geofence, the perception of that arrival is switched to the geofence. Note that AI is not a part of this process yet, but when it is integrated, the AI will be swapped in where it belongs, whether is in perception, thinking, or actions.

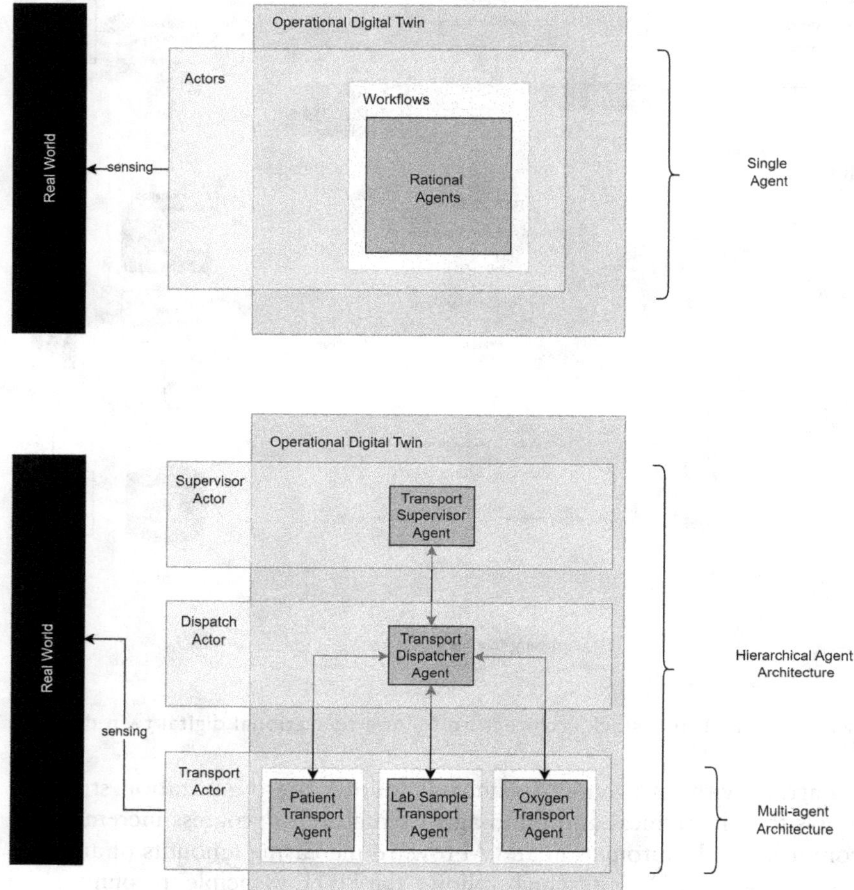

Figure 17.8 Agent architecture within the operational digital twin.

IMPLEMENTATION PROCESS FOR AN AGENT

At every stage of the implementation, agents will be created. The goal for each stage is to maximize the agent architecture so that the human actors can have all the assistance the agents can provide. All of this is done within the limits and direction set by the governance set in place by the organization. Initially, conventional methods will be used to design the agents, but when AI is added, the need for many of these methods will disappear. Below is a sequence of tools that can get the process started for the agents who are in the early stages of implementation. Later, agents will assist in the development of new agents.

1. Create a business process management (BPM) diagram of the "as-is"
    a. This is the process as is currently being used.

   b. Identify the systems that are currently used in the workflow.
   c. Ensure that the current systems are represented in the as-is BPM diagram.
2. Process Mining
   a. Connect the process mining tools to the current systems of record.
   b. Analyze the events from the current systems of record.
   c. Conformance analysis compares the process mining results with the as-is BPM.
3. Find Bottlenecks and Anomalies
   a. Find the queues and delays in the process mining results.
   b. Find process anomalies in the process mining results.
   c. Find both in the BPM and adapt the BPM accordingly.
4. Observability Analysis
   a. Find the blind spots in the workflow that mask visibility to the bottlenecks.
   b. Determine what sensing and context is necessary to make the bottlenecks observable.
   c. Determine what sensing and context is necessary to detect the anomalies.
   d. Propose additions to the agent to add observability to the blind spots.
   e. Propose additions to the agent to detect anomalies.
5. Cost Analysis
   a. Determine the time value economics for automating the nominal flow.
   b. Determine the economics of additions to observe the bottlenecks.
   c. Determine the economics of detecting the anomalies (Figure 17.9).

Business process management (BPM)

Chapter 2, "Core geospatial concepts" introduced modeling the agents from the perceive>think>act perspective. Here, we will create an "as-is" model for the workflow that we are trying to automate. To get started, we will rely on the structure that is provided by the existing workflows and make the environment as deterministic as possible. To do that, we can use BPM tools to create the flows in the format that aligns with the rational agent structure.

BPM is a process improvement tool for the Digital Transformation. Business process modeling notation (BPMN) is a standardized modeling language for documenting business processes and workflows. It includes a graphical representation and standardized symbology for complex workflows. However, BPMN is much more than just a graphical notation for processes. Workflows built using these tools include a standardized output that is serialized in xml. This means that systems can consume these workflows and process them to execute the flows. This has given rise to something called the workflow engine. These come with varying capabilities, but

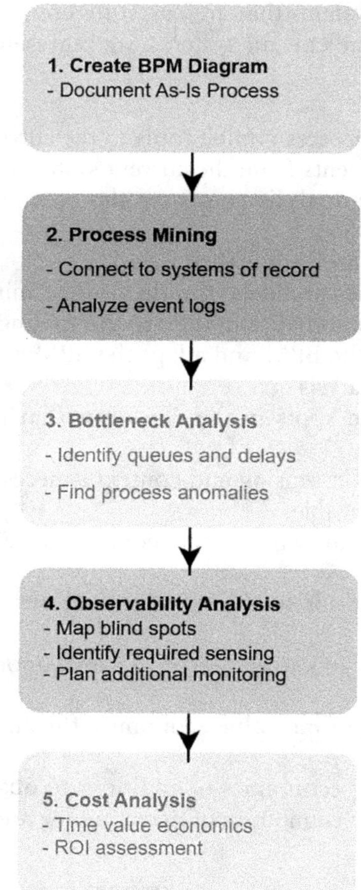

Figure 17.9 Steps for implementing an agent for process improvement.

they offer a great deal of potential for automating processes. Camunda (Camunda.com) is one such product that has these capabilities.

The workflow engine thrives in fully observable, deterministic environments. It typically uses condition/action sequences that involve very little AI. It also works well in processes with short planning horizons. With or without AI, the BPM exercise is good at understanding what the current workflow looks like.

Using BPM as first step in our workflow modeling process enables workflow automation from a workflow engine. We will use a structure for creating the BPM that aligns with the creation of the agents. The structure divides the workflow into people, property, and places. The people who are performing the work will be identified by role, the property will be only what is necessary for the workflow, and the places will be rooms and spaces that are important to the workflow.

Process mining

An important part of our CTC ecosystem is understanding how the core systems participate holistically. The core systems and "systems of record" produce events that they use to monitor their processes. The events, which are used to register the interaction with the users, can be accessed by processing mining tools. *Process mining* tools analyze event logs to discover, monitor, and improve real business processes by providing insights into their actual execution and performance. Celonis (celonis.com) is a process mining tool that provides the outputs necessary to analyze these workflows. Process mining can reveal the actual process that is being used, allowing the results can be compared with the outcomes that the system is designed for. If it is a favorable or unfavorable outcome, the process can be adjusted accordingly. It is extremely important to compare this analysis with the BPM diagrams, so that a reconciliation can be done. This conformance analysis is very helpful, as we move forward with further automation.

Bottleneck analysis

The process mining provides a bottleneck analysis for the events that are contained in the system that is currently part of the workflow. Combining the BPM and the process mining will show any blind spots. These blind spots can be covered with additional monitoring, such as user inputs, integration points, and sensors. The blind spots can be shown in the "as-is" version of the BPM diagram and filled in the "to-be" version of the BPM diagram. Since the BPM is still just a diagram, the comparison with the process mining is a better "real-world" representation. The bottleneck analysis could be anecdotal, but because it includes the entire process, it will help make a case for ensuring the blind spots are filled. The bottleneck analysis shows what delays can be seen and where the blind spots are. When the blind spots are filled, more bottlenecks may be revealed. This is why the methodology is iterative.

Observability analysis

Where the bottleneck analysis reveals the bottlenecks and where the blind spots are, the Observability Analysis addresses how to fill the blind spots. This might be a user input, a scan, location percepts from the 4Ps, or integration from an external system. This is why the catalog of percepts that was described in Chapter 11 becomes an important input. The goal is to fill the blind spots with minimal input from the user. There are cases where user input will lead to further automation that creates a net reduction in effort. Maybe the workflow asks a question and the answer from the user allows them to skip steps. The other consideration is the fidelity of the information used in observability. This needs to be tested thoroughly so that inaccurate information is not automated into the workflow. At this stage of the process, the BPM is enhanced with the means of observability that is proposed for this cycle in the methodology.

Workflow automation economics

The bottlenecks are delays that, if associated with the cost of the delay, can produce a measurement of the total cost of delay for each episode that the agent is involved in. This will allow us to make recommendations on whether to add observability or to change the process.

ROBOTS

Robots and Drones are going to be an important part of the future of Healthcare Delivery Organizations (HDO). Autonomous mobile robots (AMRs) are already providing transport services in a growing number of HDOs.

In hospitals, operating costs divide loosely around people, equipment, and supplies. Otherwise known as "staff and stuff." We know that to drive some of the costs out of hospital operations, we can get the huge return by optimizing the supply chain. When we look at the equipment side, we know that we want to drive up utilization and availability and drive down the cost of maintaining the fleet. When we think about the hospital of the future, robots are a part of that vision, but there is no reason to wait for the hospital of the future. The technology is here but the operational processes to get the most out of the robots are what is missing.

Micro-logistics is most familiar to people when you see a warehouse with robots moving items into bins to be prepared for shipment. This model can be expanded to automate the movement of "stuff" in any indoor space. The warehouse is an orderly environment to this, but these warehouses are often highly automated. Hospitals are much more chaotic, but there is a way to add order, increase the automation, and improve efficiency with micro-logistics.

Autonomous mobile robots (AMRs)

AMRs in healthcare have a huge amount of potential. Let us look at how the devices would work in a CTC environment. These robots need three things to work: locomotion, navigation, and dexterity. The current state of indoor robots is that, of the three, dexterity is the most expensive, which creates an upper limit for the automation that the robot can provide. This is because someone must load and unload the robot, which adds a human to the equation. That does not mean that there is not a huge value over the traditional delivery system, but it is important to recognize the limits and adapt to them. The goal is to transfer the transport motion to the robots and keep the robot's duty cycle maximized. Then, ensure that the role of the human in the operation is minimized and appropriate.

When we think about hospital operations holistically, and from our CTC perspective, there is a way to create the proper balance between human and machine, and use a human to provide the dexterity necessary for our micrologistics operation. Let us think about this from a departmental perspective: What is coming into the department, what is leaving the department, and what is moving around in the department?

What is coming into the department? Medications, supplies, linens, clean medical equipment, blood, medical gases, and, of course, patients. In that list, there are many different people who are doing the transport which is highly inefficient.

What is leaving the department? Medical waste, garbage, sharps, dirty medical equipment, empty tanks, lab specimens, and, of course, patients. The same goes here, many different people coming into the department to pick up things.

What is moving around in the department? Medical equipment, medical gases, supplies, and, of course, patients, all of which add to the chaos.

Let us come back to robots. If we take the dexterity part out and concede that a human needs to provide that dexterity, how do we ensure that the hospital gets the value they want? We know that for deliveries, usually there is a central location, and a human is needed to load the transport for whatever is being delivered. Those people exist now as they are currently doing the transport. Now, we will rely on the robot to do the transport to the destination with what has been loaded. At the destination, we will have a person who is called a "Department Orderly." This is kind of a catchall role, but what will this orderly do? The robot will bring things into the department on a schedule, and the orderly will put it in its proper place. The orderly will also send the robot back with the things that need to leave the department. This improves the duty cycles of the robot. The only time the robot is not doing work is when it is charging.

What else is the orderly going to do? Remember, this is in our CTC-enabled hospital. Going back to our list above, dirty IV pumps need to be put in the dirty utility closet, and the PAR levels for everything need to be maintained so stretchers in the ED, wheelchairs in the lobbies, and so on. Lean Six Sigma tells us everything has a place, and everything should be in its place. This is the concept of shadow boards where we have a map of where things are supposed to be, and the orderly makes sure they are put in their place. The RTLS helps them recover lost equipment, missing supplies, and even missing patients. The orderly is truly responsible for "order" in the department or departments they support.

The orderly will have a mobile device and an app. The same goes for the department that is the source of the delivery. The source will schedule deliveries, and the robots will come to pick up on that schedule. When a load is scanned into the robot, the destination will be assigned to the job, and the orderly for that destination will get a notification that the job has started, and see the location of the robot. Another notification will be sent at the time of arrival. The job cannot start unless the orderly has signed in because they need to be ready to receive the delivery when it comes. Upon arrival, the orderly will be tasked with ensuring the dwell time for the robot is minimized, so they will be sure to be ready and offload the robot quickly. Using the app, the orderly will be able to "log" the work, track what is accomplished, and take work orders from the nurses in the department they support.

This model will allow the caregivers to focus on the patients, as they will not spend time looking for things or ordering things. The work that is being done to keep things stocked and available will be the responsibility of the source department like supply chain instead of the nurses and managers who often must create orders and stock shelves. CTC will provide tight monitoring of everything coming into the department and leaving the department. Between the source, the transport, and the destination, the balance of work between human and machine can be optimized. Whether there are more robots or less robots, there is plenty of work to get done by the orderly.

Unmanned aerial vehicles (UAVs)

Unmanned aerial vehicles (UAVs) are most familiar to us as drones. The devices offer another transport mechanism that can address time critical medical services. They also offer access in remote and hard-to-reach locations. The main challenge for using drones is that the distance they need to travel means they would be flying beyond-visual-line-of-sight (BVLOS). This is not yet allowed for civilian UAVs, but many of these issues are being worked out with the FAA (Federal Aviation Administration).

When drones are used, real-time location is already a part of the operation. However, there will be some additional management infrastructure required as a part of the implementation. These drones will have all the makings of transport agents and will need to operate with as much situational awareness as possible. The urgency around the workflows that they are involved in creates a perfect fit for CTC.

Benefits:

1. Organ Transport: Because the viability of a donor organ diminishes with time, organ transport by drone is getting a lot of attention. A key advantage of a drone is that they can fly hospital to hospital eliminating the delays associated with airports and ground transportation.
2. Blood Transport: Within a metropolitan area, a drone can make a smooth and timely delivery of blood between hospitals, the Red Cross, or other facilities.

3. Medical Supply Delivery: Essential medical supplies, such as vaccines, medications, and diagnostic samples, can be delivered to hard to serve areas.
4. Emergency Response: In emergencies or disasters, life-saving equipment can be delivered where it is needed quickly.
5. Telemedicine Support: Telemedicine kits can be delivered to places where medical providers are needed but unable to access otherwise. These kits have all the technology necessary to enable someone to make a connection to a provider on the other end.

Apart from the obvious benefits, there are additional challenges associated with using this mode of transport.

Challenges:

Regulations: The FAA is not the only regulatory agency that must approve drone services. If hazardous materials are part of any payload, the EPA (Environmental Protection Agency) would need to approve. Additionally, the FDA (Food and Drug Administration) would regulate the transport of any medications that are being transported as well.

Safety and Reliability: Weather, air traffic, and the airworthiness of the aircraft play into the approval process by the FAA.

Infrastructure and Integration: The operational digital twin can play a role here. The fleet management and traffic control technologies are an important part of embedding this service into the operations.

Cost and Funding: Investments will need to be made for the infrastructure as well as the UAVs themselves, so that they can fit the unique needs of the medical use cases.

Public Acceptance: Introducing a device like a UAV into the public airspace will need public acceptance, as the drones will introduce noise and privacy concerns, no matter what their function is advertised to be. Transparency and awareness will be critical to obtaining the acceptance of these devices.

Unmanned Traffic Management (UTM):

Unmanned Traffic Management is the overarching concept of safely integrating drones into the national airspace.

Cooperative Interaction: Because of the ability to terminate these flights at places other than airports, there needs to be a cooperative interaction between operators, service providers, and the FAA. This drives the need to share real-time information and ensure the situational awareness that is necessary for the safe and reliable control of these devices.

Scalability and Efficiency: The UTM system will need to support many drone operations and in the case of healthcare, many of these missions will be emergent.

Automated Systems: Reducing the need for voice communication and manual intervention is going to be a required attribute for UTM because of the scale and dynamics at play.

Integration with existing ATC (Air Traffic Control): Because drones are going to share the airspace, they will need to be integrated with traditional air traffic systems, so that the situational awareness can be complete and comprehensive.

Safety and Risk Management: Standards and protocols will be developed and implemented to reduce the risk of collisions. These will be adapted to the scale and the capabilities for the services and equipment that are a part of drone operations.

ARTIFICIAL INTELLIGENCE (AI)

The digital twin benefits from its agentic design because we start with a foundation that allows the agents to advance in their intelligence as the implementation journey proceeds. The HITL allows us to build confidence in the agents as things progress and rely on them only when that confidence supports it. Initially, the agents can exist with little or no AI because the human is built into the agentic design.

Starting with the definition of intelligence, we see that an intelligent entity:

- Does what is appropriate for its circumstances.
- Does what is appropriate for its goals.
- Does what is appropriate for its perceptual limitations.
- Does what is appropriate for its computational limitations.
- Accounts for the short-term and long-term consequences of its actions.
- Accounts for its effects on society and the environment.
- Learns from experience.
- Is flexible to changing environments.
- Is flexible to changing goals.

Given this definition, we see that we expect a lot from such an entity. Fortunately, intelligence is measured along a continuum. When we use the agentic design, we can parse the application of intelligence between the human and machines to address these as requirements. Some of these are required for autonomy, and we can equally use a gradient to assess the agent's level of autonomy.

Human reasoning

Agents model the same cycle of reasoning that humans use. The human brain processes what we perceive through our senses into our sensory memory for a brief period (less than one second), where it moves into our short-term memory, where the percept is processed against other pieces of information that create associations. For instance, when we see a cat, we process that it is a cat when the percept is compared against other memories in the short-term memory. Long-term memory adds much more to the processing such as emotion and other associations. Based on this reasoning, decisions are made about what actions to take that make changes in the environment.

The AI process for CTC agents will start with careful determination of where AI can be the most effective and produce the best outcomes. The agents that are participating in the mobile workflows will use the most perception and will produce the data that we can use to train the models.

Data processing is the first step in the process and is usually

1. Data requirements
   a. Includes the goals for the AI.
   b. Establish the types of data necessary.
2. Data Sourcing
   a. Core systems like EHR, ERP, Computerized Maintenance Management System (CMMS), Lab Information Management System (LIMS), etc.
   b. Location engines from locator service's SaaS.
   c. Raw data from gateway devices.
3. Data Collection
   a. Use APIs to access data from internal and external platforms.
   b. Employ web scrapers to extracting data from websites if necessary.
   c. Obtain real-time data streaming from sensing IoT devices and mobile devices.
4. Data Preprocessing
   a. Clean to removing duplicates, correct errors, and correct missing values.
   b. Perform normalization to standardize data formats.
   c. Transform to put data into the correct format for analysis.
5. Data Annotation
   a. Label the data with tags or annotations (supervised learning).
6. Data Storage
   a. Databases, data lakes and cloud storage.
7. Data Integration
   a. Combine the data where necessary to get centralized access, additional contextual insights and reduce bias.
   b. Employ ETL (Extract Transform Load) for data integration.
8. Data Quality Assurance
   a. Validation: Ensuring the accuracy, completeness, and reliability of the data.
   b. Auditing: Regular checks and balances to maintain data integrity.

Feature Extraction

- Spatial Features: Identifying key patterns like walkways, buildings, points of interest.
- Temporal Features: Observing changes over time (e.g., mobile equipment location). Traffic patterns are temporal features that can be associated with specific jobs or tasks.

Model Training

- Algorithms: Machine learning models like Convolutional Neural Networks (CNN) and Recurrent Neural Network (RNN) trained on geospatial data to recognize patterns and make predictions.
- Training: Using labeled data to teach the model how to identify specific features or predict outcomes.

Analysis

- Spatial Analysis: Understanding relationships and patterns in the data (e.g., heat maps, clustering).
- Predictive Analysis: Forecasting future events or trends based on historical data (e.g., predicting traffic congestion).

Visualization

- If user interfaces are designed with the agentic design, the UI can more easily adapt to the new capabilities. By being aware of the perception--> thinking-->actions that are a part of the workflow, the appropriate UI will be the result.
- Maps and Graphs: Using GIS tools to create visual representations of the data and analysis results.
- Dashboards: Providing interactive platforms for users to explore the data and insights.

EDENVALE'S CTC JOURNEY

Edenvale's joint venture with Big-tech company was paying off. The internal LBS Program had expanded and was renamed to the CTC Team. For Big-tech, the ability to prove that an operational digital twin is a repeatable and beneficial initiative was a strategic priority. For Edenvale, the benefits made the entire program a strategic imperative. The digital twin had started from using the LBS 1.0 infrastructure and siloed use cases to a core system that made their most important applications situationally aware. While location played a significant role, there was more to the perception than just location.

Most people saw the operational digital twin as something in the background, if they even knew it existed. People related to it through the agents that were being created. The agents were more than just bots. Not only could you ask it a question and get an answer, but you could also tell your agent to do things for you. One interesting feature that Kirk created was harvesting the things that were asked, but the agent was unable to either answer or act because of its limitations. This was used to create new capabilities when there was a trend. Everyone was encouraged to ask anything of the agent. It was interesting to see what was being asked and sometimes it was very amusing.

Denise Henry was in her weekly meeting with Gail and was showing Gail her new agent. Denise was the director for Surgical Services, and she had worked with the Big-tech engineers to train the AI that was a part of the agent. The accuracy of some of the predictions was astonishing, and she wanted to show a couple of the things it could do. She told Gail that Kirk, the architect from Big-tech, had explained that the agent works like we do, where it might have the answer to some questions, but if it does not know the answer, it asks another agent. Surgery had many utility agents that did not directly interface with humans. These agents were performing tasks and computations in the background.

Denise said,

> Kirk said that specifically for the surgeries, the utility agent would work a lot like a sports betting platform. I can't say I know too much about sports betting but here is how he explained it. The team that is involved in the surgery has stats and the agent looks at the historical stats and the real-time stats and evaluates the surgery to give a probability if the surgery will be delayed or finished early based on the block time. One of those utility agents uses computer vision to keep track of the surgical procedure. It knows when the incision is made, when certain instruments are used, and it keeps track of any objects that go into the patient, so we don't have any retained foreign objects. It knows the procedures well enough for us to get a heads up when they are close to closing.

Denise went on, "So my agent can ask that utility agent anything that is going on in the surgical suite. It monitors turnarounds and keeps track of the equipment that comes and goes from the room. So, let's ask it a couple of questions." Gail asked, "Did you name your agent yet?" Denise laughed and said, "No, I know a lot of people have named their agents, but I haven't yet." Denise put the phone near her mouth and said, "Which surgeries will exceed their block time today?" The agent said back, "Dr, Gripen's reverse total shoulder replacement has a 75% likelihood it will exceed its block time." Denise said, "By how much?" The agent said, "The overrun could be as long as 2 hours." Denise said, "Why might the surgery overrun"? The agent said, "the notes say they will try to repair the shoulder but if it cannot be repaired the replacement will proceed."

Denise said,

> this has all been accounted for in the surgery schedule. She said we don't automatically push the block time to lower the probability of the overrun because if we do that we have to deal with underutilization. What we do is balance these probabilities with the amount of delay to find the sweet spot. The next patient might wait a little while longer, but we don't have to reschedule surgeries like we used to. All of our utilization numbers have gone up. Outcomes are better as well.

Denise went on to say,

> The scheduling is all being done in the command center because what disrupts the schedule the most are emergency surgeries. With the controller in the command center there is more awareness about what might lead to an emergency surgery. The trauma bay in the ED (Emergency Department) has its own computer vision system that feeds another utility agent. It creates probabilities and it is getting good at what types of surgeries we might need to prep for when a patient is in the trauma bay. Every second of advance warning helps.

PLAYBOOK FOR THE DIGITAL TWIN IMPLEMENTATION STRATEGY

The operational digital twin is as much of an architectural construct as it is a system. It will start as a fragmented set of solutions that will merge into a core system. This should not dissuade the commitment to the strategy. There is plenty of opportunity for progress with CTC even if the core system is behind in its formation. The strategy to get to the Late Stages of CTC maturity is spread across years. If there is commitment to the vision, the architecture will remain intact and there will be steady improvement.

Improvers

For the improvers, the objective at this stage of the strategy is to create the agents that are leveraging the digital twin. Active participation from the workforce is critical, as is transparency and communication. The potential to create amazing features and efficiency is great as is the potential for misperception and misuse.

1. Implementation assessment
    - Map current digital twin capabilities.
    - Identify opportunities for new agents to be implemented.

- Document integration requirements for agents.
- Create readiness assessment.
- Define success criteria and include value stream analysis.

2. Development strategy
   - Start with high-value components.
   - Build digital twin incrementally.
   - Focus on workflow automation first.
   - Create validation processes.
   - Establish feedback mechanisms.
3. Data integration
   - Map data sources and requirements.
   - Define data quality standards.
   - Create integration frameworks.
   - Establish synchronization protocols.
   - Monitor data accuracy.
4. Performance monitoring
   - Define performance metrics.
   - Create monitoring systems.
   - Track synchronization accuracy.
   - Measure automation effectiveness.
   - Document improvements.

Leaders

Leaders are going to be critical to the success of CTC by committing the organization to the long-term vision of an operational digital twin. Because the digital twin is a platform, many teams and individuals will have opportunities to contribute innovative ideas for constructing new agents.

The perception of the operation digital twin as a valuable assistant or an oppressive authority is in the control of the leadership. It is unlikely there will be success if it is viewed as a means to measure the performance of people. It is equally unlikely there will be success if no monitoring is done. The transparency and participation of the workforce are vital if there is going to be progress. Location information can be misused, so policies need to allow progress, but be smart and detailed enough to create a positive working environment.

Creating the digital twin ecosystem is the biggest challenge for leaders. The most valuable assets that the digital twin can leverage are in the core HIS systems. Ensuring they are available and that there is a secure way to access those systems is the difference between success and mediocrity.

1. Strategic planning
   - Develop digital twin vision.
   - Create implementation roadmap.
   - Set clear priorities.
   - Allocate resources.
   - Enable cross-functional collaboration.

2. Change management
   - Build organizational understanding.
   - Support cultural transformation.
   - Manage expectations.
   - Enable skill development.
   - Foster innovation culture.
3. Resource allocation
   - Invest in foundation technologies.
   - Support training initiatives.
   - Plan for ongoing maintenance.
   - Enable technology adoption.
   - Provide implementation resources.
4. Risk management
   - Identify implementation risks.
   - Create mitigation strategies.
   - Establish oversight mechanisms.
   - Monitor implementation progress.
   - Develop contingency plans.

Creators

When CTC and the operational digital twin are solutions in the market, they will require a level of standardization that is only achievable with industry cooperation. That is demonstrated in organizations like the Digital Twin Consortium. Creators should encourage participation in organizations like this that can enable entire industries. The more diverse the community within the consortia, the better the outcomes are for everyone.

1. Solution development
   - Create scalable architectures.
   - Enable flexible integration.
   - Support standard protocols.
   - Build validation tools.
   - Provide monitoring capabilities.
2. Implementation support
   - Provide implementation guidance.
   - Offer training programs.
   - Support system optimization.
   - Maintain documentation.
   - Enable performance monitoring.
3. Innovation focus
   - Develop new capabilities.
   - Enhance existing features.
   - Support emerging standards.
   - Enable future expansion.
   - Build adaptive systems.

Chapter 18

Systems management

Ali Youssef

The power of Location-Based Services (LBS) lies in its ability to provide real-time, actionable location data that can drive decision-making processes at both operational and strategic levels. By offering visibility into the movement and status of assets, personnel, and even customers, LBS enables organizations to make informed decisions that can significantly impact efficiency, productivity, and bottom-line results.

REMOTE MANAGEMENT IN LBS

As LBS becomes increasingly integral to organizational operations, the need for robust remote management capabilities has become essential. Remote management is not just a convenience; it is a critical factor in ensuring that LBS systems operate reliably and efficiently, maximizing uptime and responsiveness.

Ensuring system reliability through remote management

System reliability is a cornerstone of effective LBS implementation. In environments where timely access to location information is crucial, such as hospitals or smart cities, even minor system disruptions can have significant consequences. For example, in a smart city setting, a malfunction in the LBS could disrupt traffic management systems, affecting thousands of commuters.

To mitigate such risks, organizations must implement robust remote management practices that allow for continuous monitoring of system health. This proactive approach involves deploying automated monitoring tools that can alert IT teams to potential issues before they escalate into major problems. By leveraging remote management capabilities, organizations can:

- Conduct real-time system health checks
- Perform software updates and patches without on-site visits
- Troubleshoot issues promptly, minimizing downtime
- Optimize system performance based on usage patterns and load

DOI: 10.1201/9781003625483-21

Remote management also enables organizations to scale their LBS implementations more effectively. As the system grows to encompass more assets, locations, or functionalities, remote management tools allow IT teams to maintain control and visibility across the entire network, regardless of geographical dispersion.

Maximizing uptime and responsiveness

Uptime is a critical factor for any organization utilizing location services, especially in environments where continuous operation is essential. Remote management plays a crucial role in maximizing uptime by enabling quick responses to potential issues. Through remote monitoring and diagnostics, IT teams can:

- Identify and address performance bottlenecks
- Preemptively replace failing hardware components
- Balance network load to prevent overloads
- Implement redundancy measures to ensure continuous operation

By leveraging these capabilities, organizations can significantly reduce the mean time to repair (MTTR) for any issues that arise, thereby minimizing the impact on operations and maintaining high levels of system availability.

THE ROLE OF THE LOCATION SERVICES ARCHITECT

In the evolving landscape of LBS, the role of the Location Services Architect has emerged as central to the successful implementation and integration of these systems within the organizational framework. This specialized position bridges the gap between technical expertise and strategic business objectives, ensuring that LBS deployments align with and support overall organizational goals.

Justifying the need for a location services architect

The complexity of modern LBS implementations, coupled with the critical nature of the data they provide, necessitates a dedicated role to oversee their design, implementation, and ongoing management. The Location Services Architect fills this crucial gap, bringing a unique blend of technical knowledge, strategic thinking, and cross-functional leadership to the table.

Several factors justify the need for this specialized role:

- Technical Complexity: LBS systems involve a complex interplay of hardware, software, and network infrastructure. The Location Services Architect possesses the deep technical knowledge required to navigate these complexities, ensuring that the chosen solutions are robust, scalable, and aligned with organizational needs.

- Strategic Alignment: LBS implementations must support broader organizational objectives. The Location Services Architect works closely with leadership to understand these goals and translates them into technical requirements, ensuring that the LBS deployment delivers tangible business value.
- Cross-Functional Coordination: Successful LBS implementation requires collaboration across multiple departments, including IT, operations, facilities management, and end-users. The Location Services Architect serves as a bridge between these diverse stakeholders, facilitating communication and ensuring that all perspectives are considered in the system design and deployment.
- Continuous Evolution: The field of location services is rapidly evolving, with new technologies and use cases emerging regularly. The Location Services Architect stays abreast of these developments, continuously evaluating opportunities to enhance the organization's LBS capabilities and ensuring that the system remains cutting-edge and effective.
- Risk Management: LBS systems often handle sensitive data and are critical to operational efficiency. The Location Services Architect plays a key role in identifying and mitigating potential risks, ensuring that the system is secure, compliant with relevant regulations, and resilient to potential disruptions.

Responsibilities of the location services architect

The Location Services Architect's role encompasses a wide range of responsibilities, spanning from strategic planning to technical implementation and ongoing optimization. Key responsibilities include:

- Strategic planning: Developing a comprehensive LBS strategy that aligns with organizational objectives, considering factors such as scalability, interoperability, and future technological trends.
- System design: Creating the overall architecture for the LBS implementation, including hardware selection, software integration, network design, and data management strategies.
- Vendor management: Evaluating and selecting LBS vendors, negotiating contracts, and managing ongoing relationships to ensure that the chosen solutions meet organizational needs.
- Integration planning: Designing strategies for integrating LBS with existing systems, such as enterprise resource planning (ERP), CRM, or facility management software, to maximize the value of location data across the organization.
- Performance optimization: Continuously monitoring system performance, identifying bottlenecks, and implementing improvements to enhance efficiency and effectiveness.

- Security and compliance: Ensuring that the LBS implementation adheres to relevant security standards and regulatory requirements, particularly in industries handling sensitive data.
- Training and change management: Developing training programs for end-users and IT staff and leading change management initiatives to facilitate smooth adoption of LBS technologies.
- Innovation leadership: Staying informed about emerging technologies and use cases in the field of location services and driving innovation within the organization to maintain a competitive edge.
- ROI analysis: Developing metrics and conducting regular analyses to quantify the return on investment of LBS implementations, providing leadership with clear insights into the value delivered by these systems.
- Disaster recovery planning: Creating and maintaining robust disaster recovery and business continuity plans specific to the LBS infrastructure, ensuring minimal disruption in case of system failures or other emergencies.

By fulfilling these responsibilities, the Location Services Architect plays a pivotal role in ensuring that LBS implementations deliver maximum value to the organization, driving operational efficiency, enhancing decision-making capabilities, and fostering innovation across various business functions.

THE IMPORTANCE OF INTEROPERABILITY AND API INTEGRATIONS

In the realm of LBS management, interoperability stands as one of the most critical components. The ability to seamlessly integrate with existing systems through Application Programming Interfaces (APIs) is fundamental for creating an operational framework that maximizes the value of location data.

Seamless integration with legacy systems

Organizations often operate with a complex tapestry of legacy systems that may not naturally align with modern LBS solutions. The challenge lies in designing a framework that allows for effective integration, bridging the gap between old and new technologies. APIs serve as essential tools in this regard, acting as connectors that enable different systems to communicate and share data efficiently.

Consider, for example, a manufacturing facility seeking to implement an LBS solution. The facility likely operates with an existing ERP system that manages various aspects of production, inventory, and supply chain. By leveraging APIs, the LBS can be seamlessly integrated with the ERP system, allowing real-time location data of equipment and materials to flow directly into the broader operational framework.

This integration offers numerous benefits:

- Enhanced Visibility: Management gains a holistic view of inventory levels, asset utilization, and production efficiency, all updated in real-time.
- Improved Decision-Making: With access to real-time location data within familiar systems, decision-makers can make more informed choices about resource allocation and operational adjustments.
- Streamlined Workflows: Employees can access location information without switching between multiple systems, reducing friction and improving productivity.
- Data Consistency: Integration ensures that location data is consistent across all systems, reducing errors and improving overall data integrity.

Enhancing data utilization through API integration

The integration of LBS with other data sources through APIs opens up new avenues for analysis and decision-making. By combining location data with other operational metrics, organizations can gain deeper insights into their processes and identify opportunities for optimization.

For instance, in a retail environment, integrating LBS with customer relationship management (CRM) systems can significantly enhance the shopping experience. By tracking customer movements within the store and correlating this data with purchase history and preferences stored in the CRM, retailers can:

- Analyze shopping patterns to optimize store layouts
- Deliver personalized promotions based on a customer's real-time location within the store
- Improve staff allocation by predicting high-traffic areas and times
- Enhance inventory management by correlating product locations with customer interest

APIs facilitate this seamless flow of location data into and out of the CRM and other systems, enabling retailers to create a more responsive, data-driven shopping environment that enhances customer satisfaction and drives sales.

Supporting future scalability and innovation

As organizations evolve, their systems must adapt to meet new challenges and capitalize on emerging opportunities. Interoperability through APIs supports current operational needs while positioning organizations for future growth and innovation. A well-integrated LBS can easily connect with emerging technologies, enabling businesses to remain agile in a rapidly changing technological landscape.

The potential for integrating LBS with advanced technologies such as artificial intelligence (AI) and the Internet of Things (IoT) illustrates the importance of maintaining a flexible, interoperable system architecture. For instance, a logistics company could use LBS to track shipments and integrate that data with AI algorithms to predict delivery times more accurately. This predictive capability can optimize logistics operations, improve resource allocation, and enhance customer satisfaction through more reliable service.

Moreover, as new IoT devices and sensors enter the market, organizations with interoperable LBS systems can quickly incorporate these new data sources, expanding their tracking capabilities and deriving new insights from the combined data streams.

By prioritizing interoperability and robust API integrations, organizations create a future-proof LBS infrastructure that can adapt to new technologies, scale with organizational growth, and continue to drive value over the long term.

IMPLEMENTING BEST PRACTICES IN LBS MANAGEMENT

To maximize the effectiveness of LBS management, organizations should adopt a set of best practices that emphasize strategic planning, change management, and continuous improvement. These practices ensure that LBS implementations not only meet current needs but also remain adaptable to future challenges and opportunities.

Strategic planning and assessment

The implementation of an LBS solution begins with comprehensive planning and assessment. This critical phase involves evaluating the existing technological landscape, identifying integration points, and aligning the LBS strategy with broader organizational goals.

Key steps in the strategic planning process include:

- Stakeholder Engagement: Involve representatives from various departments, including IT, operations, finance, and end-users. This diverse input ensures that the LBS solution addresses the needs of all stakeholders and aligns with organizational objectives.
- Current State Analysis: Conduct a thorough assessment of existing systems, workflows, and pain points. This analysis helps identify areas where LBS can deliver the most significant impact and informs decisions about system design and integration.

- Use case definition: Clearly define the primary use cases for the LBS implementation. Whether it's asset tracking, personnel safety, or process optimization, having well-defined use cases helps focus the implementation and set clear success criteria.
- Technology evaluation: Assess various LBS technologies (e.g., GPS, Wi-Fi, BLE, UWB) against the defined use cases and existing infrastructure. Consider factors such as accuracy requirements, environmental conditions, and scalability needs.
- Integration planning: Map out potential integration points and data flow pathways between the LBS and existing systems. This step is crucial for ensuring seamless interoperability and maximizing the value of location data across the organization.
- ROI projection: Develop a comprehensive return on investment (ROI) model that accounts for both tangible and intangible benefits of the LBS implementation. This projection helps secure buy-in from leadership and sets benchmarks for measuring success.
- Risk assessment: Identify potential risks associated with the LBS implementation, including technical challenges, data security concerns, and adoption barriers. Develop mitigation strategies for each identified risk.

By engaging in thorough strategic planning, organizations lay a solid foundation for successful LBS implementation, ensuring that the chosen solution aligns with business needs and delivers measurable value.

Robust change management

Implementing LBS solutions often represents a significant change in how organizations operate, track assets, and make decisions. Effective change management is crucial for ensuring successful adoption and realizing the full potential of the LBS investment.

Key components of a robust change management strategy include:

- Clear Communication: Develop a comprehensive communication plan that articulates the benefits of the LBS implementation to all stakeholders. Address concerns proactively and highlight how the new system will improve day-to-day operations.
- Leadership Engagement: Secure visible support from leadership to underscore the importance of the LBS implementation. Leaders should champion the initiative and demonstrate commitment to its success.
- User Training: Provide thorough, role-specific training to all users of the LBS system. This training should cover not only the technical aspects of using the system but also how it integrates into existing workflows and processes.

- Phased Implementation: Consider a phased rollout approach, starting with a pilot program in a specific area or department. This approach allows for testing and refinement of the system before full-scale deployment.
- Support Systems: Establish robust support systems, including help-desk services and on-site support during the initial rollout. Ensure that users have easy access to assistance when needed.
- Feedback Mechanisms: Implement channels for users to provide feedback on the LBS system. This ongoing input is invaluable for identifying areas for improvement and addressing user concerns promptly.
- Celebration of Successes: Recognize and celebrate early wins and successes with the LBS implementation. This positive reinforcement helps build momentum and encourages continued adoption.
- Continuous Education: Develop a program for ongoing education and training, ensuring that users remain up-to-date with system updates and new features.

By prioritizing change management, organizations can overcome resistance to new technologies, foster a culture of innovation, and ensure that the LBS system is fully utilized to drive operational improvements.

Continuous monitoring and evaluation

Once the LBS is implemented, ongoing monitoring and evaluation are essential for maintaining optimal performance and ensuring that the system continues to meet organizational needs. This process involves regular assessment of system performance, user satisfaction, and alignment with business objectives.

Key aspects of continuous monitoring and evaluation include:

- Performance Metrics: Establish key performance indicators (KPIs) that align with organizational objectives. These might include metrics such as system uptime, data accuracy, asset utilization rates, or process efficiency improvements.
- Regular Audits: Conduct periodic audits of the LBS system to ensure that it is operating as intended. These audits should cover aspects such as hardware functionality, software performance, and data integrity.
- User Feedback: Regularly solicit and analyze feedback from system users. This input can provide valuable insights into the practical benefits and challenges of the LBS implementation.
- Data Analysis: Leverage the wealth of data generated by the LBS to identify trends, patterns, and opportunities for optimization. Advanced analytics can uncover insights that drive continuous improvement.
- Compliance Checks: Ensure ongoing compliance with relevant regulations and industry standards, particularly in sectors like healthcare where data privacy is paramount.

- Technology Updates: Stay informed about advancements in LBS technology and evaluate opportunities to upgrade or enhance the system to maintain its effectiveness and competitive edge.
- ROI Assessment: Regularly assess the return on investment of the LBS implementation against the projections made during the planning phase. Use this information to justify further investments or adjustments to the system.
- Scalability Planning: Continuously evaluate the system's ability to scale with organizational growth. Plan for expansions or upgrades well in advance to ensure seamless scaling.

By implementing a rigorous monitoring and evaluation process, organizations can ensure that their LBS investment continues to deliver value over time, adapting to changing needs and leveraging new technologies as they emerge.

EDENVALE'S CTC JOURNEY

When Edenvale first started its care traffic control journey, it knew it needed someone to oversee the growing complexity of its location-based services infrastructure. Imani Jefferson, who had started as their program manager and evolved into their Location Services Architect, was instrumental in establishing strong systems management practices.

One particular incident highlighted the importance of their investment in remote management capabilities. It was 2 AM on a Sunday when Imani received an automated alert on her phone indicating that several Real Time Location Services (RTLS) sensors in the Emergency Department were showing degraded performance. In the past, this would have required an on-site visit, but thanks to the remote management infrastructure they had put in place, she was able to diagnose and resolve the issue from home.

"The automated monitoring system showed that the sensors were experiencing interference from some newly installed equipment," Imani explained later to Suresh Mehta, the applications VP. "I was able to remotely adjust the frequency channels of the affected sensors and restore normal operation within minutes. Before we had these capabilities, this could have disrupted ED operations for hours."

This incident became a turning point in how Edenvale approached systems management. The hospital's CIO, Johnathon Bennett, used it as an example when justifying further investment in their systems management infrastructure. "Every minute of downtime in our location services affects patient care," he explained to the board. "Remote management isn't just about convenience – it's about maintaining the high reliability our care traffic control system requires."

The success of their systems management approach was particularly evident during the hospital-wide upgrade of their RTLS infrastructure. The upgrade, which involved updating firmware on hundreds of sensors and tags, was completed over three nights with minimal disruption to hospital operations. The remote management capabilities allowed the IT team to monitor the upgrade process in real-time and quickly address any issues that arose.

Frank McDermid, the security shift sergeant who had been initially skeptical about the complexity of the new systems, became one of their strongest advocates. "The system's reliability has been remarkable," he noted. "When we do have issues, they're usually resolved before most staff even notice there was a problem. That's exactly what we need in a 24/7 healthcare environment."

As Edenvale continued to expand its care traffic control capabilities, it maintained its focus on strong systems management. Its integrated monitoring dashboard in the command center now provides real-time visibility into the health of all its location-based service components, from individual sensors to application performance metrics.

This comprehensive approach to systems management has become a model for other hospitals implementing care traffic control. As Imani often says, "The best technology in the world doesn't matter if you can't keep it running reliably. Systems management isn't just about fixing problems – it's about preventing them from occurring in the first place."

Chapter 19

Operational roadmap

Paul E. Zieske

The ongoing digital transformation in healthcare offers benefits that can only be fully realized when paired with thoughtful organizational change management. Real-time technologies create tight feedback loops that enable actions within short planning horizons but their true value emerges when operations adapt to leverage these new capabilities.

As we saw in earlier chapters, situational awareness alone provides diminishing returns without corresponding operational changes that can act on this information. Early in the journey, this awareness can be provided to existing roles who can respond with appropriate actions. As the organization matures, new roles can be introduced to address expanding capabilities, ultimately leading to unprecedented levels of efficiency that may actually reduce the total number of roles needed for operations.

This chapter examines how care traffic control shapes organizational structure, particularly as the command center takes form in alignment with the digital twin's capabilities. We'll explore how the multi-agent architecture means each workflow and its actors will have automation assistance, functioning as true human-in-the-loop relationships. We'll describe both new roles that emerge and how existing roles evolve to leverage these capabilities.

Because care traffic control is closely related to the broader concept of Real-Time Healthcare (RTHC), we'll begin by establishing this context before exploring the organizational changes that typically occur as care traffic control matures. While many timeframes are involved in healthcare operations, this chapter focuses primarily on the real-time planning horizon, as this is where operational changes have the most immediate and visible impact.

REAL-TIME HEALTHCARE

Real-time healthcare (RTHC) is a concept described in several articles by Gartner in 2018. RTHC was characterized as a megatrend for the future, and Gartner said, "The real-time health system is a management and operating

DOI: 10.1201/9781003625483-22

paradigm and technology archetype for the next-generation health delivery organization." This statement describes something that will transform operations, but moving from a technology archetype to the next-generation health delivery organization will become a new domain and require a large knowledge base. Some groundwork has been laid, but much more is needed.

The Real-Time Healthcare system is centered around situational awareness, and operational intelligence across functional domains and includes location and motion in its scope. It is an overarching framework that includes care delivery as much as it looks at operations and support services. Location services are important to RTHC, but RTHC is more than location, so using CTC we are taking the elements of RTHC that take the most advantage of LBS 2.0.

NEW ROLES FOR A NEW ERA

The digital twin will provide an intelligent workspace that will interact with the agents that are part of the workflow automation. This will enable new roles and a restructuring of old roles. The CTC goal of optimizing mobile workflows will involve some sort of **mobile worker**, even if that worker is an Autonomous Mobile Robot (AMR). These workflows will need to be orchestrated, and that will come from the digital twin and eventually a command center. This is in line with the human-in-the-loop structure we have already talked about. The role that will emerge for the command center is the controller. Much like the air traffic controller, the **care traffic controller** is responsible for flow within the domain they support.

Most mobile workflows involve a destination that is some unit or department. When the workflow is a courier service to pick up something or drop something off, the traffic into the units increases. The **courier** is a visitor to the unit like a grocery delivery driver is a visitor to your house. You don't allow the driver to come into your house to put away the groceries. It sounds nice, but you have a way you organize your groceries so that you can be most efficient. It would be hard for the driver to get that right. The same goes for the patient care units, so having someone responsible for keeping things in *order* is important. That is where the **orderly** comes in. The orderly is part of the unit they support. They work with the people in the unit to create a system of organization that works best for them. The orderly ensures that things are according to the system of organization. The orderly receives things coming in from the couriers and puts them where they go. The deliveries to the unit are dropped off at the entrance to the unit, and the orderly brings them into the unit. The same goes for things going out of the unit. The orderly takes them to the exit for the unit where the couriers move them out of the unit.

The digital twin will even allow for **gig work** when certain tasks can be assigned to people who have free cycles that they would like to contribute.

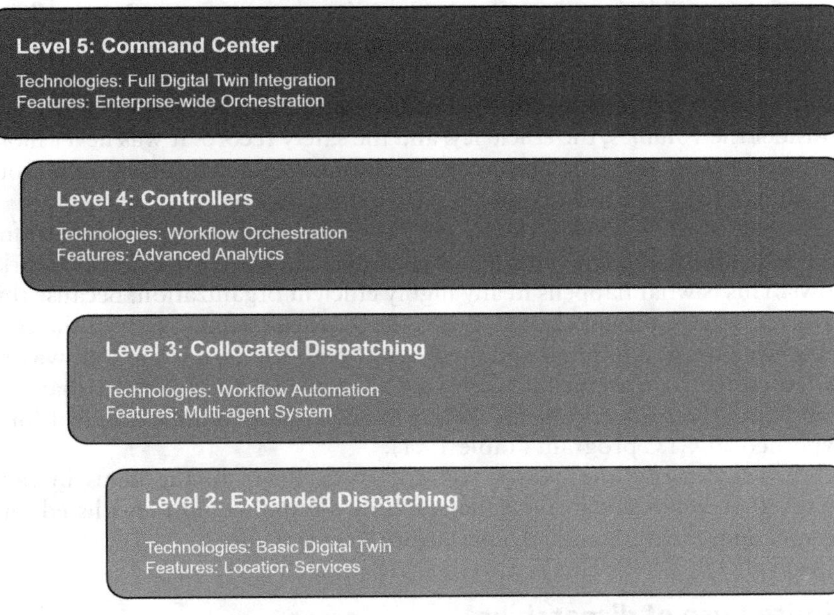

Figure 19.1 Moving from dispatching to controllers.

These behaviors can be incentivized in various ways. For instance, a doctor could take the job of moving a patient to the discharge lounge on their way out of the building for the day. It is a matter of matching the job to the person with the free cycles (Figure 19.1).

DISPATCHING TO CONTROLLING AND DISPATCHERS TO CONTROLLERS

The role of an air traffic controller brings up images of people in headsets in a dark room filled with radar screens. Air traffic controllers are highly trained and deal with high cognitive loads in complex airspaces. Communications with the pilots, weather data, traffic separation, and flight transitions are orchestrated, and sometimes there are multiple of both coming in at the same time. They have knowledge about airline operations as well as private and general aviation. They know the technology, the communications, and the details of the airspace. The role is rewarding, and it is a prestigious career path.

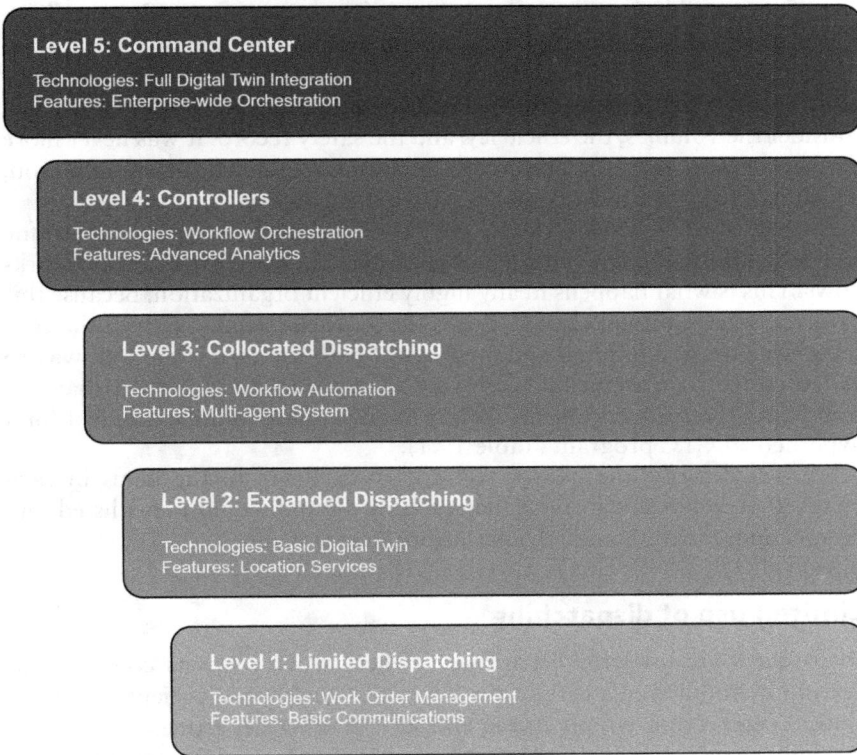

ATC is possible because of real-time information from radar, satellites, and communications systems. The surveillance and automation systems on the aircraft are critical as are the weather observation and the hundreds of other systems that contribute. It is truly a technological wonder when you consider the volumes, the efficiency, and the safety record. It was never more on display than on 9-11. The controllers safely grounded the entire nation, which had to be the most complex ATC maneuver ever accomplished.

If we want to see a world where we have real-time health care, care traffic control, or both, there will be tighter controls put on all processes and workflows. This is what happens in any highly efficient organization. Because this involves organizational change, this is the most challenging part of the concept. This means a gradual and methodical path forward is the best way to get sustained improvement. There will be new and exciting roles that will come from these advancements. Below are five phases of advancement for a hypothetical CTC program (Table 19.1).

We will describe the phases and add more detail to the items in each phase. It is important to note that each of the individual items listed will become more mature and advance as progress is made.

Limited use of dispatching

Dispatchers are used for departments where work requests come in and need to be fulfilled in a certain timeframe. In healthcare, patient transport, clinical engineering, supply chain, and several other departments are places you will see dispatching. It is almost always a mobile workflow that uses dispatching. The systems that are usually available to the dispatchers are some work request or *work order management systems*, and communications.

Table 19.1

	Control	*Digital Twin*	*Communications*
1	Limited use of dispatching	No digital twin Work order Management	Asynchronous Comms
2	Expanded use of dispatching	Work order Management Locator System	Asynchronous Comms Synchronous Comms
3	Dispatching is collocated	Workflow Automation Locator System Multi-agent System	Asynchronous Comms Synchronous Comms
4	Dispatchers become controllers	Workflow Orchestration Locator System Multi-agent System	Asynchronous Comms Synchronous Comms
5	Command Center Established	Workflow Orchestration Locator System Multi-agent System Hierarchical Agent Architecture	Asynchronous Comms Synchronous Comms Broadcasting

Sometimes the communications are limited to a verbal assignment from the dispatcher to the worker to deploy to address a request. In this phase, the dispatchers cannot observe the nominal flow of the work nor can they detect anomalies.

As a department advances, it will have a more robust work order management system, and communications will improve. In this phase, the communications should advance toward using mobile devices for receiving asynchronous communications like texting. These devices will also be used to receive work orders and report status.

Expanded use of dispatching

When the dispatchers can communicate synchronously, locate the workers, and conduct work order management electronically, several things can happen. First, the dispatchers no longer need to be collocated with the workers. The dispatchers don't even need to be in the same building as the workers or the work. Second, dispatching can be expanded to campuses where there is no dispatching currently. For instance, a health system where only the largest hospital gets the benefit of dispatching will be able to offer their smaller hospitals the service. Lastly, departments that have mobile workflows but traditionally did not have dispatching can now use dispatching to improve efficiency.

The digital twin is in an early state of formation. It is used for observation and some situational awareness, but it is not robust enough for any meaningful automation. The building is digitized into a GIS map, and the workers are streaming their location on the map to the dispatcher's console. This provides the digital representation and synchronization with the real world that qualifies it as a digital twin, but it is limited in its utility. The locator system is used for observing the workflow, and it could include the location of any equipment that is necessary to support the workflow.

Communications, using mobile devices, are both synchronous and asynchronous in the form of voice and text, respectively. The work order management system sends communications to the devices, and some status is manually sent back to the system and the dispatcher.

Collocation of dispatching

With the expanded use of dispatching and the advancing technology, the opportunity to synchronize interdependent workflows will become the next target for CTC. This means getting the dispatchers in the same location. Collocated department dispatchers coordinate their transitions, and tighter handoffs will be possible. A critical enabling technology will be workflow automation. The mobile devices will interact directly with the digital twin, and the beginnings of multi-agent systems will start to take shape. The dispatchers are monitoring the nominal flow for the work they manage and are focusing more on the anomalies. In this phase, they can help the workers solve problems more directly and manage by exception.

The increased fidelity of the locator system will make workflow automation possible. The workers will have less responsibility for reporting any status because the system will do that for them. The workers will use mobile devices to find the resources they need and keep track of the steps in the workflow. The agents will become more personalized, and the workers will interact with the agents more than they interact with dispatchers.

There is an overall reduction in the amount of human-to-human communication because of automation, and communication is usually only about anomalies. There is, however, an increase in communications between workers and the other workers in the dependent workflows, making the transitions even tighter.

Dispatchers become controllers

In this phase, the dispatchers are challenged to drive out as much delay as possible and deal with anomalies in real-time. The precision of the monitoring has increased to allow for greater automation, but the tolerances have tightened as well. Many more departments are using dispatching, and it no longer resembles what it was in the previous phases. The organization has moved to a just-in-time approach to mobile workflows, meaning the importance of "on-time" has never been higher. It is time to rethink the role of the dispatcher and move them into the role of "Controllers." The Controllers use the Observe, Orient, Decide, and Act (OODA loop) process for making decisions. They know the building, the upstream and downstream workflows, and most of the anomalies. They know all the emergency protocols and how to react when they are triggered.

The capabilities of CTC are showing so much return that some restructuring of the workflows is happening. Orderlies are now part of the different departments, and this has enabled some of the transport workflows to restructure the way transporting things is being done. AMRs are doing some of the transport as well. The AMRs are recognized as actor in the workflows they support and are a part of the CTC framework. The multi-agent architecture for the digital twin has expanded the workflow automation from automation to orchestration. This is because the agents from different departments are collaborating on handoffs. This has reduced the number of communications between workers, allowing them to accomplish more.

Command center established

The capabilities of the CTC ecosystem and the change to using controllers made collocation inevitable. Having the controllers all in one location has made it easier with the increased traffic in the building. CTC allows people who are not assigned the role of a transporter to transport, and there have been incentives created to promote the idea. This has also mitigated

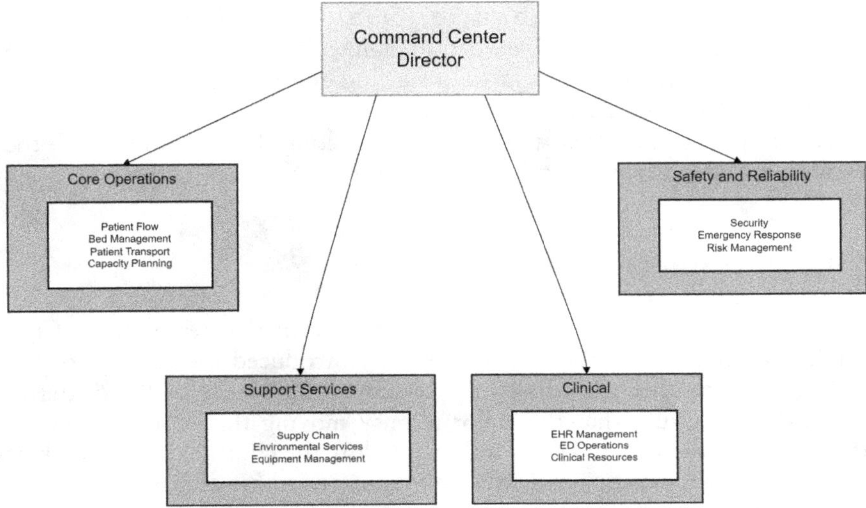

Figure 19.2 Command center organizational chart.

the traffic increases because people who are traversing the building for a single purpose are transporting things, decreasing the aggregate motion in the building.

The departments represented in the command center have expanded beyond CTC to RTHC, and workflows that are not mobile are being monitored. The operational digital twin is a robust representation of enterprise operations that is connected to every core system the enterprise has. The command center is used for disaster drills and stands ready for other emergency responses. Simulators are an important part of planning and training for responding to any scenario. There is a rich library of available simulations. Simulations are an important part of performance improvement and systems modeling.

In addition to the multi-agent system, the architecture has expanded to a hierarchical agent architecture. This incorporates agents in more supervisory and strategic roles. Because the hierarchical agents have direct access to subordinate agents, there is an enhanced ability to make informed decisions for topics that have a longer planning horizon (Figure 19.2).

COURIER SERVICES

Currently, there are many ways that things get to the units and departments. Each department that delivers things has a role that is assigned to be the transport for their department. Supply chain, medications, labs, patients, food, blood gases, blood, and equipment are all moved by different departments. There are very few special skills that go into transporting these items. Consolidating all this transport into an overarching courier service will allow for more adaptation when unplanned deliveries are added to the workload. With the orderlies at the receiving end of this all resembles the Lean concept of "standard work."

The process of standardizing the transport could follow in line with the evolution of the dispatching that oversees these services.

THE ORDERLY

In Chapter 17, we talked about the orderly from the perspective of the implementation of AMRs, and in this way introduced the concept of the hospital orderly. For the robots, the orderly would serve as the dexterity function and ensure that the robot is busy moving things in and out of their area of operations. The orderly will allow the clinical staff to work at the "top of their license" and will make the care traffic control operations function much more efficiently. Another benefit is to reduce the traffic in the units, which is a benefit from an infection control perspective. Let's go into more detail regarding this role.

History of the orderly

The orderly role dates to the Byzantine Era when hospitals were first created as physical locations dedicated to caring for the ill. Orderlies assisted physicians and nurses with various tasks, but the most physically demanding ones were solely their domain. In the 19th and early 20th centuries, orderlies were common in military hospitals. They were also prevalent in the mid-20th century for patient transport, emergency departments, operating rooms, and long-term care facilities.

While not the most prestigious role, the orderly position was crucial, especially when equipment like patient lifts didn't exist. As the role became less physical and more clinical, it was phased out in the mid to late 20th century when the role of the Certified Nursing Assistant (CNA) emerged as a certified clinical position.

Some physical tasks that orderlies used to perform are still being done by nurses and CNAs, albeit with assistive equipment. However, the proliferation of technology has brought a raft of administrative tasks, many of which require no medical training. When nurses are overwhelmed, they must prioritize tasks, often resulting in poor management of medical equipment and supplies. This is where much of the hoarding and missing equipment issues stem from.

The 21st century orderly

Structurally, the orderly would be assigned to a hospital unit or department. Depending on the workload, there may be more than one orderly.

The reason for this is because the orderly needs to have a good knowledge of the operations of the unit so that they can anticipate the needs of the unit they support. It will be important that the agent that the orderly is working with can tell the orderly when things are arriving at the unit. If not, the very purpose of having the orderly will be defeated. If things queue up at the entrance to the unit, the whole concept collapses.

The agent that orchestrates the deliveries will communicate with the orderly's agent, which will alert the orderly. The digital twin will even know if a queue is building. This is why the pace of automation will be in lockstep with the organizational changes. Below is a list of things that can be done by the orderly. All of these could be location-aware mobile workflows on their own.

- Organize and put things in their place
- Receive things into the unit
- Load things going out of the unit
- Find patients who wander or elope
- Find missing equipment
- Walk with patients as a part of their PT
- Check on patients who are a fall risk
- Find the equipment that is missing

Loss prevention, inventory control, and orderly

A measure of the success of a locator system is how little the front-line staff uses it to locate the things they need. That is because we want to rely on the 5Ss from Lean and merely train the staff to go to the places where they need to go to get things and trust that they will be there. That might sound a bit idealistic, but the point is, the focus should be on the 5S, not the remediation step of finding something that is missing. It comes back to our Desmond Tutu quote about stopping pulling people out of the river and going upstream to find out why they are falling in.

The ability to use the locator systems to drive equipment utilization up and address shrinkage from loss is a huge benefit. I have seen hospitals that implement a locator system steadily lose equipment, and all they can do is measure it because they have not designated a role to address the issue. This is an example where the role of the orderly could be used in support services for a function like a Central Equipment department. Central equipment has the function of retrieving, cleaning, and resupplying shared mobile medical equipment. The Central Equipment Orderly would have an inventory management function to ensure that the flow of equipment is efficient, utilization is high, and loss is low.

This combined with the role of the orderly assigned to the clinical department would cover almost all the mobile medical equipment, and the reduction in lost equipment would contribute greatly to the cost of the resources.

A relatively small increase in staffing, the role of the orderly would have a large impact on improving the efficiency of the already overtaxed nursing resource.

THE EDENVALE JOURNEY: THE NEW COURIER SERVICE

The command center at Edenvale General Hospital is fully functional. It has advanced from care traffic control to real-time healthcare. CTC is a big part of what goes on in the command center, but not everything involves mobile workflows. This advancement has been important because RTHC has become the parent to CTC and helps streamline operations at an even higher level.

EGH implemented a courier service that moved a great percentage of the things that needed to be moved around the hospital. The courier service is called "The Vale Express" (aka Express), and they have a controller stationed in the command center. The controller monitors the flow of the scheduled deliveries and helps ensure the stat deliveries are accommodated when they come in. All the couriers are carrying smartphones called CarePros that have their agents loaded on them.

The courier services operate on an hourly schedule. The courier staffing follows the demand that comes from how many deliveries are scheduled for each hourly run. The departures are staggered to ensure that they depart at regular intervals. For instance, if there are six couriers for the 1 pm to 2 pm segment, they leave every 10 minutes. This allows the pickups to be more frequent and accommodates more frequent deliveries to more departments.

The job starts with the departure from the first pickup location. Some jobs are batched, and some are dedicated. A batched job might have multiple pickup locations from multiple departments. When the courier gets to the drop off location, they scan the items that they are dropping off. If it is what is called amount-based packaging, like a box of supplies or linens, they are put in a designated location where the orderly will retrieve them and take them into the unit.

The orderly has a CarePro, and the agent keeps the orderly informed when things are showing up to the unit. The orderly knows all the PAR levels for every piece of equipment and all the supplies. Most of the PAR levels are lean because EGH is trending toward just-in-time deliveries. This keeps the orderly busy, but stockouts are almost nonexistent, and the nurses never need to hunt for equipment.

The nurses have CarePros that they use to register their interactions with the patient. Workflows like nurse calls, medication administration, vitals, and other processes are recorded with little effort from the nurse. They also wear a badge that is used in case they feel threatened or in need of immediate emergency assistance.

Edenvale wanted to drive down the cost of mobile medical equipment by increasing the utilization of the existing equipment and sharing equipment between departments more. This initiative was being led by the Central Sterile Processing (CSPD) department. They had a controller in the command center that was currently monitoring the PAR stocking and stat orders for equipment. This initiative was going to increase the volume of equipment in CSPD and the cleaning and distribution of the equipment for the entire hospital. This meant that they would rely on distribution to ensure they didn't have to wait for the equipment that was needed. The goal was to have two service level agreements (SLAs) with CSPD. One was called "just-in-time," and the other was called "just-enough." Just-in-time was for equipment that would be brought to the unit just-in-time for it to be used, and just-enough was for equipment that was needed on hand with tight PAR levels.

They worked with the Express team to ensure that the distribution of equipment would meet the SLAs. They also worked with the nursing units because they had to give up a lot of their equipment to CSPD. There was a tremendous amount of trust that would be needed to make this all work. PAR stocking had been working, but the CSPD agent had pointed out that there was still a lot of underutilized equipment. When CSPD created their agent, the RTLS sensors were installed in all the storage locations, and the agent could see when replenishment was needed. The orderlies were stocking the closets, and they were also ensuring that there was never a stockout. Just-in-time would be very new to everyone.

After the process went live, they still found a few units hoarding some IV pumps, but as they could see from the data that there were no stockouts at the PAR locations they started to trust, and hoarding stopped. Then they picked equipment for JIT (Just in Time) and got started with that. Express promised that if the scheduled deliveries were not going to meet the JIT SLA, they would use stat deliveries to get them there. The result was they were able to get rid of the old worn-out equipment and drove up the utilization of the equipment twofold. The entire fleet of mobile medical equipment was reduced by 25%. The quality of the equipment went way up. They were looking at leasing for increased savings so that they had much more control over the whole operation (Figure 19.3).

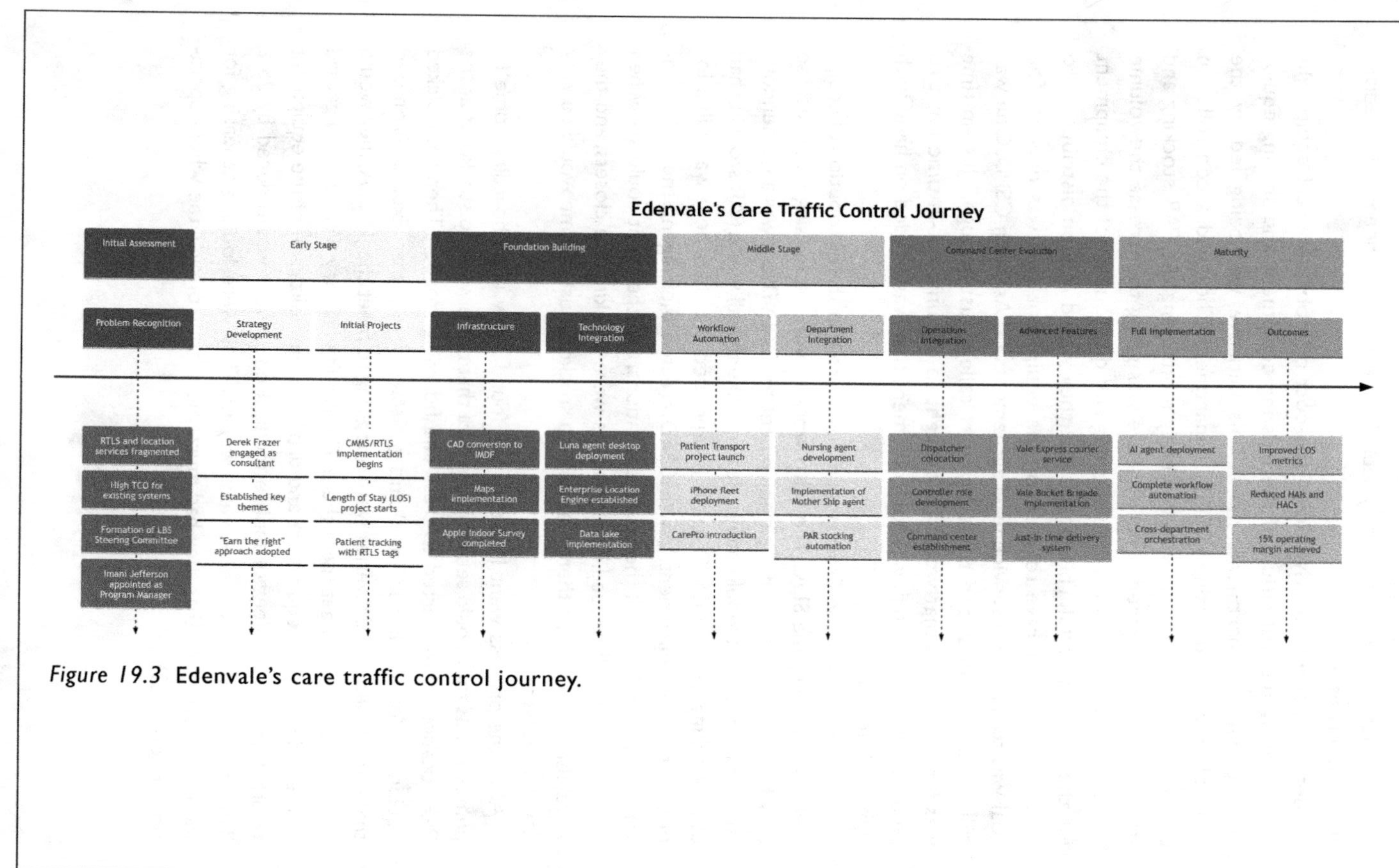

Figure 19.3 Edenvale's care traffic control journey.

PLAYBOOK FOR OPERATIONAL ENHANCEMENTS

Care traffic control should cause us to envision a command center where the participating departments have controllers who are taking in the real-time data and interacting to ensure that the flow of materials and services within the enterprise is moving seamlessly. Many of the controller functions may be fully automated, and only anomalies are attended to by a human controller.

When an emergency occurs, the team of controllers can react immediately, and there is no setup time to get the command center in emergency mode because it is merely a change in protocol.

Improver

Using the automation methodology, the adaptation phase is the place to take a good look at the roles that are using situational awareness and see what expanding those roles might mean to improve flow. The adaptation phase is not just about the workflow that is under study. Adaptation should look at the bottleneck analysis that takes into consideration an expanded scope for examining the ripple effect of change.

1. Operational Assessment
    - Document the current operational state
    - Map existing workflows and roles
    - Identify transformation opportunities
    - Evaluate readiness for new roles
    - Create baseline measurements
2. Role Development
    - Define new operational roles
        - Controllers
        - Orderlies
        - Command center staff
    - Create role transition plans
    - Establish training requirements
    - Design performance metrics
3. Command Center Planning
    - Map command center functions
    - Define operational protocols
    - Create communication frameworks
    - Establish escalation procedures
    - Design workflow orchestration
4. Implementation Strategy
    - Phase operational changes
    - Build new capabilities incrementally
    - Create transition timelines
    - Establish feedback mechanisms
    - Monitor operational impacts

Leader

When there is evidence that process changes will make improvements that have a high value, leadership commitment can be the difference between success and failure. The analysis should provide the economic benefit, but all benefits should be considered. Tight partnerships with the improvers will yield high value outcomes that come from that commitment.

1. Strategic Planning
    - Create an operational vision
    - Develop a transformation roadmap
    - Set clear milestones
    - Allocate transformation resources
    - Enable organizational change
2. Organizational Development
    - Design a new organizational structure
    - Plan role transitions
    - Support skill development
    - Create career paths
    - Enable cross-functional collaboration
3. Change Management
    - Build organizational buy-in
    - Manage transition impacts
    - Support cultural transformation
    - Address resistance
    - Celebrate successes
4. Resource Management
    - Plan staffing requirements
    - Allocate training resources
    - Support technology adoption
    - Enable skill development
    - Maintain operational continuity

Creator

As these automation capabilities become more composable, best practices will emerge around the workflows and roles that support those workflows. As rational agents can relieve people from some of the effort associated with workflow automation, composability will become a priority.

1. Solution Support
    - Align solutions with new roles
    - Enable operational transformation
    - Support workflow changes
    - Provide transition tools
    - Enable performance monitoring

2. Implementation Support
    - Provide transition guidance
    - Offer role-based training
    - Support operational changes
    - Maintain documentation
    - Enable success measurement
3. Innovation Focus
    - Develop role-specific tools
    - Enhance operational capabilities
    - Support emerging needs
    - Enable future expansion
    - Build adaptive solutions

Chapter 20

Care traffic control for support services

Paul E. Zieske

Support services offers a good place to get started with care traffic control (CTC) because it is both an enabler for the clinical operations and a way to demonstrate the power of the agentic design more broadly. Because CTC focuses on mobile workflows, there is a great deal of opportunity to get a CTC program off to a good start.

CTC is transformational, so some organizational transformation is required to reap its benefits. In this chapter, we describe a CTC entity established to be the transport service for the entire hospital. This type of centralization will have benefits within and beyond the support services that are directly affected. This chapter describes a framework, but many details need to be addressed according to the organizational needs and constraints.

The required technologies are available in the market now, and the workflow-centered implementation trims the cost to only what is necessary for the successful implementation of the CTC service. Although agents will not be a part of this initial implementation, the agentic design will be used to ensure that the workflows are adequately instrumented. Using PEAS, we will create the structure for the digital twin, but it might fall short of the fidelity we would like, so for now we will call it a "digital shadow."

New roles will be created and many existing tasks will be absorbed into the responsibilities of the CTC team. This will create a net benefit by appropriately distributing the transport workload and increasing the efficiency of the entire operations.

THE CURRENT STATE OF HOSPITAL TRANSPORT

In today's hospitals, the movement of people and property is highly fragmented, with each service managing its own transport needs. Patient transport is a transport function that exists as a dedicated service, but it operates in isolation, handling only patient movement. This siloed approach to hospital logistics creates significant inefficiencies that cost hospitals millions in waste and directly impacts the quality of patient care.

DOI: 10.1201/9781003625483-23

The sheer volume of motion within a hospital is staggering. This constant movement creates numerous challenges, including:

- Delays in services, supplies, and equipment delivery
- Lost or misplaced medical equipment and supplies
- Missing laboratory samples and medications
- Inventory stockouts and oversupply situations.

Additionally, this uncoordinated movement obscures operational visibility. Staff often lack real-time information about:

- When items transition from storage to active use
- When patients will arrive at or depart from various services
- When critical services will be available.

Motion is inherent in patient care and cannot be entirely eliminated; it can be managed far more efficiently by establishing a centralized CTC team. This CTC team represents a fundamental rethinking of hospital transport operations.

Fragmented systems and their impact

The existing system of hospital transport operates through multiple separate mechanisms, each tied to specific departments or services. This fragmented approach creates numerous operational challenges. When equipment or supplies arrive at their destinations, staff must interact with multiple transport services to resolve any issues, creating confusion and inefficiency.

A particularly concerning aspect of the current system is the misallocation of specialized staff. Healthcare professionals, trained as specialists in their departments, frequently find themselves tasked with moving equipment and supplies to their final destinations. These trained individuals end up spending valuable time on transport tasks instead of focusing on their core responsibilities and expertise. Some examples are:

- Pharm Techs doing deliveries
- Lab Techs picking up Labs
- Sterile processing tech picking and delivering medical equipment
- Nursing hunting for medical equipment
- Clinical engineers retrieving and delivering equipment.

The technology gap

While location-based services (LBS) represent a transformational technology in healthcare, few health systems have realized their true potential. As noted by Gartner in their 2018 strategic roadmap to real-time healthcare, these technologies hold immense promise. However, progress has been remarkably slow for several reasons:

1. The transformational nature of these technologies requires fundamental changes in how hospital operations function
2. Many hospital operations need significant restructuring to fully realize the benefits
3. Current implementation approaches often create tools rather than comprehensive solutions to business problems
4. The burden of using these systems typically falls on already overwhelmed staff.

The workflow challenge

Traditional approaches to implementing LBS often focus on individual use cases rather than comprehensive workflows. This limited perspective creates several problems:

- Use cases create tools instead of solutions to business problems
- Partial effectiveness due to fragmented implementation
- Additional burden on already taxed staff
- Lack of focus on overall outcomes.

A workflow-centered approach requires more than basic locator systems like RTLS (real-time location systems). It demands:

- Integration of multiple technologies including indoor positioning and mobile systems
- Specialized training for proper system utilization
- Understanding of sensing technology limitations
- Dedicated resources with developed "muscle memory" for efficient task execution
- An organizational structure that supports transformation to workflow-based operations.

The cost of inefficiency

The current fragmented approach to hospital transport and logistics results in substantial waste and inefficiency. Major areas of impact include:

1. **Resource utilization:** Specialized staff spending time on transport tasks instead of their primary duties
2. **Equipment management:** Poor tracking leading to lost or misplaced equipment
3. **Service delays:** Inefficient transport systems causing delays in patient care and services

4. **Inventory control:** Suboptimal management of supplies leading to both stockouts and oversupply
5. **Operational visibility:** Limited ability to track and optimize the flow of people and resources throughout the facility.

This inefficient state of operations not only impacts the hospital's bottom line but also affects the quality and timeliness of patient care, staff satisfaction, and overall operational effectiveness.

CORE COMPONENTS AND IMPLEMENTATION

System overview

CTC operates much like an air traffic control system for hospitals, with carefully orchestrated movements and coordinated handoffs. The system combines human resources, technology, and standardized processes to create a seamless flow of people and materials throughout the facility.

Key components

The control center

The CTC control center serves as the operational hub, similar to an air traffic control tower. Staffed by trained dispatchers, it provides:

- Real-time monitoring of all transport activities
- Centralized dispatch for scheduled and stat requests
- Coordination of multiple service lines
- Response to alerts and anomalies
- Performance monitoring and SLA tracking.

Human resources structure

The human resource structure of the CTC support services is designed to realign the transport tasks that are part of the departments that are supported. The goal is to remove the workload that is associated with the transport and stocking of equipment and supplies from its current teams and assign it to the CTC support services function.

This will result in a net reduction in the work that is associated with many services and allows the optimization techniques to further reduce the work and remove delays. This transformation will result in a reduction in workload in the affected departments that will allow staffing of the CTC transport function.

The CTC system relies on several key roles, each with specific responsibilities. Some specialties are required but a central function will allow cross-training and provide oversight and governance.

Manager

- Ensures appropriate staffing levels
- Monitors long-term planning horizons
- Acts as a servant leader, providing support where needed
- Serves as point of escalation for complex situations
- Drives continuous improvement initiatives

Dispatcher

- Monitor and coordinate all transport activities
- Assign jobs based on workorder management systems
- Track scheduled assignments against SLAs
- Monitor real-time systems (indoor positioning systems (IPS) and RTLS) for issues
- Utilize OODA (observe, orient, decide, act) decision-making techniques
- Can operate from any location with appropriate technology access

Transporter

- Execute the movement of people and property
- Follow assigned routes and schedules
- Handle both scheduled assignments and stat orders
- Log relevant activities and events
- Maintain efficient routing and timing
- Follow the appropriate protocols for transporting special items

Unit Orderly

- Serve as the equivalent of gate agents and ground crew
- Receive and coordinate arrivals within departments
- Manage point-of-use stocking for equipment and supplies
- Maintain organization according to department standards
- Drive utilization rates and minimize holding costs
- Ensure care providers don't need to hunt for supplies
- Coordinate with other orderlies across departments
- Handle ground-level RTLS tasks (Figure 20.1)

Technology infrastructure

The CTC system utilizes several integrated technologies:

Dispatching Systems

- Workorder Management Console
- Real-time location monitoring

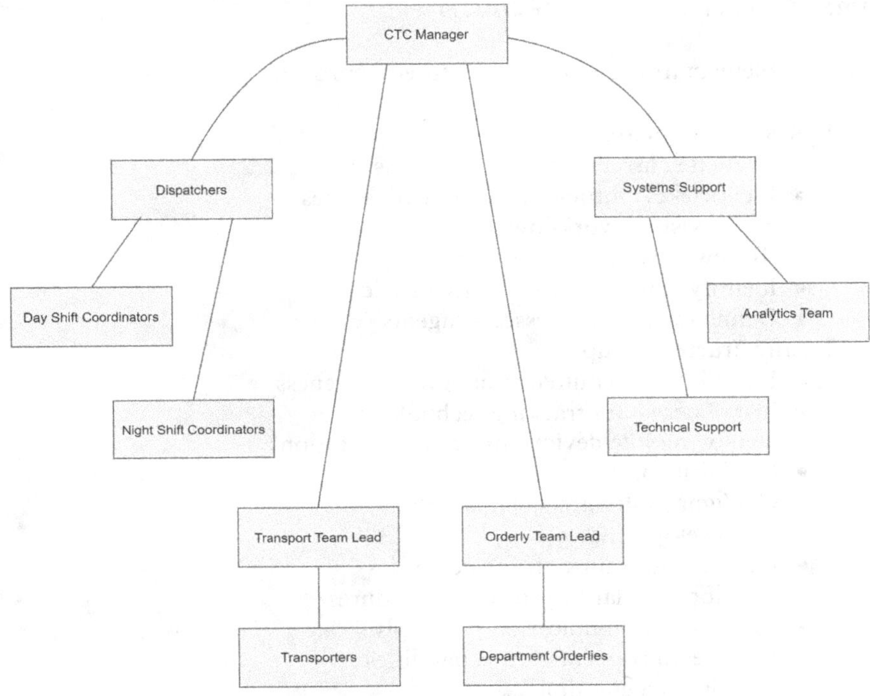

Figure 20.1 CTC human resources structure.

- Voice and messaging communications
- Mobile fleet management tools

Mobile Solutions

- iPhones for all transport staff
- Charging infrastructure
- Purpose-built mobile applications
- Location telemetry capabilities
- Status event tracking

Tracking Technologies

- RTLS (real-time location systems)
- IPS
- Workflow-oriented implementation
- Zone-level monitoring
- Choke point and egress tracking

IMPLEMENTATION APPROACH

CTC implementation follows a structured approach:

1. **Assessment phase**
   - Evaluate current transport patterns
   - Identify key bottlenecks and inefficiencies
   - Map existing workflows
   - Review existing technologies
   - Identify existing performance metrics
   - Define the new processes as agents
2. **Infrastructure setup**
   - Establish the required situational awareness
   - Install necessary tracking technologies
   - Deploy mobile devices and charging stations
   - Establish control center
   - Configure software systems
3. **Team development**
   - Recruit and train staff for new roles
   - Develop standard operating procedures
   - Establish communication protocols
   - Build team coordination capabilities
4. **Process implementation**
   - Begin with core services
   - Gradually expand scope
   - Monitor and adjust based on performance
   - Implement continuous improvement cycles
5. **Integration and optimization**
   - Connect with existing hospital systems
   - Fine-tune routing and scheduling
   - Optimize resource allocation
   - Enhance predictive capabilities

The implementation can start small but has a compounding effect as additional services are integrated and more data becomes available for optimization.

AGENTIC DESIGN

By extracting the PEAS model from the agentic design process outlined in Section 2, we will describe each service as an agent. This will allow us to better see where the agents interact with each other and the multiagent design will be easier to visualize. This is a good example of how agentic design does not require AI to get started on our journey toward more automated and assistive technology. The application of AI will be informed by using this approach.

The goal of this exercise is to create a new process that is streamlined, suits the organization, and will serve the consolidated transport function. Another goal is to create technology requirements for the CTC transport function that will endure as the product market matures. As agents enter the market, they will be assistive technologies that can only be successful if they match the requirements that come from exercises like these.

1. Organize the service/agent into the PEAS structure
   a. Performance measures
      i. Evaluate the quality of the data that is currently being captured for each performance measure.
      ii. Target performance measures where the data needs to be improved.
      iii. Identify any subordinate performance measures that are critical to the targeted performance measures and run them through the process.
   b. Environment
      i. Identify the people, property, and places that are a part of the service.
      ii. Itemize how they are represented digitally.
      iii. Prepare the state space for the service/agent.
      iv. Identify the states that are necessary to capture the performance measures.
   c. Actuators
      i. Ensure there is a process diagram. If not create one.
      ii. Identify the state changes and events that are part of the process.
   d. Sensors
      i. Determine the technologies necessary to detect the state changes for the targeted performance measures.
2. Find the states for both the environment and the actuators
   a. Decide which state changes must be processed into digital events.
   b. Consider human-in-the-loop states (e.g., human observes, decides and acts).
3. Determine what sensing is necessary to detect the required states
   a. Determine which technologies in the market now can detect the state changes.
   b. Determine how the actions change the state to the desired state.
   c. Ensure that there is sensing to validate that the desired state has been reached.
   d. Use human-in-the-loop to detect state changes that are not going to be detected with technology.
4. Adapt the process (actuators)
   a. Use the sense→decide→act model to develop control loops.

b. Determine if any new steps are needed and remove any unnecessary steps.
c. Ensure any new roles (people) are represented in the new process.
d. Ensure the new actions (actuators) are merged into the new process.

KEY SERVICES AND OPERATIONS

Patient transport

Patient transport serves as a critical component of CTC, directly impacting hospital throughput and patient care quality. This service manages the safe and efficient movement of patients throughout the facility while maintaining strict protocols for patient safety and comfort.

Key Features:

- Integrated EMR order processing
- Real-time status tracking
- Priority-based scheduling
- Equipment coordination
- Infection control protocols

PEAS for patient transport

Performance Measures:

- Request to pickup time
- Pickup to drop-off duration
- Total transport time
- Turnaround time
- On-time arrival rate
- Patient satisfaction scores
- Transporter utilization rate

Environment

- Places: Hospital building, patient rooms, clinical service locations, and discharge
  - Identify the routes that are required for patient transport.
  - Compile the state space for places by listing the states for patient rooms and service locations.
- Property: Mobility equipment (wheelchairs, stretchers, lifts, and beds), iPhones
  - Compile the state space for the property by listing the states for wheelchairs, stretchers, lifts, and beds.

- People: Patients, nurses, orderlys, transporters, dispatchers
  - Compile the state space for people by listing the states for the patients, nurses, orderlys, transporters, and dispatchers.

Actuators (Process)

- A request comes in when a nurse puts an order in the EHR
- The CTC dispatcher assigns a transporter that is in "available" state
- The transporter acknowledges the assignment
- The unit orderly for the departing department acknowledges the assignment
- The CTC transporter gets the equipment that is necessary for the transport
- The transporter proceeds to the pickup location
- At the same time, the unit orderly ensures that the patient is ready by assisting the nurse
- The transporter arrives at the pickup location, the patient is put in the transport device, and safety checks are done
- The transporter moves the patient
- The receiving staff acknowledge the handoff
- Documentation for the completed transport is completed (Figure 20.2)
- State space
  - Order status states: ordered, pending, scheduled, assigned, acknowledged
  - Active transport states: enRoute, atPickup, inProgress, atDestination
  - Hold states: onHold, medicalHold, equipmentHold, destinationHold
  - Completion states: complete, documented, verified, equipmentReturned
  - Cancellation states: canceled, cancelledMedical, cancelledDestination
  - Exception states: delayed, escalated, emergency, diverted, incident Reported
  - System states: error, pending, review, dataIncomplete, validation Failed

Sensors (example)

- RTLS shows the position of the mobility equipment
- IPS sends a departure event to the workflow engine for the "pickup" state
- IPS sends an arrival event to the workflow engine at the pickup location
- IPS sends a departure event to the workflow engine for the "in progress" state
- IPS sends an arrival event to the workflow engine at the destination location
- Workflow engine calculates the "complete" state.

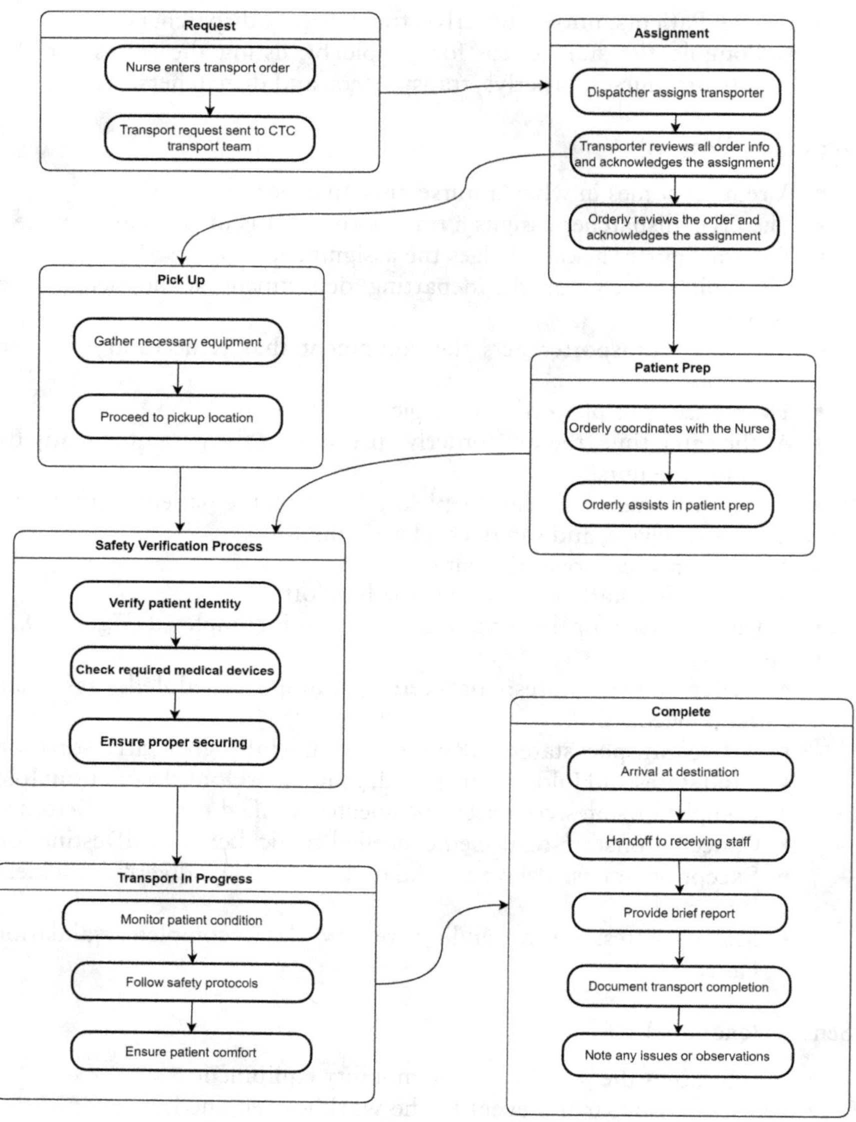

Figure 20.2 Patient transport process diagram.

When transporting the patients, the transporters will use the same workflow automation tools they do for their other jobs. That means that IPS and mobile devices will be required. RTLS is optional, but beneficial, if used to track patients or the mobility equipment.

Indoor positioning and workflow automation tools are necessary so the dispatcher can help monitor the nominal flow of the process. If the unit orderly can see the location of the patient transporter, it will be easier for them to avoid delays. The tools must show a schedule of all the tasks so patient transport can be coordinated with all their other duties. Situational awareness requires that alerting and communications with dispatching and nursing are seamless. Mobile communication is essential because the potential for tasks to collide with one another would be high with good tools to synchronize them.

Work order management systems usually have strong mobile tools, but this must be evaluated if they already exist in the health system. As the platforms mature, there will be some consolidation, but expect that the team will need multiple mobile apps to be successful.

A significant finding shows that 80% of transport delays are associated with patients not being ready for transport, highlighting the importance of coordinated preparation and communication. By adding the unit orderly to the existing process, the orderly ensures the patient is ready for reporting the delay to the dispatcher so that the transport can be rescheduled.

Medical device micro-logistics

The management of medical devices represents a substantial portion of hospital operational costs. CTC approaches this through systematic tracking and distribution. By implementing this process, the availability of medical devices and the utilization rates will increase significantly. The administrative overhead, and the time spent looking for devices will decrease significantly as well.

Reduces time to find devices

From the nurse's perspective, they will communicate the need for the device to the CTC service and the device will be put in the location that it is needed by the unit orderly. Not only will the nurse not have to hunt for the device, but also they will not have to move it from the periodic automatic replenishment (PAR) stocking location to the patient room. Shifting the burden to orderly allows for a tighter control loop for the medical devices because the orderly can scan the device indicating it is "in-use."

Reduces the effort for central processing

When central sterile supply is involved in distributing the devices, it often means that trained and certified technicians are taking on the burden of either retrieving or distributing the devices.

Core Components

- Real-time device tracking
- Transport to a centralized cleaning function

- PAR level implementation
- Just-in-time delivery
- Loss prevention integration

The system standardizes device flow through:

- Scheduled pickups from soiled utility areas
- Centralized cleaning and maintenance
- Coordinated redistribution
- Point-of-use availability tracking
- Precise demand signals to optimize PAR levels

PEAS for medical device micro-logistics

Performance Measures:
Performance measures for the function of PAR stocking IV pumps in nursing can help ensure that the process is efficient, accurate, and meets the needs of patients and staff. Here are some key performance measures to consider:

- Stockout rate – The frequency at which IV pumps are unavailable when needed.
- Replenishment time – The time it takes to restock IV pumps once a request is made.
- Inventory accuracy – The accuracy of inventory records compared to actual stock levels.
- Utilization rate – The percentage of IV pumps in use compared to the total available.
- Turnover rate – The rate at which IV pumps are cycled through the inventory.
- Maintenance and downtime – The frequency and duration of maintenance and downtime for IV pumps.
- Compliance with PAR Levels – The adherence to established PAR levels for IV pumps.
- User satisfaction – Feedback from nursing staff regarding the availability and functionality of IV pumps.
- Cost efficiency – The cost associated with maintaining and replenishing IV pumps.

Environment

- Places – Hospital building, soiled and clean utility closets, drop-off locations, central equipment
- Property – Mobility, medical equipment that is being cleaned in the central equipment, iPhones
- People – Patients, nurses, orderly, transporters, dispatchers, central equipment techs

Actuators – IV pump example (closed-loop):

- Soiled cycle
  - Orderly is notified when a pump is coming off the patient
  - The orderly gets the pump from the patient's location
  - The orderly puts the pump in the designated soiled utility closet
  - Pumps accumulate in the soiled utility closet until a pickup is triggered
  - Orderly and dispatcher are alerted that the pickup is required
  - Orderly gathers the soiled pumps and prepares them to be transported
  - Orderly puts the soiled pumps in the pickup location for transport
  - During their rounds, the transporter sees the pumps at the pickup location and adds them to the cart
  - Transport drops them off at the central cleaning facility
- Clean cycle
  - Pump supply at point of use drops below PAR
  - Orderly and dispatcher are alerted that restocking is required
  - Clean pumps are added to the manifest for one of the transport rounds
  - Transporter adds the required pumps to the cart for the schedule round
  - Pumps are dropped off at the designated drop-off location and the orderly is notified
  - Orderly retrieves the pumps from the drop-off location and puts them in the PAR location
- Use cycle
  - The nurse orders a device for the patient and the pump is assigned to the patient room
  - Orderly retrieves the device from the PAR location and scans the pump to put the pump "in-use"
  - The on-hand number is decremented from the PAR location
  - The orderly puts the pump in the patient room (Figure 20.3)

Sensors

- Room-level RTLS to count the number of devices in the soiled utility
  - The closet's state (increment) will identify that a device has put in the closet.
  - The closet's state (number) will trigger a job to retrieve the pumps.
  - The state of the pump will be "soiled."
- IPS to track the location of the transporter to pick up the pumps
- Room-level RTLS to count the number of devices in the clean utility
  - The closet's state (below PAR) will trigger a job to restock the pumps
- IPS to track the location of the transporter delivering the devices for restocking

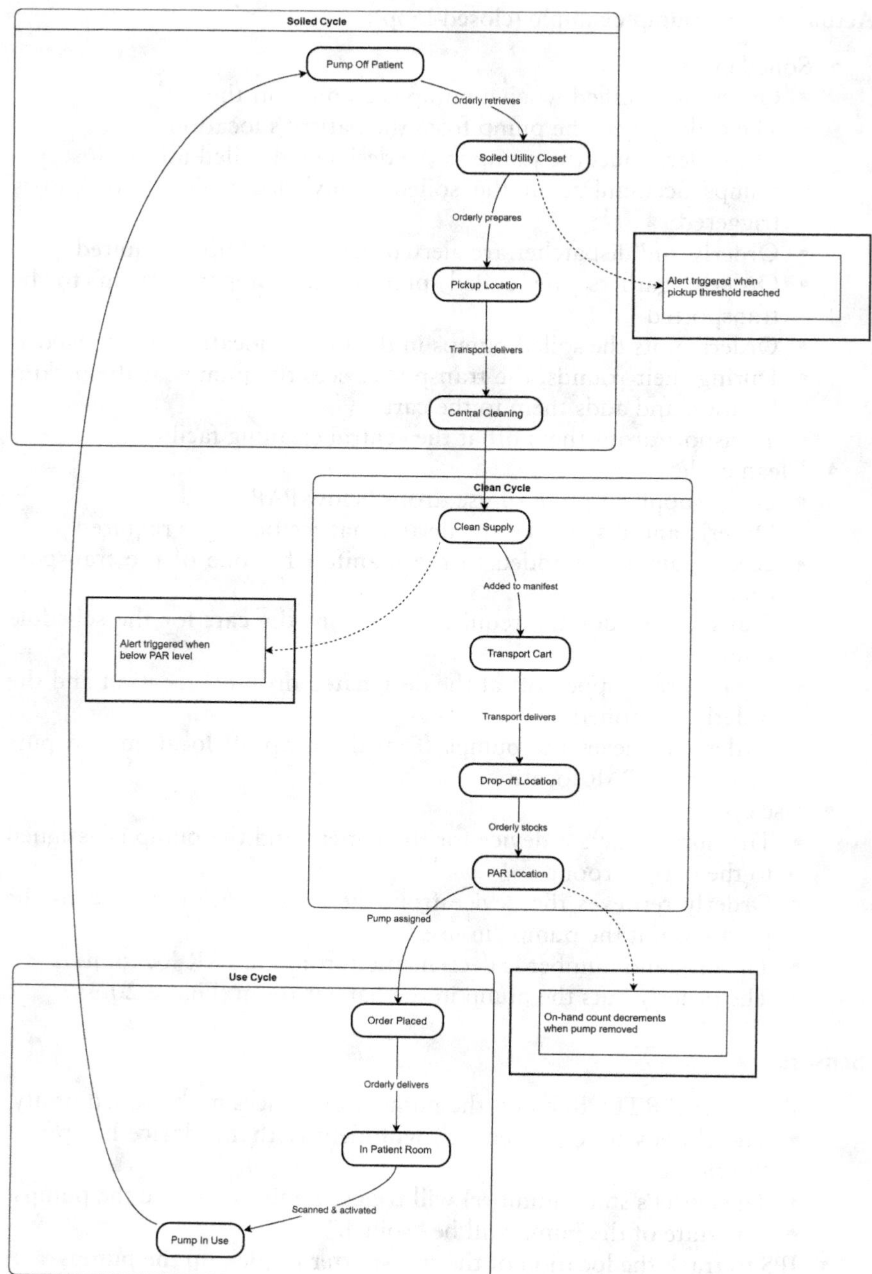

Figure 20.3 IV Pump micro-logistics process diagram.

    - The closet's state (at PAR) will identify that the closet has the PAR number of pumps
    - The closet's state (number) will identify available devices
    - The state of the pump will be "available"
    - The closet's state (decrement) will indicate a device has been retrieved
- Orderly will identify when the devices are in use with a patient (scan)
    - The state of the pump will be "in-use"

The biggest challenge with PAR stocking medical equipment has been ensuring that the soiled devices are put in the soiled utility closets. By making this the responsibility of the unit orderly, the number of hoarded devices will decrease as will the quality of the demand signals. Better demand signals allow optimization of PAR levels and stocking frequency.

RTLS is installed in the PAR locations and the soiled utility closets. This is assistive to the unit orderly so that the demand signals can be used to make the operation efficient.

Indoor positioning and workflow automation tools are helpful to the unit orderly so that the work in the department can be optimized. Situational awareness requires that alerting and communications with dispatching and nursing is seamless.

Supply chain micro-logistics

Supply chain micro-logistics operates as an indoor logistics system, like Amazon's delivery model but within the hospital environment. The system utilizes a two-bin Kanban approach for optimal inventory management. A typical pitfall for the system is that the restocking order must wait until the supply chain tech shows up at the stocking location. With the CTC structure, the unit orderly will be responsible for signaling the replenishment of the unit's supply closets. This will mean that the scanning will be done locally instead of waiting for a supply technician. This will tighten the demand signals dramatically.

System Features

- Track and trace capability
- Chain of custody documentation
- Two-bin Kanban implementation
- Last-meter delivery service
- Real-time inventory visibility

Performance Measures

- Stockout rate – The frequency at which supplies run out before the next replenishment.

- Replenishment time – The time it takes to restock supplies once a bin is empty.
- Inventory accuracy – The accuracy of inventory records compared to actual stock levels.
- Utilization rate – The percentage of supplies used compared to the total available.
- Turnover rate – The rate at which supplies are cycled through the inventory.
- Compliance with Kanban signals – The adherence to Kanban signals for replenishment.
- Cost efficiency – The cost associated with maintaining and replenishing supplies.
- User satisfaction – Feedback from nursing staff regarding the availability and functionality of supplies.
- Waste reduction – The amount of expired or unused supplies.
- Lead time variability – The consistency of lead times for replenishment.

Environment

- Places: Hospital building, storage closets, drop-off locations, central supply
- Property: Supplies, carts, iPhones
- People: Patients, nurses, orderly, transporters, dispatchers, central supply techs

Actuators (Process)

1. Active bin supplies daily operations.
2. Empty bin triggers automatic reorder.
3. The unit orderly scans the empty bins.
4. Supply chain prepares the items for restocking.
5. CTC transport picks up the items from the supply chain.
6. CTC transport delivers to the unit drop off location.
7. The unit orderly restocks the supply closets.
8. The unit orderly scans any empty bins.
9. Replenishment arrives before depletion.
10. Continuous rotation maintains stock levels (Figure 20.4).

Sensors

- When the orderly scans the bins, the reorders accumulate until a delivery is triggered.
- Scanning creates the demand signals that are used to determine optimum PAR levels.
- IPS tracks the location of the transporters who are delivering to the drop-off location.

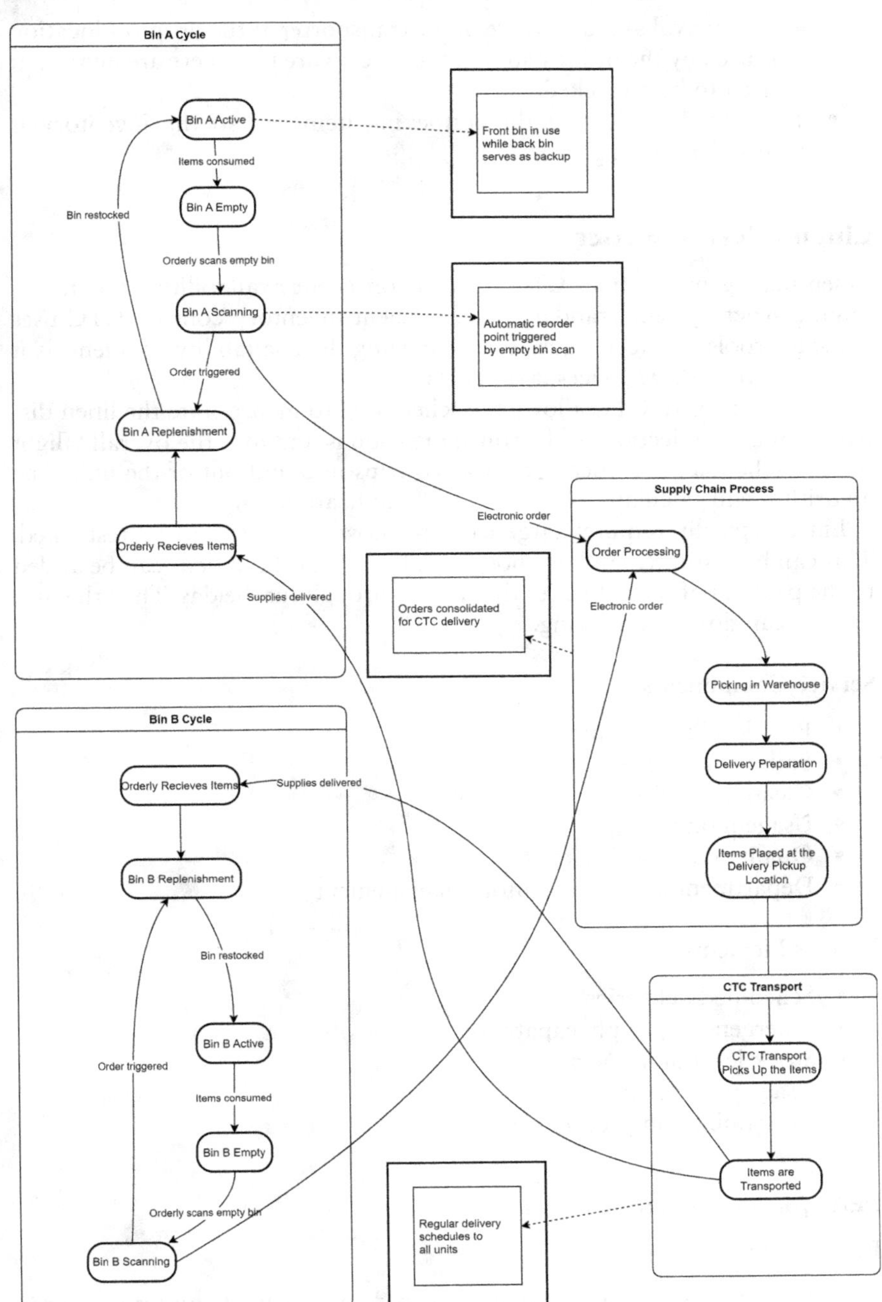

Figure 20.4 Supply chain micro-logistics process diagram.

    - The arrival and departure of the transporter at the drop-off location is used by the orderly so that they are aware that there are items that need to be restocked.
- The orderly will scan the restocking items in, so the inventory is adjusted accordingly.

Linen micro-logistics

Linen management under CTC ensures consistent availability while maintaining strict hygiene standards and efficient inventory control. CTC uses the same tools and techniques for optimizing the availability of linens as it does with the other services it supports.

Adding linens to CTC allows the scheduling to incorporate the linen distribution and collection to the transport rounds and into the overall "flight board" schedule. This means no wasted trips into and out of the unit. The algorithm will calculate to achieve 100% utilization.

Linen typically requires large carts to move the linens to be restocked. This can be disruptive in busy hospitals. By using CTC, linens can be added to the payload of the deliveries that occur throughout the day. Then the unit orderly can do the restocking.

Service Components

- PAR level management
- Soiled linen collection
- Clean linen distribution
- Usage monitoring
- Quality control checks
- Department-specific inventory management

Process Elements

- Scheduled deliveries
- Emergency resupply capability
- Stock level monitoring
- Usage pattern analysis
- Contamination prevention

PEAS for linen micro-logistics

Performance Measures

- Timeliness – The percentage of linen deliveries made on time according to the schedule.
- Stockout rate – The frequency at which departments run out of clean linens before the next delivery.

- Turnaround time – The time it takes to collect soiled linens, launder them, and deliver them back as clean linens.
- Inventory accuracy – The accuracy of inventory records compared to actual stock levels.
- Utilization rate – The percentage of linens in use compared with the total available.
- Linen Loss rate – The percentage of linens lost or damaged during the collection, laundering, and delivery process.
- Compliance with hygiene standards – The adherence to hygiene and safety standards during the laundering and handling of linens.
- Cost efficiency – The cost associated with laundering and delivering linens.
- User satisfaction – Feedback from hospital staff regarding the availability and quality of linens.
- Waste reduction – The amount of expired or unused linens.

Environment

- Places – Hospital building, linen closets, soiled pickup location, central linen
- Property – Linens, linen carts, iPhones
- People – Patients, nurses, orderly, transporters, dispatchers, central linen tech

Actuators (Process)

- Central storage and preparation (linen team)
  - Clean linens arrive from the laundry facility to central storage
  - PAR levels monitored for each type of linen
  - Carts prepared based on department orders and par levels
- Distribution schedule (CTC transport)
  - Regular delivery rounds scheduled (typically morning and evening)
  - Routes optimized based on department locations
  - Specialty areas (OR, ED) may have additional delivery times
  - Delivery schedules coordinated with other department deliveries
  - Emergency deliveries accommodated between regular rounds
- Cart preparation (linen team)
  - Carts loaded according to department par sheets
  - Items counted and verified against order
  - Special requests clearly marked
  - Cart integrity and cleanliness verified
  - Proper cart covers installed
  - Documentation attached for delivery verification
- Transport process (CTC transport)
  - Designated clean elevators and routes used
  - No transport through public areas when possible

- Temperature and humidity monitored during transport
- Clean linen protected from contamination
- Cart covers remain in place during transport
- Dedicated CTC staff for clean linen transport

- Department delivery (CTC transport)
  - Cart delivered to designated clean storage area
  - Department staff notified of delivery
  - PAR levels checked against delivery
  - Shortages or discrepancies noted
  - Delivery documented and verified
  - Empty carts retrieved
- Department storage (CTC orderly)
  - Clean linen stored in designated clean utility rooms
  - Proper shelving and storage conditions maintained
  - First-in-first-out (FIFO) rotation followed
  - PAR levels marked on shelves
  - Storage areas kept locked/secure
  - Temperature and humidity monitored
- Usage monitoring (linen team)
  - PAR levels checked regularly (by orderly)
  - Usage patterns tracked
  - Adjustments made based on census
  - Special events or increased usage anticipated
  - Emergency stock maintained
  - Regular audits conducted
- Quality control (linen team)
  - Regular inspection of storage conditions
  - Monitoring of linen quality
  - Check for proper storage practices
  - Verification of rotation practices
  - Cleanliness of storage areas verified
  - Staff compliance with protocols checked
- Emergency procedures (CTC transport and linen team)
  - Process for STAT requests established
  - Emergency par levels defined
  - After-hours access protocols in place
  - Backup supplies identified
  - Emergency contact list maintained
  - Escalation procedures documented (Figure 20.5)

Sensors

- IPS tracks the location of the transporters who are moving the linens
  - The arrivals and departures trigger notifications to the orderly so they can stock the linen closets.

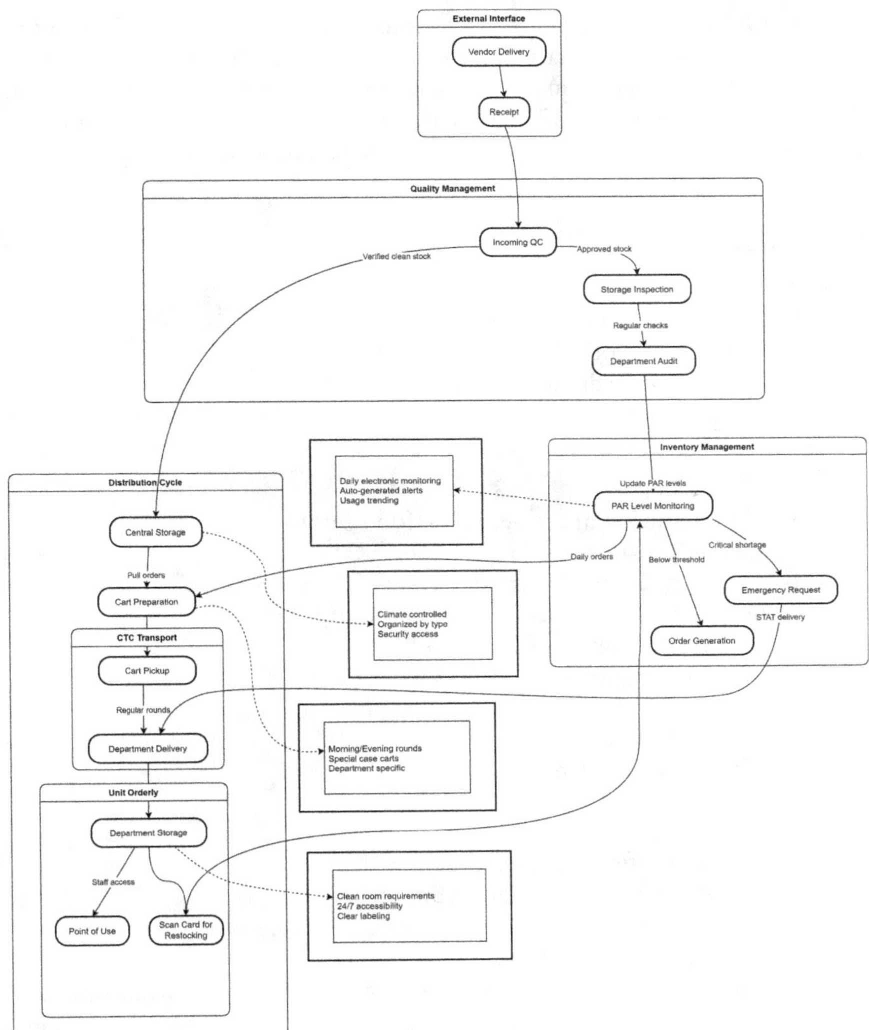

Figure 20.5 Linen distribution process diagram.

Food service deliveries

Food service integration within CTC ensures timely, temperature-controlled meal delivery while maintaining patient satisfaction and dietary compliance. Food services teams are challenged with the time constraints of feeding patients within the normal meal hours and keeping the food warm in insulated carts. CTC control can assist in the delivery cycle of food services and relieve the food services staff from retrieving the trays and silverware.

The successful delivery of food to its intended recipients is still the responsibility of food services, but using the CTC will help address the time constraints that are inherent in the process. Because the orderly is assigned to the unit, the interaction with the patient is with someone the patient is familiar with. This will allow rapport to be established and better patient satisfaction.

Key Features

- Temperature monitoring
- Dietary restriction tracking
- Delivery route optimization
- Meal timing coordination
- Tray retrieval management

Process Flow

1. Meal preparation and assembly – food service
2. Route optimization – CTC transporter
3. Temperature-controlled transport – CTC transporter
4. Point-of-service verification – CTC orderly
5. Prompt tray retrieval – CTC orderly
6. Satisfaction monitoring – Food services and CTC

PEAS for food services transport

Performance measures

- Clinical and safety measures:
  - Time between meal ordering and delivery
  - Meal tray completeness (all ordered items present)
- Patient experience metrics:
  - Delivery timeliness (meals arriving within scheduled windows)
  - Rate of missed meals or late deliveries
  - Special request fulfillment rate
- Operational efficiency:
  - Average delivery time per unit/floor
  - Number of trays delivered per hour
  - Labor hours per meal served
  - Food waste percentage
  - Cart return and cleaning turnaround times
  - Rate of equipment malfunctions (carts, warming/cooling systems)
- Quality control:
  - Sanitation compliance scores
  - Number of food safety incidents
  - Rate of tray assembly errors

- Cross-contamination prevention effectiveness
- Storage temperature monitoring compliance

Environment

- Places – Hospital building, patient rooms, drop-off locations, kitchen
- Property – Food, food carts, iPhones
- People – Patients, orderly, transporters, dispatchers, food services

Actuators

1. Cart preparation, tray verification, and cart loading are done by food services.
2. Transport team coordination is by food services.
3. Floor delivery could be any combination of food services and/or CTC transport.
4. Tray retrieval could also be done with the assistance of CTC transport (Figure 20.6).

Sensors

- IPS to track the location of the transporters as they take the carts to the floors
  - The arrivals and departures trigger notifications to the orderly so they can complete the delivery of the food to the patients
  - Other deliveries are done entirely by the transporters
- Temperature sensors on the carts to monitor the temperature throughout the delivery process

Food transport inside the hospital is designed to reduce the duration of the food must cool. In a given hospital, this could be a combination of CTC and food services. Each hospital will have requirements that must be considered when deciding how much CTC transport can participate in food delivery.

Courier services

Courier services handle time-sensitive items requiring special handling or documentation. These deliveries and retrievals are done on a scheduled basis, and some could be added to the manifest for other deliveries that are being done as a part of the CTC transport service.

Service Types

- Lab sample retrieval to the central lab
- Medication delivery from the inpatient pharmacy to the units
- Blood from the blood bank
- Medical gas distribution

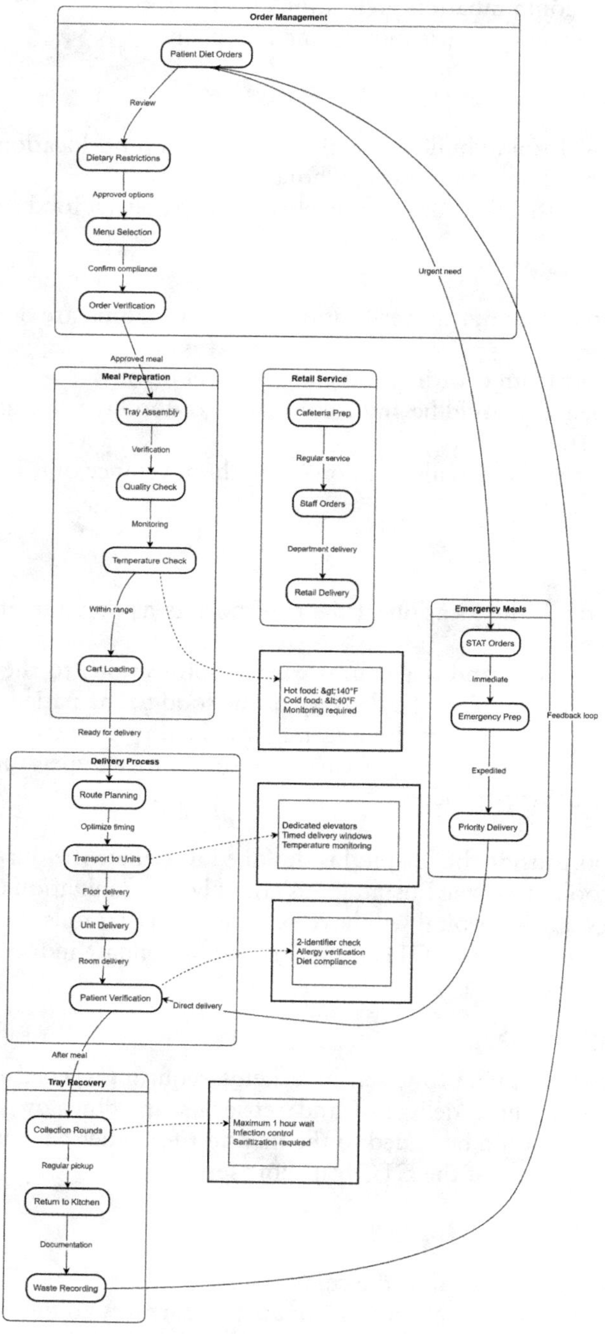

Figure 20.6 Food services process diagram.

- Specialized material handling
- Mail and document delivery

Operational Features

- Scheduled route service
- STAT delivery capability
- Track and trace monitoring
- Chain of custody documentation
- Priority-based routing

PEAS for courier services

Performance Measures

- Delivery time – The time taken from request submission to delivery completion.
- On-time delivery rate – Percentage of deliveries completed within the expected time frame.
- Accuracy – Number of deliveries made without errors (e.g., correct items delivered to the right location).
- Utilization rate – Percentage of time transport personnel and vehicles are engaged in deliveries.
- Request volume – Total number of transport requests received and completed.
- STAT delivery rate – Percentage of urgent deliveries completed on time.
- Customer satisfaction – Feedback from hospital staff on the quality and reliability of the transport service.
- Incident rate – Number of incidents or issues reported during deliveries (e.g., damaged items, delays).
- Cost efficiency – Cost per delivery and overall cost savings achieved through centralization.
- Compliance – Adherence to safety protocols and handling procedures for specialized materials.

Actuators

- Dispatching
  - Dispatchers start each shift by reviewing the day's scheduled routes and any special requirements or maintenance issues.
  - Electronic dashboard displays all scheduled pickups, deliveries, and real-time tracking of transport staff locations.
  - System automatically generates the daily schedule with predetermined routes and timing for each transport type.

- Route execution
  - Transport staff use the app to receive their route assignments and specialized equipment for the shift.
  - Each transporter is equipped with a mobile device with an app showing their route schedule, pickup/delivery locations, and special instructions.
  - Regular cycles run at set intervals (e.g., every 30 mins) with predetermined stops for each type of delivery.
  - Routes are designed to create a "milk run" style operation where one transporter can handle multiple types of deliveries along their assigned path.
- Communication and tracking:
  - Transporters scan or log each pickup and delivery using mobile devices to maintain real-time tracking.
  - Digital system automatically notifies receiving departments of estimated arrival times.
  - Command center monitors progress and can adjust routes in real-time for urgent requests or delays.
  - Any delays or issues are immediately reported through the mobile system to the command center.
- Quality control and monitoring:
  - Supervisors conduct random route audits to ensure compliance with procedures and timing.
  - System tracks key performance indicators like on-time delivery rates and route completion times.
  - Regular review of route efficiency and adjustment of schedules based on volume patterns (Figure 20.7).

Environment

- Places – Hospital building, medication alcoves, lab pickup locations, central lab, unit drop-off locations, misc. designated drop-off locations
- Property – Medications, lab samples, medical gases, blood, specialty intem, mail and documents, iPhones
- People – Patients, nurses, orderly, transporters, dispatchers

Sensors

- IPS for tracking the arrival, departures, and dwell time for the delivery routes.
- Scanning for the proof of delivery features.

Waste management

Waste management in a hospital is a critical component of infection control. The movement of waste needs to be accomplished with care due to the

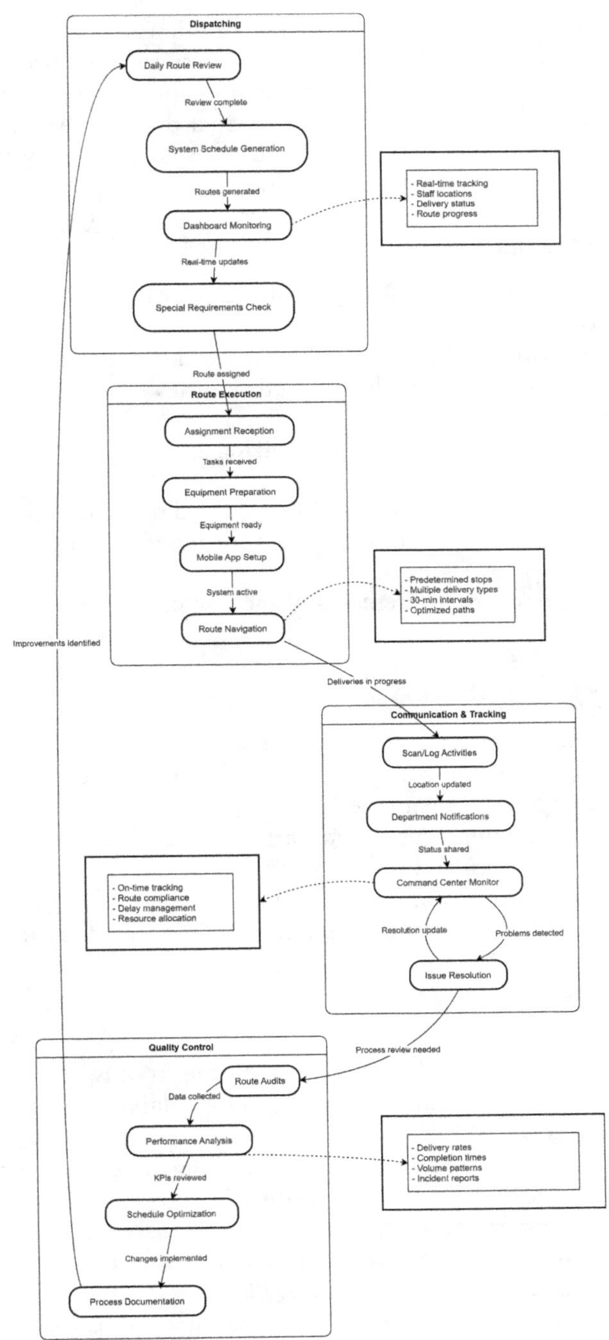

Figure 20.7 Courier service process diagram.

hazardous nature of what is being transported. The CTC waste management function optimizes the transport of waste to minimize the risk and maximize efficiency. The visibility and data of the waste traffic are helpful to ensure compliance with protocols for proper disposal. Additionally, with waste transport and loss prevention under the same entity, waste disposal can be addressed as a threat vector for loss.

Performance Measures

- Waste segregation – Ensuring waste segregation is maintained during transport.
- Transport time – Time from collection to disposal.
- Incident rate – Spills, leaks, and injuries associated with waste transport.
- Compliance with protocols – Utilizing designated carts, trolleys, or bins and proper PPE.
- Route compliance – Using established fixed transport routes.
- Low activity transport times – Transporting waste during low activity times.
- Waste volume – Measurements of the volume of waste collected.

Environment

- People:
  - CTC waste management team: Transporters, dispatchers, supervisors (for infection control purposes the orderlies do not participate)
- Property (equipment/supplies):
  - Collection equipment: Waste carts, linen hampers, bin lifters, transport containers, and spill kits
  - Administrative equipment: iPhone
  - Safety equipment: PPE supplies, safety signage, first aid kits, emergency response kits

Places

- Collection points: Patient rooms, operating rooms, treatment rooms, nursing stations, department utility rooms, laboratories, pharmacies, food service areas
- Transport routes: Service corridors, designated elevators, loading dock, transport paths, collection routes
- Storage areas: Soiled utility rooms, hazardous waste storage, regular waste holding, recycling areas, clean supply storage
- Support areas: Staff locker rooms, PPE storage areas, cart wash stations, equipment maintenance areas, training rooms
- Administrative areas: Management offices, control center, documentation stations, meeting rooms, training facilities

Actuators

- Order/request phase:
  - Department reaches capacity in waste holding areas
  - Automatic alerts generated from fill sensors/weight monitors
  - Manual requests entered into the system
  - Regular scheduled pickups programmed
  - Emergency/STAT requests initiated
- Assignment/dispatch:
  - Work orders prioritized by type and urgency
  - Routes optimized for efficient collection
  - Staff assigned to specific zones/areas
  - Equipment and PPE requirements identified
  - Special handling requirements noted
- Collection process:
  - Staff arrives with appropriate carts/containers
  - Scans location/container barcodes
  - Verifies waste segregation is correct
  - Replaces containers/bags as needed
  - Documents weights/volumes collected
  - Logs any compliance issues
  - Performs any required cleaning
- Transport requirements:
  - Use designated "dirty" elevators
  - Follow prescribed transport routes
  - Maintain proper separation of waste types
  - Monitor for spills/leaks
  - Ensure proper cart coverage
  - Avoid public areas when possible
- Staging/storage:
  - Transport to appropriate holding areas
  - Bins are scanned for loss prevention to detect medical equipment
  - Scan items into storage location
  - Monitor storage conditions
  - Ensure proper segregation is maintained
  - Track holding times
  - Manage storage capacity
- Pickup:
  - Schedule coordination with vendors
  - Preparation of shipping documents
  - Weight verification
  - Proper container loading
  - Documentation of chain of custody
  - Verification of vendor compliance (Figure 20.8)

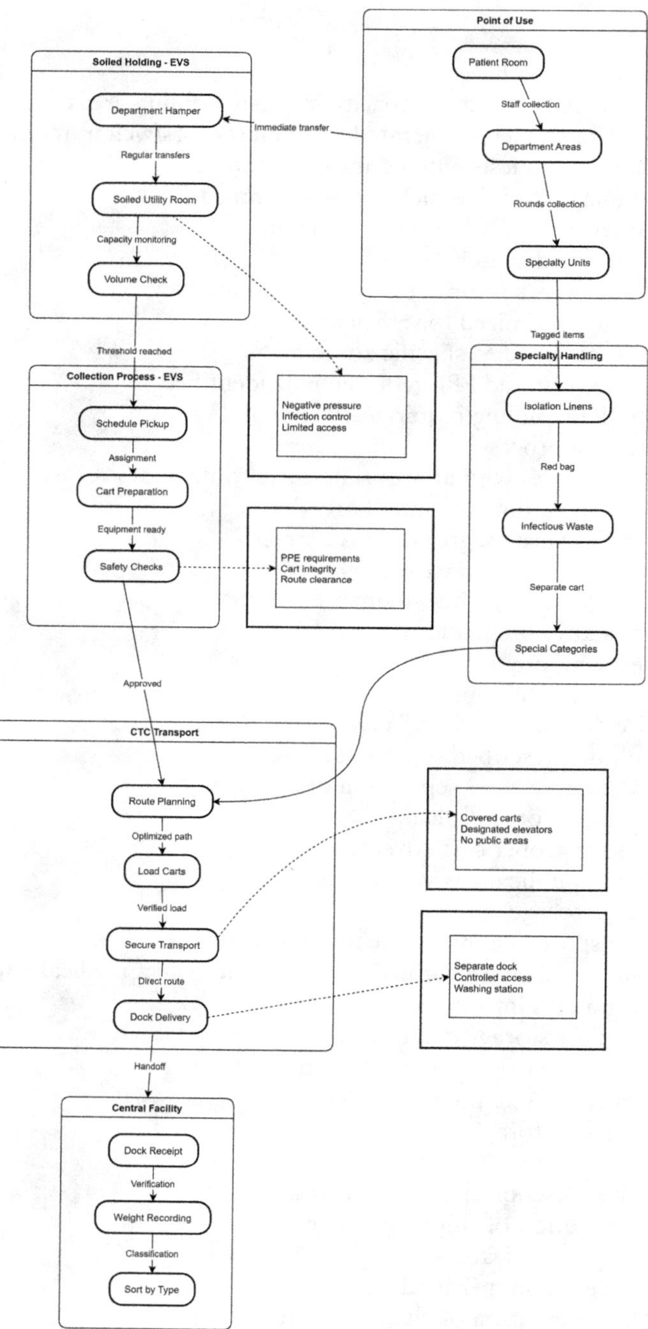

Figure 20.8 Waste management process diagram.

Sensors

- IPS to track the location of the transporters as they cover the locations on the route
  - The arrivals and departures trigger notifications to the orderlys so they

Loss prevention

The CTC loss prevention program addresses the significant challenge of missing mobile medical devices. Loss of medical equipment affects 10–20% of a hospital's mobile assets during their useful life, with an average cost of $3,000 per item. Although technology is a part of this system, the process of properly managing the inventory will have a positive impact even without the loss prevention system.

Where the Medical Device Micro-logistics services address the nominal flow of the equipment, the loss prevention program focuses on anomalies. This means understanding the conditions where loss occurs as well as addressing the events that indicate a response. The two programs must work together to be successful, but they have different processes.

Probabilities will be used to indicate if a device is at the risk of loss. The risk will indicate if an alert is created or if it some that is addressed in the daily processing.

Prevention Strategies

- Real-time location tracking
- Exit point monitoring
- Asset utilization tracking
- Pattern analysis
- Automated alerts

Common Issues Addressed

- Accidental disposal
- Patient discharge oversight
- Unauthorized removal
- Department hoarding
- Misplacement during high-activity periods

Integrating these services under the CTC framework creates a coordinated, efficient system that reduces waste, improves resource utilization, and enhances patient care delivery. Each service benefits from shared infrastructure and coordinated management while maintaining its specialized functions and requirements.

PEAS for loss prevention

Performance Measures

- Device utilization rate
- Device tracking compliance
- Loss incident rate
- Recovery rate
- Inventory accuracy
- Maintenance compliance
- Access control compliance
- Incident response time
- Employee training participation
- Vendor performance

Environment

- People:
  - Dispatchers monitor the console for alerts or conditions that indicate an incident should be created.
  - Transporters receive the jobs that are the response to the incident.
  - Orderlys can participate with incident response when the part of the response is in the unit.
- Property: Mobile medical equipment (tagged and untagged).
- Places: Hospital building and beyond, points of egress, points of use, anomalous locations.

Actuators

- Daily processing:
  - Dispatcher reviews the risk profile.
    - Devices that are missing status.
    - Devices with old last-known-location.
    - Devices in anomalous locations.
  - Dispatcher creates jobs for the transporters to address the risk items.
  - These jobs can be processed routinely.
- Incident response:
  - Dispatcher is alerted to conditions that indicate a device is at the risk of loss.
  - Dispatcher creates an incident.
  - Dispatcher assigns a job to the transporter.
  - The transporter attempts to correct the condition.
- Loss prevention tactical response:
  - Continuous review of incidents to determine how to better prevent loss.
  - Better detection of anomalies through precise risk profiles.
  - Tightening the nominal flow to keep the compliance high.

Sensors

- RTLS at points of egress and choke points in the building.
- IPS to track the location of the transporters as they respond to incidents.

BENEFITS AND OUTCOMES FOR CTC FOR SUPPORT SERVICES

Operational efficiency

CTC implementation delivers unprecedented levels of operational efficiency through systematic optimization of hospital logistics. Proven models of efficiency are replicated key improvements include:

Workflow Optimization

- Reduced transport delays
- Streamlined handoffs
- Coordinated scheduling
- Optimized routing
- Real-time adjustment capability

Resource Utilization

- Higher equipment availability
- Reduced search time
- Optimal staff deployment
- Better space utilization
- Improved inventory management

Financial impact

The financial benefits of CTC extend beyond direct cost savings to include operational efficiencies and asset optimization. Asset utilization increases go beyond the mobile equipment that comes to the patient. Utilization for fixed equipment, where the patient is moved to the location of the equipment, is improved by optimizing the patient traffic flow to the equipment.

Direct Cost Reduction

- Decreased equipment loss
- Reduced inventory holding costs
- Lower staffing overhead
- Minimized redundant transport
- Optimized asset utilization

Indirect Cost Benefits

- Reduced staff overtime
- Decreased equipment rentals
- Lower emergency purchases
- Minimized expedited shipping
- Better maintenance scheduling

Staff empowerment

CTC significantly impacts staff satisfaction and effectiveness by allowing healthcare professionals to focus on their primary responsibilities.

Professional Focus

- Specialists work at license level
- Reduced nonclinical tasks
- Enhanced job satisfaction
- Improved skill utilization
- Greater care time availability

Workflow Improvements

- Clear task assignments
- Reduced hunting for equipment
- Streamlined communications
- Better task coordination
- Enhanced predictability

Patient care enhancement

The implementation of CTC directly contributes to improved patient care through various mechanisms. Above-the-wing improvements with a concierge approach to the patients' needs for things like food delivery. Below-the-wing assistance for nurses with things like preparing patients for transport.

Service Improvements

- Faster response times
- Reduced delays
- Better care coordination
- Enhanced patient satisfaction
- Improved safety measures

Clinical Impact

- More direct care time
- Better equipment availability

- Reduced wait times
- Enhanced care transitions
- Improved treatment timing

Performance metrics

CTC success is measured through comprehensive performance metrics across multiple dimensions.

Operational Metrics

- Transport completion times
- Equipment utilization rates
- Inventory accuracy
- Response time compliance
- Service level achievement

Quality Indicators

- Patient satisfaction scores
- Staff satisfaction ratings
- Error reduction rates
- Safety incident reduction
- Service reliability measures

Evidence-based results

Healthcare facilities implementing CTC have documented significant improvements across multiple areas:

Quantitative Improvements

- 30–40% reduction in transport delays
- 50% decrease in lost equipment
- 20–25% improvement in asset utilization
- 15–20% reduction in inventory costs
- 40% decrease in stat requests

Qualitative Improvements

- Enhanced staff satisfaction
- Improved patient experience
- Better departmental coordination
- Increased operational visibility
- Stronger regulatory compliance

The comprehensive benefits of CTC implementation extend throughout the hospital organization, creating a more efficient, effective, and satisfying healthcare environment for both staff and patients.

IMPLEMENTATION AND GETTING STARTED

Initial assessment

Before beginning CTC implementation, organizations must evaluate their current state and readiness for change.

Operational Assessment

- Current workflow analysis
- Pain point identification
- Resource utilization review
- Technology infrastructure evaluation
- Staff capability assessment

Stakeholder Engagement

- Leadership buy-in
- Department coordination
- Staff feedback collection
- Union consideration
- Change readiness evaluation

Technology foundation

CTC implementation requires a carefully planned technology infrastructure that balances functionality with practical limitations.

Basic Infrastructure Requirements

- Indoor positioning system
  - Apple indoor positioning for transporter tracking
  - Mobile device integration
  - Navigation capability
- RTLS implementation
  - Room-level coverage in critical areas
  - Zone-level monitoring for asset tracking
  - Egress point coverage
  - Choke point monitoring
- Mobile device deployment
  - iPhone 12 or newer devices
  - Charging infrastructure

- Mobile app distribution
- User access management

Phased implementation approach

A successful CTC implementation follows a strategic, phased approach to ensure minimal disruption and maximum adoption.

Phase 1: Foundation Building

- Control center establishment
- Core technology deployment
- Initial staff training
- Basic workflow implementation

Phase 2: Service Integration

- Patient transport integration
- Courier service implementation
- Basic supply chain coordination
- Initial performance monitoring

Phase 3: Advanced Services

- Medical device management
- Advanced supply chain logistics
- Linen and food service integration
- Complete workflow optimization

Phase 4: Optimization

- Performance fine-tuning
- Advanced analytics implementation
- Workflow refinement
- System integration completion

Change management

Successful implementation requires careful attention to change management principles and practices.

Key Elements

- Clear communication strategy
- Stakeholder engagement plan
- Training and support programs
- Feedback collection mechanisms
- Success celebration protocols

Staff Development

- Role-specific training
- Workflow education
- Technology familiarization
- Process documentation
- Ongoing support structure

Common challenges and solutions

Understanding and preparing for common implementation challenges helps ensure success.

Technical Challenges

- Integration complexity
- System reliability
- Data accuracy
- Coverage gaps
- Device management

Solutions

- Phased testing
- Redundant systems
- Regular calibration
- Coverage mapping
- Device protocols

Operational Challenges

- Staff resistance
- Process adherence
- Workflow disruption
- Resource allocation
- Communication gaps

Solutions

- Change champions
- Clear protocols
- Flexible adaptation
- Resource planning
- Communication structure

Monitoring and optimization

Continuous monitoring and optimization ensure long-term success and maximum benefit realization.

Performance Monitoring

- Real-time metrics tracking
- SLA compliance monitoring
- Resource utilization analysis
- Cost tracking
- Quality measurements

Continuous Improvement

- Regular performance review
- Staff feedback integration
- Process refinement
- Technology updates
- Service expansion

PLAYBOOK FOR CTC FOR SUPPORT SERVICES

These are complex processes that have many compliance factors to consider. This chapter is only a partial examination of what the CTC service would need to get started. A comprehensive and incremental approach would allow a thorough implementation of this change.

To begin the CTC journey, organizations should follow these initial steps:

1. **Form implementation team**
   - **Identify project leader**
   - **Select core team members**
   - **Define roles and responsibilities**
   - **Establish governance structure**
2. **Conduct readiness assessment**
   - **Technology infrastructure review**
   - **Staff capability evaluation**
   - **Process gap analysis**
   - **Resource availability assessment**
3. **Develop implementation plan**
   - **Set clear objectives**
   - **Define success metrics**
   - **Create timeline**
   - **Allocate resources**
   - **Plan communication strategy**
4. **Begin pilot program**
   - **Select initial service area**
   - **Deploy basic infrastructure**
   - **Train pilot team**
   - **Monitor and adjust**
   - **Document learnings**

The successful implementation of CTC requires careful planning, strong leadership commitment, and a systematic approach to change. By following these guidelines and focusing on long-term objectives while managing short-term challenges, organizations can successfully transform their operations and realize the full benefits of CTC.

Chapter 21

Care traffic control capabilities maturity model

Paul E. Zieske

A capabilities maturity model provides organizations with a framework to assess their current state and plan their growth journey in implementing new technologies and processes. For care traffic control (CTC), this model helps organizations understand where they are and chart a course toward greater operational excellence.

These models guide us to create efficiency, consistency, and quality in the domain they represent.

We are introducing a CTC capability maturity model here to help organizations set some expectations as they proceed through the different levels that are a part of the model. The levels have some unavoidable overlap, but these tools remain valuable for measuring progress (Figure 21.1).

CARE TRAFFIC CONTROL CAPABILITY GROUPINGS

Infrastructure and technology capabilities

Definition: The technical foundation that enables real-time location tracking, data processing, and system integration.

Components:

- **Location technologies**
  - Real-time location systems (RTLS)
  - Indoor positioning systems (IPS)
  - Mobile device tracking
  - Sensor networks
- **Computing infrastructure**
  - Edge computing capabilities
  - Cloud infrastructure
  - Network capacity
  - Data storage systems
- **Integration platform**
  - API management

DOI: 10.1201/9781003625483-24

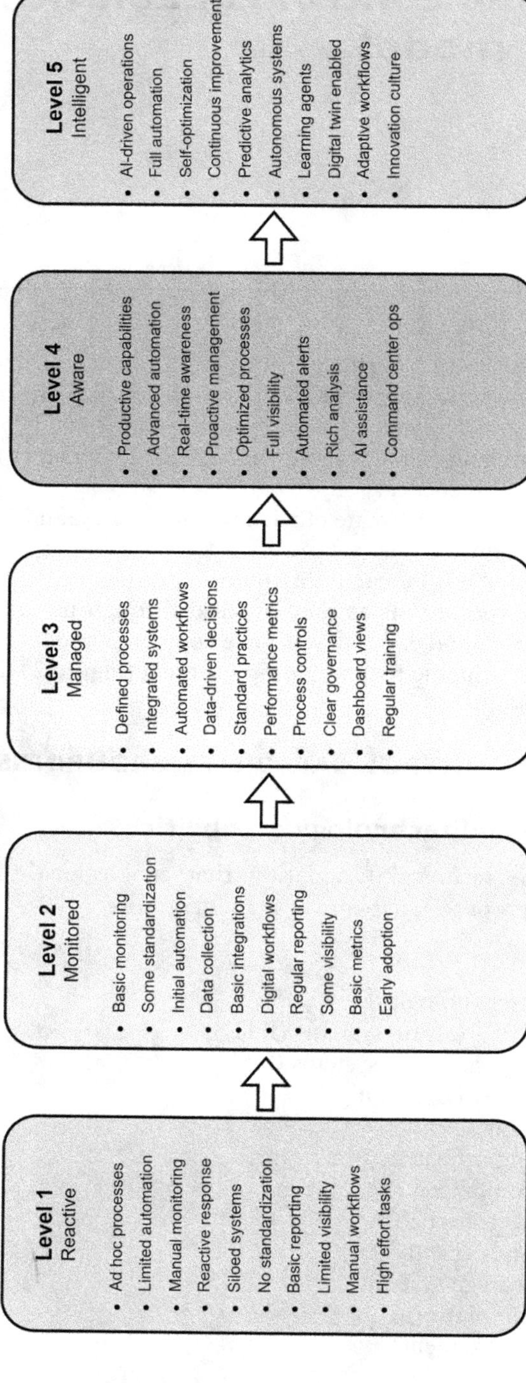
Level 1
Reactive
Ad hoc processes
Limited automation
Manual monitoring
Reactive response
Siloed systems
No standardization
Basic reporting
Limited visibility
Manual workflows
High effort tasks
Level 2
Monitored
Basic monitoring
Some standardization
Initial automation
Data collection
Basic integrations
Digital workflows
Regular reporting
Some visibility
Basic metrics
Early adoption
Level 3
Managed
Defined processes
Integrated systems
Automated workflows
Data-driven decisions
Standard practices
Performance metrics
Process controls
Clear governance
Dashboard views
Regular training
Level 4
Aware
Productive capabilities
Advanced automation
Real-time awareness
Proactive management
Optimized processes
Full visibility
Automated alerts
Rich analysis
AI assistance
Command center ops
Level 5
Intelligent
AI-driven operations
Full automation
Self-optimization
Continuous improvement
Predictive analytics
Autonomous systems
Learning agents
Digital twin enabled
Adaptive workflows
Innovation culture

Figure 21.1 Care traffic control capability maturity model.

- Enterprise service bus
- Data exchange protocols
- System interoperability

Workflow and process capabilities

Definition: The operational procedures and automated processes that enable efficient care delivery and resource management.

Components:

- **Workflow design**
  - Process standardization
  - Workflow automation
  - Exception handling
  - Change management
- **Process optimization**
  - Performance metrics
  - Continuous improvement
  - Bottleneck identification
  - Resource allocation
- **Operational control**
  - Real-time monitoring
  - Command center operations
  - Dispatch management
  - Resource coordination

Data and analytics capabilities

Definition: The ability to collect, process, analyze, and derive insights from operational data.

Components:

- **Data management**
  - Data collection
  - Data quality
  - Data governance
  - Master data management
- **Analytics**
  - Real-time analytics
  - Predictive modeling
  - Performance dashboards
  - Reporting systems
- **Intelligence**
  - AI/ML capabilities
  - Decision support

  - Pattern recognition
  - Anomaly detection

People and organization capabilities

Definition: The human and organizational elements required to effectively implement and operate CTC.
Components:

- **Skills and training**
  - Technical proficiency
  - Operational expertise
  - Change management
  - Continuous learning
- **Organizational structure**
  - Roles and responsibilities
  - Team composition
  - Governance model
  - Performance management
- **Culture and adoption**
  - Innovation mindset
  - Digital literacy
  - User acceptance
  - Continuous improvement culture

Security and compliance capabilities

Definition: The ability to maintain security, privacy, and regulatory compliance while operating CTC systems.
Components:

- **Security management**
  - Access control
  - Data protection
  - Network security
  - Incident response
- **Compliance**
  - Regulatory adherence
  - Policy management
  - Audit capabilities
  - Risk management
- **Privacy**
  - Data privacy
  - Consent management
  - Information governance

- Privacy impact assessment

Capability interdependencies

- Infrastructure enables workflow automation
- Data capabilities support process optimization
- People capabilities drive adoption and improvement
- Security ensures trust and compliance
- All capabilities contribute to overall maturity

Measurement approaches

Each capability group should be assessed using:

1. Quantitative metrics
2. Qualitative assessments
3. Maturity indicators
4. Performance benchmarks

Development considerations

When developing these capabilities:

1. Start with foundational elements
2. Build incrementally
3. Maintain balance across groups
4. Align with organizational strategy
5. Consider resource constraints
6. Plan for scalability

CARE TRAFFIC CONTROL MATURITY LEVELS

Level 1 – Reactive

Definition: Organization operates in a primarily reactive mode with manual processes and limited automation.

In the beginning, the workflows are reactive because they get the assignments from the core systems, and detecting anomalies must come from the customers or the workers during the execution of the workflow because the systems cannot detect them. Situational awareness is limited to the worker. The supervisor or dispatcher has very little information except what comes from phone calls. As the workflow matures, it will get more status from the workers through the core systems, but this is usually untrustworthy data. Nominal flow is established through training and deviations from the process are difficult to determine.

- Nominal flow is documented and taught but strict conformance is unverifiable.

- Anomalies directly impact outcomes.
- Detecting anomalies comes from customers and workers.
- Dispatchers coordinate transactional administrative functions.
- Dispatchers have few problem-solving tools.

Characteristics

- **Infrastructure and technology**
  - Basic location tracking systems
  - Standalone systems with minimal integration
  - Manual data collection and processing
  - Limited mobile device usage
- **Workflow and process**
  - Ad-hoc processes with minimal documentation
  - Manual workflows with high effort
  - Reactive problem-solving
  - Limited process standardization
- **Data and analytics**
  - Basic reporting capabilities
  - Manual data collection and analysis
  - Limited real-time visibility
  - Siloed data sources
- **People and organization**
  - Basic training on existing systems
  - Undefined roles and responsibilities
  - Limited change management
  - Resistance to new technology
- **Security and compliance**
  - Basic security controls
  - Manual compliance checking
  - Limited privacy considerations
  - Reactive incident response

Common Challenges

1. High manual effort
2. Limited visibility into operations
3. Inconsistent processes
4. Delayed response to issues
5. Limited technology adoption

Success Indicators

- Basic location tracking implemented
- Initial process documentation
- Basic reporting capabilities
- Staff awareness of systems

Level 2 – Monitored

Definition: Organization has implemented basic monitoring and begun standardizing processes with some automation.

In Level 2, the workflows use situational awareness provided by the sensors that are installed specifically for observing the tasks in the workflow. Situational awareness could be from mobile devices or locator systems like RTLS. This observation would be at the department or supervisory level.

Monitoring allows the creation of standard work and the enforcement of the standardization through observation and also allows orchestration where orchestration can remove delays and errors. Anomalies are addressed with manual workarounds.

- Workflows are locked down with a mostly linear flow
- Synchronous and asynchronous communications are used for anomalies
- Some status is captured electronically
- Anomalies are not directly visible to the system
- Outcomes are measured in a short planning horizon
- Observation and corrective actions are over a longer planning horizon

Characteristics

- **Infrastructure and technology**
  - Expanded location tracking coverage
  - Initial system integration efforts
  - Basic automation capabilities
  - Growing mobile device adoption
- **Workflow and process**
  - Documented standard processes
  - Some workflow automation
  - Proactive monitoring
  - Regular process review
- **Data and analytics**
  - Regular reporting processes
  - Some real-time monitoring
  - Basic data integration
  - Initial metrics tracking
- **People and organization**
  - Structured training programs
  - Defined key roles
  - Basic change management
  - Growing technology acceptance

- **Security and compliance**
  - Documented security procedures
  - Regular compliance checks
  - Basic privacy protocols
  - Incident response procedures

Common Challenges

1. Inconsistent automation
2. Partial system integration
3. Limited data utilization
4. Varying adoption rates
5. Resource constraints

Success Indicators

- Monitoring systems in place
- Standard processes documented
- Regular reporting established
- Initial automation benefits realized

Level 3 – Managed

Definition: An organization that has established standardized processes with significant automation and active management.

In the managed phase, technology drives the situational awareness that is presented to the actors in the workflows. The agents can manage the tasks in the workflow, and changes in the flow are captured with condition/action decision points. Outcomes are captured by the system and the system can learn what conditions are causing certain paths through the flow to be followed so they can be matched with the outcomes.

- Increased situational awareness allows more decision-making
- Synchronous and asynchronous communications
- Workflows are locked down but with many decision points
- The status of the tasks is captured electronically
- The anomalies are visible to the system, but corrections are ad hoc

Characteristics

- **Infrastructure and technology**
  - Comprehensive location tracking
  - Integrated systems architecture
  - Significant automation
  - Enterprise mobile strategy

- **Workflow and process**
  - Optimized standard processes
  - Automated workflows
  - Proactive management
  - Continuous improvement
- **Data and analytics**
  - Advanced reporting capabilities
  - Comprehensive monitoring
  - Integrated data systems
  - Performance analytics
- **People and organization**
  - Comprehensive training
  - Clear roles and accountability
  - Effective change management
  - Strong technology adoption
- **Security and compliance**
  - Robust security framework
  - Proactive compliance
  - Privacy by design
  - Effective incident management

Common Challenges

1. Maintaining consistency
2. Balancing automation
3. Managing complexity
4. Resource optimization
5. Change resistance

Success Indicators

- High automation levels
- Integrated systems
- Data-driven decisions
- Strong user adoption

Level 4 – Aware

Definition: An organization operates with advanced automation, predictive capabilities, and real-time awareness.

An aware workflow can process both the context from the core system and the perception from the sensors to find opportunities for further optimization. This is where the concept of belief comes into play for the agents. An AI assistive agent benefits from the perception accumulated from all the agents in the system to establish belief based on the experience of all the other agents. An aware workflow can adapt to the situation and make changes to create a better outcome.

- Conditions are formed from both sensors and context from the core systems
- Conditions are processed into situational awareness by agents
- Situation awareness allows workflows to adapt to conditions in real time
- Only high-level status is presented to the actors to reduce cognitive load
- Anomalies are captured by the system, and flows are adjusted with corrective actions

Characteristics

- **Infrastructure and technology**
  - Advanced location services
  - Fully integrated systems
  - Extensive automation
  - Ubiquitous mobile access
- **Workflow and process**
  - Intelligent workflows
  - Predictive operations
  - Real-time optimization
  - Continuous adaptation
- **Data and analytics**
  - Predictive analytics
  - Real-time insights
  - Advanced visualization
  - AI/ML implementation
- **People and organization**
  - Advanced skill development
  - Optimized roles
  - Proactive change management
  - Innovation culture
- **Security and compliance**
  - Advanced security measures
  - Automated compliance
  - Privacy enhancement
  - Proactive risk management

Common Challenges

1. Maintaining advanced systems
2. Managing complexity
3. Keeping pace with technology
4. Skill development
5. Change acceleration

Success Indicators

- Predictive capabilities
- Real-time optimization
- Advanced automation
- Innovation adoption

Level 5 – Intelligent

Definition: Organization achieves intelligent operations with AI-driven decision-making and self-optimization.

When the workflows are intelligent, they have the combined knowledge of all the agents in the multiagent system. Multimodal sensing is very effective because the agents can deliberate and correlate their perception to form a combined belief. This belief allows the agents to provide very reliable decision support. In many cases, the agents will decide, and a deepened trust is established between the actors and the agents.

Characteristics

- **Infrastructure and technology**
  - Intelligent location services
  - Self-optimizing systems
  - Autonomous operations
  - Advanced mobile capabilities
- **Workflow and process**
  - Self-optimizing workflows
  - AI-driven operations
  - Autonomous decision-making
  - Continuous innovation
- **Data and analytics**
  - Advanced AI/ML
  - Autonomous analytics
  - Prescriptive insights
  - Intelligent automation
- **People and organization**
  - Expert-level capabilities
  - Optimal organization
  - Innovation leadership
  - Digital transformation
- **Security and compliance**
  - Intelligent security
  - Automated compliance
  - Privacy leadership
  - Predictive risk management

Common Challenges

1. Maintaining leadership
2. Innovation pace
3. Skill availability
4. Technology evolution
5. Complexity management

Success Indicators

- AI-driven operations
- Self-optimization
- Innovation leadership
- Digital excellence

CTC MATURITY ASSESSMENT SCORECARD

Assessment scale

1 = Initial/reactive (basic capabilities, largely manual)
2 = Monitored (emerging capabilities, some automation)
3 = Managed (established capabilities, partial automation)
4 = Aware (advanced capabilities, significant automation)
5 = Intelligent (optimized capabilities, comprehensive automation) (Tables 21.1–21.7)

Table 21.1 Technology and infrastructure

Capability area	*Score (1–5)*	*Evidence/notes*
Location Tracking Systems		
Mobile Device Infrastructure		
Integration Capabilities		
Real-time Data Processing		
Automation Tools		
System Reliability		

Table 21.2 Process and workflows

Capability area	*Score (1–5)*	*Evidence/notes*
Process Documentation		
Workflow Standardization		
Automation Level		
Performance Monitoring		
Exception Handling		
Continuous Improvement		

Table 21.3 People and organization

Capability area	*Score (1–5)*	*Evidence/notes*
Staff Training		
Change Management		
Leadership Support		
User Adoption		
Role Definition		
Skills Development		

Table 21.4 Data and analytics

Capability area	*Score (1–5)*	*Evidence/Notes*
Data Quality		
Analytics Capabilities		
Reporting Tools		
Predictive Capabilities		
Decision Support		
Data Governance		

Table 21.5 Integration and interoperability

Capability area	*Score (1–5)*	*Evidence/notes*
System Integration		
API Management		
Data Exchange		
Standards Compliance		
External Systems		
Cross-platform Support		

Table 21.6 Scoring summary

Domain	*Average score*	*Target score*	*Gap*
Technology and Infrastructure			
Process and Workflows			
People and Organization			
Data and Analytics			
Integration and Interoperability			
Overall Maturity Score			

Table 21.7 Action planning

Priority	Domain	Gap	Action items	Timeline	Owner

Notes

- Score each capability area based on current state evidence
- Document supporting evidence and observations
- Identify gaps and opportunities for improvement
- Develop action plans for priority areas
- Review and update quarterly

PLAYBOOK FOR CARE TRAFFIC CONTROL MATURITY MODEL

Improvers

1. Maturity assessment
    - Evaluate current maturity level
    - Document capabilities across domains
        - Workflows
        - Systems and technology
        - Operations
        - Performance improvement
    - Identify gaps and opportunities
    - Create baseline measurements
2. Progression planning
    - Map path through maturity levels
    - Define milestone requirements
    - Create capability development plans
    - Establish measurement criteria
    - Set realistic timelines
3. Implementation strategy
    - Focus on foundational capabilities first
    - Build capabilities incrementally
    - Create validation processes
    - Establish feedback loops
    - Document progress
4. Performance monitoring
    - Define level-specific metrics
    - Create progress tracking systems

- Measure capability improvements
- Document maturity advances
- Share success stories

Leaders

1. Strategic planning
    - Understand maturity progression
    - Set organizational maturity goals
    - Create capability roadmap
    - Allocate development resources
    - Enable systematic advancement
2. Resource management
    - Invest in capability development
    - Support training initiatives
    - Plan for ongoing advancement
    - Enable technology adoption
    - Maintain progress momentum
3. Change management
    - Build understanding of maturity model
    - Support systematic progression
    - Manage expectations
    - Foster improvement culture
    - Celebrate advancement
4. Risk management
    - Identify progression risks
    - Create mitigation strategies
    - Establish oversight mechanisms
    - Monitor advancement progress
    - Develop contingency plans

Vendors

1. Solution development
    - Align solutions with maturity levels
    - Enable capability progression
    - Support advancement needs
    - Create validation tools
    - Enable progress monitoring
2. Implementation support
    - Provide progression guidance
    - Offer maturity-based training
    - Support capability development
    - Maintain documentation
    - Enable success measurement

3. Innovation focus
    - Develop advanced capabilities
    - Support emerging needs
    - Enable future progression
    - Build adaptive solutions
    - Support continuous improvement

Epilogue

You are starting your day at Edenvale General Hospital (EGH, aka "The Vale"). As the Director of Command Center Operations, you will be giving another tour to a group of five VIPs who have heard how successful EGH has been since they implemented care traffic control. People sometimes think this was something that happened overnight, but the digital transformation started years ago. It was shortly after the opening of the Command Center that the recognition came, even though EGH had been steadily improving for years.

Edenvale achieved length of stay (LOS) numbers that were eye-popping. Hospital-acquired infections (HAIs) and hospital-acquired conditions (HACs) were way down. Readmission rates were down as well. There is a strong bed utilization rate and a low average cost per discharge. OR utilization is high. Overall, the 15% operating margin has contributed greatly to the financial success. Patient satisfaction scores are high and employee satisfaction scores are just as high. How did this all happen at a place that was dismal at all these metrics 7 years prior?

This is what everyone wants to see today. There never seems to be enough time to cover everything people want to know. You gather everyone in the command center conference room (CCCR) and explain the agenda quickly and move right into the background.

In the conference room, you explain,

> The Digital Transformation has been steady and methodical. It started with the electronic health record, then care traffic control and last was the Command Center. It really is three journeys; they are all related and always moving forward. The EHR was the start. Admittedly, it was a rough beginning because even though the data was beneficial, the impact to the patient experience was somewhat negative. Doctors felt like they were spending their time 'treating the technology instead of treating the patient,' and I am quoting one doctor. We struggled through it and amassed a great deal of good data and started a period where we were integrating the EHR with many of their other systems to make use of the data and enrich it.

DOI: 10.1201/9781003625483-25

> Then came care traffic control. We knew that using care traffic control to optimize the mobile workflows was a big benefit and tried to educate everyone on how the technology worked. When we did that, we got back some innovative ideas that came from staff and patient suggestions. Those changes were implemented and that helped with adoption and patient experience.
>
> The building is an active participant in workflows and makes the work easier by removing a lot of steps. We use something we call 'Vale'; it is the EGH digital twin. The digital twin is a virtual replica of the building. The building is filled with sensors that allow us to see where people and things are around the building. That is how Vale participates in the workflows. Vale works with the Command Center, and the Command Center monitors the operations in real time.

You explain, "Everyone carries a mobile device called a CarePro." You show them the smartphone and say,

> This is my CarePro. The CarePro helps with our workflows and keeps us aware of many things that are going on, all day long. The CarePro functions as something called an 'AI agent' and it helps us adhere to the structure of the workflows. It looks for problems and alerts us and it helps keep us safe while we are in the building. I have this whole tour set up as a job so you will see, and feel, a little bit of how the CarePro works on the tour.
>
> The CarePros, Vale and the Command Center are where we get situational awareness. These are the main three components of the system, and they have helped us automate many of the steps in the workflows. The controllers are problem solvers who ensure the teams are aware, safe, and always informed. They interact with their department's customers, but usually only when there is a problem. So, let's talk about the Command Center because it really was the third part of the journey.

You explain,

> The Command Center was something that started long before the day the doors opened on it. When EGH started thinking about a Command Center, we assessed all the team huddles that were going on each day. There was a morning safety huddle with the hospital leaders and many departments that had distributed teams that would huddle. We had six different departments that had dispatching. We also had other locations and departments that could benefit from dispatching, but the expense was too high before we had the digital twin. The digital twin meant we could do more with much less.
>
> As the digital twin was providing us more and more real-time information, we were able to consolidate the dispatching into a couple

> locations. That put the dispatchers in the same room where they could interact. This helped make sure that transitions were smooth. We also expanded the dispatching to several new departments. Problems were being solved and the employees saw the dispatchers as people who could help them in the field.

You hold up your CarePro and show them how it alerted you it was time to visit the Command Center. The group enters the Command Center and sees a perfectly square room with each wall covered with video monitors. You explain each wall shows the data that is necessary for monitoring the operations for teams that are organized together. The groups are Patient Flow, Support Services, Safety and Reliability, and Clinical. There are rows of tables facing each wall and radiating out from the center. The tables have workstations with people busily working. Some have headsets and some do not. In the center is a single chair with someone who appears to be in charge. You tell everyone,

> This is not a call center. They take calls but they do much more than that. The folks working here are controllers. They are focused on outcomes and can make decisions that attain the outcomes. Because the goal of the Command Center is to provide anticipatory responses to demand, if calls are coming in, they see that as a failure. If there is a scheduled surgery that needs to be done stat, the OR controller can change the schedule and trigger the protocol that is used to get ready for that surgery. The impact is assessed and the schedule is adjusted accordingly. The ripple effects of changes are much easier to see because of the monitoring provided by the digital twin and having everyone in the same place.

You tell everyone, "Each wall has a map that shows the location of anomalies that are being addressed for that team. The monitors at the individual workstations can access their version of the map and their features of the digital twin."

You ask, "Are there any questions so far?" One person asks, "I see all of this monitoring and controlling tech, do the staff feel like the Command Center is Big Brother and are you seeing any burnout from it?". You say,

> Great Question. The system does so much to reduce the cognitive load on people that it is actually reducing burnout. It was important to build in the automation so that we could ensure that the pace for the workers was something they could sustain. Efficiency reduces frustration, which reduces anxiety, which reduces burnout. Remember too, this was not overnight. It took 7 years to get this implemented so people had a lot of time to adjust. Another thing that happened was that we added more breaks and down time because of exactly what you said. That still didn't offset the efficiency gains. The system became part of the culture and

that wasn't for everybody. Some people didn't like it, and we probably lost some people because of it. But we have lots of people who want to be a part of this, and the net is that we have less issues with retention because of the Digital Transformation. Thanks so much for that question.

It is 10:40 and the CarePro told you it is time to go to the ED. It popped up a map and a route to where you are going. You let the group know, and while you are on the way to the ED, you see a doctor pushing a patient in a wheelchair, and this gets people's attention. Someone asks about it. You tell everyone,

> Anyone who wants to get the training can move patients. The CarePro knows when someone is signed up to move patients. If you are near the pickup location and it can see if you are going to the same place, you will likely get offered the job. Some people love to interact with patients, so they volunteer to transport patients. Some do it on their breaks and accumulate steps that way. This is done with other things that need to get moved as well. We love to see doctors moving patients and it is a thrill for the patients as well.

You explain to everyone that, "The employees are incentivized to help move things from one place to another. The program is called the 'Vale Bucket Brigade' (VBB). We will see carts that are parked at various pickup and drop-off locations. You hit the button on your CarePro and say your destination. Sometimes, it will know your destination. You start on your way, and you will see an alert for the job, and if you accept the job, you go to the pickup location. The CarePro will beep, telling you it is the correct cart. You transport the cart, and at the drop-off location, it will beep again. Pretty simple. It adds about 2 mins to your trip. If you sign up, you are given points for the things you move and accumulating those points contributes to various kinds of bonuses. You will understand why this is important a little later."

You tell the group,

> Instead of meeting with a manager or leader, we are going to meet someone else who is just as important; the Orderly. Dave Simmons is the ED orderly, and he has one of the most challenging jobs in the hospital because he is responsible for anticipating the needs of the ED.

You are in the walkway just outside of the ED, and Dave is there to meet you. He introduces himself and you ask him to show the group his CarePro. Everyone can see that he saw "Tour arrived" on the CarePro. Dave explains,

> The flow of supplies, meds, labs, and equipment goes through me. There are some scheduled deliveries as well, but they are happening less frequently. I have carts come in from people and there are four different robots (AMRs) that show up many times a day. The CarePro tells me

when things are coming and the ETA. You saw how the CarePro told me this tour was showing up and that is how I was able to be here exactly when you arrived.

Dave walks the group through the ED and shows how they have everything organized. He mentions, "If there is any equipment missing, I use the CarePro to find it. Sometimes, I have to use the scanner, but I can usually find it on the map. Last resort, the Command Center will find it for me."

You tell them, "This is a good time to talk about the JIT or the just-in-time initiative. Because of care traffic control, we are using JIT a lot more." You ask, "Does everyone know what just-in-time is? Another word for it is on-demand". Everyone nods. You go on,

> JIT doesn't mean we don't store anything, but it has reduced the storage significantly. It does increase the motion in the building because of the increased frequency of deliveries. This can negatively offset the return on the JIT approach, so EGH introduced the Vale Bucket Brigade as well as a large fleet of AMRs (autonomous mobile robots). JIT has had a dramatic positive impact and has helped address the space concerns and expiry issues for drugs and other items as well.

Dave says,

> I know you don't have time to meet with the clinical manager, but she asked me to talk about the employee duress feature on the CarePro. The staff all carry employee badges that have buttons on them in case there is some sort of safety issue with a threatening patient or visitor in the ED. The system works where the badge, the CarePro, and the sensors all work together so that we can have high confidence that when we push that button there will be an immediate response. It is our 'see something say something' system, and it has been very important to help everyone feel secure in the ED.

The CarePro alerts you that you need to head up to the OR. You thank Dave and head to the OR.

You tell the group,

> This time we are meeting a department leader. We are going to talk to Terri Fanconi who is the Director for Surgical Services. She is responsible for those amazing OR utilization numbers that we showed you. The OR is an amazing place for care traffic control because of all the processes and workflows that need to be so tightly orchestrated.

The first place you stop is the waiting area, where, like the ED, Terri is there waiting for you. You introduce Terri, and Terri asks, "What was the first thing you noticed about the waiting area." One person says, "It is almost empty." She says,

> Yes that is exactly it. The Patient app tells the patient exactly when to show up and when they get here, they go directly to the preop. They can check in on the app and reception can see they are in the building or even in the parking lot. If there is a delay, there are some very pleasant spaces in the Atrium where people usually like to wait, and we buy them a snack and a coffee if we cause them to wait. Usually, the delays are minimal, so things sync up quite well. The family will usually wait in the Atrium as well. There are far better amenities in the Atrium. There they are kept up to date on the patient's surgery with the app and there is a 'flight board' there that keeps them aware of the status.

Terri goes on,

> The OR has two orderly's and four robots that visit as well. The OR is a place where the CarePro's really shine because they provide real-time awareness for each step in the process for things like turning around an OR. The reduction of turnaround time has been important to the good numbers the OR has.
>
> The exact location of the patient is known from the time they get to preop to when they are in the PACU. The doctors, nurses, CRNA's, specialists, techs, EVS staff, and orderlys are streaming their location from their CarePros, at all times. When someone is on a case, it is easy to see they are busy and what case they are on. The staff never have to log in to a workstation or machine, nor do they have to bring up the patient or the case. They simply have a verification step. The ORs have computer vision cameras that help the staff with things like foreign objects and infection risk during surgery and they monitor the room turnover before and after surgery.

Both Terri and you get the notification that it is time to end the visit. You move on to the Observation unit. You say,

> We are going to go to the Observation unit now. Obs is critical to patient flow because we use it for short-term admits, and it helps ensure that the ED is never boarding patients. It is a good place to see how the patient and employee experiences are benefiting from care traffic control.

When you get there, you swing by the nurse's station and let them know you are there. There is an empty patient room, and you stand in front of the door with the group. You say,

> We have this room set up as a simulation. We can do this with any room. First, I am going to demonstrate being a physician and then the patient. Let's all go into the room, and I will leave and come back as

> Doctor Warner. I need someone to be the patient, Stephanie Bradford. You don't have to get in the bed, but just answer the questions. You are being observed for a possible concussion.

You all enter the room and then you leave. You come back in and grab the roller stool and pull it up to the bed. You say, "Hi Stephanie Bradford, right?" She says, "Yes." You say, "Ok Stephanie, I am Doctor Warner and you and I, and our friend Vale here are going to have a conversation." You all here "Hi Stephanie" from the speaker in the room. You go on, "Vale is here so I can focus on you and not type into a computer. Vale mostly just dings at me to tell me the record is being filled out. I wanted you to know what all this dinging is when you hear it. OK, are we good?" Stephanie says, "Yes." Doctor Warner says, "Tell me your name and date of birth." Stephanie says, "Stephanie Bradford, 11/10/99" and you all hear a ding. Doctor Warner says, "Tell me why you are here." Stephanie says, "I fell and hit my head." Doctor Warner says, "OK, so you fell and hit your head and do you have a headache?" She says, "Yes." Doctor Warner says, "We will confirm you are experiencing a headache." There is another ding and everybody smiles at the roleplay. Doctor Warner says, "Vital signs are BP 120/80, HR 72, RR 16, Temp 98.6°F." There is another ding. He goes on, "Neurological exam: Alert and oriented x3. Cranial nerves II-XII intact. No focal neurological deficits observed. Gait steady but slow." Another ding. He says, "Physical exam: No signs of external trauma. Pupils equal, round, and reactive to light. No nystagmus." There is another ding. You stop and say, "I could finish the exam, but you get it, I am no doctor." Everyone laughs.

You say,

> What you all saw was a hands-off-computer exam with the progress notes being filled in automatically. All the authentication was done with the sensors, and each ding was a little different to let the doctor know which part of the record was being completed. It is a simple exercise for the doctor to edit and attest to the progress notes. That is done on the CarePro and he can do that whenever he has time.

Now, let's move on to the patient side of this.

You grab the remote control for the monitor, and you say, "I am going to bring up the patient on what we call 'Vale tv.' You can see the monitor shows Stephanie Bradford. First, I need to address the warning here." The warning says, "There are people other than you, the patient, and your caregivers present. Click here to authorize me to display protected health information." You say, "I will click Authorized, and now my information appears."

You go on,

> There it is. I am scheduled for an MRI and the transport is on the way. Here is the transport and I can see it coming on the map. The person coming is Brian Jackson, and in this case, Brian is a transporter. I will

say, if the transport is someone from the Bucket Brigade, you don't get much warning because it means they were already very close to the patient's pickup location. I can go back in time here and see every time a nurse has visited the room and what they did. Here you can see my vitals, meds, and other reasons for the visits. I can see the food, when it comes, and I can even see how much I ate which is based on what is left so it is more about what I didn't eat. The system is even aware of when I am in the presence of people who shouldn't be seeing my private information, and it suppresses private information. The patient can override that as well by approving the override. This is only part of what the patient can see, and observation is not as complex as some other units so you can imagine there is a lot more that is shown in other units.

You get an alert that the job says you are off to Support Services. You head down to the basement of the hospital and tell everyone, "This is where some of the most important work in operations happens."

You remind them that everyone carries a CarePro. You go to a large room and introduce Nguyen Linh. Nguyen thanks you and says,

> Welcome to The Vale and Patient Transport. It might seem strange to meet here, but we are here because this is where patient transport used to be before we had care traffic control. Now, transport uses a small office, and the transporters are distributed around the building. You can see we use it to store some of the carts, wheelchairs, and stretchers that need to be repaired. Transporters move equipment and supplies as well as patients. The transporters get jobs ahead of the Bucket Brigade, so they get the jobs before they go out to the other members, but part of the algorithm is who is closest to the pickup location. It does create some friendly competition as the transporters have financial incentives to move more things in a day. Because of the algorithm, the transporters do end up moving most of the patients, but the bottom line is the wait time is very short. In the office, we can see the location of everyone on the transport team, and the people are available for the VBB. The Transport Controller can see the same thing. Are there any questions?

One person asks, "Is the Transport Controller someone from your team?" Nguyen says, "Yes the controller on duty today used to be a dispatcher that sat in this very office. Any more questions?" After a few seconds he says, "I hope you have a great tour."

The CarePro alerts you that it is time to go to Supply Chain. On the way, you stop at Clinical Engineering. You say, "You see the carts parked by Clinical Engineering. That is equipment that is coming down for repair.

The orderlies loaded it at the units and the Bucket Brigade usually picks it up and drops it off there." You stop again at the Linen dock, and you explain,

> The linens come here on the trailers from the central laundry, and the trailers are connected to the AMRs by the staff. That is, literally all they do is connect the carts. The AMRs are told which patient care units they are going to, and when they get there, the orderly's will unload them and put them in the closets.

You continue on to Supply Chain where some carts are being connected to AMR's there as well. You meet Beth Sutton who is the manager. Beth says, "Hi everybody, Welcome to Supply Chain." You follow Beth to the bay with several AMRs that are parked against the wall. She says, "This is the charging bay where our AMRs are charged." She points to one with a small trailer attached. She says,

> Here is one that is ready to go out. Some of the carts are going to pick up locations where a transporter or someone from the Bucket Brigade will move them to the drop-off location. I have people on my team who move things, but most of the transport is done by the AMRs and the VBB. Pretty cool, huh? Are there any questions?

One person asks, "I see one of the AMR over there that has two trailers. How does that work at the drop-off location." Beth says,

> Great question. First, that only works for one of our routes because it uses a freight elevator that is big enough for both carts. But that route is the ICU and we have a lot of supplies that go up there so it is great that we can accommodate both trailers. Thanks for the question.

The CarePro alerts you that it is time to go back to the Command Center, and you thank Beth for her time. The group follows you to the elevator, and when you get to the Command Center, you find one of the spare workstations near the Supply Chain Controller. You have everybody huddle around the workstation, and you bring up a job that says "VIP Tour." The map comes up and everyone can see the trace of the entire morning of touring The Vale. You put the trace back to the beginning and hit play, and the trace starts to play back showing the exact location of the CarePro as the tour was going on. Each location that was visited shows an icon for the task that is called "Visit." You explain,

> This jobs board is something we can create for any job. I created it for the tour today and added it to the schedule. This is what scheduled work looks like but because of the just-in-time processes, a lot of the jobs pop up on the schedule with very little notice. This is where the Command Center helps a lot.

You introduce the Supply Chain Controller, Gina, to the group. You say, "Gina is probably one of the busiest controllers because of the amount of traffic she manages." Gina says, "Thanks, yes we have a lot of traffic that we manage, but did you talk about the Bucket Brigade?" You say, "Yes we did." She says,

> Good, yes. The Bucket Brigade is great, and they do an amazing number of jobs everyday but remember they are volunteers. The system rates them on the on time and successful accomplishment of the jobs they do. If they don't do the job right, their rating goes down and they don't get any more jobs, but someone has to fix the jobs that were not done right. We can see much of the job like you saw with your 'Tour Job,' but we can't see everything in the system, so sometimes the orderlies report issues or even other members of the Bucket Brigade, but they do have to be fixed. Certain jobs don't go out to the VBB because they are too important. All in all, it works well.

You say thanks Stephanie. Let's grab some time with Ken. He is the Patient Flow Controller. He also has a busy job. He also has some interesting responsibilities. I will let him tell you. Ken smiles and looks at you wryly. He says thanks, "I think I know what you mean. We have bed management responsibilities, and yes, flow is the primary responsibility, but we also deal with wandering patients, infant protection, and patient elopement. We have seen some 'interesting' things like patients who are trying to steal drugs or even ICU patients who are on oxygen and have made their way outside for a smoke. We usually catch these clever people before there is a problem, but it keeps us busy."

You say, "Thanks Ken. OK, let's head back to the CCCR and wrap it up." You walk into the conference room and ask what everyone's impression was. The overwhelming response is, it was amazing and exciting, but we wish we had a lot more time to learn more. You say,

> Yes, we keep hearing that. We are trying to do more tours, and we are working on extending them. Thanks for visiting the Vale today and we hope you keep in touch. We want to hear how your own journey is going. Bye everybody.

FINAL NOTE TO THE READER

Paul's note to the reader. I want to thank Ali for being my partner on this journey. His background and knowledge have complemented my experience in so many ways. I was a healthcare outsider when I first met Ali having come from aviation and air traffic control. Ali's biomedical background gave him the same experience of working on systems that people trust with their lives. Location was a passion we shared because of the potential as well as the challenge.

Writing this book has been an almost cathartic experience for me. I have been in trenches with users and wanted their message of change to come through in this book. We wanted this book to be more than an instructional text about location services. The playbook and the story appeared to be a way to do something different from other books like this. Creating a vision for what might be possible with the Edenvale story was not meant to be utopian; however, it was meant to be futuristic. Utopias are only in our mind, but the one thing we can be sure of is the future is coming.

Ali's note to the reader. Writing this book has been a long journey, and I truly appreciated crossing paths with Paul, who brings endless passion and vision to reimagining location-based services. When I began to have deep conversations with Paul on this topic, it made me excited about the possibilities of reimagining LBS. Healthcare operations have long struggled with two persistent challenges: widespread operational waste and the failure to successfully adopt new technologies. The countless stories of abandoned real-time location systems (RTLS), unused asset tracking implementations, and failed workflow automation initiatives all share common themes – insufficient planning, lack of strategic vision, and failure to consider the human elements of change.

Where Matters aims to break this cycle by providing a comprehensive framework for implementation that addresses both the technical and human aspects of operational transformation. Rather than presenting a rigid prescription for success, this book offers a flexible roadmap that can be adapted to each organization's unique circumstances, culture, and goals.

The journey toward care traffic control requires patience, commitment, and a willingness to think differently about how healthcare operations can be improved. By taking an incremental approach that delivers value at each stage, organizations can build momentum while maintaining stakeholder engagement. Remember that no single book can provide all the answers. *Where Matters* is intended to spark conversations, challenge assumptions, and provide a structure for thinking about how location-based services can transform healthcare operations. The real work begins when you and your team start applying these concepts to your unique situation.

We encourage you to share your experiences, successes, and challenges with others in the healthcare community. Only through open dialogue and shared learning can we collectively advance toward more efficient, effective, and human-centered healthcare operations.

The future of healthcare operations lies not just in new technologies, but in our ability to thoughtfully apply them in ways that enhance rather than burden our workforce. We hope this book helps light the way forward on your journey toward operational excellence.

Glossary

A

Accuracy (Location): The degree of correctness in a measured position's alignment with its actual position in physical space, involving both precision (repeatability and consistency of measurements) and trueness (proximity of a measurement to the true value). This is crucial in applications like global positioning system (GPS) and geolocation services.

Access Control: A combination of systems, protocols, and policies designed to regulate who or what can view or use resources within a computing environment. This includes physical entry (such as keycard access to rooms) and digital access (like passwords or biometrics) to ensure that only authorized individuals can access sensitive areas or information.

Active RFID: Radio frequency identification (RFID) tags that use an internal power source (such as a battery) to actively transmit signals to a reader, allowing for longer-range detection. Active RFID is often used in real-time location systems (RTLS) for tracking high-value assets and inventory across large areas.

Adaptive Routing: A network or logistics system feature that dynamically selects routes based on current network conditions, traffic patterns, or other environmental factors. Adaptive routing is especially valuable in networks or supply chains where flexibility and responsiveness are needed to manage changing conditions.

Advanced Analytics: Sophisticated data analysis methods that leverage machine learning, artificial intelligence, and statistical algorithms to autonomously or semi-autonomously analyze large volumes of data. These analytics provide deeper insights into trends, predictive capabilities, and prescriptive recommendations.

Agent Architecture: The structured design governing how software agents, or autonomous programs, are organized, interact, and execute tasks within a system. It defines protocols for communication, decision-making, and execution strategies, often applied in artificial intelligence (AI) systems or robotics.

Agent: A software entity capable of perceiving its environment, processing information, and making autonomous decisions or taking actions based on predefined goals or objectives. Agents can vary in complexity from simple automated tasks to complex AI systems that interact with humans or other agents.

Air Traffic Control (ATC): A critical aviation service that organizes and manages the movement of aircraft on the ground and in the airspace to ensure safety and efficiency. ATC uses communication, radar, and navigation systems to maintain safe distances between aircraft, handle flight paths, and manage airport operations.

Alarm Management: Systems designed to process, prioritize, and respond to alerts from various sources. Effective alarm management ensures that critical alerts are noticed and acted upon while reducing false alarms or unnecessary interruptions, thus preventing alert fatigue.

Alert Fatigue: A phenomenon where users become desensitized to frequent alerts and notifications, resulting in slower or missed responses to significant alerts. Common in high-stakes fields like healthcare and IT, managing alert fatigue is essential for maintaining safety and efficiency.

Ambient Intelligence (AmI): An advanced computing environment where technology becomes seamlessly embedded in everyday surroundings and adapts in response to human presence and activity. This creates intuitive, responsive spaces that enhance comfort, efficiency, and safety.

Ambient IoT: The use of Internet of Things (IoT) devices that operate without traditional batteries, instead using energy harvesting methods such as solar power or electromagnetic waves. These devices contribute to a sustainable, low-maintenance IoT ecosystem by reducing dependency on replaceable power sources.

Anomaly Detection: A technique in data analysis and machine learning for identifying patterns, behaviors, or values that deviate significantly from expected norms. Anomaly detection is widely applied in fraud detection, cybersecurity, and quality control to identify irregularities early.

API (Application Programming Interface): A set of protocols, tools, and definitions that allow software applications to communicate with each other. APIs enable developers to integrate different applications, access external data or services, and create complex, interoperable systems.

Asset Management: A systematic approach to tracking, maintaining, and optimizing an organization's physical assets. Effective asset management reduces costs, extends asset lifecycles, and improves operational efficiency by ensuring assets are available, well-maintained, and used optimally.

Authentication: The process of verifying the identity of a user, device, or system to control access to digital resources. Authentication may involve various methods, such as passwords, biometrics, or tokens, often implemented in multi-factor forms for increased security.

B

Bandwidth: The maximum data transfer rate of a network or internet connection, measured in bits per second (bps). Bandwidth determines how much data can be transmitted over a network at any given time, impacting the speed and quality of internet or network communications.

Beacon Management: The process of deploying, monitoring, and maintaining devices that transmit location or identification signals at regular intervals. Effective beacon management enables accurate location-based services in environments such as retail, logistics, or large public spaces.

Beacon: A small wireless device that periodically broadcasts a signal to nearby devices, typically using Bluetooth low energy (BLE). Beacons enable location-based services, providing context-aware information to users' mobile devices in physical spaces.

Below-the-wing: In healthcare, refers to operational support services that enable front-line medical care. This can include administrative functions, logistics, and other non-clinical tasks that support care delivery but do not involve direct patient interaction.

Bi-directional Communication: Communication that allows two parties, systems, or devices to exchange information in both directions. This type of communication is essential for systems that need real-time feedback or updates, like IoT devices or customer service systems.

Biometric Authentication: A security process that uses unique biological characteristics (like fingerprints, facial recognition, or voiceprints) to verify identity. Biometric authentication adds an extra layer of security by requiring something inherently unique to each individual.

Blockchain: A distributed, decentralized ledger technology that records transactions in a secure and transparent way. Blockchain ensures immutability and trust by using cryptographic protocols, enabling applications in finance, supply chain, and more.

Bluetooth Low Energy (BLE): A wireless communication standard that enables low-power data transfer between devices. BLE is commonly used in wearable devices, smart home gadgets, and other IoT applications to conserve battery life.

Bluetooth Mesh: A network topology that enables many-to-many communications among Bluetooth devices, allowing large-scale networks with long-distance range capabilities, particularly useful for IoT devices in smart buildings or industrial settings.

Bottleneck Analysis: The process of identifying and analyzing constraints that limit the efficiency of a system. Bottleneck analysis helps organizations optimize workflows, increase productivity, and reduce costs by addressing points of delay or congestion.

Business Analytics: The application of statistical, data-driven techniques to business data in order to extract insights, identify trends, and support decision-making. Business analytics often leverages data visualization and predictive modeling to guide strategies.

Business Intelligence (BI): The technologies, applications, and practices for collecting, integrating, and analyzing business information. BI provides actionable insights to help organizations make informed decisions, improve performance, and gain competitive advantage.

Business Process Management (BPM): A systematic approach to designing, executing, and optimizing organizational workflows. BPM focuses on enhancing efficiency, quality, and adaptability in business processes through modeling, analysis, and automation.

Business Process Modeling: The graphical representation of an organization's workflows and business processes. Business process modeling facilitates analysis, improvement, and communication of processes within an organization.

Business Rules Engine: A software system that manages and enforces a company's operational rules and policies. Business rules engines automate decision-making processes, ensuring consistency and compliance across applications.

BYOD (Bring Your Own Device): A policy that allows employees to use personal devices (like smartphones, laptops, or tablets) for work purposes. BYOD policies can improve flexibility and satisfaction but require security measures to protect corporate data.

C

Calibration: The process of adjusting and aligning measurement instruments to standard values to ensure accuracy and precision. Calibration is essential in fields requiring highly accurate measurements, such as manufacturing, healthcare, and scientific research.

Capacity Management: The practice of optimizing an organization's resources to meet demand without overutilization or underutilization. Effective capacity management ensures that services are delivered efficiently and at the right cost.

Care Traffic Control (CTC): A healthcare coordination approach that uses real-time data, situational awareness, and automated processes to optimize patient flow, resource allocation, and clinical operations, enhancing overall healthcare delivery.

Change Management: A structured approach to transitioning individuals, teams, and organizations to a desired future state. Change management addresses the human and operational aspects of implementing organizational changes effectively.

Clean Data: Data that is accurate, complete, and properly formatted. Clean data is essential for reliable analysis and decision-making, as errors and inconsistencies can lead to incorrect insights and flawed business outcomes.

Client-Server Architecture: A computing model where multiple client devices connect to a centralized server to access shared resources, data, or applications. This architecture underpins many web services and business applications.

Cloud Computing: The on-demand delivery of computing resources (such as storage, databases, servers, and software) over the internet, enabling scalability and reducing the need for on-premises infrastructure.

Cognitive Computing: Technologies designed to simulate human cognitive processes, including reasoning, learning, and perception. Cognitive computing applications are commonly seen in natural language processing, machine learning, and decision support systems.

Cognitive Load: The amount of mental effort required to perform a task or process information. Managing cognitive load is crucial in user-centered design and education to improve performance and reduce errors.

Command Center: A centralized facility where real-time monitoring, decision-making, and coordination of operations are carried out. Command centers are common in critical operations such as emergency response, IT, and military applications.

Communication Protocol: A set of rules and standards that enable data exchange between devices in a network. Protocols ensure that devices can communicate effectively and reliably, forming the basis of the internet and other networks.

D

Dashboard: A real-time visual interface that displays key performance indicators (KPIs), metrics, and other relevant data points for monitoring and decision-making. Dashboards consolidate information from various sources into an easily interpretable format, allowing users to quickly assess performance and make data-driven decisions.

Data Acquisition: The process of sampling real-world signals, such as temperature or pressure, and converting them into digital values that can be analyzed. Data acquisition is often used in scientific research, industrial monitoring, and IoT applications to bridge the gap between the physical world and digital analysis.

Data Analytics: A systematic and scientific approach to examining raw data to identify patterns, trends, and insights. Data analytics spans from simple descriptive statistics to complex predictive and prescriptive analytics, supporting business decisions, optimizing processes, and uncovering hidden insights.

Data Architecture: A framework outlining how an organization's data is collected, stored, transformed, and used. This includes data models, structures, policies, and standards, providing the blueprint for data management that aligns with business goals and ensures data accessibility, security, and quality.

Data Fusion: The process of integrating data from multiple sources to create more accurate, reliable, and actionable information. Data fusion is commonly used in fields like sensor networks, surveillance, and autonomous systems, where combining multiple data points improves overall understanding and decision-making.

Data Governance: A set of policies, procedures, and responsibilities that guide the management of an organization's data assets. Effective data governance ensures that data is accurate, accessible, consistent, and compliant with regulations, providing accountability for data-related decisions.

Data Integration: The process of combining data from different sources into a unified view, making it more accessible and meaningful. Data integration is essential in analytics, enabling organizations to analyze comprehensive datasets from disparate systems or applications.

Data Lake: A centralized storage repository that can hold vast amounts of structured and unstructured data at any scale. Data lakes enable organizations to store data in its raw format, allowing for flexible access, analytics, and the application of machine learning on varied data types.

Data Lifecycle Management: The governance of data through its entire lifecycle, from creation or acquisition to archival and deletion. Data lifecycle management ensures that data is properly managed, secured, and stored according to compliance and organizational standards.

Data Mining: The practice of exploring large datasets to identify patterns, correlations, or insights that can inform business decisions or improve processes. Techniques in data mining, like clustering, classification, and association rule learning, help uncover previously hidden insights.

Data Quality: A measure of how well data meets its intended purpose, considering attributes like accuracy, completeness, consistency, and timeliness. High data quality is crucial for effective decision-making, as poor data quality can lead to inaccurate insights and flawed conclusions.

Data Streaming: The continuous flow and processing of data as it is generated, allowing for real-time analytics and rapid response. Common in IoT and event-driven applications, data streaming enables organizations to act immediately on incoming data, such as sensor readings or transactional information.

Data Validation: The process of ensuring that data is accurate, complete, and compliant with specified formats or rules before it is used in analysis or operations. Data validation helps maintain data integrity, reduces errors, and ensures that only quality data is stored.

Data Visualization: The graphical representation of data in the form of charts, graphs, or maps to make complex data more accessible and understandable. Data visualization enables users to spot trends, anomalies, and patterns easily, aiding in data-driven decision-making.

Database Management System (DBMS): Software that allows users to create, manage, and retrieve data from databases. A DBMS provides a systematic way to organize, store, and access data, supporting multi-user environments and ensuring data security and integrity.

Deep Learning: A type of machine learning that uses layered neural networks to model complex patterns in large datasets. Deep learning is behind many advanced AI applications, including image recognition, natural language processing, and autonomous systems.

E

Edge Computing: A distributed computing model where data processing occurs close to the data source or at the "edge" of the network, rather than in a centralized cloud. Edge computing reduces latency, conserves bandwidth, and enables real-time processing, particularly important in IoT and mobile applications.

Edge Device: A piece of hardware located at the boundary of a network that processes data locally and controls data flow to central systems. Edge devices, such as sensors, cameras, or IoT gateways, play a key role in edge computing by reducing the need for data transmission to central servers.

Enterprise Architecture: A strategic framework that defines the structure and operation of an organization's technology systems in alignment with its business goals. Enterprise architecture guides decisions on IT infrastructure, applications, and data, ensuring interoperability and scalability.

Enterprise Integration: The process of linking applications, systems, and data sources across an organization to enable seamless data sharing and improved efficiency. Enterprise integration supports better decision-making and operational cohesion.

Enterprise Location Engine: A software system that processes and manages location data across an organization. This enables tracking and analysis of assets, people, and events within enterprise environments, supporting applications like security, logistics, and resource allocation.

Enterprise Resource Planning (ERP): A software system that integrates core business processes, such as finance, HR, supply chain, and manufacturing, into a unified platform. ERP helps streamline operations, reduce costs, and improve cross-departmental collaboration.

Entity Resolution: The process of identifying and consolidating different data records that refer to the same real-world entity, such as a person or product. Entity resolution reduces redundancy and improves data consistency in databases.

Environmental Monitoring: The tracking and analysis of environmental factors like temperature, humidity, air quality, and noise, which can impact operations or personnel health. Common in industries such as manufacturing and healthcare, environmental monitoring supports compliance, safety, and efficiency.

Environmental Services (EVS): A department responsible for maintaining cleanliness, hygiene, and environmental standards within facilities, often in healthcare. EVS supports patient safety and comfort through cleaning, waste management, and infection control.

Error Detection: Techniques and processes used to identify discrepancies or faults in data, software, or systems. Error detection helps maintain accuracy, prevent data corruption, and ensure reliable operations, particularly in critical applications.

Event Detection: The process of identifying significant occurrences or changes within a data stream, such as a security breach or equipment failure. Event detection is essential for real-time monitoring systems, enabling prompt responses to critical events.

Event Processing: The continuous analysis and transformation of event data as it is generated. Event processing is used in real-time systems, where the fast handling of events, such as in finance or IoT, is necessary for effective decision-making.

Event-Driven Architecture: A software design pattern in which services communicate through events, allowing for asynchronous, scalable systems. Event-driven architecture is used in applications that require real-time responses to changing conditions.

Exception Handling: Mechanisms within software to manage unexpected situations or errors that deviate from normal operation. Effective exception handling improves system robustness by ensuring that disruptions do not halt operations entirely.

Extended Reality (XR): An umbrella term encompassing technologies that enhance or replace real-world experiences through virtual, augmented, or mixed reality. XR is widely used in entertainment, training, and remote collaboration.

Extensibility: The capability of a system to be extended or enhanced by adding new features or components without affecting its core functionality. Extensibility ensures a system can adapt to future needs or integrate with additional tools.

F

Failover: The automatic switching to a backup or redundant system when the primary system fails. Failover ensures continuity of operations in critical systems by minimizing downtime in case of failure.

False Positive: An incorrect result in which a test or system indicates a condition is present when it is not. False positives can lead to unnecessary actions or alerts, impacting efficiency and user trust in the system.

Feature Extraction: The process of identifying and isolating key variables or patterns in data that are relevant for analysis. In machine learning, feature extraction helps in simplifying data and improving the performance of models.

Feedback Loop: A process where the output of a system is fed back into the system as input, enabling it to self-correct or optimize. Feedback loops are common in control systems and decision-making models.

Field Device: Physical hardware, such as sensors or actuators, deployed in operational environments to collect data or perform actions. Field devices are essential for monitoring and controlling industrial and IoT applications.

File Transfer Protocol (FTP): A standard protocol used to transfer files between computers over a network. FTP supports data exchange in collaborative environments but has been largely replaced by more secure protocols.

Filter: A tool, device, or process that removes unwanted components from data, signals, or content. Filters are widely used in data processing, image analysis, and audio applications to improve quality or extract relevant information.

Fingerprinting: A technique used to estimate indoor location based on distinct signal patterns from sources like Wi-Fi, Bluetooth, or RFID. Often used for indoor navigation where GPS signals are weak.

First In, First Out (FIFO): A queue management principle where the first item added is the first item processed. FIFO is commonly used in data processing, manufacturing, and inventory management to ensure orderly handling.

Fleet Management: The coordination, monitoring, and maintenance of a group of mobile assets like vehicles. Fleet management optimizes logistics, improves asset utilization, and enhances safety.

Flow Control: Mechanisms used to manage the rate of data transmission between devices, preventing network congestion and ensuring efficient communication.

Frequency Hopping: A radio transmission technique that rapidly switches frequencies to reduce interference and enhance security. Often used in wireless communications, such as Bluetooth.

Fully Observable Environment: A setting where all relevant information about the state of the environment is known and accessible. Fully observable environments are ideal for certain types of decision-making models and simulations.

Function Point: A standardized unit for measuring the functional complexity of software based on the functionality provided to users. Used in project management to estimate development effort and productivity.

Functional Requirements: Specifications detailing what a system should do under certain conditions, focusing on behavior rather than implementation. Functional requirements provide a basis for system design and testing.

Fuzzy Logic: A mathematical logic framework that allows for varying degrees of truth, rather than strictly true/false outcomes. Fuzzy logic is useful in handling uncertainty in complex decision-making and control systems.

G

Gateway: A network device that acts as a bridge between different networks, facilitating communication and data exchange. Gateways can manage traffic between local networks and the internet, ensuring data security and efficient routing.

Geofencing: A virtual boundary set around a specific geographic area, triggering actions or alerts when devices enter or exit the defined zone. Geofencing is used in applications like security, logistics, and marketing.

Geographic Information System (GIS): A system that captures, stores, analyzes, and displays spatial or geographic data. GIS supports applications in urban planning, environmental monitoring, and logistics by providing insights through maps and spatial analysis.

Geolocation: The process of determining the geographic location of an object or individual, typically using GPS or network data. Geolocation enables location-based services like navigation, tracking, and location-based marketing.

Geospatial Analysis: The study of geographic data patterns and relationships. Geospatial analysis is commonly used for environmental management, urban planning, and disaster response.

Geospatial Database: A specialized database optimized for storing and querying spatial data. Geospatial databases support GIS applications, allowing for efficient storage and analysis of geographic data.

Global Positioning System (GPS): A satellite-based navigation system providing real-time location and time data to receivers anywhere on Earth. GPS is widely used for navigation, mapping, and location-based services.

Graph Database: A database that represents data as a network of nodes and relationships, making it ideal for analyzing complex connections, like social networks or recommendation systems.

Grid Computing: A distributed computing model where a network of computers works together to perform large computations in parallel. Grid computing enables complex calculations across multiple devices, optimizing processing power.

Ground Truth: The actual, real-world condition or status used as a benchmark for testing and validating models, particularly in fields like machine learning, remote sensing, and autonomous vehicles.

Group Policy: A set of rules that control the configuration of user and computer accounts within an organization. Group policies are commonly used in IT environments to enforce security, control settings, and manage permissions.

Guided Path: A pre-established route for autonomous systems to navigate, helping robots or vehicles avoid obstacles and complete tasks efficiently in a controlled environment.

GUI (Graphical User Interface): A visual interface that allows users to interact with software through graphical elements like icons, buttons, and windows, making it more user-friendly than command-line interfaces.

Gyroscope: A device that measures angular velocity and orientation, commonly used in smartphones, drones, and other electronics for motion detection and stabilization.

Graceful Degradation: The ability of a system to continue operating at a reduced level when parts of it fail or are compromised, ensuring that core functionalities are maintained even under failure conditions.

Granularity: The level of detail or refinement in a dataset or system. High granularity means more detailed information, while low granularity indicates more general data. Granularity can impact the precision of analysis and decision-making.

H

Hand-off: The coordinated transfer of responsibility, tasks, or data between systems, teams, or individuals, ensuring smooth continuation of operations without interruptions or errors. Common in healthcare, customer service, and automated systems.

Hardware Abstraction Layer: A software layer that masks hardware complexities from higher-level applications, providing a standardized interface. This allows software to interact with hardware without needing to manage hardware-specific details.

Hash Function: An algorithm that transforms data of arbitrary size into a fixed-size value, known as a hash. Commonly used in data security, hash functions provide a unique representation of data, supporting data integrity and authentication.

Healthcare Information System (HIS): An integrated software system designed to manage administrative, clinical, and financial aspects of healthcare facilities. HIS supports patient management, electronic health records, and billing functions.

Heat Map: A graphical data visualization tool that uses color intensity to represent data values, highlighting areas of higher or lower concentration. Common in analytics, heat maps reveal patterns in geographical data, website activity, and resource usage.

Heterogeneous Network: A network composed of diverse types of devices, operating systems, and network protocols. Heterogeneous networks improve flexibility and resilience but require careful management to ensure compatibility and security.

Hierarchical Agent Architecture: A multi-level structure that organizes autonomous agents into a hierarchy. Agents at higher levels coordinate or oversee the activities of agents at lower levels, often used in robotics and distributed systems.

High Availability: A system design strategy that minimizes downtime and ensures continuous operation. High availability solutions include redundancy, failover mechanisms, and fault-tolerant architectures, critical in mission-critical systems.

Historical Data: Data that has been collected over time and is stored for later analysis. Historical data allows for trend analysis, forecasting, and decision-making based on past performance.

Host System: A computer or device that provides services, resources, or applications to other computers or devices within a network. Host systems often serve as servers, offering centralized control and access.

Hot Spot: A location or area with a high level of activity, connectivity, or demand. In networking, a hot spot refers to a Wi-Fi-enabled area; in data, it highlights areas with intense data activity or interest.

Human-Computer Interaction: The study and design of interfaces that allow effective interaction between humans and computers. HCI focuses on user experience, usability, and accessibility, aiming to make digital systems intuitive and user-friendly.

Human-in-the-Loop (HITL): Systems that combine human intelligence and machine processing, typically in decision-making or complex tasks where human insight is beneficial. HITL is widely used in areas like AI training, autonomous systems, and quality control.

Hybrid Architecture: A system that combines different architectural approaches, such as combining monolithic and microservices architectures, to achieve a balance between flexibility and scalability.

Hybrid Cloud: A computing environment that combines private cloud resources with public cloud services, allowing for greater flexibility, cost savings, and control over sensitive data.

Hypervisor: Software that allows multiple operating systems to run concurrently on a single physical machine by creating virtual machines. Hypervisors enable efficient resource use and are key to virtualization and cloud computing.

I

Identity Management: The administration and control of digital identities within an organization. Identity management systems verify, authenticate, and manage user roles and permissions, enhancing security and compliance.

IMDF (Indoor Mapping Data Format): A standard format developed by Apple for indoor mapping. IMDF enables the creation of maps for indoor spaces, facilitating indoor navigation and location-based services.

Impedance: In a system, impedance refers to the resistance or opposition to flow, whether of electrical current, data, or processes. In communications, impedance mismatch can reduce efficiency and signal quality.

Implementation: The process of executing a design or plan into practical operation. Implementation turns concepts into functioning systems, requiring testing, adaptation, and integration within an organization's ecosystem.

Independent Surveillance: A form of passive tracking that does not require participation or active cooperation from the subject. Common in areas like radar and video monitoring, independent surveillance enables covert or remote observation.

Indoor Positioning System (IPS): A technology solution for determining the location of people or assets within indoor environments, often using Wi-Fi, Bluetooth, or RFID, as GPS signals are unreliable indoors.

Information Architecture: The organization, structuring, and labeling of information within a system, focusing on accessibility, usability, and logical grouping. Information architecture is essential in web design, libraries, and knowledge management systems.

Infrastructure as Code: A DevOps practice that manages and provisions IT infrastructure using machine-readable configuration files rather than physical hardware. This approach improves automation, version control, and repeatability.

Input/Output (I/O): The communication or transfer of data between an information system and the external environment, such as user devices or other systems. Efficient I/O management is critical to system performance.

Integration Testing: A testing phase that verifies the interaction between different system components, ensuring they work together as expected. Integration testing is essential in uncovering issues in system communication and workflows.

Intelligence Amplification: The use of technology to enhance human intelligence and decision-making capabilities. This concept supports areas like analytics, problem-solving, and situational awareness by augmenting human cognitive abilities.

Interface: The point of connection between different systems, components, or users, allowing interaction or data exchange. Interfaces can be hardware (like USB ports) or software (like APIs).

Internet of Things (IoT): The network of physical devices connected to the internet, capable of collecting, exchanging, and acting on data. IoT has applications in smart homes, industrial automation, healthcare, and more.

Interoperability: The ability of different systems, devices, or applications to work together seamlessly. Interoperability is essential in healthcare, government, and enterprise environments, where data exchange and cross-system communication are critical.

Intrusion Detection: A security mechanism that monitors for unauthorized access or anomalies in a system. Intrusion detection systems (IDS) identify potential threats, protecting networks and data from malicious activities.

Inventory Management: The process of tracking, managing, and controlling inventory levels and stock. Inventory management ensures that resources are available when needed while minimizing excess stock.

J

Job Queue: An ordered list of tasks waiting to be processed. Job queues are used in computing and workflow management to prioritize and manage tasks systematically.

Job Scheduling: The allocation of resources to tasks, managing when and how tasks are executed within a system. Effective job scheduling ensures optimal use of resources and minimizes processing delays.

Join Operation: A database operation that combines data from multiple tables based on related fields. Join operations enable comprehensive data analysis by connecting relevant data points.

JSON (JavaScript Object Notation): A lightweight data interchange format that is easy to read and write. JSON is commonly used for data exchange between web applications and servers due to its simplicity and flexibility.

Just-in-Time (JIT): An inventory management strategy where materials or products are ordered and produced as needed, reducing inventory costs. JIT aims to minimize waste by aligning production with demand.

Just-in-Time Compilation: A technique that compiles code during execution rather than before, improving performance by optimizing code for the current execution environment. Often used in virtual machines like Java and.NET.

Junction Point: A connection point where different paths, networks, or processes meet. In workflows, a junction point allows for decision-making or routing based on specific conditions.

Jitter: The variation in signal timing or processing delay, often considered undesirable in real-time communications. Jitter can affect the quality of voice, video, and other time-sensitive data.

Journey Mapping: The visual representation of a user's experience or a process over time, identifying key touchpoints, challenges, and opportunities for improvement. Journey mapping is valuable in UX design and customer experience.

Jurisdiction: A defined area where specific authority or control is exercised. In legal and regulatory contexts, jurisdiction dictates where laws, regulations, or responsibilities apply.

Junction Analysis: The examination of intersection points within workflows, identifying bottlenecks or inefficiencies. Junction analysis is useful for process optimization and workflow management.

Jupyter Notebook: A web-based application for creating and sharing live code, data visualizations, and documentation. Jupyter Notebooks are popular in data science and education for interactive exploration and collaboration.

JWT (JSON Web Token): A secure way of transmitting information between parties as a JSON object, often used in authentication and data exchange in web applications.

Job Assignment Algorithm: A method for allocating tasks across resources efficiently. Job assignment algorithms are used in fields like workforce management and load balancing.

Join Optimization: The process of enhancing the efficiency of join operations in databases. Join optimization improves query performance, especially in large datasets or complex queries.

Jurisdictional Boundaries: The limits within which authority, control, or legal regulations apply. Jurisdictional boundaries help clarify roles, responsibilities, and rules in multi-organizational or cross-border environments.

K

Kanban: A visual workflow management system that tracks work items through stages of a process. Originally developed for manufacturing, Kanban is now used in project management to improve transparency and productivity.

Kernel: The core component of an operating system, managing system resources and facilitating communication between hardware and software. The kernel is responsible for tasks like memory management, device control, and process scheduling.

Key Performance Indicator (KPI): A quantifiable measure used to evaluate the success or performance of an organization, team, or individual against set objectives. KPIs help track progress and inform strategic decision-making.

Key-Value Store: A data storage paradigm where data is stored as pairs of unique keys and values. Key-value stores are simple, fast, and commonly used in NoSQL databases.

Knowledge Base: An organized repository of information, including articles, documentation, and FAQs, that aids users in finding information quickly. Knowledge bases support customer service and technical support.

Knowledge Discovery: The process of analyzing data to uncover patterns, relationships, or insights. Knowledge discovery is fundamental in fields like data mining, machine learning, and business intelligence.

Knowledge Graph: A networked representation of entities and their relationships, often used in AI, search engines, and data integration. Knowledge graphs enable structured data organization and facilitate knowledge-based reasoning.

Knowledge Management: The practices and strategies for capturing, sharing, and using organizational information effectively. Knowledge management enhances collaboration and decision-making.

Known State: The verified condition or status of a system or component, typically used in troubleshooting and configuration management. A known state serves as a benchmark for testing or reverting to a stable condition.

Kubernetes: An open-source platform for managing containerized applications in clusters. Kubernetes automates deployment, scaling, and management of applications, supporting modern DevOps practices.

Key Distribution: The process of securely managing and distributing cryptographic keys among users and devices to ensure data privacy and authentication.

Kiosk Mode: A restricted mode of operation that limits device functions to a specific application or interface, commonly used in public displays, ATMs, and check-in kiosks.

Knockback: A system response to control or limit requests in response to excessive demand. Knockback mechanisms prevent server overload and ensure fair resource distribution.

Key Risk Indicator (KRI): A metric used to measure the level of risk associated with an activity or process. KRIs help organizations anticipate and manage potential risk exposure.

Kinematic Analysis: The study of motion without considering the forces that cause it, used in robotics, biomechanics, and animation to analyze movement patterns.

Knowledge Mining: The process of extracting valuable insights from unstructured data sources like text, images, and social media. Knowledge mining combines text analytics, machine learning, and data processing techniques.

L

Latency: The time delay between an input or stimulus and the system's response. Latency impacts performance and is critical in systems like networking, gaming, and real-time processing.

Layer 2 Network: The data link layer in the OSI networking model responsible for transferring data between adjacent network nodes. Layer 2 includes protocols like Ethernet, ensuring error detection and data framing.

Lead Time: The time elapsed between the initiation and completion of a process or task. Lead time is a key metric in manufacturing, supply chain, and project management to measure efficiency.

Legacy System: An outdated or obsolete technology or application that is still in use. Legacy systems may lack compatibility with newer technologies but are often retained due to cost or complexity of replacement.

Load Balancing: The process of distributing workloads across multiple resources to optimize system performance, prevent overload, and enhance reliability. Load balancing is commonly used in cloud computing and web servers.

Location Analytics: The analysis of spatial and geographic data to gain insights about locations, trends, and behaviors. Location analytics supports decision-making in fields like retail, logistics, and urban planning.

Location Engine: A system that processes spatial positioning data to determine accurate geographic locations, often used in GPS and indoor positioning systems.

Location Fidelity: The accuracy and reliability of location data. High location fidelity is essential in navigation, tracking, and other applications that require precise positioning.

Location Services: Systems that provide position-based functionalities, such as navigation, tracking, and geo-tagging. Location services are used in mobile applications, IoT devices, and GIS.

Location-Based Services (LBS): Services that use geographic location data to deliver information, entertainment, or security features. Examples include mapping, navigation, and location-based advertising.

Log Analysis: The examination of log files to understand system events, troubleshoot issues, and improve system security. Log analysis is key in IT operations and cybersecurity.

Logical Architecture: The conceptual arrangement of system components, defining their interactions and dependencies without specifying physical details. Logical architecture guides system design and planning.

Long-Range Navigation: Navigation systems or techniques that enable positioning and tracking over extended distances. Used in fields like aviation, maritime, and outdoor recreation.

Low-Code Platform: A development environment that simplifies application building with minimal hand-coding, using visual interfaces. Low-code platforms accelerate software development for businesses and developers.

Low-Power Wide-Area Network (LPWAN): A wireless communication network designed for long-range, low-energy usage. LPWANs are used in IoT for connecting devices over large areas.

Lossless Compression: A method of data compression that reduces file size without any loss of data, enabling exact reconstruction. Common in text, image, and audio compression.

M

Machine Learning: A branch of artificial intelligence where systems improve their performance on tasks over time with experience and data without explicit programming. Machine learning underlies applications like image recognition and predictive analytics.

Maintenance Window: A scheduled period for performing system updates, upgrades, or repairs with minimal impact on users. Maintenance windows help organizations manage downtime effectively.

Managed Services: Outsourced IT services where a provider manages and monitors systems, networks, or applications on behalf of a client, enhancing operational efficiency and support.

Manual Override: A mechanism that allows human intervention to take control of an automated process, typically used to ensure safety, address malfunctions, or respond to changing conditions.

Master Data Management (MDM): The process of defining and managing an organization's critical data to ensure consistency and accuracy. MDM supports data integrity across various business applications.

Material Requirements Planning (MRP): An inventory control and production planning system used to ensure materials are available for production, balancing supply with demand.

Mesh Network: A decentralized network topology where each node connects to multiple others, enhancing network reliability and coverage. Mesh networks are popular in IoT and wireless communications.

Message Broker: Software that transfers messages between applications, enabling communication and integration. Message brokers ensure reliable data exchange in distributed systems.

Message Queue: A buffer or holding area where messages are temporarily stored before processing, facilitating asynchronous communication between processes or services.

Metadata: Data that describes or provides information about other data, such as file size, creation date, or author. Metadata aids in data organization, retrieval, and management.

Microservices: An architectural style where applications are built as a collection of small, independent services, each focused on a specific function. Microservices improve scalability and agility in software development.

Middleware: Software that connects different applications, systems, or devices, enabling communication and data exchange. Middleware supports interoperability in complex IT environments.

Migration: The process of moving data, applications, or systems from one environment to another, often done for system upgrades, data center relocations, or cloud transitions.

Mobile Device Management (MDM): Software that controls the deployment, security, and management of mobile devices within an organization. MDM enhances data security and enforces usage policies.

Monitoring: The continuous observation of a system's performance, health, or security status. Monitoring helps detect issues early and maintain system reliability.

Multi-tenancy: An architecture in which multiple users or organizations (tenants) share the same system or application instance, while their data remains isolated. Multi-tenancy is common in cloud computing.

N

Network Address Translation (NAT): A method of modifying network address information in IP packet headers. NAT allows multiple devices on a local network to share a single public IP address.

Network Latency: The delay experienced during data transmission over a network. High network latency can affect application performance and user experience.

Network Monitoring: The continuous observation of network performance, traffic, and security status. Network monitoring tools help detect outages, bottlenecks, and intrusions.

Network Topology: The arrangement of network devices and connections, including physical (e.g., layout of cables) and logical (e.g., data paths) configurations. Common topologies include star, ring, and mesh.

Neural Network: A computing model inspired by the structure of the human brain, consisting of interconnected nodes (neurons). Neural networks are foundational in deep learning and artificial intelligence.

Node: A connection point within a network, system, or data structure. Nodes can represent devices, servers, or data elements, facilitating communication or data storage.

Noise: Unwanted variations in data, signals, or system performance. Noise can obscure meaningful information and reduce data accuracy or quality.

Nominal Flow: The standard or expected progression of a process or sequence of events. Nominal flow helps establish baselines for normal operations.

Non-functional Requirements (NFR): System qualities, such as performance, security, and usability, that define how a system operates rather than specific functionalities.

Normalization: The organization of data to reduce redundancy and dependency, commonly used in relational databases to optimize structure and efficiency.

Notification System: Infrastructure for distributing alerts or messages, often in real time, to keep users informed of events or issues. Notification systems are common in IT, business, and security.

Near-Field Communication (NFC): A short-range wireless communication technology that enables devices to exchange data when in close proximity. NFC is widely used in mobile payments and access control.

Network Edge: The boundary between two networks, typically where a local network connects to the internet. Network edge devices handle traffic routing, security, and data processing.

Network Interface: The hardware or software point that enables a device to connect to and communicate within a network. Examples include network interface cards (NICs) and wireless adapters.

Network Protocol: A set of rules governing data exchange across networks. Protocols ensure devices can communicate effectively and include standards like TCP/IP, HTTP, and FTP.

Network Segmentation: The division of a network into smaller sub-networks to improve performance and security. Segmentation reduces broadcast traffic and limits access to sensitive resources.

O

Object Detection: The identification and classification of objects within an image or sensor data, often using computer vision techniques. Object detection has applications in autonomous vehicles, surveillance, and augmented reality.

Observable State: The aspects or conditions of a system that can be monitored or measured. Observing system states allows for performance tracking, troubleshooting, and decision-making.

Occupancy Detection: The sensing or identification of people or objects within a defined space. Occupancy detection is used in smart buildings, security, and resource management.

Off-peak Processing: The scheduling of tasks during times of lower demand to reduce strain on resources and improve efficiency. Off-peak processing is common in data processing and batch jobs.

On-premises: Refers to software, hardware, or systems physically located within an organization's facility, rather than hosted remotely or in the cloud.

Online Analytical Processing (OLAP): A data analysis approach used for complex querying and reporting. OLAP enables multidimensional data analysis, supporting decision-making in business intelligence.

Open Architecture: A system design that provides publicly accessible standards and interfaces, enabling interoperability and customization. Open architecture promotes flexibility and extensibility.

Operating System (OS): The primary software that manages computer hardware and software resources, providing services for applications. Examples include Windows, macOS, and Linux.

Operational Data: Information generated from day-to-day business activities. Operational data is typically transactional and reflects real-time system performance.

Operational Intelligence (OI): The real-time analysis of operational data to support decision-making and improve performance. OI is often used in industries like finance, retail, and IT.

Optimization: The process of improving a system, application, or process to be more effective or efficient. Optimization often involves minimizing costs, increasing speed, or enhancing quality.

Orchestration: The automated configuration, coordination, and management of complex workflows and systems. Orchestration helps ensure that processes run smoothly and efficiently.

Output Device: Hardware used to present information to a user, such as monitors, printers, and speakers.

Overhead: The additional resources or processes required to perform a task. Overhead can include computation, memory usage, or administrative tasks, and reducing overhead improves efficiency.

Override Protocol: A procedure allowing for manual control of an automated system, often used in emergencies or unusual conditions.

Over-the-Air Updates (OTA): The wireless distribution of software updates, commonly used in mobile devices, IoT, and automotive software to keep systems current without physical intervention.

P

Packet: A formatted unit of data used for transmission across networks. Packets are broken down and reassembled, enabling efficient and reliable data transfer.

Parameter: A variable that defines specific characteristics within a system or function, often used to control operations or customize system behavior.

PAR Level: The minimum level of inventory required before restocking, ensuring optimal inventory management without overstocking or shortages.

Parallel Processing: The simultaneous execution of multiple tasks, improving efficiency and performance in computing systems.

Pattern Recognition: The identification of repeated data structures or features in data, often used in machine learning, signal processing, and image analysis.

PEAS Framework: A model used in AI design, standing for Performance-Environment-Actuators-Sensors, which defines the attributes necessary for an intelligent agent to function.

Peer-to-Peer (P2P): A decentralized network architecture where devices communicate directly with each other without a central server.

Performance Metrics: Measurements used to assess the effectiveness, efficiency, and reliability of a system, application, or process.

Perimeter Security: Security measures focused on protecting the boundary of a network or system to prevent unauthorized access.

Persistent Storage: A type of non-volatile storage that retains data even when the system is powered off, commonly used for long-term data storage.

Physical Layer: The lowest level of the OSI networking model, responsible for the physical connection between devices and data transmission over cables or wireless signals.

Platform as a Service (PaaS): A cloud-based environment providing tools and infrastructure for application development, allowing developers to build, test, and deploy applications.

Point of Interest (POI): A specific location or place of significance, often used in mapping and navigation applications.

Polling: The regular checking of devices or systems to determine their status, used in system monitoring and data collection.

Port: An endpoint for communication in a network, identified by a unique number, which allows data to flow between devices or applications.

Predictive Analytics: The use of statistical and machine learning techniques to forecast future trends and behaviors based on historical data.

Q

Quality Assurance (QA): The systematic monitoring of production and development processes to ensure quality standards are met, often including testing and process improvements.

Quality Control (QC): A process focused on maintaining quality standards in products or services, often through inspection and testing.

Quality of Service (QoS): The measurement of performance levels in a network or service, ensuring reliable and efficient service delivery.

Queue Management: The organization and prioritization of tasks or items waiting to be processed, optimizing system performance and reducing wait times.

Query: A request for specific information from a database, typically written in a query language like SQL.

Query Optimization: Techniques used to improve the efficiency and speed of database queries, enhancing performance for complex data retrieval.

Queue Theory: The mathematical study of waiting lines or queues, used to model and predict system behavior in fields like telecommunications and operations management.

Quick Response (QR) Code: A two-dimensional barcode that stores information and can be quickly scanned to retrieve it, commonly used in mobile payments and information sharing.

Queueing Model: A mathematical representation of waiting lines, used to predict queue lengths, waiting times, and system performance.

Quota: A limit on the use of specific resources within a system, ensuring resources are allocated fairly and efficiently.

Quantum Computing: An advanced computing paradigm based on quantum mechanics, which performs calculations using quantum bits (qubits) and enables complex problem-solving.

Quarantine: The isolation of suspicious or potentially harmful elements within a system to prevent damage or spread, often used in cybersecurity.

Queue Priority: The determination of the order in which tasks or processes are handled, typically based on urgency or importance.

Query Language: A specialized language used to interact with databases and retrieve specific information, such as SQL.

Query Plan: A strategy created by a database to execute a query, outlining the most efficient way to retrieve data.

Quorum: The minimum number of participants or votes required for a decision or action to be considered valid within a system or organization.

R

Radio Frequency (RF): Electromagnetic wave frequencies used for wireless communication, including applications in radio, television, and mobile communications.

Radio Frequency Identification (RFID): A technology that uses electromagnetic fields to automatically identify and track tags attached to objects.

Random Access Memory (RAM): A type of volatile computer memory that temporarily stores data for active processes, allowing for fast data access and manipulation.

Range Finding: A process for measuring the distance between two points, used in navigation, surveying, and location-based technologies.

Rate Limiting: A technique to control the frequency of requests or data processing to prevent overloads and ensure fair resource distribution.

Real-Time Analytics: The immediate analysis of data as it is received, enabling quick decision-making and responses in time-sensitive applications.

Real-Time Location System (RTLS): A system that tracks and identifies the location of objects or people in real time, commonly used in logistics, healthcare, and asset tracking.

Real-Time Processing: The immediate processing of data as it is received, essential in applications that require instant feedback, like financial trading and monitoring systems.

Recovery Point Objective (RPO): The maximum acceptable amount of data loss during a disaster or system failure, used to determine backup frequency.

Recovery Time Objective (RTO): The maximum acceptable amount of time a system can be down before recovery, guiding disaster recovery planning.

Redundancy: The inclusion of duplicate systems, data, or components to increase reliability and reduce the risk of failure.

Reference Architecture: A template or blueprint for designing a system, providing best practices and standardized approaches.

Refresh Rate: The frequency at which a display or data source is updated, affecting visual smoothness and accuracy in real-time displays.

Registration: The process of enrolling or signing up a user or system component to enable access or participation.

Remote Monitoring: Observing and tracking a system's status from a distance, often used in IT, healthcare, and industrial applications.

Resource Allocation: The distribution of available resources, such as processing power, storage, or personnel, to maximize efficiency.

S

Scalability: A system's ability to handle increased demand or growth in workload without performance degradation, crucial for cloud computing and distributed systems.

Scheduling Algorithm: A method for assigning tasks or processes to resources over time, optimizing task completion and system efficiency.

Security Information and Event Management (SIEM): A system that collects, analyzes, and monitors security-related data and events in real time, enhancing threat detection and incident response.

Sensor Fusion: The integration of data from multiple sensors to produce a more accurate and reliable output, commonly used in autonomous vehicles and robotics.

Sensor Network: A network of interconnected measurement devices that collect and transmit data, often used for environmental monitoring and IoT applications.

Service Level Agreement (SLA): A contractual agreement outlining the performance expectations, responsibilities, and guarantees between a service provider and client.

Signal Processing: The analysis, manipulation, and interpretation of signals, which can be audio, video, or sensor data, to improve quality or extract information.

Simulation: A model that replicates the behavior of a system, used for testing, training, and predicting outcomes in various fields.

Single Point of Failure (SPOF): A critical component whose failure would bring down the entire system. Avoiding SPOFs is essential in resilient system design.

Software as a Service (SaaS): A cloud-based software delivery model in which applications are hosted by a provider and accessed over the internet, reducing infrastructure needs.

Spatial Analysis: The study of geographic or spatial data to identify patterns and relationships, used in fields like geography, urban planning, and epidemiology.

State Machine: A model representing the states and transitions of a system, often used in programming, game design, and automation.

Storage Area Network (SAN): A dedicated network that provides access to consolidated storage, enhancing storage performance and scalability.

Stream Processing: The continuous processing of data in real time, used in applications requiring immediate insights, like social media monitoring and financial trading.

System Architecture: The foundational structure of a system, defining components, interactions, and design principles to meet specific requirements.

System Integration: The process of combining different subsystems into a unified, functioning whole, essential for interoperability and cohesive system performance.

T

Tag Management: The administration and control of tracking systems that attach tags to items, devices, or data, allowing for easier monitoring and management, especially in IoT and analytics contexts.

Task Automation: The process of configuring systems to perform tasks autonomously, reducing manual intervention and increasing efficiency.

Task Queue: An ordered list of tasks or operations waiting to be processed by a system, ensuring efficient task management and resource allocation.

Technical Debt: The long-term cost incurred by taking shortcuts or choosing suboptimal solutions in software development to expedite delivery, leading to future maintenance challenges.

Telemetry: The collection and remote transmission of data from sensors or systems, commonly used in healthcare, environmental monitoring, and space exploration.

Throughput: The rate at which a system processes or transmits data, often used as a performance measure in computing and networking systems.

Time Division Multiple Access (TDMA): A method of sharing communication channels by dividing time into distinct slots for different users, commonly used in cellular networks.

Time of Flight (ToF): A technique for measuring the distance between two points based on the time it takes for a signal (often light or radio) to travel between them.

Time Series Analysis: The study of data points ordered in time, used to identify trends, seasonal patterns, or irregular behaviors in a dataset over time.

Time Synchronization: The process of aligning the clocks of different systems or devices to ensure they operate in a coordinated manner, especially critical in distributed systems and communication networks.

Token: A digital object that represents the right to perform a specific operation or action within a system, often used in authentication and authorization processes.

Topology: The physical or logical arrangement of components within a network or system, which can affect performance, scalability, and reliability.

Track and Trace: The ability to monitor the location and history of an object, often used in logistics and inventory management to improve efficiency and accountability.

Traffic Analysis: The study of network data flow, identifying patterns and monitoring for security threats or performance bottlenecks in data transmission.

Transaction Processing: The handling of data exchanges or transactions, ensuring accurate and secure recording of business operations, such as financial transactions or order processing.

Triangulation: A method for determining the location of an object by measuring angles to it from two or more known points.

U

Ubiquitous Computing: A computing paradigm where devices and technologies are integrated seamlessly into daily life, often invisible or unobtrusive to the user.

Ultra-Wideband (UWB): A radio technology that uses a broad spectrum of frequencies, allowing for high-speed data transmission over short distances, often used for precise location tracking and high-performance wireless communication.

Unicast: A method of communication where data is sent from a single sender to a single receiver, commonly used in networking for point-to-point communication.

Unified Communications (UC): The integration of various communication methods (email, voice, video, messaging, etc.) into a single, streamlined system, improving collaboration and efficiency.

Universal Serial Bus (USB): A widely used standard for connecting peripheral devices to a computer, providing both power and data transfer capabilities.

Update Propagation: The distribution of changes or updates across a system or network, ensuring that all components reflect the most current version or state.

Uplink: Communication from a local system or device to a central or higher-level system, typically referring to data sent from a client to a server or from a satellite to ground control.

Uptime: The percentage of time a system is operational and available, used as a key metric for measuring system reliability and performance.

Use Case: A specific scenario or example of how a system or application will be used, often used in design and development to ensure that functional requirements are met.

User Authentication: The process of verifying the identity of a user attempting to access a system, typically through credentials like passwords, biometric data, or security tokens.

User Experience (UX): The overall experience and satisfaction a person has when interacting with a system or product, focusing on ease of use, functionality, and accessibility.

User Interface (UI): The point of interaction between a user and a computer or application, typically involving visual elements like buttons, menus, and layouts that facilitate user interaction.

User Profile: A collection of settings, preferences, and information that customize a user's experience in a system, often used for personalization.

Utilization: A measure of how efficiently resources (such as computing power, storage, or bandwidth) are being used, often expressed as a percentage of total capacity.

UUID (Universally Unique Identifier): A unique reference number used to identify information in systems, ensuring no two identifiers are the same across time and space.

UX Design: The process of designing systems, applications, or websites to ensure a positive, intuitive, and efficient user experience, focusing on usability, accessibility, and interaction.

V

Validation: Process of confirming that a system or process meets specified requirements and produces intended results through systematic testing and verification.

Value Stream: Complete sequence of activities required to deliver a product or service, from initial request through final delivery and completion.

Vector Data: Geographic data represented through points, lines, and polygons with precise coordinates and mathematical descriptions.

Version Control: System managing changes to documents, programs, and other information collections, tracking modifications and enabling rollback capabilities.

Virtual Machine: Software-based emulation of a computer system, enabling isolation of computing environments within a single physical machine.

Virtual Reality: Computer-generated simulation of three-dimensional environment that can be interacted with using specialized electronic equipment.

Virtualization: Creation of virtual versions of computing resources, enabling multiple logical resources to operate on shared physical hardware.

Visibility: Degree to which system components and their status can be observed, monitored, and analyzed in real time.

Visual Analytics: Science of analytical reasoning supported by interactive visual interfaces, combining automated analysis with human insight.

Voice over IP: Technology enabling voice communications over Internet Protocol networks, supporting integrated communications in healthcare settings.

Volume: Quantity measurement of data, transactions, or activities within a system over a specified time period.

Vulnerability: Weakness in system security or design that could be exploited to compromise system integrity or performance.

W

Warehouse Management System: Software application supporting daily operations in warehouse environments, including inventory tracking and order fulfillment.

Wayfinding: System of information systems helping people navigate through physical spaces, particularly important in complex healthcare environments.

Web Service: Software system supporting machine-to-machine interaction over networks using standardized messaging formats.

Workflow Automation: Technology-enabled automation of repeatable processes based on predefined business rules and triggers.

X

XR (Extended Reality): An umbrella term for all immersive technologies, including virtual reality (VR), augmented reality (AR), and mixed reality (MR), which blend physical and digital worlds to create interactive experiences.

Z

Zero Trust Architecture: A security framework that assumes no user or device, whether inside or outside the network, can be trusted by default. Every access request is verified based on strict identity authentication and authorization, minimizing risks from internal threats and unauthorized access.

Zone-based Location: A method of tracking that focuses on identifying the presence of an individual or object within specific zones or areas, rather than providing precise geographic coordinates. This is commonly used for applications where high-level location information is sufficient, such as in indoor navigation or asset tracking within a building.

Special Concepts

4Ps (Position, Proximity, Presence, Possession): Core concepts in Care Traffic Control that define the key elements used to manage and track individuals or assets. These concepts help determine the location and movement of items or people within a system:

Position: The exact or general location of an entity.
Proximity: The closeness of an entity to a defined point or another entity.
Presence: The state of being located within a defined area or system.
Possession: The ownership or control over an item or asset.

5S (Sort, Set in Order, Shine, Standardize, Sustain): A workplace organization methodology developed in Japan to improve efficiency and safety by ensuring systematic organization and cleanliness. The five principles are:

Sort: Remove unnecessary items from the workplace.
Set in Order: Organize remaining items for easy access and use.
Shine: Keep the workspace clean and maintained.
Standardize: Establish standardized practices for consistency.
Sustain: Ensure continuous adherence to the standards and practices.

Index

Pages in *italics* refer to figures and pages in **bold** refer to tables.

For Product Safety Concerns and Information please contact our EU representative GPSR@taylorandfrancis.com
Taylor & Francis Verlag GmbH, Kaufingerstraße 24, 80331 München, Germany

www.ingramcontent.com/pod-product-compliance
Lightning Source LLC
Chambersburg PA
CBHW052010230326
41598CB00078B/2348

* 9 7 8 1 0 4 1 0 3 8 1 2 2 *